OXFORD STUDIES IN ANCIENT CULTURE
AND REPRESENTATION

General Editors
Simon Price   R. R. R. Smith   Oliver Taplin

OXFORD STUDIES IN ANCIENT CULTURE AND REPRESENTATION

Oxford Studies in Ancient Culture and Representation publishes significant interdisciplinary research into the visual, social, political, and religious cultures of the ancient Mediterranean world. The series includes work which combines different kinds of representations which are usually treated separately. The overarching programme is to integrate images, monuments, texts, performances, and rituals with the places, participants, and broader historical environment that gave them meaning.

Greek Athletics in the Roman World

Victory and Virtue

ZAHRA NEWBY

OXFORD
UNIVERSITY PRESS

OXFORD

UNIVERSITY PRESS

Great Clarendon Street, Oxford OX2 6DP

Oxford University Press is a department of the University of Oxford.
It furthers the University's objective of excellence in research, scholarship,
and education by publishing worldwide in

Oxford New York

Auckland Cape Town Dar es Salaam Hong Kong Karachi
Kuala Lumpur Madrid Melbourne Mexico City Nairobi
New Delhi Shanghai Taipei Toronto

With offices in

Argentina Austria Brazil Chile Czech Republic France Greece
Guatemala Hungary Italy Japan Poland Portugal Singapore
South Korea Switzerland Thailand Turkey Ukraine Vietnam

Oxford is a registered trade mark of Oxford University Press
in the UK and in certain other countries

Published in the United States
by Oxford University Press Inc., New York

British Library Cataloguing in Publication Data

Data available

Library of Congress Cataloging in Publication Data

Data available

Typeset by Graphicraft Limited, Hong Kong
Printed in Great Britain
on acid-free paper by
Antony Rowe, Chippenham, Wilts.
ISBN 0-19-927930-6   978-0-19-927930-2

1 3 5 7 9 10 8 6 4 2

ACKNOWLEDGEMENTS

The material in this book has its roots in a section of my Ph.D. thesis. Both during and since that period of research I have acquired numerous debts which I am pleased to acknowledge here. My first thanks go to Jas' Elsner, my Ph.D. supervisor, for his eternal enthusiasm, acute criticism, and support, which I have been lucky enough to enjoy ever since. For first introducing me to the Second Sophistic, and for his continuing interest in my work, I also thank Ewen Bowie. Numerous people have volunteered to read part or all of this work, in its various drafts. I am particularly grateful to the editors of this series who offered many helpful suggestions, and especially to Bert Smith whose reports as my Ph.D. examiner also helped me to refine my ideas, as well as to the external reader for the Press.

My colleagues at Warwick have been most supportive throughout the preparation of this work; for their willingness to read and advise on parts of the book I am very grateful to Alison Cooley and James Davidson, as well as to Simon Swain, who generously read the whole draft and helped to improve it in many ways. My thanks also go to Nigel Kennell for reading Chapters 5 and 6, and to Jason König, with whom I have shared many conversations on athletics, for showing me the manuscript of his forthcoming book and commenting on my own. Julie Van Voorhis also kindly let me see a copy of her article before publication. I would also like to thank the staff of Oxford University Press for seeing this into press and saving me from numerous errors. Any errors that remain are, of course, my own.

For enabling my access to sites and museums and helping with photographs I am grateful to Helen Clarke of the British School at Athens, Maria Pia Malvezzi of the British School at Rome and Gülgün Girdivan of the British Institute of Archaeology at Ankara. Numerous individuals helped me with access to collections including Mhammed Behel (St-Romaine-en-Gal), Adriano D'Offizi (Villa Adriana), Anna Gallina Zevi (Ostia), Paolo Liverani (Castel Gandolfo), Olga Vikatou (Olympia Museum), and Elena Zavvou (Sparta Museum). For last-minute help with photographs I am also indebted to Orhan Atvur, Sheila Dillon, and Bert Smith. I have tried to contact all those holding copyright over the images used, but if notified I will be pleased to correct any omissions.

Research for the book was carried out in Italy with the help of a Rome Award from the British School at Rome, in Greece with a British Academy Small Research Grant, and in Turkey with a grant from the Teaching and Research Development Fund at Warwick University. The M. Aylwin Cotton Foundation and the Warwick University Humanities Research Fund generously contributed to the cost of illustrations. I am most grateful to all for their support.

Finally, some personal thanks. Thanks to all the friends who have discussed these ideas, advised me, or offered insights from the sciences. Many thanks to Andrew, for listening to my niggles in the final stages, and for both encouraging and distracting me. I am also especially grateful to my family for all their support and interest. Nick, Ruth, and Sarah have provided support in so many different ways, from photographic skills and discussion to simple entertainment! Finally, I owe my parents a huge debt of thanks for being unstintingly generous with their love, interest, and support both throughout this project, and always. I dedicate this book to them.

Kidlington
February 2005

CONTENTS

Illustrations   viii

Abbreviations   xiii

1. Introduction: Greeks, Romans, and Athletics in
   the Roman World   1

Part I Athletics in the Roman West   19

2. Greek Athletics in the Heart of Rome   21

3. Visualizing Athletics in the Roman Baths   45

4. Idealized Statues in Roman Villas   88

Part II Athletics and Identity in the Greek East   141

5. Training Warriors: The Merits of a Physical Education   143

6. The Athenian *Ephēbeia*: Performing the Past   168

7. Olympia and Pausanias' Construction of Greece   202

8. Gymnasia, Festivals, and Euergetism in Asia Minor   229

9. Conclusions   272

Bibliography   282

Index   307

ILLUSTRATIONS

FIGURES

2.1   Terracotta lamp in the British Museum, Q1718. Photo: © Copyright
      The British Museum   29

2.2   Aureus of Septimius Severus. *BMCRE* Septimius Severus and
      Caracalla no. 319. Photo: © Copyright The British Museum   37

2.3   Child sarcophagus with athletic scenes. Vatican, Museo
      Gregoriano Profano 1019. Photo: DAIR 80.1697, by permission
      of the Vatican Museums   42

3.1   Mosaic from the 'Palaestra', Pompeii VIII.ii.23. Photo: Z. Newby   47

3.2   Mosaic from the Baths of Neptune, Ostia. Photo: Soprintendenza
      di Ostia Antica   51

3.3   Mosaic from the Baths of Porta Marina, Ostia. Photo: N. Newby   53

3.4   Mosaic from the Terme Marittime, Ostia. Photo: Fototeca Unione   57

3.5   Mosaic from the Inn of Alexander Helix, Ostia. Photo: Soprintendenza
      di Ostia Antica   59

3.6   Mosaic from a bath complex on the Via Portuense, Rome.
      Museo Nazionale Romano. Photo: original by A. M. Reggiani,
      taken from M. Floriani Squarciapino, *AttiPontAccRomRend*
      58 (1985–6), 175, fig. 6; Bodleian Library, University of Oxford,
      shelfmark Soc. 20500d.42   61

3.7   Mosaic from the Baths on the Via Severiana, Ostia. Photo:
      Soprintendenza di Ostia Antica   64

3.8   Mosaic from the Great Baths at Aquileia. Aquileia Museum.
      Photo: DAIR 82.154   65

3.9   Mosaic from the Great Baths at Aquileia. Aquileia Museum.
      Photo: DAIR 82.156   66

3.10 Plan of the Baths of Caracalla at Rome. J. DeLaine, *The Baths
      of Caracalla*, JRA Supplement 25 (Portsmouth, RI, 1997), 23,
      fig. 11. Copyright *JRA*   68

3.11 Watercolour showing the mosaics from the Baths of Caracalla.
      Photo: from B. Nogara, *I mosaici antichi conservati nei palazzi
      pontifici del Vaticano e del Laterano* (Milan, 1910), pl. IV;
      Bodleian Library, University of Oxford, shelfmark 17505b1   69

3.12 Statue of the Polycleitan Heracles type. Museo Nazionale
      Romano, inv. 106184. Photo: DAIR 60.658   72

3.13 Farnese Heracles. Naples, Museo Nazionale, inv. 6001.
      Photo: DAIR 80.2908   73

3.14 Detail of an athletic mosaic from ancient Vienna in Gaul.
      St-Romain-en-Gal, Museum. Photo: Z. Newby   80

3.15 Detail of an athletic mosaic from ancient Vienna in Gaul.
      St-Romain-en-Gal, Museum. Photo: Z. Newby   81

4.1   Statue of a boxer. Museo Nazionale Romano, inv. 1055.
      Photo: DAIR 66.1689   94

4.2   Rosa's Map of Domitian's villa at Castel Gandolfo. G. Lugli,
      BullCom 46 (1918), pl. 1, annotated   97

4.3   Basalt torso, from Domitian's villa. Castel Gandolfo Antiquarium,
      inv. 36405. Photo: Vatican Museums.   98

4.4   Statue of the Westmacott athlete type from Domitian's villa.
      Castel Gandolfo Antiquarium, inv. 36420. Photo: Vatican Museums   100

4.5   Statue of the Dresden youth type from Domitian's villa.
      Castel Gandolfo Antiquarium, inv. 36408. Photo: Vatican Museums.   101

4.6   Statue of the Dresden youth type from Domitian's villa.
      Castel Gandolfo Antiquarium, inv. 36407. Photo: Vatican Museums   102

4.7   Statue of an athlete from Domitian's villa. Castel Gandolfo
      Antiquarium, inv. 36406. Photo: Vatican Museums   103

4.8   Terracotta relief showing a statue of an athlete beneath a portico.
      British Museum, D632. Photo: © Copyright The British Museum   106

4.9   Map of Hadrian's villa at Tivoli. S. Aurigemma, *Villa Adriana*
      (Rome, 1961), 18, fig. 6; relabelled.   108

4.10 Map of Hadrian's villa at Tivoli by F. Contini, 1668, detail. British
      Library Maps 7 Tab 45. Photo: By permission of the British Library   109

4.11 Map of Hadrian's villa at Tivoli, signed by F. Piranesi, 1871,
      detail. British Library 1899 d 19 (5). Photo: By permission
      of the British Library   110

4.12 Statue of an athlete. Louvre, MA 889. Photo: Réunion des
      Musées Nationaux   112

4.13 Statue of the 'Amelung athlete' type from Hadrian's villa.
      Villa Antiquarium, inv. 1060. Photo: DAIR 82.1341   114

4.14 The 'Townley Discobolus' from Hadrian's villa. British Museum,
      Sc. 250. Photo: © Copyright The British Museum   115

4.15 Statue of Hermes of the 'Sandalbinder' type. Ny Carlsberg Glyptotek,
      cat. 273. Photo: Ny Carlsberg Glyptotek, Copenhagen   117

4.16 The 'Lansdowne Heracles' from Hadrian's villa. The J. Paul Getty
      Museum, Malibu, Calif., inv. 70.AA.109. Photo: Courtesy of
      the J. Paul Getty Museum   118

4.17 Herm of Heracles wearing a wreath. Vatican, Museo Pio-Clementino,
      inv. 2842. Photo: DAIR 6505, by permission of the Vatican Museums   120

4.18 Statue of a youthful satyr, from the theatre of Domitian's villa
      at Castel Gandolfo. British Museum, Sc. 1648. Photo: © Copyright
      The British Museum   131

4.19 Statue of a youth, from the Ninfeo Bergantino. Castel Gandolfo
      Antiquarium, inv. 36413. Photo: Vatican Museums   133

4.20 Statue of a youth, from the Ninfeo Bergantino. Castel Gandolfo
      Antiquarium, inv. 36413. Photo: Vatican Museums   135

5.1 Sanctuary of Artemis Orthia, Sparta. Photo: Z. Newby, by permission of the Archaeological Receipts Fund 158

5.2 Sickle dedication. Sparta Museum, inv. 1526. Photo: Z. Newby, by permission of the Archaeological Receipts Fund 159

5.3 Sickle dedication. Sparta Museum, inv. 1515. Photo: Z. Newby, by permission of the Archaeological Receipts Fund 160

5.4 Statue base, Sanctuary of Artemis Orthia, Sparta. Photo: Z. Newby, by permission of the Archaeological Receipts Fund 161

5.5 Statue base. Sparta Museum, inv. 252. Photo: Z. Newby, by permission of the Archaeological Receipts Fund 162

5.6 Hip herm of Heracles. Sparta Museum, inv. 1126. Photo: Z. Newby, by permission of the Archaeological Receipts Fund 164

5.7 Remains of the so-called 'Arapissa' bath complex, Sparta. Photo: Z. Newby, by permission of the Archaeological Receipts Fund 165

5.8 Excavation plan of the baths. A. J. B. Wace, *ABSA* 12 (1905–6), 408, figure 1. Reproduced with permission of the British School at Athens 166

6.1 Ephebic relief. Athens, National Museum, inv. 1469. Photo: Athens, National Museum 172

6.2 Ephebic relief. Athens, National Museum, inv. 1468. Photo: Athens, National Museum 173

6.3 Ephebic relief. Athens, National Museum, inv. 1484. Photo: Athens, National Museum 175

6.4 Ephebic relief. Athens, National Museum, inv. 1465. Photo: Athens, National Museum 176

6.5 Herm portrait of a cosmetes. Athens, National Museum, inv. 388. Photo: Athens, National Museum 177

6.6 Ephebic relief. Athens, National Museum, inv. 1466. Photo: Athens, National Museum 181

6.7 Detail of Fig. 6.6. Photo: Z. Newby, by permission of Athens National Museum 182

6.8 Ephebic relief. Athens, National Museum, inv. 1470. Photo: Athens, National Museum 183

6.9 Detail of Fig. 6.8. Photo: Z. Newby, by permission of Athens National Museum 184

6.10 Detail of Fig. 6.8. Photo: Z. Newby, by permission of Athens National Museum 185

6.11 Detail of Fig. 6.4. Photo: Z. Newby, by permission of Athens National Museum 187

6.12 Detail of an ephebic relief. Athens, Epigraphical Museum, inv. 12554. Photo: Z. Newby, by permission of Athens Epigraphical Museum 190

6.13 Herm portrait. Athens, Epigraphic Museum, inv. 10323. Photo: Z. Newby, by permission of Athens Epigraphical Museum 193

6.14 Ephebic dedication. Oxford, Ashmolean Museum (Michaelis 135). Photo: Z. Newby 197

7.1 Entrance to stadium, Olympia. Photo: Z. Newby   206

7.2 Pausanias' tour of the victor statues in the Altis at
Olympia. H.-V. Herrmann, *Nikephoros* 1 (1988), 133; relabelled.   207

7.3 View of the sanctuary at Olympia. Photo: Z. Newby   208

8.1 Statue of an athlete. Vienna, Kunsthistorisches Museum, inv. 3168.
Photo: Vienna, Kunsthistorisches Museum   233

8.2 Plan of the Harbour Baths at Ephesus. O. Benndorf, *Forschungen
in Ephesos* 1 (1906), 183, fig. 130.   234

8.3 Plan of the Vedius Bath-Gymnasium, Ephesus. J. Keil, *JÖAI* 26 (1930),
supplement, 19, fig. 6, annotated. Copyright: Österreichisches
Archäologisches Institut, Vienna   236

8.4 Plan of the East Bath-Gymnasium, Ephesus. J. Keil, *JÖAI* 28 (1933),
supplement, 7, fig. 2, annotated. Copyright: Österreichisches
Archäologisches Institut, Vienna   237

8.5 The marble room in the bath-gymnasium at Sardis, restored.
Photo: Z. Newby   239

8.6 Portrait statue. Izmir Museum, inv. 570. Photo: Izmir Museum   241

8.7 Portrait statue. Izmir Museum, inv. 648. Photo: Izmir Museum   242

8.8 Bronze coin of Hierapolis in Phrygia. *BMC Phrygia*, Hierapolis 66.
Photo: © Copyright The British Museum   248

8.9 Bronze coin of Hierapolis in Phrygia. *BMC Phrygia*, Hierapolis 71.
Photo: © Copyright The British Museum   248

8.10 Central panel of *scaenae frons*, Hierapolis theatre. Hierapolis Museum
Photo: Z. Newby, by permission of the Director of the Missione
Archeologica Italiana at Hierapolis   250

8.11 Panel of *scaenae frons*, Hierapolis theatre. Hierapolis Museum
Photo: Z. Newby, by permission of the Director of the Missione
Archeologica Italiana at Hierapolis   251

8.12 Statue of the Polycleitan Discophorus type. Aphrodisias
Museum, inv. 70-502/3. Photo: Aphrodisias Excavations,
New York University   256

8.13 Statue of a boxer. Aphrodisias Museum, inv. 70-508-511.
Photo: Aphrodisias Excavations   258

8.14 Statue of a boxer. Aphrodisias Museum, inv. 60-287.
Photo: Aphrodisias Excavations   259

8.15 Sarcophagus of an athlete, Aphrodisias. Photo: Z. Newby
by permission of Aphrodisias Excavations   261

8.16 Detail of architectural decoration of Building M, Side.
Photo: Z. Newby   262

8.17 Reconstruction view of Building M, A. M. Mansel,
Die Ruinen von Side (Berlin, 1963), 113, fig. 90 (M. Beken)   263

8.18 Discobolus torso. Side Museum, inv. 93. Photo: Z. Newby,
by permission of Side Museum   264

8.19 Ludovisi Discobolus. Side Museum, inv. 92. Photo: Z. Newby,
by permission of Side Museum   265

8.20 Diadoumenus torso. Side Museum, inv. 91. Photo: Z. Newby, by permission of Side Museum   266

8.21 Sandalbinder torso. Side Museum, inv. 95. Photo: Z. Newby, by permission of Side Museum   267

8.22 Podium from Side. Side Museum. Photo: Z. Newby, by permission of Side Museum   268

8.23 Coffer from nymphaeum. Side Museum. Photo: Z. Newby, by permission of Side Museum   269

8.24 Coffer from nymphaeum. Side Museum. Photo: Z. Newby, by permission of Side Museum   270

COLOUR PLATES

1a Mosaic from the Baths of Caracalla, Rome. Vatican, Museo Gregoriano Profano. Photo: Z. Newby, by permission of the Vatican Museums.

1b Mosaic from the Baths of Caracalla, Rome. Vatican, Museo Gregoriano Profano. Photo: Z. Newby, by permission of the Vatican Museums.

2a Paintings from the latrines at Vienna in Gaul. Photo: Paul Veysseyre, Musée gallo-romain de Saint-Romain-en-Gal.

2b Paintings from the latrines at Vienna in Gaul, detail of a boxer. Photo: Paul Veysseyre, Musée gallo-romain de Saint-Romain-en-Gal.

2c Paintings from the latrines at Vienna in Gaul, detail of the umpire. Photo: Paul Veysseyre, Musée gallo-romain de Saint-Romain-en-Gal.

3 Mosaic from ancient Vienna in Gaul. Photo: Alain Basset, Musée gallo-romain de Saint-Romain-en-Gal.

4a Mosaic found at Baten Zammour in Tunisia. Gafsa Museum. Photo: Z. Newby.

4b Mosaic found at Baten Zammour in Tunisia, detail of a victorious athlete. Gafsa Museum. Photo: Z. Newby.

4c Mosaic found at Baten Zammour in Tunisia, detail of wrestling match and torch race. Gafsa Museum. Photo: Z. Newby.

ABBREVIATIONS

AA	*Archäologischer Anzeiger*
ABSA	*Annual of the British School at Athens*
AC	*L'antiquité classique*
AJA	*American Journal of Archaeology*
AJP	*American Journal of Philology*
ANRW	*Aufstieg und Niedergang der römischen Welt*
AthMitt	*Mitteilungen des Deutschen Archäologischen Instituts, Athenische Abteilung*
AttiPontAccRomMem	*Atti della Pontificia Accademia Romana di Archeologia: Memorie*
AttiPontAccRomRend	*Atti della Pontificia Accademia Romana di Archeologia: Rendiconti*
BCH	*Bulletin de Correspondance Hellenique*
BICS	*Bulletin of the Institute of Classical Studies*
BMC Phrygia	B. V. Head, *Catalogue of the Greek Coins of Phrygia* (London, 1906)
BMCRE	H. Mattingly, *Coins of the Roman Empire in the British Museum* (London, 1923–62)
BM Papyri	F. G. Kenyon and H. I. Bell, eds., *Greek Papyri in the British Museum* (London, 1899–1917)
BullCom	*Bullettino della Commissione Archeologica Comunale di Roma*
CIA	*Corpus Inscriptionum Atticarum*
CIL	*Corpus Inscriptionum Latinarum*
CQ	*Classical Quarterly*
CRAI	*Comptes Rendus de l'Académie des Inscriptions*
DAIR	*Deutsches Archaeologisches Institut, Rome*
Hyde, *OVM*	W. W. Hyde, *Olympic Victor Monuments and Greek Athletic Art* (Washington, 1921)
IEphesos	*Inschriften von Ephesos*
IG	*Inscriptiones Graecae*
ILAlg	S. Gsell, ed., *Inscriptions Latines de l'Algérie*, i (Paris, 1922)
IOlympia	*Inschriften von Olympia*
JHS	*Journal of Hellenic Studies*
JÖAI	*Jahreshefte des Österreichischen Archäologischen Institutes in Wien*
JRA	*Journal of Roman Archaeology*
JRS	*Journal of Roman Studies*
Lugli I	G. Lugli, 'La villa di Domiziano sui Colli Albani', *BullCom* 45 (1917), 29–78
Lugli II	G. Lugli, 'La villa di Domiziano sui Colli Albani', *BullCom* 46 (1918), 3–68
Lugli III	G. Lugli, 'La villa di Domiziano sui Colli Albani', *BullCom* 47 (1919), 153–205
Lugli IV	G. Lugli, 'La villa di Domiziano sui Colli Albani', *BullCom* 48 (1920), 3–72

MEFRA	*Mélanges de l'École française de Rome: Antiquité*
Moretti, *IAG*	L. Moretti, *Iscrizioni agonistiche greche* (Rome, 1953)
Moretti, *IGUR* i	L. Moretti, *Inscriptiones Graecae Urbis Romae*, i (Rome, 1968)
NSc	*Notizie degli Scavi*
PBSR	*Papers of the British School at Rome*
PCPS	*Proceedings of the Cambridge Philological Society*
REA	*Revue des Études Anciennes*
RömMitt	*Mitteilungen des Deutschen Archäologischen Instituts, Römische Abteilung*
SEG	*Supplementum epigraphicum Graecum*
SIG	W. Dittenberger, ed., *Sylloge Inscriptionum Graecarum*, 3rd edn. (Lipsiae, 1915–24)
YCS	*Yale Classical Studies*
ZPE	*Zeitschrift für Papyrologie und Epigraphik*

ONE

Introduction
Greeks, Romans, and Athletics in the Roman World

During the course of the first three centuries AD, Greek athletics came to play a dominant role in the cultural life of the Roman empire. From ancient Games such as those at Olympia or Delphi, to the newer festivals which sprang up around the Mediterranean world, festival culture was thriving, and successful athletes could achieve an almost heroic status. In art and literature too, athletic subjects were omnipresent. Idealized statues of athletes thronged baths, gymnasia, and villas across both east and west of the empire, while floor mosaics decorated with athletic scenes attested to the popularity of Greek athletics as a spectacle in the Roman west. The Greek literature of the period also included a number of pieces which take athletics as their theme, such as Dio Chrysostom's orations for the dead athlete Melancomas, Lucian's comic debate between Solon and Anacharsis on the values of athletic activity, or Philostratus' defence of gymnastic training in the *Gymnasticus*.[1] All these suggest the prominence of athletic activity in the contemporary world—both in the stadium and the gymnasium—and the ways that it could provide a cultural model with which to consider fundamental themes of human life such as fame, virtue, education, and the relationship between the present and the past.

My aim in this book is to explore the different roles played by athletic activity during this period, and the ways it was adopted and adapted by both Greeks and Romans, by focusing in particular on the abundant visual evidence. Through examining the ways that athletic activity was understood and represented, I aim also to cast light on the many different roles played by elements of Greek culture in the world of the Roman empire. Athletic activity provides a particularly good case study within which to examine wider issues. Throughout Greek history, athletics played a crucial role in formulating Greek culture and identity. The practice of exercising naked and competing in public at religious festivals was a sign marking

---

[1] Dio Chrysostom, *Orations* 28, 29; Lucian, *Anacharsis*; Philostratus, *Gymnasticus*.

Greeks out from non-Greeks, whose pale and puny bodies could be mocked.[2] Adoption of athletic practices also became a clear sign of Hellenization, a point made particularly clear by the description of the Hellenizing Jews which we find in 1 Maccabees.[3] Athletic contests and training continued to grow in popularity during the Roman period, and a central aim of this work is to explore the ways that athletic activity continued to be used to assert Greek identity once the Greek world came under the dominance of Roman power.

Athletic activity was also adopted with alacrity by the Romans themselves. While a number of Latin literary sources suggest hostility to the idea of exercising naked and competing publicly, there is extensive evidence that Greek-style athletic training came to be a popular leisure activity in Rome itself, while Greek-style festivals (which included both athletic and musical contests) became an important part of Rome's spectacle culture.[4] The emperor himself also exerted a profound effect on festival culture across the empire. Any city planning to institute one of the most prestigious 'crown' or 'sacred' games had first to secure imperial permission.[5] Numerous festivals also bore the name of the reigning emperor, and accommodated the imperial family in their sacrifices and processions. Athletics thus lies at the heart of the ways in which Greek cultural practices were used by individuals and communities in both east and west of the empire to reflect upon and construct their

---

[2] Cf. Lucian, *Anacharsis* 16, where the unathletic Anacharsis asks Solon to continue their discussion in the shade. On the importance of athletics in constructions of difference, see M. Golden, *Sport and Society in Ancient Greece* (Cambridge, 1998). There have been many general accounts of ancient athletics, mostly concentrating on the classical period. See esp. E. N. Gardiner, *Greek Athletic Sports and Festivals* (London, 1910); id., *Athletics of the Ancient World* (London, 1930); J. Jüthner, *Die athletischen Leibesübungen der Griechen*, ed. F. Brein (Vienna, 1965; 1968); H. A. Harris, *Greek Athletes and Athletics* (London, 1964); id., *Sport in Greece and Rome* (London, 1972); M. B. Poliakoff, *Combat Sports in the Ancient World: Competition, Violence and Culture* (New Haven and London, 1987); and, most recently, S. G. Miller, *Ancient Greek Athletics* (New Haven and London, 2004); N. Spivey, *The Ancient Olympics* (Oxford, 2004). For recent attempts to set athletics into its social and historical contexts, see D. Sansone, *Greek Athletics and the Genesis of Sport* (Berkeley, Los Angeles, and London, 1988); S. Müller, *Das Volk der Athleten: Untersuchungen zur Ideologie und Kritik des Sports in der griechisch-römischen Antike* (Trier, 1995); C. Mann, *Athlet und Polis im archaischen und frühklassischen Griechenland* (Göttingen, 2001); T. F. Scanlon, *Eros and Greek Athletics* (Oxford, 2002). For further bibliographies see D. Kyle, 'Directions in Ancient Sport History', *Journal of Sport History* 10 (1983), 7–34; T. F. Scanlon, *Greek and Roman Athletics: A Bibliography* (Chicago, 1984); N. B. Crowther, 'Studies in Greek Athletics', *Classical World* 78 (1984–5), 497–558, and 79 (1985–6), 73–135; id., 'Recent Trends in the Study of Greek Athletics', *AC* 59 (1990), 246–55; Golden, *Sport and Society*, 179–82. Collections of source material are provided by R. S. Robinson, *Sources for the History of Greek Athletics in English Translation* (Cincinnati, 1955); W. E. Sweet, *Sport and Recreation in Ancient Greece* (Oxford and New York, 1987); S. G. Miller, *Arete: Greek Sports from Ancient Sources*, 2nd edn. (Berkeley and Los Angeles, 1991) and for an athletic dictionary see M. Golden, *Sport in the Ancient World from A to Z* (London and New York, 2004). The journal *Nikephoros* is also dedicated to the discussion of ancient athletics and games.

[3] 1 Maccabees 1.10–14; 2 Maccabees 4.7–14. See G. Shipley, *The Greek World after Alexander 323–30 BC* (London and New York, 2000), 308–10.

[4] For bibliography on this, see Ch. 2, n. 1.

[5] F. Millar, *The Emperor in the Roman World*, 2nd edn. (London, 1992), 449, 451.

own senses of identity, and to negotiate their positions with others from across the Mediterranean.

ACTING GREEK AND THE BENEFITS OF EMPIRE

Ever since first coming into contact with the Greek world in the third century BC, and with growing impetus from the first century BC onwards, the Romans had eagerly embraced certain aspects of Greek culture, such as literature and philosophy, art and architecture. Greek intellectuals came to Rome as tutors, rhetoricians, or philosophers, while elite Romans themselves might spend a few years of their youth attending lectures in Athens.[6] Excessive engagement with Greek culture could be a cause for concern, though even individuals who were famed as being the most hostile to Greek culture, such as the elder Cato, were themselves also steeped in Greek learning.[7] It would appear that there were certain contexts in which Hellenism was appropriate and others where it was not, and it often seems to be inappropriate or excessive Hellenism that attracted the disapproval of moralists rather than Hellenism *per se*. Indeed, within these permitted contexts (e.g. a country villa or the Hellenized cities of Campania), the proper use of Greek culture could become a crucial sign of one's own identity as an educated elite Roman.[8] Of course, what constituted excessive Hellenism or an appropriate context could be a question for debate, with individuals adopting a range of views from the enthusiastically philhellenic to a more limited engagement with Greek culture. Some aspects of this culture were also slower to take hold than others. Involvement in Greek athletics seems to have been particularly problematic.[9] Traditional Roman morality was hostile to the public nudity and performance which were such characteristic features of Greek athletics and attacked the gymnasium as lustful and enervating.[10] However, both the literary and visual evidence suggest that during

---

[6] On the third and second centuries BC see J.-L. Ferrary, *Philhellénisme et Impérialisme: Aspects idéologiques de la conquête romaine du monde Hellénistique* (Rome, 1988), esp. 495–615; and E. S. Gruen, *Culture and National Identity in Republican Rome* (Ithaca, 1993). The first century BC is discussed by E. Rawson, *Intellectual Life in the Late Roman Republic* (London, 1985).

[7] Gruen, *Culture and Identity*, 52–83.

[8] A. Wallace-Hadrill, 'Greek Knowledge, Roman Power', *Classical Philology* 83 (1988), 224–33; id., 'Rome's Cultural Revolution', *JRS* 79 (1989), 157–64; id., 'Roman Arches and Greek Honours: The Language of Power at Rome', *PCPS* 36 (1990), 143–81; id., 'Mutatio Morum: The Idea of a Cultural Revolution', in T. Habinek and A. Schiesaro, eds., *The Roman Cultural Revolution* (Cambridge, 1997), 3–22; id., 'To be Roman, go Greek: Thoughts on Hellenization of Rome', in M. Austin, J. Harries, and C. Smith, eds., *Modus Operandi: Essays in Honour of Geoffrey Rickman*, BICS Supplement 71 (London, 1998), 79–91.

[9] See Ferrary, *Philhellénisme*, 517–26 on Roman attitudes to the gymnasium in the Republican period. S. Goldhill, *Being Greek under Rome: Cultural Identity, the Second Sophistic and the Development of Empire* (Cambridge, 2001), 10–13 discusses Roman attacks on excessive Greek culture at a later period.

[10] Cicero, *Tusculan Disputations* 4.70; Tacitus, *Annals* 14.20. For further discussion see Ch. 2.

the course of the first three centuries AD Greek-style athletic activity in the palaestra areas of public baths increasingly became the norm.

From Horace's declaration that 'captive Greece ensnared her wild conqueror' to Juvenal's satirical characterization of Rome as a Greek city, Latin sources acknowledge, relish, or lament the extensive influence that Greek culture exerted in diffuse areas of Roman life.[11] Concerns about the extent to which foreign luxuries had corrupted Roman morality went hand-in-hand with a delight in adopting them. Indeed, the very figures who were most outspoken in attacking this cultural trend were also those who were themselves most heavily implicated in it.[12] Yet while a satirist like Juvenal could suggest that the Romans were losing their own cultural identity by their keen adoption of all things eastern, this adoption was in fact more a case of adaptation and appropriation than of a wholesale acceptance of Greek values. Greek literature, philosophy, rhetoric, and art were indeed taken over by Romans, but in the process they were turned to the service of Roman needs. So Virgil's *First Eclogue* adapted the conventions of Theocritean bucolic poetry to allude to the contemporary realities of land confiscations, while Augustus appropriated the styles and themes of classical Greek art to serve his own self-representational purposes.[13]

This use of Greek culture to serve Roman concerns was, as I have said, a feature going back to the Republican period. Yet a number of changes and intensifications took place during the course of the Imperial period, particularly in respect to the Roman attitude to Greek athletics. While Roman villas of the Republican period had often included areas designed to evoke the intellectual and philosophical associations of the Greek gymnasium, interest in physical athletics, both as a form of personal training and as an object of spectatorship, seems only to have come to the fore in the Imperial period. A number of factors contributed to this. Imperial sponsorship of athletic festivals, such as those promoted by the emperors Augustus, Nero, and Domitian, must have been important. Yet these acts were probably themselves signs that feeling at Rome, in at least some quarters, was sympathetic to such a move, though the pattern traced in Chapter 2 shows that this was a steadily developing process during the course of the first century AD.

The population of Rome itself was also changing. Of course, Greeks had been present there as either slaves, freedmen, or visitors even in the Republic. Yet throughout the first century the areas from which Roman senators were drawn increasingly came to include the Greek-speaking eastern provinces, as well as other

---

[11] Horace, *Letters* 2.1.156; Juvenal, *Satire* 3.61.

[12] See especially C. Edwards, *The Politics of Immorality* (Cambridge, 1993), 24–8.

[13] *Eclogues*: G. Williams, *Tradition and Originality in Roman Poetry* (Oxford, 1968), 307–13; P. Hardie, *Virgil* (Oxford, 1998), 5–10; Augustus: P. Zanker, *The Power of Images in the Age of Augustus*, trans. A. Shapiro (Ann Arbor, 1988).

areas of the empire.[14] By the early third century, the imperial family itself had its roots partly in Syrian Emesa, through the intermarriage of the North African emperor Septimius Severus with the Syrian Julia Domna. Indeed, the eastern origins of the Severan emperors is likely to have played a significant part in their promotion of athletic culture at Rome, as we shall see in Chapter 3. Roman imperial society thus became increasingly cosmopolitan as time progressed, bringing together elites from different areas of the empire.

One thing which these elites shared was a common level of education, based in large part upon a knowledge of classical Greek culture. In the Republican period a figure like Cicero could quote Greek words or throw out learned allusions as a means of presenting himself as a member of the Roman aristocracy.[15] Yet as time went on, this marker of elite identity could also increasingly be used to bind together members of the elite from disparate areas of the Roman empire. This can be seen particularly clearly in the case of the North African orator and philosopher Apuleius. After an education first in Carthage and then Athens, and travels in Rome, Greece, and Asia Minor, Apuleius settled in North Africa and a career in Latin oratory.[16] He claims to have written Greek works too, and often refers to his knowledge of the Greek language.[17] Stephen Harrison has characterized Apuleius as a 'Latin sophist' and his literary interests do share many similarities with those appearing in contemporary Greek literature and oratory. However, when his audience is Roman, Apuleius can also be seen as acting in the time-honoured fashion of a Roman aristocrat, flaunting his knowledge of Greek language, literature, and philosophy as a means of showing his educated, elite status. This is especially clear in the *Apology*, where Apuleius' quotation of long passages of Greek seems designed to create a bond with his Roman judge which is based on their shared education, *paideia*, while distancing them both from the boorish prosecutors.[18]

While Greek culture may have afforded a means of communication between members of the elite, and while its delights were increasingly enjoyed in cities around the empire, it never took over completely in the west. 'Greek' practices, such as athletics, seem to have kept their veneer of Greekness, and hostility or ambivalence towards the influence of eastern culture, and particularly the perceived degeneracy of modern-day Greeks could still be shown as a marker of

---

[14] See further below, pp. 139–40.

[15] On Cicero see S. Swain, 'Bilingualism in Cicero? The Evidence of Code-Switching', in J. N. Adams, M. Janse, and S. Swain, eds., *Bilingualism in Ancient Society: Language Contact and the Written Text* (Oxford, 2002), 128–67.

[16] S. Harrison, *Apuleius: A Latin Sophist* (Oxford, 2000), 5–9.

[17] e.g. Apuleius, *Florida* 9.29, ed. V. Hunink (Amsterdam, 2001). On Apuleius' bilingualism see Anderson, *Second Sophistic*, 123.

[18] e.g. Apuleius, *Apology*, 10. See Harrison, *Apuleius*, 45–7.

Roman morality. The Roman elite were characterized both by their selective adoption and adaptation of elements of Greek culture and, simultaneously, by a moralizing attitude towards those who let themselves slip too far into these delights.

Part I of this book focuses on Rome's engagement with athletic culture with the broader aim of investigating her changing involvement with Greek culture more generally. Chapter 2 looks at the introduction of Greek athletic festivals to Rome, and the increased interest shown in physical training within the Roman baths, arguing that athletic activity, still strongly signalled as an element of 'Greek' rather than 'Roman' culture, came to exert a pervasive effect on the leisure and spectacle culture of the city of Rome. In Chapter 3 I take a closer look at the visual evidence relating to Greek athletics, particularly the scenes of athletic activity which decorated bath complexes in Ostia and Rome, as well as the spread of athletic activity to other areas in the west of the empire. My focus here is on how this decoration helped to reflect and give meaning to the activities which took place within the baths, allowing bathers to see their own activities as parallel to those of their sporting heroes, even if few of them actually took part in public competitions themselves.

Chapter 4 turns to the world of elite villas, and especially the idealizing statues of athletes which were used to define certain areas as gymnasium spaces. While this use of statues can be traced back to the Republican period too, the increased interest in Greek athletics in the Imperial age added to the range of associations such statues provoked. Yet the continuities with the past also remained strong, the forms of the statues evoking the values of classical Greece and the wider cultural and educational ideals of the gymnasium. The preference shown in certain villas for youthful boyish figures might also have provoked a sensual or erotic appreciation of these idealized beautiful bodies.

In all these areas—spectacle culture, exercise at the baths, and idealized sculptural display in villas—the exotic and foreign connotations of Greek athletics seem to have remained a major part of its attraction. Roman bathers might indulge in a little light wrestling at the baths, or delight in looking at beautifully honed athletic naked bodies, but these versions of athletics were tailored to Roman needs and desires. The Greek ideal of victory in public athletic competition as embodying the height of masculine physical prowess, and the associations of a gymnasium education with the training of worthy citizens and soldiers, never entered into the Roman experience of athletics. Whether experienced by a spectator, bather, or villa owner, athletics remained part of the world of relaxation, leisure, and *otium*, a sign of cosmopolitan delights rather than a crucial element in the creation of a Roman citizen. Debates on Roman attitudes towards Greek culture tend to become polarized between those who see the situation in the third century AD as roughly the same as that under Augustus and those who argue that in the course of those three centuries Greek and Roman culture gradually came to be almost interchangeable.[19] As with any such stark dichotomy, the truth rather lies somewhere in the middle. My examination of the Roman attitude to athletics does suggest the gradual integration and absorption of this key element of Greek culture. However, it also shows that it was never completely adopted, never fully taken over as an integral part of Roman identity. Like the pleasures afforded by art, food, or philosophy, athletics finds its place in the world of pleasure, part and parcel of the benefits of empire and indulgences of Greek culture.

ATHLETICS, THE PAST, AND GREEK IDENTITY IN THE SECOND SOPHISTIC

In Part II of the book I turn from the west to the Greek east of the Empire. Many of the features of athletics in the west can also be found here, but in the east athletics also played a much deeper, more significant, role in the creation of individual and civic identities. Many aspects of this flourishing of athletic activity in the Imperial period can, of course, be seen in earlier centuries too. The Olympic games had continued to attract both competitors and spectators since the conventional date of its foundation in 776 BC, though its appeal may have weakened slightly in the late Hellenistic period.[20] Similarly the numerous new festivals instituted around the Greek world during the course of the second and third centuries AD carried on a trend begun in the Hellenistic period.[21] The role played by athletic training in the gymnasium, particularly as part of the *ephēbeia* (the training of citizen youths) can also be traced back to the Classical and Hellenistic periods.[22] Yet there was also something new both about the intensity of athletic and festival activity in the Roman east, and in the historical and cultural circumstances in which it took place. This is the period which has become known as the Greek Renaissance, a period when the political and military instability of the late Republican period was past

---

[19] G. Woolf, 'Becoming Roman, Staying Greek: Culture, Identity and the Civilising Process in the Roman East', *PCPS* 40 (1994), 116–43, at 130, arguing in favour of the former.

[20] A. Farrington, 'Olympic Victors and the Popularity of the Olympic Games in the Imperial Period', *Tyche* 12 (1997), 15–46; Scanlon, *Eros*, 41–5. For a good general discussion of the festival see M. I. Finley and H. W. Pleket, *The Olympic Games: The First Thousand Years* (London, 1976). Other accounts are given by L. Drees, *Olympia, Gods, Artists, and Athletes* (London, 1967); J. Swaddling, *The Ancient Olympic Games*, 2nd edn. (London, 1999); U. Sinn, *Olympia: Cult, Sport, and Ancient Festival*, trans. T. Thornton (Princeton, 2000).

[21] For discussions of festivals see L. Robert, 'Discours d'ouverture', in *Praktika of the Eighth International Congress of Greek and Latin Epigraphy* (Athens, 1984), i. 35–45; A. J. S. Spawforth, 'Agonistic Festivals in Roman Greece', in S. Walker and A. Cameron, eds., *The Greek Renaissance in the Roman Empire*, BICS Supplement 55 (London, 1989), 193–7; S. Mitchell, 'Festivals, Games and Civic Life in Roman Asia Minor', *JRS* 80 (1990), 183–93; H. Pleket, 'Games, Prizes, Athletes and Ideology: Some Aspects of the History of Sport in the Greco-Roman World', *Stadion* (=*Arena*) 1 (1975), 49–89 at 54–71.

[22] J. Delorme, *Gymnasion: Étude sur les monuments consacrés à l'éducation en Grèce* (Paris, 1960).

and the cities of the Greek east, particularly those in Asia Minor, could use their citizens' wealth in public building projects and festival foundations.[23] It is also the period which witnessed the flourishing of the 'Second Sophistic', a rhetorical movement described by Philostratus as beginning in the middle of the first century AD and lasting at least until his own period in the mid-third century AD.[24]

The characteristics of the Second Sophistic and the literary production associated with it have attracted increased scholarly attention over the last thirty or so years.[25] While scholars used to despair of the imitative quality of much Greek imperial literature, we now see the complex series of allusions and reworkings as signs of a creative engagement with the past, a way of harnessing the greats of classical Greek culture, from Homer to Plato and Euripides, in the service of the creation of new senses of Greek identity under Roman power.[26] The sophists themselves, whose lives are recorded in Philostratus' *Lives of the Sophists*, are well described by Bowersock as 'virtuoso rhetor[s] with . . . big public reputation[s]'.[27] These figures were primarily orators, performing improvised speeches on themes taken from Greek history to vast and enthusiastic audiences, as well as imparting their knowledge to bands of students who followed them from city to city, acting as entourage and groupies while imbibing oratorical skills in the process.[28] Like other members of the wealthy and educated elite from which they mostly came, the sophists could also act as ambassadors and benefactors to their own, or adopted, cities and might include among their friends members of the Roman elite, extending even to the emperor.[29] Indeed, some remarkable figures could themselves combine their

---

[23] S. Walker and A. Cameron, eds., *The Greek Renaissance in the Roman Empire*, BICS Supplement 55 (London, 1989). See P. Veyne, *Bread and Circuses: Historical Sociology and Political Pluralism*, trans. B. Pearce (London, 1990), 70–200 on euergetism.

[24] Philostratus, *Lives of the Sophists* 1.481.

[25] e.g. G. W. Bowersock, *Greek Sophists in the Roman Empire* (Oxford, 1969); E. L. Bowie, 'The Greeks and their Past in the Second Sophistic', *Past and Present* 46 (1970), 3–41 (reprinted in M. I. Finley, ed., *Studies in Ancient Society* (London, 1974), 166–209); G. W. Bowersock, ed., *Approaches to the Second Sophistic* (University Park, Pa., 1974); G. Anderson, *Philostratus: Biography and Belles Lettres in the Third Century AD* (London, 1986); id., *The Second Sophistic: A Cultural Phenomenon in the Roman Empire* (London and New York, 1993); S. Swain, *Hellenism and Empire: Language, Classicism and Power in the Greek World AD 50–250* (Oxford, 1996); T. Schmitz, *Bildung und Macht: zur sozialen und politischen Funktion der zweiten Sophistik in der griechischen Welt*, Zetemata 97 (Munich, 1997); Goldhill, *Being Greek*; T. Whitmarsh, *Greek Literature and the Roman Empire: The Politics of Imitation* (Oxford, 2001).

[26] Whitmarsh, *Greek Literature*, 41–5 discusses the history of scholarship.

[27] Bowersock, *Greek Sophists*, 13. Much discussion has focused on what precisely the sophists did, how 'new' they were and the occasionally pejorative associations of the word. Against the sceptical view expressed by P. Brunt, 'The Bubble of the Second Sophistic', *BICS* 39 (1994), 25–52 see Schmitz, *Bildung und Macht*, 9–18 and G. W. Bowersock, 'Philosophy in the Second Sophistic', in G. Clark and T. Rajak, eds., *Philosophy and Power in the Graeco-Roman World: Essays in Honour of Miriam Griffin* (Oxford, 2002), 157–70, at 159–60.

[28] Anderson, *Second Sophistic*, esp. 13–46.

[29] See Bowersock, *Greek Sophists* with the corrective provided by E. L. Bowie, 'The Importance of the Sophists', *YCS* 27 (1982), 29–60.

performance and teaching lives with duties within both civic and imperial administration, as did the Athenian sophist Herodes Atticus, who served as archon at Athens and as Roman consul as well as being a major sophist and performer.

What has all this to do with athletics? The answer is that the overwhelming interest in Greek culture and identity which permeates the speeches of the sophists, as well as much of the contemporary Greek literature, can also be seen in the culture of Greek civic life more generally. Thomas Schmitz has defined the sophists as exemplary figures, embodying through their superior grasp of the classical past the superiority of the educated elite more generally.[30] Yet while the elite were indeed literally speaking a different language from the majority of ordinary Greeks (Attic Greek as opposed to the *koinē* form used in normal speech), they also embodied an attitude to the Greek past which was crucial to the construction of *civic* as well as *elite* identities.[31]

Indeed, the audiences who attended oratorical displays, or watched athletic performances during civic festivals, would have been drawn from the whole range of society. Wealth and education were usually necessary to become a successful sophist, orator, or athlete, but the prowess of these figures also helped to assert that of their city as a whole. Their performances marked them out as belonging to a privileged elite, but they also contributed towards the creation of civic identities. While this was true in the cases of oratory and competitive euergetism, it seems to have been particularly noticeable in the area of athletics. As I show in Chapters 5 and 6, the ephebic competitions of Athens and Sparta, which primarily involved the wealthy elite of those cities, also embodied and performed the civic identity of the whole city. The victory statues set up in Olympia and around the Greek world certainly commemorated the achievements of particular individuals, but they also acted as signs that the city from which the victor came was firmly part of the Greek world. When looking at euergetism too, as I show in Chapter 8, the benefactors may be members of the wealthy elite, but through their bequests they open up the ideals and associations of Greek culture to be enjoyed by all, albeit at different levels of engagement.

Although some may have worked their way up from more lowly beginnings, many of the most successful athletes of the imperial period do seem to come from elite families, or to have achieved elite status through their successes.[32] It is now

---

[30] Schmitz, *Bildung und Macht*, 39–66.

[31] On language, see Swain, *Hellenism and Empire*, 17–64. As an account of the many ways in which the Greeks responded to their past, Bowie, 'Greeks and their Past' is still crucial.

[32] For discussions of the social background of competitors see H. W. Pleket, 'Zur Soziologie des antiken Sports', *Mededelingen van het Nederlands Instituut te Rome* 36 (1974), 57–87; id., 'The Participants in the Ancient Olympic Games: Social Background and Mentality', in W. Coulson and H. Kyrieleis, eds., *Proceedings of an International Symposium on the Olympic Games, 5–9 September 1988* (Athens, 1992), 147–52; O. van Nijf, 'Athletics, Festivals and Greek Identity in the Roman East', *PCPS* 45 (1999), 176–200; id., 'Local Heroes: Athletics, Festivals and Elite Self-Fashioning in the Roman East', in Goldhill, *Being Greek*, 306–34.

widely recognized that earlier assertions about the debasement of athletics in the Roman period have more to do with a nineteenth-century amateur ideal than with the realities of the ancient world.[33] As van Nijf and König have recently argued, athletic activity could play a crucial role in the construction of elite masculine identities, one which has often been underplayed by the stress that has been put on rhetorical skills, though these were also, of course, of great importance.[34] Athletic victors were often members of the wealthy elite and athletic competition could play an important part in the rivalries and jostlings for position that took place between members of that elite.

Yet what I want to concentrate on in this book is the way in which these figures could represent and embody ideals which were relevant not just to the elite but also to the whole city. Through their activities they helped to reinforce civic senses of identity and the engagement with the values of the classical past. In concentrating on civic identities, as well as the ways that they were enabled and expressed by the activities of a few, I want to suggest that while extensive involvement in athletics may have been restricted to a fairly small group, that group served to embody ideals and values which were crucial for their wider communities as a whole.

Much of the scholarship on the Second Sophistic has divided between seeing the Greeks' interest in their culture and past either as a means of accommodating Roman rule or as a sign of resistance to or escape from it.[35] Others have turned instead to the ways that literature playfully constructs and performs a variety of Hellenic identities.[36] Certainly there were a variety of different versions of Hellenic identity, and Greek culture, the past, and identity were understood in many different ways by different people. Yet here I wish to concentrate more on similarities than differences. While the Greek literary texts often play complex games with aspects of Greek culture and their associations, a number of repeated features recur again and again.[37] Much of the literature concerning athletics examines the relationship between the athletics of the present and the past, and considers the role that athletic training and competition played within education, particularly its

---

[33] D. C. Young, *The Olympic Myth of Greek Amateur Athletics* (Chicago, 1984).

[34] van Nijf, 'Local Heroes', esp. 321; J. König, *Athletics and Literature in the Roman Empire* (Cambridge, forthcoming), introduction. See also Pleket, 'Games, Prizes', 74–89 and contrast M. Gleason, *Making Men: Sophists and Self-presentation in Ancient Rome* (Princeton, 1995); Schmitz, *Bildung und Macht*. For an analysis of the way that this agonistic culture pervaded other areas of elite life, see T. Barton, *Power and Knowledge: Astrology, Physiognomics and Medicine under the Roman Empire* (Ann Arbor, 1994).

[35] Accommodation: Bowersock, *Greek Sophists*; Resistance: Bowie, 'Greeks and their Past'. For accounts of the ways Greek authors responded to Roman rule see J. Palm, *Rom, Römertum und Imperium in der griechischen Literatur der Kaiserzeit* (Lund, 1959) and Swain, *Hellenism and Empire*. See also the overview in Bowersock, 'Philosophy', 157–60.

[36] Whitmarsh, *Greek Literature*, taking a New Historicist approach. See also the papers in Goldhill, *Being Greek*.

[37] The varied performances of athletic culture shown in Greek imperial literature are explored by König, *Athletics and Literature*.

associations with military training and the overlaps between athletic competition and warfare. While not all authors fully subscribe to all the values with which athletics is invested, their very discussion of and engagement with those values is itself strong evidence for their continuing importance in the world of the Roman empire.

Identity is a notoriously slippery concept to grasp and individuals may often have had a number of competing self-identities, both as members of the imperial Roman elite and as loyal citizens of a particular town. Within the eastern Roman empire there was also a whole range of different sorts of Greek identity to which individuals and cities could lay claim. The ancient cities of the Greek mainland, such as Athens and Sparta, had long-standing historical and cultural claims to be seen as authentic 'Greek' cities. The major cities of Asia Minor, such as Pergamum or Ephesus, could not claim such an integral role in classical Greek history. However, their wealth and thriving cultural life in the Roman period could instead entitle them to an equally powerful counter-claim to be the new inheritors of the Greek past.[38] Other cities had weaker claims, the Hellenized cities of Syria or Egypt, for example, or the native cities of Asia Minor such as those in Lycia and Pamphylia. Yet many of these chose to acquire a Greek identity, proclaiming ancestral links with the cities of the Greek mainland, or using their cultural lives to assert their adherence to all the values of Greek civic life.[39] The very fact that cities like Side, discussed here in Chapter 8, chose to institute and advertise athletic festivals, is a powerful sign of the pervasive role that athletic activity played within Greek culture, and the importance placed on claims to be a part of the Greek world.

In order to look at the ways in which athletic activity helped to assert Greek identities for a range of different sorts of cities I have chosen to investigate a number of case studies. In Chapters 5 and 6 I focus on the 'old' Greek cities of Athens and Sparta, and particularly on the ways that the *ephēbeia* in these cities helped to reassert the individual virtues to which they had laid claim since the Classical period. In both cities ephebic training was strongly associated with traditional ideas about the training of citizen soldiers, showing that the ideological link between athletics and warfare was still pervasive in the Roman period. It seems likely that the *ephēbeia* in other Greek cities too would also have evoked similar ideas. Yet a comparison of Athens and Sparta also shows that the *ephēbeia* played specific roles relating to the individual ways in which these cities wished to present themselves. The continuance of brutal and unusual contests as part of the Spartan

---

[38] On the claims of cities in Asia Minor to their own particular brand of Hellenic identity, see Z. Newby, 'Art and Identity in Asia Minor', in S. Scott and J. Webster, eds., *Roman Imperialism and Provincial Art* (Cambridge, 2003), 192–213.

[39] On civic genealogies see Bowie, 'Greeks and their Past', 19–22; S. Mitchell, 'Iconium and Ninica: Two Double Communities in Roman Asia Minor', *Historia* 28 (1979), 409–38; L. Robert, 'Deux inscriptions de Tarse et d'Argos', *BCH* 101 (1977), 80–132, especially 120–9.

agōgē was a way of asserting Sparta's individuality, her specific claims to a particular sort of warlikeness. In Athens too, the images decorating ephebic stelae suggest that the *ephēbeia* here was seen as asserting the continued importance of Athens' naval heritage and her key role during the Persian wars. The situations in Athens and Sparta show a number of broad similarities, but they also suggest that ephebic training could be tailored to the specific representational needs of individual cities. This is emblematic of the ways that civic involvement in athletic activity could be used to assert values held across the Greek world, but also to show an individual city's specific claims to prestige within those broader ideals.

This combined assertion of a broad Greek identity and particular local importance is also a key feature of Pausanias' description of Greece. In Chapter 7 I turn from the *ephēbeia* to athletic festivals to consider the importance which the key athletic festival, that of Olympia, played within Greek constructions of identity in the Roman world. Pausanias strongly asserts the centrality of Olympia as crucial to Hellenic identity, particularly through its status as a place of Panhellenic unity—a place where representatives of all Greek states could meet, but which could also be used as a forum for expressions of rivalry and competition. Pausanias' construction of Greece is, of course, an individual one, and his privileging of Olympia may in part be due to a desire to modify or challenge other constructions of Greece, such as the Athenocentric version propagated especially by Hadrian. However, his discussion of the Olympic victory monuments which were scattered throughout the cities of Greece, and the ways in which a victory at Olympia serves to justify not only individual, but also civic, claims to identity, can also be traced elsewhere, in other literary texts such as Philostratus' *Life of Apollonius*, as well as in the epigraphical evidence.

In Chapter 8 I turn away from the Greek mainland to look instead at some of the cities of Asia Minor. As mentioned above, these cities had a different sort of relationship to Greek culture and identity. While the great cities of the western coast, such as Ephesus, had thriving cultural lives, and indeed produced and educated a number of the sophists themselves, their claims to Greek culture differed from those of the cities in mainland Greece. At least Ephesus could claim to be a Greek foundation. Many other cities, such as Hierapolis and Aphrodisias, only became Greek cities in the Hellenistic period, and even Ephesus had only existed on her current site since the third century BC.[40] Yet it was these cities who increasingly furnished Olympic victors in the Roman period, and their elites who rose to positions of civic and imperial power. While they might not have had the historical advantages of cities like Athens and Sparta, they exceeded those cities in wealth and

---

[40] P. Scherrer, 'The City of Ephesos from the Roman Period to Late Antiquity', in H. Koester, ed., *Ephesos: Metropolis of Asia* (Valley Forge, Pa., 1995), 1–25, at 3–4.

often possessed flourishing religious sanctuaries that drew in visitors.[41] Chapter 8 focuses on the ways in which the elites of cities in Asia Minor used their wealth to found festivals and erect and decorate complexes dedicated to athletic activity. Here too my selection of examples is designed to give an idea of the range of ways in which euergetism associated with athletics was used to assert individual and civic senses of identity. While a great city like Ephesus could boast of four separate bath-gymnasia, all lavishly decorated with idealizing statues linking contemporary pursuits to the values of classical Greece, other smaller cities chose to advertise their Hellenic credentials through the institution of a festival, or the commemoration of their Olympic victors. While the basis of their claims to Greek identity varied, all of these cities show the importance placed on festivals and gymnasia as symbols of belonging to the wider Greek world.

GREEK CULTURE AND ROMAN POWER

This book is divided into two halves, looking respectively at the Roman appropriation of Greek athletics in the service of luxury, entertainment, and elite self-fashioning, and at the use of Greek athletics in the Greek world, where it was also involved with the creation of deeper identities situated around the Greeks' understanding of their own culture and past. Yet these two halves cannot be so easily divided. Through the institution of the Capitoline Games at Rome in AD 86, Rome herself became part of the Greek festival circuit. While never attaining the status of Olympia, Rome exercised a dominant effect on Greek festival culture through the involvement of the emperor in regulating the institution of new festivals, and through the erection here in the mid-second century AD of the headquarters for the international guild of athletes.

Imperial interest in the institution of new 'sacred' or 'crown' games was certainly in part financial.[42] These prestigious festivals awarded only a prize of foliage to their victors, instead of the monetary prizes awarded in the lesser 'thematic' or 'prize' games, but this prize was far from being purely symbolic.[43] Instead it entitled the victor to numerous benefits from his home city, ranging from meals at public expense to exemption from taxation and triumphal entrance into the city (the *eiselasis* which led to these festivals sometimes being called *eiselastikos*). Yet imperial involvement in international festival culture would have had other motivations as well. The evidence suggests that this was a key area for cities to assert their claims to Greek identity. It was probably wise, then, for emperors to infiltrate themselves into it as fully as possible.

---

[41] On the renown of Ephesus in the Imperial period see Pausanias 4.31.8.

[42] Millar, *Emperor*, 451.   [43] For a fuller discussion see Pleket, 'Games, Prizes', 54–71.

Indeed, as we will see in Chapter 8, emperors were highly visible in civic festivals, mentioned in sacrifices, represented in processions of statues, and often included either in the name of the festival or in visual representations such as those on the theatre at Hierapolis.[44] Sometimes this would have been due to imperial actions, when an emperor himself gave a sacred festival to a city as a mark of honour and prestige. Yet at others the impetus must have come from the city itself, as a mark of loyalty and respect to the imperial house.[45] Indeed, often it is hard to know where the impetus first arose and a diplomatic dialogue of civic honours and imperial acceptances should probably be imagined. To see the presence of the imperial family in all areas of civic life, from the statues decorating the gymnasium to those carried in public procession, as a matter of either domination from above or accommodation from below, is overly simplistic. It was both simultaneously. It allowed the emperor to keep an eye on Greek expressions of cultural hierarchy and present himself as the supreme benefactor preserving and cherishing Greek culture. Yet, at the same time, it allowed the Greek cities themselves to assert their belief in the superiority of their own cultural values, while also signalling their loyalty to Rome. While some individuals may have seen imperial control as intrusive, in the end this solution allowed both sides to save face, asserting the emperor's right to interfere in all aspects of imperial culture, while also upholding and respecting the superior cultural values of the Greek heritage.

CHOICES AND CASE STUDIES

In order to get closer to the ideals and associations which congregated around athletic activity in the Roman period I have chosen to focus in particular on visual and material evidence, pairing this with the representations of athletics which we find in both Greek and Latin literary texts. A number of recent studies have focused on the epigraphical evidence relating to Greek athletics in the Imperial period.[46]

---

[44] On the ubiquity of the imperial presence in all areas of civic life see S. R. F. Price, *Rituals and Power: The Roman Imperial Cult in Asia Minor* (Cambridge, 1984), which is crucial reading for any understanding of the relationship between the Greek cities and Roman power. For a focus on one particular festival, see G. M. Rogers, *The Sacred Identity of Ephesos: Foundation Myths of a Roman City* (London, 1991), esp. 80–126.

[45] On the difficulties of distinguishing initial motivation: M. T. Boatwright, *Hadrian and the Cities of the Roman Empire* (Princeton, 2000), 94, 104–5.

[46] Much early work was done by Louis Robert, e.g. L. Robert, 'Deux concours grecs à Rome', *CRAI* (1970), 6–27; id., 'Discours d'ouverture' and Luigi Moretti; esp. L. Moretti, *Olympionikai: i vincitori negli antichi agoni olympici*, Atti della Accademia Nazionale dei Lincei 8 (Rome, 1957), with three supplements in *Klio* 52 (1970), 295–303, in *Miscellanea greca e romana* 12 (1987), 67–91, and in W. Coulson and H. Kyrieleis eds., *Proceedings of an International Symposium on the Olympic Games, 5–9 September 1988* (Athens, 1992), 119–28; also Moretti, *IAG*. For accounts of Greek festivals in the west see M. L. Caldelli, *L'Agon Capitolinus* (Rome, 1993), and ead., *Gli agoni alla greca nelle regioni occidentali dell'impero: La Gallia Narbonensis* (Rome, 1997) and on athletics in the Greek east, van Nijf, 'Athletics'; id., 'Local Heroes'.

The Greek literary texts, so often in the past mined simply for the information which they can shed on athletics of an earlier period, have also recently been studied within their cultural and historical contexts by Jason König.[47] Yet little work has been done on the prolific visual evidence. Earlier studies of athletic sculpture, such as those by Hyde and Rausa, have concentrated instead on the Classical period, using Roman statues primarily as a means of reconstructing the lost originals.[48]

In fact, the visual evidence relating to athletics is extensive, and it allows us access to a wider spectrum of society than is represented in the literary texts. Thus the picture painted by material evidence from Italy, particularly the mosaic pavements from Rome and Ostia, helps to clarify that given in the moralizing Latin sources, identifying their hostility to Greek athletics as a response to its incredible popularity among all levels of society. In the Greek east too, while the values associated with athletic activity in the literary sources have more in common with the visual material, this also helps to show the breadth across which athletic activity was advertised, showing its importance on a civic level and giving a positive picture of the values associated with athletics which the playfulness of literary texts such as Lucian's *Anacharsis* sometimes challenged or exploited.

By putting together visual, literary, and epigraphic evidence, I hope to provide a deeper insight into the ways Greek athletics were used and experienced by both Greeks and Romans which also illuminates the wider roles played by Greek culture in the middle Roman empire. While I am using athletics in part as one example of the many uses of Greek culture, the extensive evidence relating to it suggests that it was indeed a major area in which engagement with the Greek past, identity, and culture centred. The enduring importance of Greek athletics in the Roman period can be seen as a last stage in the history of its place within Greek culture and history more generally, a history which has until now mostly been focused on earlier periods. A proper understanding of the roles played by athletics in the Roman period is also crucial for our understanding of those earlier periods, since so much

---

[47] J. König, 'Athletic Training and Athletic Festivals in the Greek Literature of the Roman Empire', D.Phil. thesis (Cambridge, 2000), revised as *Athletics and Literature*. Earlier accounts looking at the historical background behind these texts can be found in B. Bilinski, *L'agonistica sportiva nella grecia antica: aspetti sociali e ispirazioni letterarie* (Rome, 1959), 107–28 and Müller, *Volk*, 296–330.

[48] Hyde, *OVM*; F. Rausa, *L'immagine del vincitore: L'atleta nella statuaria greca dell'età arcaica all' ellenismo* (Rome, 1994). See also N. J. Serwint, 'Greek Athletic Sculpture from the Fifth and Fourth Centuries BC: An Iconographic Study', Ph.D. thesis (Princeton, 1987) and W. J. Raschke, 'Images of Victory: Some New Considerations of Athletic Monuments', in ead., ed., *Archaeology of the Olympics: The Olympics and Other Games in Antiquity* (Madison, Wis., 1988), 38–54. L. Kurke, 'The Economy of Kudos', in C. Dougherty and L. Kurke, eds., *Cultural Poetics in Archaic Greece: Cult, Performance, Politics* (Cambridge, 1993), 131–63 and D. Steiner, 'Moving Images: Fifth-Century Victory Monuments and the Athlete's Allure', *Classical Antiquity* 17 (1998), 123–49; ead., *Images in Mind: Statues in Archaic and Classical Greek Literature and Thought* (Princeton and Oxford, 2001), 222–34 give contextual accounts of the roles played by these statues in classical Greece.

of the literary and visual evidence used to investigate them was actually produced during the period of the Roman empire.

In taking Greek athletics as my subject, I have chosen to concentrate on personal physical activity, events such as running, wrestling, boxing, and the pancratium (a combination of boxing and wrestling), leaving aside equestrian events. While the contests of Greek festivals often included chariot and horse races as well as athletic events, they are usually separated from the athletic events in the descriptions of those festivals. So Suetonius' account of the introduction of the Capitoline games at Rome describes it as 'musicum equestre gymnicum', 'musical, equestrian and gymnastic', separating out these three categories of competition.[49] Chariot racing, in particular, could often involve hired jockeys of servile status, and in the Capitoline games the factions which dominated chariot racing at Rome also seem to have taken part.[50] A comparison of Greek and Roman chariot racing, as well as one between the brutalities of boxing and gladiatorial combat, could certainly yield interesting insights into the boundaries between those activities characterized as either Greek or Roman, but is beyond the scope of this book. Similarly, while many of the comments which I make about the significance of Greek festivals relate to the festival as a whole and not purely to its athletic manifestation, I have chosen to leave aside discussion of the theatrical and musical contests which usually took place alongside the athletic ones.[51] Instead, I focus on the two major aspects of Greek athletics, summed up in my title as victory and virtue—competitive athletics as practised in public festivals and the role played by athletic training in the gymnasium as part of both education and leisure.

In choosing case studies I have been influenced most by my desire to investigate the changing use of Greek athletics at both major and minor sites around the Roman world, as well as by the spread of surviving evidence. Since I am interested in Roman appropriations of Greek athletics, Rome and her surroundings form an obvious central focus in Part I of the book. In Chapter 2 I aim to investigate the Roman reaction to both sides of Greek athletics—as spectacle and physical training—through a discussion of the introduction of Greek-style festivals to Rome and the impact which Greek athletics had on activities within the Roman baths. My focus on mosaics and bath decoration in Chapter 3 allows us to see how the world of contemporary spectacle influenced activities at the baths, as well as documenting the spread of interest in Greek athletics from Rome and Italy to other areas of the western provinces. Yet in Roman eyes the gymnasium was not just a place for athletic activity, it was also closely associated with intellectual and philosophical values. In Chapter 4 I turn to the idealized images of athletes in

---

[49] Suetonius, *Domitian* 4.4.   [50] Caldelli, *Agon*, 81–2.

[51] However, these were often discussed in connection with athletic activities as another integral part of Greek culture and education, e.g. Lucian, *Anacharsis* 22–3.

Roman villas to see how they illustrate the Roman understanding of Greek athletics as part of the classical Greek past as well as a feature of contemporary life. The two imperial villas of Domitian and Hadrian provide the opportunity to reconstruct particular displays in some detail and show a number of broad similarities both with one another and with other elite villas in their use of classicizing athletic figures. Yet the precise choices made in these statuary ensembles also show that within the broader range of options, individual owners could select particular statues to create or reflect an individual image.

Part II turns from the western empire to the east, continuing with a dual focus on both gymnasium and festival athletics. As outlined above, Chapters 5 and 6 explore the continuing ideological importance of a gymnasium education at the most prestigious cities of the Greek mainland, Sparta and Athens, both still revered for their greatness in the classical past. In particular, I argue that the material remains produced by the *ephēbeia* in both cities suggest its continuing role in the construction of civic self-representations. In Chapters 7 and 8 I turn to the wider Greek world and the role that festivals and the celebration of athletic victories had in creations of Greek civic identity. Chapter 7 focuses on Olympia, arguing for the crucial centrality of this festival site in constructions of Greekness. In Chapter 8 I turn instead to Asia Minor, to explore the ways that the importance of athletic activity—both in festivals and the gymnasium—is revealed by the choices made by elite euergetes, and the monuments or images erected in individual cities. The abundance of evidence here makes choices inevitable. My focus on Ephesus, Aphrodisias, Hierapolis, and Side is designed to give an overview of the ways that athletic culture was used in cities with varying claims to wealth, status, and Greek identity in the service of their particular creations of self-identities.

Throughout this book, I have aimed to use the detailed examination of particular case studies to illuminate both broader trends in the use of athletic culture and the particular ways that those trends were customized to serve individual needs. While it is far from being comprehensive or exhaustive, I hope that this account will help further to flesh out our picture of the appropriations and adaptations which Greek culture and the past underwent in the world of the Roman empire and of the central role which continued to be played by athletic activity.

PART I

Athletics in the Roman West

TWO

Greek Athletics in the Heart of Rome

It has been a truism of past scholarship that the Romans had no time for Greek athletics, attacking the immorality and lewdness of the Greek gymnasium and preferring the violent contests of the arena and the circus to athletics in the stadium. Plentiful quotations from Latin literature have been used to support these claims and, for the most part, scholars have been content to ignore or underplay the literary, epigraphical, and visual evidence which attests to Greek athletic activities in the heart of Rome. This can be seen especially clearly in the scholarship on Roman spectacle culture, which has long been dominated instead by the study of gladiatorial contests and chariot races. Yet the interest in Roman spectacles which is attested by these studies suggests that an examination of other types of public spectacle and performance should indeed be a welcome addition to the field.

In this chapter I intend to study the literary and archaeological evidence for the introduction of Greek athletic festivals and training to Rome, and thus to set some of the most-cited criticisms of Greek athletics more firmly into their cultural contexts. The following chapters in this section will look more closely at the visual evidence, suggesting that this shows a strong interest in contemporary athletic festivals as well as the broader cultural ideals of the Greek gymnasium, both in Rome and elsewhere around the western provinces of the empire.

ATHLETIC SPECTACLES AND PHYSICAL TRAINING

Over the last thirty years or so Roman spectacle culture has become a popular area of research, with a whole series of works investigating the Roman games, including monographs on individual forms of entertainment, such as the circus, gladiators, and aquatic displays.[1] Many of these works discuss the importance which public

[1] R. Auguet, *Cruauté et civilisation: les jeux romaines* (Paris, 1970); A. Cameron, *Circus Factions* (Oxford, 1976); G. Ville, *La Gladiature en Occident des Origines à la Mort de Domitien* (Rome, 1981); K. Hopkins, *Death and Renewal* (Cambridge, 1983), 1–30; T. Wiedemann, *Emperors and Gladiators* (London and New York, 1992); C. A. Barton, *The Sorrows of the Ancient Romans: The Gladiator and the Monster* (Princeton, 1993); K. Coleman, 'Fatal Charades: Roman Executions Staged as Mythological Enactments', *JRS* 80 (1990), 44–73; ead., 'Launching into History: Aquatic Displays in the Early Empire', *JRS* 83 (1993), 48–74. See also the catalogues of the series of exhibitions held at Lattes in France: C. Domergue, C. Landes, and J.-M. Pailler,

spectacles came to have within Roman culture, often citing Juvenal's famous observation about the Roman people: 'those who once gave power, rods of office, legions, everything, now restrain themselves and hope anxiously for two things only, bread and circuses (*panem et circenses*)'.[2] While most of these studies concentrate on the popular events of the circus and arena, only a few have begun to consider the interplay between Greek and Roman forms of spectacle and the role which Greek-style athletic contests also played within the entertainment culture of ancient Rome, subjects which were, however, prefigured in the work of the French scholar Louis Robert.[3] In particular, Maria Caldelli has started to look at the introduction of Greek-style games in the west in terms of imperial policy.[4] The impact of the spectacle culture of the ancient world on visual art has also received recent attention.[5]

A number of works have established the major role played by public spectacles in Rome in establishing and maintaining the relationship between the emperor and his people.[6] While Juvenal suggests that such entertainments served to replace the mob's desire for political power, they can also be seen as the one place where that power did continue to be exerted. It is in the circus that the people are said to have demanded tax exemptions from Gaius, in the theatre that they demanded an end to high corn prices under Tiberius, and in both that they encouraged the emperor Galba to execute the hated informer Tigellinus.[7] On a more subtle level, lines

eds., *Spectacula*, i: *Gladiateurs et amphithéatre: Actes du colloque tenu à Toulouse et à Lattes les 26, 27, 28 et 29 mai 1987* (Lattes, 1990); V. Kramérowskis and C. Landes, eds., *Spectacula*, ii: *le théâtre antique et ses spectacles: Actes du colloque tenu au Musée archéologique Henri Prades de Lattes les 27, 28, 29 et 30 avril 1989* (Lattes, 1992); C. Landes, ed., *Le stade romain et ses spectacles* (Lattes, 1994). For works focusing on the archaeological remains of circuses and amphitheatres, see J. H. Humphrey, *Roman Circuses: Arenas for Chariot Racing* (London, 1986); D. L. Bomgardner, *The Story of the Roman Amphitheatre* (London, 2000).

[2] Juvenal, *Satire* 10.81. See A. Cameron, *Bread and Circuses: The Roman Emperor and his People* (Oxford, 1974); P. Veyne, *Le pain et le cirque: Sociologie historique d'un pluralisme politique* (Paris, 1976), abridged and translated into English as *Bread and Circuses: Historical Sociology and Political Pluralism*, trans. B. Pearce (London, 1990) looking also at Greek euergetism; and K.-W. Weeber, *Panem et Circenses: Massenunterhaltung als Politik im antiken Rom*, 2nd edn. (Mainz, 1994).

[3] L. Robert, *Les gladiateurs dans l'Orient grec* (Paris, 1940); id., 'Deux concours grecs'. See Weeber, *Panem et Circenses*; D. Mancioli, *Giochi e spettacoli* (Rome, 1987); and J.-P. Thuillier, *Le Sport dans la Rome Antique* (Paris, 1996) for accounts which include some discussion of Greek-style athletic contests at Rome.

[4] Caldelli, *Agon*; ead., *Gli agoni alla greca nelle regioni occidentali dell'impero: La Gallia Narbonensis* (Rome, 1997).

[5] See the essays collected in B. Bergmann and C. Kondoleon, eds., *The Art of Ancient Spectacle* (New Haven and London, 1999).

[6] See especially Cameron, *Bread and Circuses*; Veyne, *Bread and Circuses*, 292–482 and Wiedemann, *Emperors and Gladiators*, 1–54, 165–83. See also the discussion by F. Millar, *The Emperor in the Roman World*, 2nd edn. (London, 1992), 368–75.

[7] Josephus, *Antiquities* 19.25; Tacitus, *Annals* 6.13; Plutarch, *Life of Galba* 17. See Veyne, *Bread and Circuses*, 398–402; Wiedemann, *Emperors and Gladiators*, 175.

spoken during theatrical performances could be taken to refer to current political figures or events, as when a line spoken by an actor playing a eunuch priest of Cybele was taken to allude to Augustus' supposed effeminacy.[8]

Indeed, the games appear in historical and biographical writings as a central area for observation of the emperor's conduct.[9] It was essential that an emperor be seen at the games: for his people, it provided evidence that he shared their pleasures, kept him in touch with their lives and provided a place where requests could be made of him. For the historians, the emperor's behaviour in the circus or arena was indicative of his overall nature as a ruler. Thus Tiberius' disinterest in public entertainments echoes his essentially reclusive nature while the over-enthusiasm of Nero and Caligula could be seen as symptomatic of their love of excess. Only a 'good' emperor, such as Augustus, could really get it right.

It seems clear that emperors were aware of the importance of achieving the correct balance: Suetonius tells us that Augustus always watched the games intently to avoid the example of Julius Caesar, who had earned hostility by spending the time reading letters or petitions, while Pliny praises the emperor Trajan for taking down the private box in which Domitian had sat to watch circus games, thus making himself more accessible to the people.[10] The decision to build an amphitheatre on the site of Nero's Domus Aurea was a deliberate act of policy by Vespasian, highlighting the contrast between the two reigns, and Fronto represents the emperor Trajan deliberating over the advantages of giving benefactions to the masses in the forms of shows rather than money or grain.[11]

This clear concern for the correct management of public spectacles strongly suggests that the athletic contests introduced into the Roman calendar would have been carefully considered, designed to appeal to the populace in a similar way. While references to such contests are admittedly less common in the literary sources than those to circus or gladiatorial games, where they do appear they are often in the context of the emperor's attitude to the games as a whole. This is especially true of Suetonius' *Lives of the Caesars*, where the thematic approach allows the author to group together episodes he sees as similar.[12] He describes Augustus' display of athletic contests in a specially constructed stadium on the Campus Martius in the same breath as the theatrical, gladiatorial, and wild-beast displays he

---

[8] Suetonius, *Augustus* 68; see Edwards, *Politics*, 114–19 and S. Bartsch, *Actors in the Audience: Theatricality and Doublespeak from Nero to Hadrian* (Cambridge, Mass., 1994), 63–97.

[9] See R. F. Newbold, 'Cassius Dio and the Games', *AC* 44 (1975), 589–604; Wiedemann, *Emperors and Gladiators*, 165–83.

[10] Suetonius, *Augustus* 45; Pliny, *Panegyric* 51.5.

[11] Martial, *Liber Spectaculorum* 2; Fronto, *Principia Historiae* 17.

[12] See A. Wallace-Hadrill, *Suetonius: The Scholar and his Caesars* (London, 1983), 1–25 on Suetonius' style. J. König discusses Suetonius' treatment of the emperors' relationships with Greek culture in his forthcoming book, *Athletics and Literature*, ch. 5.

also promoted, and couples his increase of the privileges given to athletes with his concern to ensure mercy in gladiatorial games.[13] When we look at his biographies of Nero or Domitian, the other two emperors particularly involved in the promotion of athletic contests, the description of their institution of Greek-style festivals is similarly included in sections dealing with their overall attitude towards public spectacles.[14]

A similar attitude can be seen in Tertullian's diatribe against public spectacles, in which he attempts to convince a Christian audience in Roman North Africa of the pernicious influences of all such entertainments. He groups together the circus, theatre, stadium, and arena as all equally worthy of disdain, on the grounds both of their immorality and their religious framework.[15] Indeed, this speech is particularly interesting for the attitudes it reveals towards Greek-style athletic contests. On the one hand these are clearly grouped together with other types of public spectacle, for example in comments such as 'non ibis in circum, non in theatrum, agonem, munus non spectabis', 'you will not go into the circus, nor into the theatre, you shall not watch the contest, nor the gladiatorial display', and in the care taken to attack all four contests equally.[16] Yet when Tertullian describes the spectacles of the stadium, he also lays great stress upon their Greek origins. Of the contests he mentions all take place in Greece except for the Capitoline games at Rome, which are said to be equivalent to the Olympic games since both are dedicated to Jupiter.[17] In chapter 18, athletes are specifically described as those fed for the 'idleness of Greece', 'Graeciae otium', and Tertullian's attacks on the unnatural diet and physique of such men can be seen echoed in contemporary Greek writings on athletic practice, such as those by Philostratus and Galen.[18]

Thus for Tertullian, athletic games are both a spectacle which corrupts the morals of those watching, like the activities of the circus, theatre, or arena, but are also marked out as of Greek origin. The evidence of both Tertullian and Suetonius, then, suggests that by the second century AD at least, athletic contests could be seen as one of a range of Roman spectacles, though at the same time they did not lose their association with Greek culture.

Greek athletic contests had, in fact, been seen at Rome sporadically since the early second century BC, though a permanent Greek-style festival was not

---

[13] Suetonius, *Augustus* 43, 45.   [14] Suetonius, *Nero* 12; *Domitian* 4.

[15] See M. Beard, J. North, and S. Price, *Religions of Rome* (Cambridge, 1998), i. 262. For an account of Christian opposition to Roman spectacles see W. Weismann, *Kirche und Schauspiele: die Schauspiele im Urteil der lateinischen Kirchenväter unter besonderer Berücksichtigung von Augustin* (Würzburg, 1972), especially 98–104 on idolatry.

[16] Tertullian, *De Spectaculis* 5. Note the use of the latinized form of the Greek word 'agon' to refer to athletic contests.

[17] Tertullian, *De Spectaculis* 11.

[18] Philostratus, *Gymnasticus* 44; Galen, *Exhortation to Study the Arts* 9–14.

established until the first century AD. First introduced in 186 BC by M. Fulvius Nobilior, Greek-style athletic contests during the Republican period were primarily put on by successful generals to celebrate military triumphs in Greece.[19] In Nobilior's games and in those of 55 BC, held by Pompey to celebrate the opening of his theatre, Greek-style contests, *certamina*, seem to have formed part of a wider spectacle, along with other events such as *venationes*, wild-beast hunts.[20] Many Roman events already included athletic contests, for example the *ludi Magni* or *ludi Romani*, held in honour of Jupiter Capitolinus, which included boxers, wrestlers, and runners as well as chariot races and theatrical displays.[21] Thus there was already a tradition of some athletic activity as part of the Roman games, though largely consisting of boxing and wrestling matches. It is possible that this native Italian tradition of athletics derived from Etruscan customs, where boxing was a major spectacle.[22] Indeed, Livy declares that Tarquinius Priscus had imported boxers from Etruria for his games celebrating victory over the Latins. Other authors, such as Tertullian, repeat the idea that the games at Rome were called *Ludi* because of their origins among the Lydians who had moved to Etruria.[23] Dionysius of Halicarnassus, however, could also use alleged Greek features in the *ludi Romani* as part of his attempt to present Rome as a Greek city, suggesting that such games could provide a fruitful area for debates over origins and self-identities.[24] What was specifically new about Nobilior's games is not clearly outlined by Livy. Presumably it lay in the use of Greek rather than Italian athletes, and the rules and customs by which they competed, perhaps including the lighter contests of the pentathlon as well as the more familiar boxing and wrestling matches.[25] It may also have referred to the nakedness of those competing.[26]

[19] A thorough discussion is given by Caldelli, *Agon*, 15–21; see also I. R. Arnold, 'Agonistic Festivals in Italy and Sicily', *AJA* 64 (1960), 245–51; N. B. Crowther, 'Greek Games in Republican Rome', *AC* 52 (1983), 268–73.

[20] Nobilior: Livy 39.22.1–2; Pompey: Plutarch, *Pompey* 52.4; Cassius Dio 39.38.1; Cicero, *Ad Familiares* 7.1. Caesar's games in 46 BC were of a similar type: Suetonius, *Julius Caesar* 39; Plutarch, *Caesar* 55; Appian, *Civil War* 2.102. Cassius Dio 43.22.

[21] J.-P. Thuillier, 'Le programme "Athlétique" des *Ludi Circenses* dans la Rome Républicaine', *Revue des Études Latines* 60 (1982), 105–22, and Crowther, 'Greek Games', both argue that such contests were native to Italy.

[22] J.-P. Thuillier, *Les Jeux athlétiques dans la civilisation étrusque* (Rome, 1985), 181–286. They competed to the music of a flute player: Athenaeus, *Deipnosophistae* 4.154a.

[23] Livy 1.35.8–9; Tertullian, *De Spectaculis* 5, cites Timaeus as the source for this etymology.

[24] Dionysius of Halicarnassus, 7.71.3–73.5; see Beard, North, and Price, *Religions*, i. 40–1; ii. 137–9. On the different layers of tradition and innovation in the Saecular Games held by Augustus, which distinguished between Greek and Latin rites and entertainments, see ibid., i. 203–4; ii. 139–44.

[25] Thuillier, *Sport*, 46–8.

[26] Dionysius of Halicarnassus, 7.72.2–4, says that the Romans adhere to the original Greek custom of wearing a loincloth, whereas Greeks now run naked, though he does not specify the dress of Greek athletes who competed in Rome. The nakedness of Greek athletes may lie behind Augustus' ban on women attending athletic contests, Suetonius, *Augustus* 44. On athletic nudity, see further bibliography in Chapter 7, n. 48.

Sometimes, however, wholesale Greek *agones* on the model of those at Olympia or Delphi were put on. So Polybius recalls with disgust the victory games (*agōnes epinikioi*) that L. Anicius Gallus held to celebrate his Illyrian victory in 166 BC. These included artists brought from Greece and a theatre set up in the circus, but the musical contest swiftly turned into a farcical free-for-all, probably because of the Roman crowd's impatience with Greek-style musical contests and a clamouring instead for physical combat.[27] Sulla's games in 80 BC, held to celebrate his victories over Mithridates, certainly included athletic contests and were said to have robbed Olympia that year of any contest except the stade race since all the athletes had been called to Rome.[28] This sounds like evidence of a Greek-style festival, with free-born contestants travelling to take part, as also seems to have been the case with the athletes performing for Nobilior in 186 BC, who are described as coming from Greece 'honoris eius causa', 'for the sake of his honour'.[29]

The commanders involved in such festivals can partly be seen as setting themselves up as the successors or rivals of the Hellenistic kings through means of such festivals, indicating their ability to call upon the full artistic resources of Greece. This is particularly true of the games in Greece, such as those held by L. Aemilius Paullus at Amphipolis in 167 BC to celebrate his victory over Perseus of Macedon. Here Paullus put on a display along Greek lines and acted in true Hellenistic fashion by sending envoys to the Greek cities and Hellenistic kings to announce the festival and invite them to send sacred envoys to attend it.[30]

Yet the fact that many such spectacles advertised victories over the Greek world must also have suggested at least to the Roman audience that the performers were in some ways like captives in a triumph—another example of *spolia* from the defeated enemy to act as a testament to the power of the conquering commander. The emphasis in these games was also very much upon athletics as spectacle, with the Roman audience clearly in the role of spectators rather than participants, even though Romans may occasionally have participated in festivals elsewhere.[31]

---

[27] Polybius 30.12.1–12, cited in Athenaeus 14. 615c. J. C. Edmondson, 'The Cultural Politics of Public Spectacle in Rome and the Greek East, 167–166 BCE', in Bergmann and Kondoleon, *Art of Ancient Spectacle*, 81–4, suggests that the crowd's desire for violence forced the disintegration of the musical contest into a fight, contra E. S. Gruen, *Culture and National Identity in Republican Rome* (Ithaca, 1993), 215–18, arguing that this mockery of Greek culture was deliberately intended by Anicius. Compare Terence, *The Hecyra* 1–42 on the disruption caused to the first and second performances of the play by news of the imminent appearance of boxers, tightrope walkers, and gladiators.

[28] Appian, *Roman History* 1.99. V. J. Matthews, 'Sulla and the Games of the 175th Olympiad (80 BC)', *Stadion* 5 (1979), 239–43, correctly notes that Appian does *not* say that Sulla transferred the Olympic games to Rome, as is sometimes stated.

[29] Livy 39.22.1–2.   [30] Livy 45.32.8–11. See Edmondson, 'Cultural Politics', 78–81.

[31] They were first invited to participate in the Isthmian games in 228 BC: Polybius, 2.12, though Roman involvement in Greek-style athletic festivals never seems to have been extensive. See M. I. Finley and H. W. Pleket, *The Olympic Games: the First Thousand Years* (London, 1976), 11. The majority of the Roman victories recorded at Olympia were by members of the imperial family in the chariot race: Moretti,

Thus the introduction of Greek athletic and dramatic events into Rome in the Republic can be seen both as indicative of an interest in Greek culture and, simultaneously, as reaffirming the military power of Rome over this conquered part of the world. The fact that all such performances seem to have taken place on an ad-hoc basis, as one-off shows associated with particular events, must have limited their influence on Roman customs and probably also prolonged their novelty value. In the Imperial period, however, we see a change with the introduction for the first time of permanent athletic festivals in Italy.

Although it was not until AD 86 during the reign of Domitian that a permanent Greek-style festival, the *Agon Capitolinus*, was finally instituted at Rome, this can be seen as the climax in a series of moves.[32] Augustus instituted a permanent Greek-style festival, the *Actia*, in Greece at Nicopolis in 30/28 BC to commemorate the victory over Antony. Another festival, the *Sebasta*, was set up by the senate and local community in 2 BC or AD 2 at Naples along the lines of the Olympic festival.[33] Both are directly associated with the figure of the emperor, and can also be associated with the 'games for the health of Caesar', 'ludi pro valetudine Caesaris', voted him by the senate in Rome in 28 BC. These included among other events a 'gymnicus agon', 'gymnastic competition', held in a wooden stadium built on the Campus Martius. They seem to have been repeated every four years at least until AD 9.[34] The regular repetition of these games and their inclusion of Greek-style athletic events clearly identifies them with the festivals declared at the Greek cities of Nicopolis and Naples, though it would seem that the time was not yet ripe for a formal Greek-style festival in Rome itself.[35]

Augustus may also have been keen to encourage Greek-style athletic training in Rome. Nielsen has argued that the development of public baths in Italy, especially large *thermae* complexes which included areas for both exercise and bathing, was closely related to the spread of Greek customs. Thus the earliest bath-gymnasium complexes are found in the Hellenized cities of Campania, like the Stabian baths at

Olympionikai 738 (Tiberius), 750 (Germanicus), 790–5 (Nero), 743, 846 (non-imperial figures). There is evidence, however, that Italians who settled in cities in the east actively took part in the athletic culture of their new cities: see R. M. Errington, 'Aspects of Roman Acculturation in the East under the Republic', in *Alte Geschichte und Wissenschaftsgeschichte: Festschrift für Karl Christ* (Darmstadt, 1988), 140–57; L. Robert, 'Catalogue Agonistique des Romaia de Xanthos', in id., *Opera Minora Selecta*, vii (Amsterdam, 1990), 681–94.

[32] Suetonius, *Domitian* 4.4. See Robert, 'Deux concours grecs'. A full discussion of the festival and the relevant epigraphic evidence is provided by Caldelli, *Agon*.

[33] *IOlympia* 56; Suetonius, *Augustus* 18.2, 98.5; Cassius Dio 51.1.1–3; Velleius Paterculus 2.123. On the date, see Caldelli, *Agon*, 28–9; M. Leiwo, *Neapolitana: A Study of Population and Language in Graeco-Roman Naples*, Commentationes Humanarum Litterarum 102 (Helsinki, 1994), 45–8.

[34] Cassius Dio 53.1.4–6; Suetonius, *Augustus* 43.1. See Caldelli, *Agon*, 21–37.

[35] On Naples as a Greek city, see Leiwo, *Neapolitana*, who emphasizes the difficulties of separating the city's Greek and Roman identities. The agonistic inscriptions are all written in Greek.

Pompeii, where the customs of the Greek gymnasium were familiar. In Rome, however, bathing seems to have been restricted to *balnea*, smaller complexes without areas for exercise, up until the time of Augustus. She suggests that the turning-point came with Agrippa's Baths on the Campus Martius, the first that seem to have combined areas for physical exercise with rooms for bathing.[36] Until this point, physical exercise had traditionally been associated instead with training for warfare, with the Romans showing hostility towards what they saw as the unmanly interest in exercise for its own sake in the Greek gymnasium.[37] Bequeathed to the Roman people upon his death, Agrippa's Baths were placed on the Campus Martius, traditionally the military training ground of Rome.[38] They thus drew together the Greek gymnasium, evoked by the prominent placement outside of Lysippus' Apoxyomenus, a statue of an athlete cleaning himself with a strigil, with the area traditionally used by the Romans for physical training.[39] This suggests a conscious desire to promote the use of certain elements of Greek culture in the service of Rome, just as Augustus also promoted athletic festivals at Naples and Nicopolis.

In fact, the establishment of these baths may also have been a response to existing interest in Greek athletic training. Harris has shown that Augustan poetry, especially that of Horace and Ovid, shows a knowledge of and delight in Greek-style athletics at this time, and elite Romans would already be familiar with the Greek gymnasium through their villas in the Hellenized south of Italy and through imperial posts abroad.[40] It seems quite likely, then, that the building and subsequent bequest of the Baths of Agrippa at Rome could have been both a response to an existing interest in Greek exercise and a further spur to it. The interests of the Augustan family in encouraging athletic pursuits can also be seen in Gaul, where a fragmentary inscribed architrave from Nemausus (Nîmes) records the dedication of a *xystus* or running track to the city by Gaius Caesar.[41]

This link between the introduction of Greek festivals and the practices of the Greek gymnasium can also be seen when we turn to Nero's institution of the *Neronia* festival, held in AD 60 and again in 65, though it failed to survive the death and disgrace of its founder. This included athletic, theatrical, and equestrian

---

[36] I. Nielsen, *Thermae et Balnea: The Architectural and Cultural History of Roman Public Baths* (Aarhus, 1990), 25–59, esp. 57–9. I follow her use of the terms *thermae* and *balnea* though note that they are not always used so precisely by ancient authors.

[37] See the views collected below, pp. 38–41.

[38] Cassius Dio 54.29.4. Nielsen, *Thermae et Balnea*, 58, suggested that they may have been used for the Iuventus, on which see M. Della Corte, *Iuventus: un nuovo aspetto della vita pubblica di Pompei finora inesplorato* (Arpino, 1924); and J. Delorme, *Gymnasion: Étude sur les monuments consacrés à l'éducation en Grèce* (Paris, 1960), 433–5.

[39] On the Apoxyomenus, see Pliny, *Natural History* 34.62.

[40] e.g. Horace, *Odes* 3.12. H. A. Harris, *Sport in Greece and Rome* (London, 1972) 55–60.

[41] *CIL* xii. 3155; Caldelli, *Agoni alla greca*, 433–5, N17.

contests, with Nero himself performing in the musical contests.[42] Margherita Guarducci has suggested that a series of lamps decorated with foliage, crowns, and scenes of actors, athletes, or other performers were probably made to commemorate these games (Fig. 2.1).[43] Further evidence of their popularity might also be seen in the satirical Greek epigrams of Lucillius, written in Nero's Rome, many of which make fun of contemporary athletes.[44] In association with the games Nero also built baths and a gymnasium close to the existing Baths of Agrippa on the Campus

[42] Suetonius, *Nero* 12.3–4; 21; Tacitus, *Annals* 14.20, 47; Cassius Dio 62.21.

[43] See M. Guarducci, 'Una nuova officina di lucernette romane: gli *Aeoli*', *RömMitt* 89 (1982), 103–31, at 103–14; with additional material in ead., 'Nuove osservazioni sulle lucernette degli Aeoli', *RömMitt* 93 (1986), 301–3.

[44] L. Robert, 'Les épigrammes satiriques de Lucilius sur les athlètes. Parodie et réalités', in *L'épigramme grecque*, Entretiens sur l'Antiquité Classique 14 (1968), 181–295, at 286–7. One is actually addressed to Nero himself: *Greek Anthology* 11.75. On Lucillius, see also G. Nisbet, *Greek Epigram in the Roman Empire: Martial's Forgotten Rivals* (Oxford, 2003), 36–81.

Martius, and provided free oil to the senatorial and equestrian classes when these were opened.[45] We should see this institution of a Greek-style festival in connection with Nero's other philhellenic interests, in particular his tour of Greece in 66–7, the highlight of which was his declaration of freedom to Greece at the Isthmus in AD 67.[46] During his time in Greece Nero competed both as a singer and as a charioteer in the four Panhellenic festivals, their dating having been specially reorganized to accommodate him, and then re-entered Italy in the style of an Olympic victor.[47]

While the literary sources are uniformly hostile to these actions, as to Nero's removal of Greek artworks to Rome and attempted cutting of the Isthmus, Susan Alcock has suggested that there may have been sound political reasoning behind the trip.[48] The emperor's engagement with Greek culture here is certainly in line with his actions in Rome. By issuing free oil on the opening of his gymnasium, and by his repeated attempts to encourage the elite to perform on the stage, Nero can be seen as encouraging a more widespread adoption of the practices of Greek culture within Rome itself.[49] If Agrippa's baths had already been successful in encouraging athletic pursuits, there may well have been a market for this.

Tacitus' discussion of the Neronia festival is illuminating. He represents the opponents of the new festival as fearful that the introduction of this new festival will further encourage the deleterious influence of foreign pursuits which have already ruined the youth of Rome, leading them to 'athletics, leisure, and shameful love affairs', 'gymnasia et otia et turpis amores'. According to this statement, an interest in Greek physical training is already popular among the Roman youth. What these conservatives then fear is that Roman nobles, who have already appeared on the public stage, might also begin to 'strip their bodies naked and take up boxing gloves, practising boxing rather than warfare and arms'.[50] The moralizing tone of this passage certainly warns us against seeing it as a straightforward representation of reality. Yet evidence that some Roman nobles, at least, did indeed take part in these games is probably to be found in the comment of a scholiast to Juvenal's *Satire* 4.53. This tells us that Palfurius Sura, the son of a consular and

[45] Suetonius, *Nero* 12.3. B. Tamm, *Neros Gymnasium in Rom* (Stockholm, 1970), 13, suggests that the gymnasium may first have been used as a place for musical performances and later as baths, but the distribution of oil would seem to make the bathing side primary right from the start. I follow Tamm and Nielsen, *Thermae et Balnea*, 45–6, in seeing the bath and gymnasium as both part of the same complex, rather than as separate ones. According to Suetonius, *Nero* 12.4, the gymnastic competitions took place in the Saepta on the Campus Martius, probably because it was easier to see them here.

[46] See K. R. Bradley, 'The Chronology of Nero's Visit to Greece AD 66/67', *Latomus* 37 (1978), 66–71; and M. T. Griffin, *Nero: The End of a Dynasty* (London, 1984), 163–4, on the chronology of the trip.

[47] Suetonius, *Nero* 22–5; Cassius Dio 62.14, 20–1.

[48] S. E. Alcock, 'Nero at Play? The Emperor's Grecian Odyssey', in J. Elsner and J. Masters, eds., *Reflections of Nero: Culture, History, and Representation* (London, 1994), 98–111.

[49] Griffin, *Nero*, 40–5, 208–20.   [50] Tacitus, *Annals* 14.20.

an infamous informer of Domitian's reign, had also been a wrestler in his youth under Nero.[51]

Despite some elite disapproval, presented by Tacitus as the typical viewpoint of a conservative Roman senator, the evidence suggests that the emperors were consistently eager to promote Greek culture in Italy in the middle decades of the first century. Nero's predecessor, Claudius, seems to have taken a keen interest in Greek-style festivals and those performing in them.[52] His attendance at the *Sebasta* in Naples in 42, in which he put on a Greek comedy written by his brother, probably raised the profile of the games, attracting performers from the Greek east as well as more local athletes.[53] Imperial involvement in these games can also be seen in the Flavian period. The imperial prince Titus attended three times running as agonothete in AD 70, 74, and 78, an interest which led to suggestions of a love affair with one of the athletes.[54] Thus the contest at Naples was put firmly on the festival map, encouraging athletes and actors from around the Mediterranean to come to Italy and laying the ground for Domitian's institution of the *Capitolia* in 86.[55]

Naples' status as a Greek city, with a festival which made it part of the Greek world, was one which was endorsed and, in part, created by Roman power. The *Sebasta* festival certainly seems to have been initiated by the Neapolitans themselves, and Cassius Dio relates it to their desire 'alone of the Campanians . . . to imitate the customs of the Greeks'.[56] Yet its institution also ties in with Augustus' foundation of the *Actia* festival at Nicopolis and was presumably welcomed and approved by the emperor himself. Later emperors also elevated the position of the festival by their own patronage. Indeed, as Kaimio has pointed out, the fact that most of the public epigraphy of the city (including that relating to the games) continued to be written in Greek is evidence not just of Naples' conception of itself as a Greek city, but also of the desire of the Roman authorities to allow it to keep that Greek identity.[57] Naples provided a space where the emperor and other elite Romans could indulge their fantasies of Greek life. In the early days those fantasies

[51] P. Wessner, ed., *Scholia in Iuvenalem Vetustiora* (Lipsiae, 1931), 57.

[52] Leiwo, *Neapolitana*, 42 n. 1, mentions an inscription recording Claudius' grant of citizenship to a citharist who had acted as chief priest in games in Rome and Naples. He also granted concessions to the international guild of athletes. See *BM Papyri* iii. 1178, ll. 8–31 (E. M. Smallwood, *Documents Illustrating the Principates of Gaius, Claudius, and Nero* (Cambridge, 1967), no. 374); C. A. Forbes, 'Ancient Athletic Guilds', *Classical Philology* 50 (1955), 238–52, at 243, and discussion below, pp. 34–6.

[53] Suetonius, *Claudius* 11.2. See Moretti, *IAG*, no. 53; Caldelli, *Agon*, 36 n. 154; Leiwo, *Neapolitana*, 42, 45; D. S. Potter, 'Entertainers in the Roman Empire', in D. S. Potter and D. J. Mattingly, eds., *Life, Death and Entertainment in the Roman Empire* (Ann Arbor, 1999), 256–325, at 279.

[54] Themistius, *Oration* 139a–b. See E. Miranda, 'Tito a Napoli: una dedica onoraria', *Epigraphica* 50 (1988), 222–6.

[55] A number of inscriptions recording the careers of victorious athletes have been discovered at Naples. See Moretti, *IAG*, nos. 67, 68, 77.

[56] Cassius Dio 55.10.9.

[57] J. Kaimio, *The Romans and the Greek Language*, Commentationes Humanarum Litterarum 64 (Helsinki, 1979), 70–2.

(such as Augustus' encouragement of a form of cultural cross-dressing where Romans dressed up as Greeks and Greeks as Romans) seem to have been permissible in public only when one was away from Rome, in the freer atmosphere of Hellenized Campania.[58] Yet by the time of Nero and Domitian they gradually seeped into the entertainment culture of Rome itself.[59]

Domitian's institution of the Capitoline festival in AD 86 is described by Suetonius. The festival was named in honour of the Capitoline Jupiter, whose image along with those of Juno and Minerva adorned the crown of Domitian as he presided over the contests.[60] Caldelli suggests that the festival might be related to the imperial cult, since the Flamen Dialis and the Flaviales, who also presided at the festival, wore the emperor's image in addition to those of the Capitoline Triad on their crowns.[61] From its appearance in victory lists the festival appears to have been successful in subsequent years and survived until well into the fourth century.[62] In association with it, Domitian built both an odeum, for the musical contests, and a stadium, the only one known of outside Greece, whose traces can be seen in the present-day Piazza Navona.[63]

Through the foundation of this festival Rome acquired the accoutrements of a Greek city.[64] Just as in the east, the festival was named after the patron god of the city and also accommodated the imperial power in the presence of the emperor as agonothete and the imperial image placed on the crown.[65] Greek structures, the odeum and stadium, were also built to accommodate these Greek contests. Why was it that by the end of the first century AD Rome seemed to require a Greek-style festival? In part, this can be attributed to Domitian's philhellenism, just as the *Neronia* can be seen as evidence of Nero's interest in Greek contests. Yet there were also deeper benefits in Rome's possession of a festival which must lie behind its endurance, despite some senatorial opposition, when other acts of Domitian were revoked.[66] I would suggest that an understanding of the role played by these festivals should look at their significance in the interactions of the *princeps* with two distinct bodies, the city of Rome itself, and the Greek-speaking provinces of the empire.

---

[58] Suetonius, *Augustus* 98, discussed by Wallace-Hadrill, 'To be Roman, go Greek'. On the Romans in Campania see J. D'Arms, *Romans on the Bay of Naples* (Cambridge, Mass., 1970), esp. 55–72, 142–52, and 165–7 on cultural life.

[59] Note that Tacitus, *Annals* 14.20, says that Greek clothes were worn by many during the celebration of the *Neronia* in AD 60.

[60] Suetonius, *Domitian* 4.   [61] Caldelli, *Agon*, 65–7.   [62] Robert, 'Deux concours grecs', 7–9.

[63] Suetonius, *Domitian* 5. On the stadium, see P. Virgili, 'Le stade de Domitien', in Landes, *Stade romain*, 107–19.

[64] Robert, 'Deux concours grecs', 8.

[65] For a discussion of crowns with images of the imperial family and civic deities, which she sees as a sign that the bearer acted as a festival agonothete, see J. Rumscheid, *Kranz und Krone: zu Insignien, Siegespreisen und Ehrenzeichen der römischen Kaiserzeit* (Tübingen, 2000), 7–51. On festivals in the east, see the discussion in Chapter 8, pp. 246–55.

[66] Opposition: Pliny, *Letters* 4.22, discussed below, p. 40.

The role played by athletic festivals in the emperor's relationship with the people of Rome has already been explored. Greek games, like other public spectacles, gave the emperor an opportunity to show his munificence to the city of Rome in a novel form. It probably both reflected and encouraged an increased interest in Greek athletics that can also be seen in the literary sources from the Augustan period onwards and would have been increased by the imperial promotion of the *Sebasta* festival in Naples. An interest in watching athletic contests can also be seen earlier in the late Republic when elite Romans appear to have regularly attended the Olympic games in Greece. So, Cicero's comment that he would not want to be thought to have gone to Olympia in the upheaval of 44 BC strongly suggests that many Romans were indeed accustomed to travel to Olympia to see the games.[67] By creating a permanent festival at Rome, Domitian allowed the inhabitants of Rome to indulge their delights in Greek culture without having to leave the city itself. There is some continuity here with the one-off displays put on in the Republican period since through this foundation Domitian allowed the citizens of Rome to reap the benefits of the multicultural empire they controlled. Yet the very fact that this festival survived suggests that the concerns over excessive Hellenization and a weakening of Roman morals which had scuppered previous attempts were gradually losing their grip. Indeed, some may have argued instead that as new festivals sprang up elsewhere and the *Sebasta* in Naples gradually gained prestige, it was only right that Rome too should have her own Greek-style festival.

While some continued to criticize an interest in the Greek gymnasium, the evidence for a gradual increase in both athletic training and spectacles throughout the course of the first century AD suggests that traditional attitudes towards Greek culture were gradually weakening in favour of an embrace of the multicultural opportunities of empire. Both literary and visual evidence suggest an increasing delight in Greek-style physical training amongst the population of Rome which must in part have been fostered by the provision of luxurious public baths such as those constructed by Agrippa, Nero, and later emperors. The provision of a Greek-style musical and athletic festival in Rome can be seen both as a response to this increasing interest and as a further spur to it, appealing both to Rome's native population and to the large numbers of eastern immigrants.[68] The fact that the *Capitolia* was not abolished on Domitian's death reflects the growing hold which Greek festival culture had on the populace of Rome.

[67] Cicero, *Ad Atticum* 16.7; Harris, *Sport*, 53–4.

[68] The large number of people from the Greek east present at Rome, in a variety of different capacities, are famously suggested by Juvenal, *Satire* 3.58–125. See also Lucian, *On Salaried Posts in Great Houses*. On the epigraphic evidence see H. Solin, *Beitrage zur Kenntnis der griechischen Personennamen in Rom*, Commentationes Humanarum Litterarum 48 (Helsinki, 1971); L. Morreti 'I Greci a Roma', *Opuscula Instituti Romani Finlandiae* 4 (1989), 6–16.

At the same time, as Louis Robert saw, the introduction of a Greek-style festival to Rome also helped to set Rome at the heart of the Greek world and its festival circuit.[69] Even before the introduction of the Neronian or Capitoline games Greek cities, guilds, and individuals had turned to Roman generals and later the emperors to request the establishment or upgrading of new festivals and to confirm the privileges granted to performers.[70] Rome was already, then, an important centre in the world of public festivals and their participants. The establishment of Greek-style festivals recognized and further encouraged Rome and the emperor's centrality in the Greek agonistic world. This can be seen particularly clearly in the history of the relationships between the emperor and the guilds of actors and athletes.

While a guild of athletes is unattested until the late first century BC, the guild of the 'Artists of Dionysus', a band of professional actors, is known in the Hellenistic world from the third century BC.[71] This group had already sought protection and privileges from Hellenistic kings such as the Attalids, and it was natural for them to turn to the Roman emperors when Rome became the major power in the Mediterranean. Yet the imperial promotion of such groups can also be seen as a way of exerting political control over them, and the changing relationships between the emperor and athletic and artistic guilds are one way to measure the imperial relationship with Hellenic culture. While I will concentrate here on athletic guilds, a similar story could be told of the Artists of Dionysus, the major guild of actors.[72]

I have already mentioned Augustus' acts to maintain and increase the privileges enjoyed by athletes.[73] While Suetonius does not specify what these privileges were, they probably included exemptions from military service and from public liturgies, as were granted to 'the synod of international sacred victors' in Asia by Mark Antony.[74] Similar privileges were also granted by Claudius and later endorsed by Vespasian.[75]

The precise nature of the various athletic guilds which existed in the Roman period is tricky to untangle. Alongside various local groups, inscriptions from the first century BC mention two separate international associations, 'the athletes from

---

[69] Robert, 'Deux concours grecs', especially 8. [70] See Millar, *Emperor*, 447–63.

[71] See E. Csapo and W. J. Slater, *The Context of Ancient Drama* (Ann Arbor, 1995), 239–55, for a discussion of this guild.

[72] e.g. see J. H. Oliver, 'The Empress Plotina and the Sacred Thymelic Synod', *Historia* 24 (1975), 125–8; and H. Lavagne, 'Rome et les associations dionysiaques en Gaule (Vienne et Nîmes)', in *L'association dionysiaque dans les sociétés anciennes* (Rome, 1986), 129–48. On guilds of athletes see Forbes, 'Ancient Athletic Guilds'; H. W. Pleket, 'Some Aspects of the History of the Athletic Guilds', *ZPE* 10 (1973), 197–227; M. L. Caldelli, 'Curia athletarum, iera xystike synodos e organizzazione delle terme a Roma', *ZPE* 93 (1992), 75–87.

[73] Suetonius, *Augustus* 45.

[74] R. K. Sherk, *Roman Documents from the Greek East: Senatus Consulta and Epistulae to the Age of Augustus* (Baltimore, 1969), 290–3, no. 57. The fact that this body included a trainer, 'aleiptes' (l. 7), shows that athletes must have been included in it, possibly with actors too. The dating is disputed between 42/1 and 33/2 BC. See Pleket, 'Some Aspects', 200–2.

[75] *BM Papyri*, iii. 214–19, no. 1178, ll. 8–36 (Smallwood, *Documents*, no. 374). See Forbes, 'Ancient Athletic Guilds', 243.

the inhabited world' and 'the sacred victors from the inhabited world'.[76] These seem to have merged in the first century AD to become 'The sacred roving athletic guild of those associated with Heracles'.[77] In the second century we find another change when this international synod moved to Rome. Some inscriptions refer to the 'sacred athletic synod of those associated with Heracles living after the dissolution (*katalusis*) in the royal city of Rome'.[78] The word *katalusis* has been interpreted in differing ways. Forbes and Moretti think that it refers to a dissolution of the synod at some point, before being re-established at Rome in the mid-first century AD.[79] However, Pleket has argued that it refers instead to the retirement of the athletes, suggesting that this is a guild for retired athletes while the second body which was based in Rome, the 'complete xystos' (*sumpas xystos*) represented both active and retired athletes.[80]

This suggestion makes sense in my view, especially since it is precisely retired athletes whom we find holding the permanent posts here and acting as overseers of festivals (*xystarchai*) around the empire.[81] It was also one such athlete, the pancratiast Marcus Ulpius Domesticus of Ephesus, who obtained for the synod the privilege of erecting their headquarters near the Baths of Trajan in Rome in the area now occupied by the church of S. Pietro in Vincoli, where a number of athletic inscriptions have been discovered. This was first granted by Hadrian in AD 134 but seems not to have been carried out by the time of his death since we find it granted again by Antoninus Pius in 143.[82] In his reply to the synod, Antoninus defines the area as that next to the baths of his grandfather (Trajan) and indicates that they can use it to store their sacred objects and documents, and especially to assemble for the *Capitolia*.[83] Domesticus is also named in this inscription as the imperial *epi balaneion*, overseer of the baths. Whilst the duties which this post entailed are nowhere set out, it was perhaps analogous to the Greek post of gymnasiarch, and seems to indicate the use of the imperial baths by the athletes during their training for the Capitoline games.[84]

Later inscriptions show the guild taking on the names of the reigning emperor, and it has been suggested that as well as having a shrine of Heracles in their Roman

---

[76] Pleket, 'Some Aspects', 199–200. The latter group seems to be that honoured by Mark Antony.

[77] The full title is given in *BM Papyri*, iii, no. 1178 (Smallwood, *Documents*, no. 374). See Pleket, 'Some Aspects', 208.

[78] *IG* xiv. 1105; Moretti, *IGUR* i, no. 243.

[79] Forbes, 'Ancient Athletic Guilds', 244; Moretti, *IAG*, no. 248.

[80] Pleket, 'Some Aspects', 213–22; see also Millar, *Emperor*, 457 n. 5.

[81] For a list of these, mostly pancratiasts, see Forbes, 'Ancient Athletic Guilds', 248.

[82] *IG* xiv. 1054, 1055; Moretti, *IGUR* i, nos. 235, 236.

[83] *IG* xiv. 1055; Moretti, *IGUR* i, no. 236b, ll. 9–12.

[84] Athletes had to attend a period of training before the games at certain festival sites, as at Olympia: Philostratus, *Life of Apollonius of Tyana* 5.43 (Olympia); *IOlympia* 56 (*Sebasta* at Naples). Caldelli, 'Curia athletarum', discusses the post of *epi balaneion*.

headquarters, the athletes may also have played a role in the imperial cult.[85] The guild had a major role in overseeing all existing festivals and in promoting new ones, with lifelong *xystarchs* for individual festivals being appointed by the emperor.[86] In addition to the honour individual ex-athletes could receive by undertaking such posts, victorious athletes also continued to be awarded privileges such as exemptions from public duties. However, the explosion of athletic festivals in the second and third centuries meant that by the time of the Tetrarchs it was necessary to limit such exemptions to those victors who had won at least three times in sacred games, including at least once in Rome or Greece.[87] This highlights the privileged position which the *Capitolia* attained, shown also by the fact that in inscriptions it is regularly rated as second only to the four great Panhellenic festivals, probably because of the association with the emperor who often seems to have presided in person.[88] The centrality of Rome as a place in which athletes from across the empire congregated can be clearly seen by the location of the guild's headquarters here, as well as by the fact that a number of athletic victory inscriptions have been found in and around the city.[89]

Along with the *Sebasta* at Naples, the *Capitolia* seems to have held the primary place among those festivals set up in the Roman empire. Indeed, along with that festival and perhaps the *Heraia* at Argos it may have constituted one of a new *periodos*, or circuit, to complement the ancient *periodos* of the festivals at Olympia, Delphi, Nemea, and the Isthmus.[90] Other festivals too were set up in Italy and Rome in the course of the second and third centuries.[91] The status and popularity of the *Capitolia* may also have influenced the establishment of similar festivals elsewhere in the western provinces, an idea which is supported by Pliny the Younger's linkage of a festival at Vienna in Gaul (Vienne) with the Capitoline games at Rome.[92]

Within Italy we hear of the *Eusebeia* games set up by Antoninus Pius in honour of Hadrian at Puteoli, the site of his death, probably in AD 142.[93] These carried on into the third century, when Rome too saw the celebration of new festivals. The 'Antonineia Pythia in Rome', recorded on an inscription from Delphi, could be the games given by Elagabalus in 219/220, mentioned by Herodian and Dio.[94] We also

---

[85] Forbes, 'Ancient Athletic Guilds', 245–6.   [86] Ibid., 247–8.

[87] *Codex Justinianus* 10.54.1; Millar, *Emperor*, 457.

[88] On the status of the *Capitolia*, see Caldelli, *Agon*, 54, 105–12, and Millar, *Emperor*, 457, for evidence of Antoninus Pius presiding in person.

[89] See Moretti, *IAG*, nos. 65, 79, and Moretti, *IGUR* i, nos. 249–63.

[90] Caldelli, *Agon*, 89, though Spawforth, 'Agonistic Festivals', 193 n. 3, suggests that the *Heraia* may have been part of the older *periodos*.

[91] Robert, 'Deux concours grecs', 9–27; Caldelli, *Agon*, 43–52.

[92] Pliny, *Letters* 4.22, discussed further below, p. 78. See Caldelli, *Agoni alla greca*, 448, 458.

[93] Scriptores Historiae Augustae, *Hadrian* 27.3; *CIL* x. 515.

[94] Herodian, 5.5.8, 6.6; Cassius Dio, 80.10.2–3; inscription published by Robert, 'Deux concours grecs', 18–27.

FIGURE 2.2 Imperial coinage could be used to commemorate the festival culture of ancient Rome. The reverse of this aureus of Septimius Severus shows athletic events taking place in Domitian's stadium, possibly during the Capitoline games of AD 206. Diameter: 0.85cm, Severan.

hear of an *Agon Herculeus* held by Severus Alexander in honour of Alexander the Great, which Caldelli suggests might be associated with the restoration of Nero's baths and the stadium carried out by this emperor in 228.[95] Both these festivals seem to have been one-off occurrences which did not survive their dedicators. However, in 242 we find the *Agon Minervae* instituted by Gordian III on the eve of his battle against the Persians, which seems to have continued into the start of the fourth century, and later, in 274, Aurelian instituted the *Agon Solis*, which survived into the reign of Julian in the mid-fourth century.[96]

All these festivals suggest that our traditional picture of Roman hostility or ambivalence to Greek athletics is far from the truth. Inscriptions show that the games at Rome were prestigious and well-attended by athletes from across the Mediterranean. They must also have been popular among Roman spectators since in other areas of spectacle culture, emperors seem to have paid attention to the crowd's delights. Indeed, it is likely that it was this popularity that ensured the survival of the Capitoline games after the downfall of their founder Domitian. Other games sometimes appear advertised on imperial coinage, as on a coin of Septimius Severus which shows athletic events taking place in Domitian's stadium (Fig. 2.2).[97] The introduction of these festivals can be seen as part of the ongoing interest in and appropriation of Greek culture that characterized much of the cultural life of Rome. By promoting Greek-style festivals at Rome the emperors both reflected and encouraged the adoption of Greek practices in the city and gave Rome a privileged place at the heart of Greek festival culture. In order to explore further the reactions that these contests evoked among their audiences at all levels of society I will turn now to the impact that they had on the literary and intellectual elite, before looking in more detail at the visual evidence in the next chapter.

[95] Scriptores Historiae Augustae, *Severus Alexander* 35.4; Caldelli, *Agon*, 47–8.

[96] Caldelli, *Agon*, 48–52.

[97] B. L. Damsky, 'The Stadium Aureus of Septimius Severus', *American Journal of Numismatics* 2 (1990), 77–105.

ROMAN ATTITUDES TO GREEK ATHLETICS

It has been repeatedly stated by numerous scholars that the Romans were not interested in Greek athletics.[98] This view has been drawn for two reasons, the passionate response of the whole Roman people to gladiators, charioteers, and the theatre which we find mentioned in the literary sources and which seem to indicate a lesser enthusiasm for the Greek games, and the hostile statements made by several elite authors. Yet, on further examination, this picture is not as uniform as it is often represented. A closer look at both literary and visual evidence will, I suggest, in fact reveal an increasing interest in both physical training and athletic spectacles amongst the populace of Rome and its surroundings.

Let us look first at the typical elite attitudes towards Greek games which are commonly offered as evidence for Roman disdain for athletics. Indeed, we can find a number of such comments. So Cicero, writing to Marius about his inability to attend the games given by Pompey in 55 BC, says that he has not missed much, and particularly comments on the athletes on whom even Pompey himself, he says, admitted that he had wasted both effort and oil.[99] Seneca too, in the mid-first century AD, has a similar dismissive attitude to athletic activity when a cheer from the stadium prompts him to exclaim how much those whose muscles we praise are in fact feeble in mind.[100]

Indeed, this unfavourable comparison between athletic and intellectual activities is one which recurs throughout our sources—lying behind the dismissive statements of both Cicero and Seneca, as well as in Vitruvius' statement that authors deserve renown much more than famous athletes since they make not only themselves stronger, but also the minds of others.[101] Yet the same contrast can also be found in the Greek sources, for example in Galen's *Exhortation to Study the Arts*, where he urges a youth not to devote himself to athletics but to literary study.[102] These comments follow a topos in philosophical writing which privileges the intellectual arts over the physical ones, a theme which can be traced back to the writings of Plato and Aristotle and which it is hardly surprising to find used by writers who wish to present themselves as intellectuals.[103]

---

[98] e.g. E. N. Gardiner, *Athletics of the Ancient World* (London, 1930), 124; Weeber, *Panem et Circenses*, 76, 83. Detailed accounts of Roman views of athletics are given by E. Mähl, *Gymnastik und Athletik im Denken der Römer* (Amsterdam, 1974) and S. Müller, *Das Volk der Athleten: Untersuchungen zur Ideologie und Kritik des Sports in der griechisch-römischen Antike* (Trier, 1995), 214–23.

[99] Cicero, *Ad Familiares* 7.1.3.   [100] Seneca, *Letters* 80.2.

[101] Vitruvius, *De Architectura* 9, preface 1.

[102] Galen, *Exhortation to Study the Arts* 9. On the attitudes to athletics expressed within Galen's writings, see König, 'Athletic Training', 118–41; König, *Athletics and Literature*, ch. 6.

[103] On Greek opposition to athletics, see B. Bilinski, *L'agonistica sportiva nella grecia antica: aspetti sociali e ispirazioni letterarie* (Rome, 1959), 74–87.

Intertwined in this physical/mental opposition is also the whole issue of spectatorship. The focus of Cicero, Vitruvius, and Seneca's comments is not upon the athletes themselves but on the reactions to them among their audiences. Cicero claims that the athletes in Pompey's show were a mistake, a waste of oil and effort. This may suggest that the public did not rate them very highly, though Cicero's own agenda here, to console Marius for missing the games as well as to denigrate Greek culture in accordance with Marius' alleged hatred of it, debars us from drawing any firm conclusions.

For Vitruvius and Seneca, however, we find a clear awareness that many people did indeed rate such athletic victors, though they themselves criticize this inappropriate privileging of physical over mental prowess. The same distancing of the writer from the pleasures of others can be found in Cicero's disparaging remarks about public spectacles in *De Officiis*.[104] Similar remarks appear in Pliny the Younger's letters where he calls the circus races, an abiding passion in Rome among all levels of society, 'childish', 'pueriliter'.[105] The criticism seems to be that all spectacles, including athletics, are simply a waste of time which would better be spent in serious academic pursuits. This, of course, is simply a strategy to elevate the intellectual status of the author himself, as Pliny's comments show so brutally:

When I think of how this futile, tedious, monotonous business can keep them sitting endlessly in their seats, I take pleasure in the fact that their pleasure is not mine. And I have been very glad to fill my idle hours with literary work during these days which others have wasted in the idlest of occupations.   (*Letters* 9.6.3–4)[106]

Yet at times this hostility to public spectacles is also suggested as due to the detrimental effect it has on the human spirit. Thus Seneca complains that going to the games leaves him 'more greedy, more ambitious, more voluptuous, even more cruel and inhumane'.[107] This concern about the troubling effects of public spectacles is typical of a Stoic viewpoint.[108] It reappears in Greek authors of the period as well as in the Christian Tertullian's attack on spectacles, where his words indicating the dangers of the stadium and arena are in line with Seneca's concerns that spectacle can induce metamorphoses of character:

The man who, in the streets, suppresses or objects to a quarrel coming to blows, in the stadium applauds much more serious fights; and he who shudders at the body of a man dead by nature's law, in the amphitheatre, looks down with most tolerant eyes on bodies mangled, torn in pieces, defiled with their own blood.   (Tertullian, *De Spectaculis* 21)

While these authors do indeed criticize a love of athletic spectacles, that criticism is as much due to elite and philosophical self-fashioning as to serious hostility

---

[104] *De Officiis* 2.16 (56–7) (citing Aristotle). See also *Ad Familiares* 7.1, 12, 18.2.   [105] Pliny, *Letters* 9.6.
[106] *The Letters of the Younger Pliny*, trans. B. Radice (Harmondsworth, 1963), 236.
[107] Seneca, *Letters* 7.3.   [108] Wiedemann, *Emperors and Gladiators*, 141–3.

towards Greek athletics, especially since similar criticisms are evoked against other public spectacles.

Sometimes, however, the Greekness of athletics is indeed at issue, blamed for the stereotypical faults of Greek culture, at least as they appear to Roman eyes—luxury, corruption, and a tendency towards vice. For Cicero, Greek athletics is directly associated with the encouragement of pederasty and effeminacy. For him, Ennius encapsulated the dangers of athletic nudity when he proclaimed, 'to strip the body naked among citizens is the fount of shame'.[109] Pliny the Younger too sees athletic games as encouraging vice. In his letter explaining the abolition of a gymnastic competition at Vienna in Gaul he quotes approvingly Junius Mauricus' comment that he wished those at Rome, the *Capitolia*, could also be abolished. Finishing his letter, he concludes, 'It was decided to abolish the games at Vienna, which had infected their morals just as ours corrupt the morals of all men.'[110]

Similar fears about the debilitating effects of Greek games can be seen in Tacitus' account of the institution of the *Neronia*, mentioned above.[111] Here, too, opponents of the festival associate this delight in foreign pursuits with luxury and degeneracy. Yet similar arguments could also be hurled against the importation of foreign marbles in domestic housing or the contemporary interest in the theatre. The moralizing attacks on these areas have been discussed by Catharine Edwards, who shows that they were a way of the elite setting itself up as guardian of public morality, while at the same time being the class which was also most often implicated in such attacks.[112]

Tacitus' traditionalists worry that this new enthusiasm for boxing will distract young men from the proper activities suitable for them, namely warfare and military training. This opposition between athletics and warfare is an enduring strand in Roman attitudes to the Greek gymnasium. So in Lucan's *Civil War*, Caesar urges on his troops by telling them that they will encounter only the youth of Greece, which has been so weakened by its time in the gymnasium and palaestra that it can scarcely bear arms.[113] The fear that Romans might give up training for war, for the gymnasium, is itself presented as a *fait accompli* by Pliny the Younger, again in a context relating to public spectacles, though here those of the arena rather than the stadium. He criticizes the public's addiction to spectacle, arguing that the Roman interest in weapons has passed from their hands to their eyes; that they prefer to

---

[109] Cicero, *Tusculan Disputations* 4.70, in the context of a discussion of the origins of pederastic relationships in the gymnasium.

[110] Pliny, *Letters* 4.22.3, 7. On athletics in Vienna, see further below, pp. 78–83.

[111] Tacitus, *Annals* 14.20, see p. 30.   [112] Edwards, *Politics*, 1–33, 98–172.

[113] Lucan, *Civil War* 7.270–2. The links between athletics and warfare in the Greek imagination are explored below, Chapters 5–7, though note that Greek intellectuals too could see increasing specialization in athletics as contrary to the training necessary for warfare, e.g. Plato, *Republic* 1404a–b; Plutarch, *Philopoemen* 3.

watch others fighting, and when they do exercise, it is under the direction not of a veteran, but of a 'Graeculus magister', a Greek trainer.[114] For Pliny, it is hard to tell which is worse—not to train at all, or to train in the Greek manner!

Traditional Roman exercise actually seems to have included a number of the features of the Greek gymnasium—throwing the javelin, running, and wrestling, albeit with a little swimming in the Tiber thrown in. Yet changes do seem to have taken place in the course of the first century. While the traditional site for such activities was the Campus Martius, over time the area was increasingly monumentalized with, among other things, the building of large bath complexes, such as those of Agrippa and Nero. Presumably much of the 'military training' which used to take place in the open became transferred to the baths, which were increasingly supplied with large palaestra areas, themselves evocative of the Greek world, though the palaestra was never as dominant a feature here as in the east.[115] While the activities which took place there might not have differed greatly from those credited to the rustic heroes of the Roman past, what mattered was the Greek veneer which could now be put upon them.

Indeed, the complaints of Juvenal about the rustic Roman who wears prizes of victory on his oiled neck, or the crafty Greek who can take on the role of personal trainer as easily as that of doctor or rhetorician, suggest that in reality Greek-style training was becoming increasingly popular in Rome.[116] The presence of Greek trainers working for Roman clients, suggested by Pliny, is also attested by Lucian, whose satire on the misfortunes of those who take up posts in elite Roman families also sneers at those who take up even more lowly positions, linking athletic trainers with parasites.[117]

The growing popularity of athletic pursuits and spectacles is also suggested by the appearance of athletic scenes on Roman sarcophagi of the second and third centuries AD, especially those of children.[118] While some of these show children or cupids engaging in athletic contests, others, like one in the Vatican, feature adult athletes, here shown competing in the pancration (a contest combining elements of both boxing and wrestling), wrestling, and boxing, and being crowned in victory (Fig. 2.3).[119] Following the lead of Franz Cumont, Margherita Bonanno Aravantinou has suggested that these athletic images should be seen as symbols of

---

[114] Pliny, *Panegyric* 13.5.   [115] Nielsen, *Thermae et Balnea*, 24–59.   [116] Juvenal, *Satire* 3.68, 76.

[117] Lucian, *On Salaried Posts in Great Houses* 4. His condescending attitude to such figures can be explained by his own pretensions to be seen as of vastly superior rank.

[118] They are collected by M. Bonanno Aravantinou, 'Un frammento di sarcofago romano con fanciulli atleti nei Musei Capitolini: contributo allo studio dei sarcofagi con scene di palestra', *Bollettino d'Arte* 15 (1982), 67–84. See also F. Castagnoli, 'Il capitello della Pigna Vaticana', *BullCom* 71 (1943–5), 1–30, on examples of victorious athletes in relief sculpture, including sarcofagi.

[119] Bonanno Aravantinou, 'Frammento di sarcofago', 73, D27.

FIGURE 2.3
The appearance of
athletic scenes on
Roman children's
sarcophagi shows
the contemporary
delight in athletic
pursuits and spec-
tacles in Rome and
their place within
childhood education
and amusements.
L: 1.24m. Turn of
second and third
centuries AD.

FIGURE 2.3 The appearance of athletic scenes on Roman children's sarcophagi shows the contemporary delight in athletic pursuits and spectacles in Rome and their place within childhood education and amusements. L: 1.24m. Turn of second and third centuries AD.

immortality, suggesting the deceased's victory over death.[120] However, other scholars have argued that much funerary imagery is concerned to commemorate the past life of the deceased rather than expressing hopes for immortality, and a reference to the delights and pursuits of the deceased seems appropriate here.[121] Like the scenes of erotes engaged in childhood games or racing chariots which appear on other children's sarcophagi, athletic scenes probably reflect the delights and pursuits of the deceased and perhaps the dashed hopes of their parents.[122] The appearance of both child and adult athletes within funerary art suggests a delight in watching Greek-style athletics comparable to that of watching chariot races as well as the imitation of such contests within childhood pursuits and education.[123]

Both literary and visual evidence thus suggest a gradual increase in Greek-style athletic training throughout the period of the first three centuries AD. The building of large imperial bath complexes with areas for exercise both responded to this interest and further encouraged it, providing facilities for both Roman citizens and others, such as the professional athletes who travelled to take part in festivals like the Capitoline games. The extent to which Roman citizens may actually have taken

[120] F. Cumont, *Recherches sur le symbolisme funéraire des Romains* (Paris, 1942), 457–84, esp. 469–75; Bonanno Aravantinou, 'Frammento di sarcofago', 82.

[121] A. D. Nock, 'Sarcophagi and Symbolism', *AJA* 50 (1946), 140–70; J. A. North, 'These He Cannot Take', *JRS* 73 (1983), 169–74. For discussions of the debate over the interpretation of funerary imagery see R. Turcan, 'Les sarcophages romains et le problème du symbolisme funéraire', in *ANRW* 16.2 (1978), 1700–35, and B. C. Ewald, 'Death and Myth: New Books on Roman Sarcophagi', *AJA* 103 (1999), 344–8.

[122] J. Huskinson, *Roman Children's Sarcophagi: Their Decoration and its Social Significance* (Oxford, 1996), 16–19.

[123] Such scenes of physical training can be compared to those of intellectual education shown by sarcophagi with figures of the Muses. On these, see H. I. Marrou, *ΜΟΥΣΙΚΟΣ ΑΝΗΡ: Etude sur les scènes de la vie intellectuelle figurant sur les monuments funéraires des Romains* (Grenoble, 1938).

part in public competitions is rather less certain. I discussed above the worries reported by Tacitus that the introduction of the *Neronia* would encourage Roman youths to take up boxing just as some had already appeared on the stage. This linking of acting with athletics suggests that these conservatives feared Roman involvement in the (to them) shameful activity of public athletic contests, and indeed one Roman senator, Palfurius Sura, does appear to have wrestled in his youth, presumably in a public capacity.[124] Yet Caldelli has shown that there is no epigraphic evidence for athletic victors in the Capitoline games coming from the Roman west, though a number of elite Roman figures do appear as victors in both the Latin poetry and oratory competitions.[125] If a few elite Romans did take part in these games, they seem not to have found much success. On the whole, Roman participation in public athletic competitions probably remained the exception rather than the norm, though the worry that the elite might take part could still attract the outrage of old-fashioned moralists.

However, what does seem certain is that a number of Romans indulged in the fantasy of Greek athletic activity, either in the baths or in the privacy of their own homes, under the supervision of an athletic trainer. This slippage between the traditional Roman hostility to Greek athletics, and especially its nakedness, and the simultaneous desire to partake in all aspects of Greek culture is perhaps best expressed in a passage in Plutarch's *Roman Questions*, dealing with the subject of athletics:

> The Romans used to be particularly suspicious of rubbing down with oil, and even today believe that nothing has been so responsible for the enslavement and effeminacy of the Greeks as their gymnasia and wrestling schools, which engender for the cities much indolence, wasting of time and pederasty . . . By these practices, they have failed to notice their collapse of military training, and have become happy to be called skilful and noble athletes rather than fine hoplites and cavalrymen. It is certainly an effort to escape this if you exercise naked in the open air. But those who oil themselves at home and care for their bodies commit no error.[126]

Here we find all the standard Roman stereotypes about athletics—that it encourages degeneracy and pederasty, and replaces the proper training for warfare. Yet at the end Plutarch tells us that while these dangers are difficult to avoid if one exercises naked in public, those who exercise at home can avoid the errors! Whether this is advice to Greeks or Romans is not specified—a curious alignment of the speaker with the Roman viewpoint seems to happen in the middle of the passage, yet any suggestion to the Greek cities in the east that they should abandon the

---

[124] Scholiast to Juvenal, *Satire* 4.53 (Wessner, *Scholia*, 57).   [125] Caldelli, *Agon*, 90–4.

[126] Plutarch, *Roman Questions* 40 (274d–e). I give the translation of S. Goldhill, 'Introduction: Setting an Agenda: "Everything is Greece to the Wise"', in id., *Being Greek*, 1–25, at 1–2, who also highlights the end of the passage.

palaestra and start exercising at home would surely be taken with disbelief.[127] Instead, it probably represents a Roman viewpoint. This, surely, is the Romans both having their cake and eating it, staying true to their traditional hostility towards Greek athletics, but also endorsed in their current athletic practices—so long as they are at home, well away from prying eyes! What in fact seems to have happened is that athletic exercises did take place in public, but within the semi-public world of the baths, where nudity could be safely accommodated, rather than in public athletic festivals such as the *Capitolia*.

Through this discussion of the gradual introduction of Greek athletic contests and physical training to Rome, I hope to have shown that there is, in fact, convincing evidence that the Romans were by no means uniformly hostile to Greek athletics. Of course, opposition to Greek athletics was indeed expressed, yet in many cases these views can be seen as part of a rhetoric of concern about the extent to which the encroachments of Greek culture might undermine Roman identity and morals. Such concerns help to illuminate the struggles that took place within Roman constructions of their own identity and suggest that Roman views of their culture and identity were far from unified. Certainly, not everyone welcomed the increasing Hellenization of Roman society, and trends that were increasingly acceptable to some could still be resisted by others.

An analogy with the attacks discussed by Edwards, with which these comments on athletics share a number of similarities, also suggests that we should not see this simply as a case of the lower classes welcoming new and varied spectacles while the upper classes remained hostile and aloof.[128] Instead, through the involvement of the emperors in promoting athletic festivals and the concerns expressed about the activities of Roman youths (by which most authors mean *elite* youths), the senatorial and equestrian classes of Roman society would appear to have been just as implicated in this adoption of Greek athletic culture as those at other levels of the social scale. In order to explore these reactions to Greek athletics in more detail, I will turn now to the figural depictions of athletic activity which we find in mosaics decorating bath complexes in and around Rome as well as elsewhere in the western provinces.

---

[127] Though the ideas about excessive athletic training being contrary to military preparation do have similarities with other viewpoints in Greek sources, e.g. Plato, *Republic* 1404a–b.

[128] Edwards, *Politics*. See above, p. 40.

THREE

Visualizing Athletics in the Roman Baths

In the previous chapter I argued that over the course of the first three centuries AD Greek athletics came to occupy an increasingly prominent place in Roman society, both through the gradual introduction of Greek festivals to Rome and through the adoption of Greek athletic training by the Romans themselves. While the literary sources are often hostile to Greek-style athletics, their very attacks also suggest its popularity. In this chapter I will examine the evidence presented by figural mosaics from bath complexes in Rome, Ostia, and elsewhere in the western provinces to show how they reflect the impact of Greek athletics both as a public spectacle and as a form of personal bodily training.[1]

In recent years a number of scholars have highlighted the important role which public bathing played within Roman culture, and have examined the development of bath complexes and their spread throughout the Roman empire.[2] The public baths were a place where those at all levels of Roman society went to socialize and advertise themselves, perhaps hoping to gain an invitation to dinner or find an audience for their poetry. A combination of literary and archaeological evidence suggests that exercise, massage, conversation, eating, drinking, and sexual activity all took place in the baths as well as the simple act of washing.[3] Over the course of the first few centuries AD a number of huge imperially sponsored bath complexes were built in the city of Rome, revealing the importance of such projects as a form of imperial munificence. The nearby city of Ostia, too, could boast three large public bath complexes as well as a plethora of smaller establishments.[4]

---

[1] Some of the material in this chapter has appeared previously as Z. Newby, 'Greek Athletics as Roman Spectacle: The Mosaics from Ostia and Rome', *PBSR* 70 (2002), 177–203.

[2] Nielsen, *Thermae et Balnea*; F. K. Yegül, *Baths and Bathing in Classical Antiquity* (Cambridge, Mass., 1992); M. Weber, *Antike Badekultur* (Munich, 1996); G. G. Fagan, *Bathing in Public in the Roman World* (Ann Arbor, 1999); J. DeLaine and D. E. Johnston, eds., *Roman Baths and Bathing*, JRA Supplement 37 (Portsmouth, RI, 1999), especially DeLaine's introduction. For a study of an individual complex see J. DeLaine, *The Baths of Caracalla: A Study in the Design, Construction and Economics of Large-Scale Building Projects in Imperial Rome*, JRA Supplement 23 (Portsmouth, RI, 1997); and on sculptural decoration, H. Manderscheid, *Die Skulpturenausstattung der kaiserzeitlichen Thermenanlagen* (Berlin, 1981).

[3] See Fagan, *Bathing in Public*, 12–39, for a description based on the epigrams of Martial.

[4] R. Meiggs, *Roman Ostia*, 2nd edn. (Oxford, 1973), 404–20. On the importance of bath complexes as a form of munificence, see J. DeLaine, 'Benefactions and Urban Renewal: Bath Buildings in Roman Italy', in DeLaine and Johnston, *Roman Baths and Bathing*, 67–74.

In addition to the rooms dedicated to bathing, the largest complexes, usually referred to as *thermae*, also included areas for exercise as well as other recreational spaces such as parks and libraries.[5] From the late first century AD, especially, athletic activity seems to have become an important part of the bathing routine. Seneca, Martial, and Juvenal all refer to bathers exercising by boxing, wrestling, or weight-lifting before bathing, though other popular pursuits included walking and ball games.[6] Some informal competitions also seem to have taken place in the baths. Thus a funerary inscription of one Ursus boasts of his success in playing ball games in the Baths of Trajan, Agrippa, Titus, and Nero in Rome and the applause that he won from those watching.[7] Such competitions could have been accommodated in stadium-like areas such as that visible along the south side of the Baths of Caracalla in Rome.[8] Juvenal's scathing reference to a Roman who wears 'niceteria', Greek-style medals, on his oiled neck may also refer to the prizes awarded in this type of informal contest.[9]

Juvenal's comment clearly associates a love of sport with the delights and encroachments of Greek culture, an association evident too in Pliny's comment that Romans now exercise under the eye of a Greek trainer rather than a Roman veteran.[10] The architecture of these large bath complexes helped to facilitate athletic activity by providing dedicated spaces for physical exercise. Yet I will suggest that their decoration too helped to create an atmosphere of fantasy and exoticism around even the most mundane scenes of physical training. In particular, a number of bath complexes were decorated with figural mosaics with athletic scenes, suggesting a comparison with the public world of athletic festivals as well as the physical training of the Greek gymnasium. Even in small complexes which lacked dedicated areas for physical exercise, decoration could help to link bathing and exercise or evoke the competitive world of public festivals.

Before turning to the evidence from Rome and Ostia, it is worth looking briefly at the material from Campania. This area was long familiar with Greek culture, particularly through the presence of the city of Naples, which boasted its own Greek festival, the *Sebasta*, recorded in inscriptions which highlight its Hellenic nature.[11] The Greek gymnasium was familiar here, and towns like Pompeii possessed their own palaestrae. They also began to build bath complexes which united rooms for bathing with areas for exercise, as we see in the Stabian baths at Pompeii.[12] Yet even

---

[5] Nielsen, *Thermae et Balnea*, 144–6.

[6] e.g. Seneca, *Epistle* 56; Juvenal, *Satire* 6.419; Martial, *Epigrams* 4.8.5; 7.32.5–9; 7.67.4–8. See Nielsen, *Thermae et Balnea*, 144.

[7] *CIL* vi. 9797.   [8] Nielsen, *Thermae et Balnea*, 53, 145; DeLaine, *Baths*, 20–1.

[9] Juvenal, *Satires* 3.67.   [10] Pliny, *Panegyric* 13.5. See above, pp. 40–1.

[11] M. Leiwo, *Neapolitana: A Study of Population and Language in Graeco-Roman Naples*, Commentationes Humanarum Litterarum 102 (Helsinki, 1994), 45–8, notes that the Sebasta is always recorded in Greek inscriptions, whereas other areas of civic life could be recorded in Latin. On the Sebasta see above, p. 27.

[12] On palaestrae and the development of baths in Campania, see Yegül, *Baths and Bathing*, 55–66.

FIGURE 3.1 A mosaic showing two wrestlers decorates the threshold of a bathing establishment at Pompeii, acting as an advertisement for the baths within and showing the link between athletics and bathing. Height of figures: *c.*1m. Claudian.

in small bath complexes where dedicated areas for exercise were restricted or lacking, the imagery could help to assert the close connection between bathing and athletics. So, in the so-called Palaestra at Pompeii, Region VIII.ii.23, the entrance to this small bath complex is advertised by a black and white mosaic showing two wrestlers (Fig. 3.1) while the small peristyle inside features later fourth-style decoration of a scaenae frons populated by athletic figures.[13]

A similar use of an athletic mosaic to act as a signpost to the baths can be seen in a private bathing suite in the villa rustica of N. Popidius Florus at Boscoreale. Here the threshold to the bathing suite is marked by a mosaic spelling the greetings 'HAVE SALVE' with the rough figures of two naked wrestlers shown above.[14]

[13] See A. Sogliano, 'Pompei: Degli edifizi recentemente scoperti e degli oggetti raccolti negli scavi dal settembre 1888 al marzo 1889', *NSc* (1889), 114–36, at 114–22; F. Noack and K. Lehmann-Hartleben, *Baugeschichtliche Untersuchungen am Stadtrand von Pompeji* (Berlin and Leipzig, 1936), 91–6; J. R. Clarke, *Roman Black-and-White Figural Mosaics* (New York, 1979), 12; I. Baldassarre, ed., *Pompei: Pitture e Mosaici*, viii (Rome, 1988), 166–90. The mosaic is dated to the Claudian period and the wall-paintings to the AD 60s.

[14] M. Della Corte, 'La "Villa rustica N. Popidi Flori" esplorata dalla signora Giovanna Zurlo-Pulzella, nel fondo di sua proprietà in contrada Pisanella, comune di Boscoreale, l'anno 1906', *NSc* (1921), 442–60, at 450–1, fig. 15.

Close by, the caldarium of a rustic villa found at Centopiedi near Boscoreale was decorated with wall-paintings showing scenes of athletic competition in a gymnasium setting.[15] Similar images appear in the caldarium of the baths of the House of the Menander at Pompeii.[16] In all these cases the rooms are small, serving only the basic washing needs of the household, yet the images decorating them allude to the wider world of the Greek gymnasium and sometimes also to the prizes which athletic success could bring in public festivals. They link together the exercises associated with bathing with the public world of the Greek gymnasium.

All these images date from the middle of the first century AD. While Campania is well-known as an area deeply imbued with Greek culture, the decision to decorate private bath suites with these images at that time may also reflect the popularity of athletic games in the contemporary world. This is the period when the games at Naples were given added status by the presence of imperial figures like Claudius and Titus as gymnasiarchs and even, in the case of Nero, as contestants.[17] The prominence of the *Sebasta* festival may have encouraged in the owners of these rustic villas or town houses a tendency to see their own simple exercises as a reflection of both the Greek gymnasium and the public world of athletic competition. In Rome, too, we can link together the gradual introduction of athletic festivals with an increased interest in athletic training within the baths themselves.

In Rome and Ostia both large thermae complexes and smaller private bath suites appear to have been decorated with athletic imagery, particularly in the form of mosaics and statues. While the evidence from Rome is more scattered, apart from the majestic Baths of Caracalla where the decorative scheme can be reconstructed in some detail, Ostia presents us with a plethora of athletic imagery especially in the form of the black and white floor mosaics for which it is so famed.[18] Recent work has focused on the differences between Rome and Ostia, pointing out the individual characteristics of Ostia's population mix and features of her civic life.[19] Yet in her bathing and spectacle culture there also seem to be a number of similarities.[20]

---

[15] R. Paribeni, 'Boscoreale: Villa rustica rinvenuta nella contrada Centopiedi, al Tirone', *NSc* (1903), 64–7. From the description, I identify one of these with a painting conserved in the Museo Archeologico at Naples, cat. 338 (Museo Nazionale di Napoli/Archivio Fotografico Pedicini, *Le collezioni del Museo Nazionale di Napoli*, i. 1. 170).

[16] R. Ling, *The Insula of the Menander at Pompeii*, i (Oxford, 1997), 276, no. 48.

[17] See above, p. 31. Nero took part in the musical contests but is also shown as a spectator of athletics in the gymnasium at Naples; Suetonius, *Nero* 40.

[18] The Baths of Caracalla are discussed below, pp. 68–76. The Ostian mosaics are published in G. Becatti, *Mosaici e pavimenti marmorei*, Scavi di Ostia 4 (Rome, 1961). See also M. E. Blake, 'Roman Mosaics of the Second Century in Italy', *Memoirs of the American Academy in Rome* 13 (1936), 69–214 and Clarke, *Black-and-White Mosaics*.

[19] C. Bruun and A. Gallina Zevi, eds., *Ostia e Portus nelle loro relazioni con Roma*, Acta Instituti Romani Finlandiae 27 (Rome, 2002).

[20] Though note C. Valeri, 'Arredi scultorei dagli edifici termali di Ostia', in Bruun and Gallina Zevi, *Ostia e Portus*, 213–28, on some trends within the sculptural display of these baths.

In particular, Caldelli's suggestion that Ostia was probably heavily influenced by the spectacle culture of nearby Rome is supported by the visual evidence which attests to a great interest in Greek athletics, despite the fact that we hear little about such contests taking place in Ostia itself.[21]

The mosaics vary in detail and complexity. Some consist of simple scenes of pairs of athletes engaged in a particular contest,[22] or of individual athletes crowning themselves[23] or being rewarded with a palm of victory.[24] Sometimes more complex scenes are presented, combining scenes of athletic contest with indications of specific prizes and the settings in which the contests take place.[25] Occasionally the figures are named, suggesting an allusion to particular famous individuals. Here I want to focus on just a few key examples, to give an idea of the variety within the representations and of the connections which they provoke within the spaces they decorate.[26]

Athletic mosaics appear in a variety of different contexts. In large public complexes such as the Baths of Neptune and the Baths of Porta Marina they tend to be located close to the palaestra, setting up a direct connection with the physical exercises taking place nearby. In smaller suites such as the Baths of the Trinacria or the Terme Marittime, however, they can be placed instead in heated rooms, evoking a link between bathing and exercise which is not actually accommodated in the layout of the building itself. While all the mosaics discussed here proclaim the popularity of athletic pursuits in second- and third-century Ostia, their precise locations and content provoke a range of differing associations pointing both to the bathing experience and to the wider popularity of public athletic spectacles.

THE BATHS OF NEPTUNE AND THE BATHS AT PORTA MARINA

If we look first at those bath complexes which possessed palaestrae, we find that two of the three *thermae* in Ostia have yielded mosaics with athletic scenes, while the third, the Forum Baths, seems to have included athletic themes within its

---

[21] M. L. Caldelli, 'Varia agonistica ostiensia', in G. Paci, ed., *Epigrafia Romana in area Adriatica: Actes de la IXe. rencontre franco-italienne sur l'épigraphie du monde romain* (Macerata, 1998), 205–47. See also Meiggs, *Roman Ostia*, 425–8, and C. Pavolini, *La vita quotidiana a Ostia* (Bari, 1986), 239–45. There are no certain references to athletic spectacles at Ostia, although boxing and wrestling contests may have occurred during *ludi*, possibly held in the theatre.

[22] e.g. Baths of Neptune, discussed below, pp. 50–1.

[23] A lost mosaic in so-called Palazzo Imperiale: C. L. Visconti, 'Escavazioni di Ostia dall'anno 1855 al 1858', *Annali dell'Istituto di corrispondenza archeologica* 29 (1857), 281–340, at 336.

[24] Baths of Trinacria: Becatti, *Mosaici*, 139–42, no. 278.

[25] Terme Marittime and Baths of Porta Marina, discussed below, pp. 51–8.

[26] For a fuller discussion, see Newby, 'Greek Athletics'.

statuary display.[27] While all three complexes could accommodate athletic activity in their palaestrae, the connections evoked by the mosaics vary according to their complexity.

The Baths of Neptune on the Decumanus can be identified with the complex which is recorded as having been built under Hadrian and completed and decorated by Antoninus Pius.[28] Their mosaic decoration, which includes the famous image of Neptune in his chariot, has thus been dated to the Antonine period, though the mosaic with which we are concerned here is a rather simpler composition than those elsewhere in the building.[29] It paves a room which originally had an opening on its western side onto the palaestra area, later closed off.[30] While part of the mosaic is now lost, it seems to have shown four pairs of athletes (Fig. 3.2). On the north side of the room are a pair of boxers wearing spiked gloves and another pair of athletes, probably pancratiasts, one of whom is already defeated and sits on the ground. The mosaic on the southern side of the room is mostly destroyed, with only the head of a figure surviving from one pair of athletes and a single figure from the other. His pose suggests that he is about to start wrestling. Thus the mosaic showed four pairs of athletes engaged in various athletic contests. There do not appear to be any prizes for victory shown on the mosaic, such as palms or vases. The impression given is one of general athletic activity rather than a representation of a particular contest, although the presence of spiked gloves and the *cirrus* or ponytail worn by one of the athletes also hint towards professional public contests.[31]

The mosaic is placed on the edge of the palaestra or exercise ground of the baths. The lack of a black border on the side opening onto the palaestra is a strong visual suggestion that it should be seen as part of that space, which was available for physical exercises such as wrestling, walking, weight-lifting, and ball-games. The mosaic image of athletic activity thus acts as a prelude to the human activities nearby. It defines the space as one for athletic activity and encourages an identification

[27] The head of an athletic statue found in a drain of the Forum Baths probably comes from a statue originally displayed in the nearby palaestra: R. Calza, *I ritratti*, Scavi di Ostia 5 (Rome, 1964), 24, no. 17; Manderscheid, *Skulpturenausstattung*, 77, no. 82.

[28] *CIL* xiv. 98, see F. Zevi and A. Granelli, 'Le Terme di Nettuno: Stratigrafia e fase edilizie pre-adrianee', *Mededelingen van het Nederlands Instituut te Rome* 58 (1999), 80–2. Earlier accounts are provided by H. Bloch, *I bolli laterizi e la storia edilizia* (Rome, 1938), 246, 276–9, and Meiggs, *Roman Ostia*, 409–10.

[29] Becatti, *Mosaici*, 52, no. 72, dates it to AD 139.   [30] Room D on Becatti's map (*Mosaici*, 48, fig. 15).

[31] On gloves, see M. B. Poliakoff, *Combat Sports in the Ancient World: Competition, Violence, and Culture* (New Haven and London, 1987), 68–79, and H. M. Lee, 'The Later Greek Boxing Glove and the "Roman" Caestus : A Centennial Reevaluation of Jüthner's "Über Antike Turngeräthe" ', *Nikephoros* 10 (1997), 161–78 with pls. 2–7. On the cirrus as a mark of professionalism, see E. N. Gardiner, *Athletics of the Ancient World* (London, 1930), caption to fig. 74, and B. Gassowska, 'Cirrus in vertice', in *Mélanges offerts à Kazimierz Michalowski* (Warsaw, 1966), 421–7, with reference to Suetonius, *Nero* 45.1. It seems likely, however, that this is often overstated, since we also find images of athletes without the cirrus. For the latest discussion, see J.-P. Thuillier, 'Le *cirrus* et la barbe: Questions d'iconographie athlétique romaine', *MEFRA* 110 (1998), 351–80, who argues that it distinguishes between different age groups of athletes.

FIGURE 3.2 This mosaic with athletic scenes decorated a room opening onto the palaestra of the baths of Neptune, inviting comparison between the figures represented here and the bathers themselves. L: 7.5m. *c*.AD 139.

between the athletes shown on the ground and the bathers themselves. Similar invitations to compare mosaic imagery with activities taking place in the baths can also be seen elsewhere. The later, fourth-century, mosaics in the villa baths at Piazza Armerina in Sicily show figures of attendants ready to massage the bathers, while in Ostia itself a mosaic in the Baths of Buticosus shows a man holding a bucket and labelled as Buticosus, probably indicating the overseer of the baths.[32] The primary frame of reference of this mosaic would seem to be the activities actually taking place within the baths themselves.

The mosaic in the Baths near the Porta Marina, sometimes called the Baths of Marciana, suggests a wider set of referents.[33] The initial construction of these baths

[32] Piazza Armerina: A. Carandini, A. Ricci, and M. de Vos, *Filosofiana: The Villa of Piazza Armerina* (Palermo, 1982), 359–62, room 5, pl. 61; Ostia: Becatti, *Mosaici*, 29–30, no. 51, dated to AD 115. Compare a similar mosaic in the Baths of the Seven Sages, Becatti, *Mosaici*, 137, no. 270, which may represent either a bather or an attendant.

[33] A portrait head of Marciana was found here, along with images of Trajan and Sabina. See Manderscheid, *Skulpturenausstattung*, 79; Meiggs, *Roman Ostia*, 407–9.

is dated to the Trajanic-Hadrianic period, though they also received later renovations in the Severan period.[34] The athletic mosaic decorates a room which opens onto the frigidarium and is placed close to the palaestra. It has been identified by Floriani Squarciapino as an apodyterium or changing room.[35] The dating of the mosaic has been debated, though in the foreshortening of the figures and the delineation of the musculature it shares a number of similarities to the Neptune mosaic in the Baths of Neptune, and the Hadrianic date suggested by Floriani Squarciapino seems, to my eye, more convincing than the Severan one proposed by Clarke.[36] It shows a palaestra-like scene (Fig. 3.3). In the centre lies a table with an ornate spiked crown and a palm. A herm stands nearby and a ball, three strigils, a bucket, and a metal vase lie in front of the table, all orientated to be viewed from the entrance to the room (which lies at the top of the photograph shown here). Around this central scene a series of figures are orientated towards the sides of the room. At the entrance is a group of two boxers and a gymnasiarch or umpire, to whom one of the boxers seems to be complaining while the other raises his hands in victory. A youthful herm is placed behind the umpire. On the opposite side of the room a pair of wrestlers are shown next to an athlete holding a strigil while the athlete in the corner carries a hoop with two strigils and an oil flask.[37] Next to him, on one of the short sides, we see an athlete lifting weights while the opposite short side shows a discus thrower and a triumphant trumpeter.

The image itself and its placement within a bath complex with a palaestra would certainly have evoked the exercises in which the bathers here took part. They could see images of themselves in the figures wrestling, throwing the discus, and weightlifting, while the shift from exercise to bathing is suggested by the athletes carrying strigils, an implement also used in the baths. Yet while the mosaic can be read on one level as an illustration of athletics within the baths, other aspects of it suggest different resonances. In particular, the prominent placement of a table with prizes in the centre of the image also evokes the world of public competition in athletic festivals. While palms and metal vases often appear elsewhere as general

---

[34] See most recently, with further bibliography, C. Valeri, 'Brevi note sulle Terme di Porta Marina a Ostia', *Archeologica Classica* 52 (2001), 307–22 and ead., 'Arredi scultorei', 214–16.

[35] M. Floriani Squarciapino, 'Un Altro Mosaico Ostiense con Atleti', *AttiPontAccRomRend* 59 (1986–7), 161–79 at 164.

[36] Floriani Squarciapino, 'Altro Mosaico Ostiense', 171–2; contra J. R. Clarke, 'Mosaic Workshops at Pompeii and Ostia Antica', in P. Johnson, R. Ling, and D. J. Smith, eds., *Fifth International Colloquium on Ancient Mosaics, held at Bath, England, on September 5–12, 1987*, JRA Supplement 9 (Ann Arbor, 1994), 89–102 at 98–101. The mosaic shares a number of similarities with the so-called Lancelloti mosaic discovered at Tusculum, which may also have decorated a changing room. See E. Pinder, 'Musaico tuscolano', *Bullettino dell'Istituto di corrispondenza archeologica comunale di Roma* (1862), 179–82; H. Hirzel, 'Musaico tuscolano', *Annali dell'Istituto di corrispondenza archeologica* (1863), 397–412; and Blake, 'Roman Mosaics', 163–4, who reasserts a Hadrianic date for the mosaic.

[37] Not visible on this photograph. See Floriani Squarciapino, 'Altro Mosaico Ostiense', 163, fig. 1.

FIGURE 3.3 This complex mosaic paved a changing room in the baths of Porta Marina and alludes to the activities taking place within the baths themselves as well as to public athletic contests and the Greek gymnasium, illustrating the varying associations of athletic activity. L: 7.30m. Hadrianic.

attributes of success, the distinctive spiked crown may allude to one festival in particular, although it is impossible now to identify which.[38] As Floriani Squarciapino suggests, we should probably see the crown on the table as an enlarged version of that which the trumpeter wears on his head, showing him as a victor in this set of games.

However, the mosaic may also allude to the Greek gymnasium. The herm in the centre of the mosaic shows a balding figure with a long beard, reminiscent of a philosopher portrait and thus perhaps evoking not just the physical but also the intellectual side of the palaestra. Herms are certainly common as features of the decoration of the Roman circus as well as the Greek gymnasium, and it could be argued that the appearance of herms in this mosaic points towards the location of these athletic events as taking place in a circus such as that at Rome.[39] However, the

[38] See Floriani Squarciapino, 'Altro Mosaico Ostiense', 164, 173–9. Rumscheid, *Kranz und Krone*, 161, cat. 99, suggests that the spikes represent flowers or leaves. It is unlikely to refer to the Capitoline games since the prize for these was a crown of oak leaves: Martial, *Epigrams* 4.1.6, 4.54.1–2. See Caldelli, *Agon*, 106, for more references.

[39] On herms as decoration of the circus see J. H. Humphrey, *Roman Circuses: Arenas for Chariot Racing* (London, 1986), 135–6 and *passim*.

elderly appearance of this particular one differs from those which we see on representations of Roman circuses, adding a wider set of allusions. The youthful herm
behind the group of two boxers and a gymnasiarch is more typical of those which
decorated the circus and could point either to the Greek gymnasium or to a location closer to home, perhaps in the circus or stadium at Rome.[40]

The two boxers standing in front of it are marked out as individuals by their lack
of the cirrus and their distinctive facial features. The combination of the youthful
victor standing with an older, bearded man in front of an umpire and a herm seems
in part to offer a snapshot of life in a Greek gymnasium. Yet at the same time, these
boxers also wear spiked gloves on their hands, symbols which seem more appropriate for public competition than for informal bouts in the gymnasium or baths.
In part their presence may simply be to mark these men out as boxers, rather than
wrestlers or pancratiasts, but it also presents a scene which is evocative of the Greek
gymnasium but also framed within the terms of Roman spectacle culture.

Thus the mosaic seems to point in several different directions simultaneously,
conflating images of physical activity in the baths or gymnasium with scenes of
athletic victory in public competitions. The figures of athletes holding strigils on
the other side of the mosaic also invite this multiplicity of viewings. While they
wear the cirrus and thus appear as 'professional' athletes, they are not involved in
any athletic activity but rather appear to be, like the bathers who would be viewing
this mosaic, engaged in the task of cleaning themselves with oil and strigils. As in
the mosaic from the Baths of Neptune, the image simultaneously invites the
bathers viewing it to identify themselves with the figures represented there, but
also separates them by the presence of attributes such as the cirrus and gloves.

Yet by showing the mosaic athletes with whom the bather is implicitly compared
as professionals, engaged in public competition, such images also link the practice
of athletics as part of the bathing routine with the world of athletic festivals. While
we have little evidence of Romans finding success in Greek athletic festivals, the
mosaics suggest that the line between athletics in the baths and in a public festival
might easily be crossed.[41] This is precisely the fear expressed in Tacitus' account by
those opposed to Nero's introduction of the *Neronia*.[42] The inscriptional record
suggests that such fears were hardly realized on an extensive scale. Yet the display in

[40] It is possible that herms also decorated the stadium of Domitian at Rome, though we have no evidence
for this. See P. Virgili, 'Le stade de Domitien', in C. Landes, ed., *Le stade romain et ses spectacles* (Lattes, 1994),
107–19, for an account of the stadium and its decoration.

[41] On Romans as athletes, see Caldelli, *Agon*, 90, who notes that no Romans are recorded as victors in the
athletic contests of the Capitoline games, though they do appear in the poetry contests. An inscription which
shows the town council of Ostia honouring one of their citizens for his victories in festivals in Syria, Arabia,
and North Africa does not specify his speciality and may honour either an athlete or a musician: *CIL* xiv. 474,
see H. Dessau, 'Due iscrizioni ostiensi', *Bullettino dell'Istituto di corrispondenza archeologica* (1881), 137–41.
Caldelli, 'Varia agonistica ostiensia' discusses this and other agonistic evidence from Ostia.

[42] Tacitus, *Annals* 14.20. See above, p. 30.

the baths of images that flirt with such ideas also suggests the attitude of the Roman public in the second century AD. Moralists and satirists might bemoan the encroachment of Greek culture, but the bathing public, at least in Ostia, seems to have increasingly enjoyed the fantasy of seeing themselves as victorious athletic figures, just as others took to the stage or the arena.[43] In the Baths of Neptune and Porta Marina the placement of the mosaics close to the palaestra, where bathers could themselves exercise, reinforces this blurring of the line between the bathers and the mosaic figures.

The presence of a philosopher herm in the centre of the mosaic also alludes to the broader educational and cultural ideals of the Greek gymnasium. This rather muted allusion to the wider cultural associations of the gymnasium and athletic activity might well have been extended by the sculptural display of the baths, as I will argue in more detail in my discussion of the Baths of Caracalla at Rome.[44] In many cases we cannot fully reconstruct the sculptural decoration. However, we do know of a few statues which were found in the Baths at Porta Marina.[45] In addition to portrait busts of Trajan, Marciana, and Sabina, indicating the imperial patronage of the baths, a number of other statues were found here by Gavin Hamilton.[46] Hamilton's letters to Lord Shelburne describe his excavations at Ostia in 1774–5.[47] More details are given in the letters written later to Charles Townley in which Hamilton says that they decided to excavate at a spot known as Porta Marina in the ruins of some public 'Thermae Maritimae'.[48] While later scholars have sometimes associated these with another set of baths on the line of the Sullan walls to the west of the city, the map drawn by P. Hol in 1804 clearly labels the set of ruins at the south of the city as those excavated by Hamilton.[49] In his letters to Townley, Hamilton says that the following statues were found in the area, 'the fine Antinous in the character of Abundance . . . an Esculapius and a large statue of his daughter Hygea . . . [and] a most excellent torso under the knees'.[50] This latter piece was

[43] See Edwards, *Politics*, 96–136. Note that in the first century BC Cornelius Nepos, *Preface* 5, linked together acting and athletics as activities which are disgraceful in Rome though they win renown in Greece.

[44] Below, pp. 67–76.   [45] See Valeri, 'Terme di Porta Marina', 311–18; ead., 'Arredi scultorei', 216–19.

[46] Manderscheid, *Skulpturenausstattung*, 79, cats. 99–101, only mentions the imperial portraits, which were found later.

[47] See the letters to Shelburne of 1 May 1774 and 16 April 1775, collected in the appendix to A. Michaelis, *A Catalogue of the Ancient Marbles at Lansdowne House*, ed. A. H. Smith (London, 1899), 71, 77–8. L. Paschetto, *Ostia Colonia Romana: Storia e Monumenti* (Rome, 1912), 490, wrongly dates the excavations to 1788.

[48] A. H. Smith, 'Gavin Hamilton's Letters to Charles Townley', *JHS* 21 (1901), 306–21 at 314–16.

[49] The map is conserved in the Archives of the Soprintendenza at Ostia Antica. The key for this area, no. 18, describes it thus: 'Ruins remaining above the earth to a height of around forty palms (palmi) called Porta Marina discovered by Monsieur Hamilton'. The tall ruins are in fact brick piers from the baths, which still tower over the surrounding ruins. Hamilton also refers to the excavation of another set of baths, which cannot be clearly identified, though they may be the set on the Sullan walls.

[50] Smith, 'Gavin Hamilton's Letters', 315. See also the description of the torso in Hamilton's letter to Shelburne of 25 March 1776 which does not, however, record the find-spot.

restored as an image of Diomedes carrying off the palladium and sold to Lord Shelburne. It is now recognized, however, as a torso of Myron's *Discobolus*.

As well as images of the gods, a version of a famous Greek artwork, an *opus nobile*, representing a discus-thrower, was chosen for display in a context close to the athletic images shown on the mosaic. I argue in Chapter 4 that such pieces would often have carried with them both their artistic prestige as works of art and the associations of the classical gymnasium which produced them. Here the sculpted image of a pentathlete, the athletic all-rounder who is so praised in Aristotle's *Rhetoric*, is complemented by the mosaic images which evoke both the activities of the baths and the contemporary contests of public festivals.[51] The ambiguous referents of the mosaic itself, combined with this idealized image of a classical Greek athlete, suggest a desire to evoke both the contemporary and ancient experience of athletics, to see the activities which took place as a prelude to bathing as parallel to those of the classical Greek gymnasium, with all its cultural cachet, and also to hold out the fantasy of an equivalence with the famous athletes who actually won success in public festivals.

Even in smaller bath complexes without palaestra areas, mosaic decoration sometimes suggests a desire to evoke the world of public athletic spectacles within the context of bathing. A small but lavish bath suite was found on the line of the Sullan walls to the west of the city and is usually referred to as the Terme Marittime.[52] This complex was partially excavated by Visconti in the nineteenth century and as it stands today appears to be a Severan expansion of an originally Hadrianic building, with the mosaics being added in the Severan period.[53] A fragmentary mosaic was found in the apodyterium of the building, showing a man carrying a sack, and two boxers, one of whom raises his hand to crown himself.[54] While most of the mosaic is missing, these figures suggest the same desire we have seen elsewhere to point out the athletic activities traditionally associated with bathing, even in a complex where space for such activities was more restricted.

Another athletic mosaic comes from one of the heated rooms in the baths, where it contrasts with the marine scenes decorating the neighbouring two rooms.[55] Only the bottom section of the mosaic survives today, but its original composition can be seen in an excavation drawing and an old photograph (Fig. 3.4). In the apse appeared two reclining figures, probably Neptune and his consort Amphitrite,

---

[51] Aristotle, *Rhetoric* 1.5.14; cf. Socrates in Xenophon, *Symposium* 2.17.

[52] See Paschetto, *Ostia*, 302–7, though the association with *CIL* xiv. 98 is now generally rejected. See Becatti, *Mosaici*, 110–13.

[53] See Bloch, *Bolli laterizi*, 277–8 and G. Calza and G. Becatti, *Ostia*, 9th edn. rev. M. Floriani Squarciapino (Rome, 1974), 44–5.

[54] Paschetto, *Ostia*, 305; Becatti, *Mosaici*, 110, no. 209; Newby, 'Greek Athletics', 189, fig. 4.

[55] On these see Clarke, *Black-and-White Mosaics*, 93–6, fig. 65. It paves room B on Becatti's plan, *Mosaici*, 110, fig. 44.

FIGURE 3.4 A mosaic paving a heated room in the Terme Marittime combined fantasy scenes of athletic cupids with indications of real contemporary public competitions. This excavation photograph shows the whole mosaic, of which only a fraction remains today. L: 7.9m. Severan.

surrounded by winged Cupids.[56] The main body of the floor was occupied by athletic scenes. At the bottom is the only section which survives today, showing two stocky athletes standing either side of a table which holds boxing gloves, a jug, and a palm. The figure to the left holds a long palm and raises his hand to a crown decorated with protrusions on his head. Above these figures the centre of the floor is occupied by the figure of a trumpeter, dressed in a cloak and holding a large tuba in front of him. On either side are pairs of athletic Cupids standing next to tables topped by large vessels, the prizes for success.

Above the trumpeter hangs a large circular object, decorated with circular protrusions. It was identified by Becatti and the original excavators as a lamp. However, it seems more likely to me that this object is intended to represent a victory crown, a more schematized version of which appears on the athlete's head at the bottom of the scene. The protrusions are flowers, similar to those which

[56] Becatti, *Mosaici*, III, no. 210, only mentions one figure, but the remains of a second are clearly visible in the photograph.

appear in a mosaic showing girls weaving crowns at Piazza Armerina, while the objects dangling from the back of the crown are ribbons.[57] As we know, prizes for the sacred games in Greece usually consisted of a crown, of olive at Olympia and of laurel at Delphi. Here too we have a crown made of flowers, possibly the prize for a set of games which was celebrated in Rome or Ostia.[58] The inclusion of this individualized crown helps to evoke the world of public competition. The mosaic thus merges reality and fantasy, equating the human delight in athletics with the amusements of the divine realm.[59]

NAMED ATHLETES ON MOSAICS

All the mosaics discussed above show narrative images of athletic activity. They often allude to the exercise which took place within the baths they decorate, while some show scenes of victory and competition which may also have evoked either simple contests held in the baths or more public athletic festivals held either in Ostia itself or in nearby Rome. In some mosaics, however, a more specific reference to historical victories in actual athletic festivals is suggested by the inclusion of individually named athletes. The clearest example is a mosaic which comes not from a bath suite, but from an inn, the eponymous Inn of Alexander Helix in Ostia (Fig. 3.5). In addition to the figures of Venus admiring herself in a mirror and two grotesquely phallic fighting dwarves, this shows two athletes named above as Alexander and Helix.[60] They both hold their fists clenched and are engaged in the pancration contest, a combination of boxing and wrestling. Between them stands a short palm and to the side is an over-lifesized representation of a metal bowl or cup, the prize for victory.

Christopher Jones has identified the figures shown here as the athletes Aurelius Alexander and Aurelius Helix, both attested in the epigraphic record as being prominent at Rome in the early third century. Alexander was high priest of the athletic synod and Helix a victor in the Capitoline games of AD 218.[61] The presence of such an image in an inn seems less to suggest a parallel between the viewers and the athletes, as the mosaics in the baths do, and can rather be compared with images on

---

[57] See Carandini, Ricci, and de Vos, *Filosofiana*, 284–91, room 45a and b. Similar crowns are shown in the mosaic of female athletes, room 34a, pl. 17. On crowns of flowers as victory prizes see Rumscheid, *Kranz und Krone*, 62–75, who also identifies this as a crown of flowers (p. 65).

[58] See Rumscheid, *Kranz und Krone*, 62–78, on floral crowns.

[59] Mythological athletic contests are also popular elsewhere, e.g. a scene of Pan and Cupid wrestling in the House of Bacchus and Ariadne; Becatti, *Mosaici*, 155–8, no. 293, pl. 80.

[60] Becatti, *Mosaici*, 205–7, no. 391.

[61] C. P. Jones, 'The Pancratiasts Helix and Alexander on an Ostian Mosaic', *JRA* 11 (1998), 293–8.

FIGURE 3.5 Part of the mosaic decorating an inn at Ostia shows two pancratiasts labelled as Alexander and Helix. They can be identified with two highly successful Greek athletes of the early third century, showing the popularity of Greek athletic spectacles at Ostia. W: 6m. Severan.

mosaics or graffiti celebrating individual charioteers or gladiators.[62] It is a sign of the fame of certain prominent athletes, and the fan-clubs they could attract. The concentration here appears to be on athletics as a spectacle, like gladiatorial shows or chariot races, rather than as an activity the viewers themselves engage in. Like images of the arena or circus, it shows the popularity of athletic contests as one in a whole range of public spectacles. In the fourth-century mosaics from the villa at Piazza Armerina in Sicily, athletic contests also appear among other representations of public shows. These mosaics show scenes of chariot races, musical performances, and mythologized contests featuring Erotes as well as scenes of female athletes (the so-called 'bikini girls') and a fragmentary scene of a torch race.[63] By

[62] For a selection of such imagery, see K.-W. Weeber, *Panem et Circenses: Massenunterhaltung als Politik im antiken Rom*, 2nd edn. (Mainz, 1994), *passim*, and D. Mancioli, *Giochi e spettacoli* (Rome, 1987). See also the mosaic paving the entrance to a guild building at Ostia, the Caseggiato del Lottatore, which shows two athletes named as Artemi and Sacal, probably shortened versions of their full names: Pavolini, *Vita Quotidiana*, 243, fig. 104. For further discussion see Newby, 'Greek Athletics', 193–4, fig. 7.

[63] The 'bikini girls' are now recognized to be athletes rather than aquatic performers, possibly associated with the Capitoline games, which included contests between female athletes. See H. M. Lee, 'Athletics and the Bikini Girls from Piazza Armerina', *Stadion* 10 (1984), 45–76; Rumscheid, *Kranz und Krone*, 64.

including scenes of athletic competition among other public spectacles they suggest that by the early fourth century athletics had come to hold a secure place among the public spectacles of ancient Rome.[64]

Elsewhere, however, named athletes also appear on mosaics in bathing suites. A couple of fragmentary examples come from Rome itself. A small bathing room excavated along the Via Nomentana in Rome probably formed part of an elite suburban villa.[65] It was paved with a black and white mosaic which showed a life-size figure of an athlete with his right hand to his head, perhaps in the act of crowning himself, and holding a palm branch in his left hand. To the right of the figure was written 'Eutyches qui et Nynnys', 'Eutyches who is also known as Ninnus'. Thus it seems to celebrate a famous athlete who was given the nickname Ninnus.[66] This may be the same athlete as the P. Pompeius Eutyches, also known as Ninnaros, who is attested as twice circuit-victor (*periodonikēs*) on an inscription from Philadelphia in Asia.[67] While the name differs slightly, it seems quite possible that this mosaic is referring to this very Olympic victor, whose victories are dated by Moretti to the first century AD.

Another mosaic from a bath complex on the Caelian hill in Rome is described by Visconti.[68] It showed four life-sized figures: a trainer, two athletes, and another figure wearing a short mantle. One of the athletes is seen from the back with his hands raised to his head and with 'A LAPONI VICTUS ES', 'Ah La(m)ponius you are conquered' written above his head. He is clearly the defeated partner. Another inscription close to a draped figure reads 'A MEL ATTICU' which has been translated either as 'Ah, Attic honey', as a reference to the origin of the victorious athlete, or instead as his name, Amelius Atticus.[69] Whichever we choose, it clearly refers to the victorious athlete, to whom the trainer is offering the palm of victory.

Another labelled athlete appears on a mosaic from a Hadrianic bath building on the Via Portuense at Rome.[70] The mosaic is now fragmentary. The left half shows a pair of wrestlers competing in front of an umpire and part of another figure.

---

[64] See Carandini, Ricci, and de Vos, *Filosofiana*, 45–82, on the representation of games in the villa, many of which may be shows put on in Rome.

[65] G. Gatti, 'Scoperte di antichità in Roma e nel suburbio', *NSc* (1888), 434–59, at 459; id., 'Scoperte recentissime', *BullCom* (1888), 327–34, at 333; Blake, 'Roman Mosaics', 166.

[66] The practice of giving nicknames to famous athletes seems to have been common, see e.g. *BM Papyri* iii. 1178 (E. M. Smallwood, *Documents Illustrating the Principates of Gaius, Claudius and Nero* (Cambridge, 1967), no. 374) for Herminus of Hermopolis, also known as Morus, or *IG* xiv. 916, which mentions M. Aurelius Demetrius, also known as Harpocration.

[67] Moretti, *Olympionikai*, 157, nos. 785, 757.

[68] C. L. Visconti, 'Trovamenti di oggetti d'arte e di antichità figurata', *BullCom* (1886), 49–53, at 49–51. He says that it was taken to the Capitoline stores, but I have not been able to track it down or find an illustration.

[69] See Visconti, 'Trovamenti', 50, and Blake, 'Roman Mosaics', 166, for the interpretations.

[70] F. Fornari, 'Roma: Scoperte di antichità nel suburbio', *NSc* (1916), 311–20, at 311–18; Blake, 'Roman Mosaics', 163.

FIGURE 3.6 This fragment of a mosaic from a bath building outside Rome shows an athlete, probably crowning himself, in front of a trumpeter. He is labelled as [D]OMESTICUS and can be identified with the pancratiast M. Ulpius Domesticus of Ephesus. His appearance here attests to the fame gained by Greek athletes in second-century Rome.

Another fragment from the right end of the mosaic shows a trumpeter and the naked legs of a frontal figure, probably shown crowning himself, and labelled [D]OMESTICUS (Fig. 3.6).[71] He is probably to be identified with the famous Ephesian pancratiast M. Ulpius Domesticus who later secured the right for the Guild of Athletes to build a headquarters in Rome. As a renowned athlete and Olympic victor it is quite likely that Domesticus had appeared in public competitions in Rome too, perhaps at the *Capitolia*.[72]

These and similar mosaics show narrative scenes of athletes being crowned, competing, or standing around after the contest has finished.[73] Apart from the fact that they add inscriptions to identify some of the individuals, their iconography is

[71] Floriani Squarciapino, 'Altro Mosaico Ostiense', 175, fig. 6.

[72] See above, p. 35, and, for more details, Newby, 'Greek Athletics', 196–8. Another mosaic with the labelled figures of boxers and a flute-player was also found here and probably relates to other public spectacles.

[73] Other examples: Santa Severa: O. Benndorf, *Bullettino dell'Istituto di corrispondenza archeologica* (1866), 231 n. 1, with the inscription Neilodorus; Reggio di Calabria: N. Putortì, 'Reggio di Calabria: Nuove scoperte in città', *NSc* (1924), 89–103, at 91–2; Blake, 'Roman Mosaics', 165, with remains of Greek inscriptions.

no different to the mosaics decorating the baths at Ostia and there seems little desire to differentiate the athletes with portrait features.[74] Rather, a general image of athletic competition is made more specific by the addition of a name label. This may refer to a particular famous competition in which an athlete had competed, or to an imagined contest between two famous victors, yet the more general associations of the image would also have remained present. Through these inscriptions the mosaics show the popularity and fame of Greek athletic spectacles, recording the names of famous athletes in the same way another mosaic might evoke famous charioteers or gladiators. Yet their iconography, especially when they decorate bathing rooms, also serves to link this idealization of particular famous athletes with the athletic activity that took place in these very baths. Through these particularized images, then, bathers were encouraged to see their own activities as parallel to those of their more famous role models. Among the bathers there would have been a variety of different nationalities represented. Examination of the epigraphical evidence from both Ostia and Rome reveals a multicultural society, including a growing number of figures from the Greek world, particularly Asia Minor and Syria.[75] Their presence may well have helped to encourage an interest in Greek athletic culture. Yet this interest was by no means limited to the Greek-speaking populations of Ostia and Rome. Along with the literary evidence discussed in the last chapter, the athletic mosaics which decorated the elite villas and baths of Rome, as well as buildings at Ostia, paint a clear picture of a widespread interest in Greek athletics in Italy throughout all levels of Roman society.

The mosaics discussed above all show narrative images of athletic activity, although some are also linked to particular individual athletes through the provision of inscriptions. In later mosaics, however, there seems to have been a change in taste towards polychrome portrait-like images of individual athletes, divided from one another by frames. Such images can be seen in mosaics from the Baths of Caracalla at Rome, a set of baths along the Via Severiana at Ostia, and a large bath complex at Aquileia.[76] The dating of all is controversial. While some scholars see the mosaics from the Baths of Caracalla as contemporary with the initial opening

---

[74] In contrast, a mosaic showing the athlete Nicostratus of Aegeae from Seleucia near Antioch in Syria does seem to show portrait features: D. Levi, *Antioch Mosaic Pavements* (Princeton, 1947), 115–16; J. Balty, 'La mosaïque antique au Proche-Orient I. Des origines à la Tétrarchie', *ANRW* II.12.2 (1981), 347–429, at 376, dates it to the Severan period.

[75] See esp. L. Morreti, 'I Greci a Roma', *Opuscula Instituti Romani Finlandiae* 4 (1989), 6–16; M. L. Lazzarini, 'I Greci di Ostia', *Scienze dell' Antichità: Storia, Archeologia, Antropologia* 6–7 (1992–3), 137–41. For differences between Ostia and Rome see O. Salomies, 'People in Ostia: Some Onomastic Observations and Comparisons with Rome', in Bruun and Gallina Zevi, *Ostia e Portus*, 135–59.

[76] Baths of Caracalla: B. Nogara, *I mosaici antichi conservati nei palazzi pontifici del Vaticano e del Laterano* (Milan, 1910); DeLaine, *Baths*; H. Werner, *Die Sammlung antiker Mosaiker in den Vatikanischen Museen* (Vatican, 1998), 217–51. Via Severiana: M. Floriani Squarciapino, 'Nuovi Mosaici Ostiensi', *AttiPontAccRomRend* 58 (1985–6), 87–144; Aquileia: G. Brusin, 'Aquileia: Scavi in un grande edificio pubblico', *NSc* (1923), 224–31; P. Lopreato, 'Le grandi terme di Aquileia: i mosaici del frigidarium', in J.-P. Darmon and A. Rebourg, eds., *La Mosaïque Gréco-Romaine IV* (Paris, 1994), 87–99.

of the Baths, others suggest a date in the fourth century on stylistic grounds.[77] Since the dating of the other mosaics hinges on that suggested for the Caracalla ones, their datings too range from early third to mid-fourth century.[78]

In my opinion, there are no concrete arguments against dating all these mosaics in the third century, which would also agree with an apparent interest in athletic festivals and training under the Severan dynasty. This can be seen in a coin issue of Septimius Severus showing athletic contests in the stadium (Fig. 2.2) and in the fact that new athletic festivals were introduced to Rome by the emperors Alexander Severus and Elagabalus, as well as later by Gordian III and Aurelian.[79] The Severans also seem to have taken care to ensure that Rome was well provided with bathing and exercise facilities. Caracalla funded an impressive new set of baths in the city and Alexander Severus completed these as well as undertaking the restoration of the Baths of Nero and Domitian's stadium.[80] According to his biographer he was also a keen athlete.[81] The first half of the third century AD seems to have been a popular time for Greek-style festivals in Rome, and it is likely that these athletic mosaics reflect that popularity.

The mosaics from the Baths of Caracalla show a combination of full-length figures and busts of athletes.[82] The others, however, concentrate on busts of athletes alone. In the baths along the Via Severiana at Ostia the mosaic decorated a small apsidal room next to the caldarium.[83] It shows five square panels, divided by a guilloche border and surrounded by small panels decorated with athletic objects. The panel in the apse depicts the bust of an elderly draped man, probably the gymnasiarch, who is labelled 'MUSICIOLUS'. The other four panels show the busts of athletes, again accompanied by inscriptions (Fig. 3.7). Two beardless athletes, one wearing the cirrus, are labelled as 'FAUSTUS' and 'URSUS', while the others, a youthful boy and an older bearded man, are labelled 'LUXSURIUS' and 'PASCENTIUS'. The names appear to be nicknames, perhaps those given to real historical athletes, 'Lucky' and 'Bear', just as we hear of the athlete known as Morus ('fool') from Hermopolis.[84] Yet they may also reveal the common qualities

[77] Severan: A. Insalaco, 'I mosaici degli atleti dalle terme di Caracalla', *Archeologia Classica* 41 (1989), 293–327; DeLaine, *Baths*, 239; K. M. D. Dunbabin, *The Mosaics of the Greek and Roman World* (Cambridge, 1999), 68. Fourth century: Darmon, in Darmon and Rebourg, *Mosaïque Gréco-Romaine IV*, 99; Floriani Squarciapino, 'Nuovi Mosaici Ostiensi', 113.

[78] Though note Lopreato, 'Grandi terme', 98, says that a coin of Constantine II was found beneath the Aquileia mosaic, suggesting a fourth-century date for at least part of it.

[79] See B. L. Damsky, 'The stadium aureus of Septimius Severus', *American Journal of Numismatics* 2 (1990), 77–105. On the festivals see Caldelli, *Agon*, 45–52, and discussion above, pp. 36–7.

[80] *Scriptores Historiae Augustae*, *Severus Alexander* 35.4.

[81] *Scriptores Historiae Augustae*, *Severus Alexander* 27.   [82] Discussed below, pp. 67–70.

[83] See Floriani Squarciapino, 'Nuovi Mosaici Ostiensi'. It was unfortunately stolen shortly after its discovery.

[84] *BM Papyri*, iii. 1178 (Smallwood, *Documents*, no. 374). On these, which were added to the name with 'qui/quae' see S. Hornblower and A. Spawforth, eds., *Oxford Classical Dictionary*, 3rd edn. (Oxford, 1996), 1025 (names, personal, Roman, 10).

FIGURE 3.7 On this polychrome mosaic from a bath complex at Ostia the figures of athletes are clearly individual-ized and labelled with nicknames, possibly those of popular contemporary athletes. From the Baths on the Via Severiana, Ostia. W: 1.9m. Probably Severan. Location unknown (stolen).

associated with athletes. While these two athletes are renowned for their luck and brute strength, the gymnasiarch is called 'Musiciolus', presumably referring to his grace and sense of rhythm. The young boy is depicted in a haughty, sensuous manner, fully agreeing with his nickname as luxurious. Indeed, he reminds us of the luxurious associations physical beauty is often given in philosophical texts, and the reputation of some athletes as decadent and sensuous.[85] The meaning of Pascentius is less clear but the pairing of this adult bearded male with the boyish Luxsurius may allude to the erotic attractions of the gymnasium and the baths. The status of the athletes is unclear. Their names could be those of Roman slaves, yet they could also be the nicknames of free-born Greek athletes, a suggestion which their pairing with the draped gymnasiarch seems to make most likely.

Here the mosaics decorated a small bath establishment. In the baths at Aquileia and Rome, however, they are found in large public *thermae*. At Aquileia they form part of a large mosaic pavement, centred around the depiction of Neptune in his

[85] See Floriani Squarciapino, 'Nuovi Mosaici Ostiensi', 101 n. 10, and Dio Chrysostom, *Oration* 28.6, 29.17.

FIGURE 3.8
This detail of the polychrome mosaic from the Great Baths at Aquileia shows an athlete wearing the cirrus in his hair, comparable to the portraits of athletes that appear in Baths at Ostia and Rome. Third or fourth century AD.

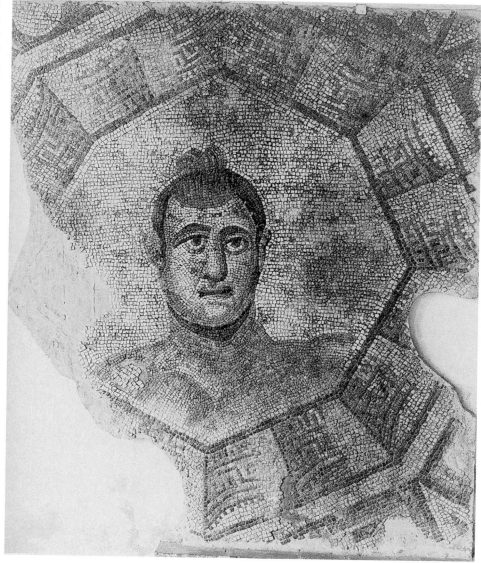

chariot.[86] Smaller panels around this central scene show a mix of marine and athletic scenes. Thus we find images of Thetis and Clymene along with those of a boy trumpeter, an athlete throwing a javelin, and another holding a palm. Geometric borders towards the edges of the room enclosed circular and octagonal panels depicting the busts of athletes. These are all depicted with portrait-like features. One is a youthful athlete, clean-shaven and wearing the cirrus on the top of his head (Fig. 3.8). Another is also youthful, but shown with close-cropped hair and a short

[86] See P. Lopreato, 'L'edificio romana della "Braida Murada": Nuove scoperte', *Aquileia Chiama* 29 (1992), 2–4; ead., 'Grandi terme'; L. Bertacchi, *Basilica, Museo e Scavi—Aquileia* (Rome, 1994), 52–3. The earlier excavations are recorded by Brusin, 'Aquileia'.

FIGURE 3.9
Another detail of
the mosaic from
the Great Baths at
Aquileia shows an
athletic official
wearing a crown
with three busts.
This identifies him
as an imperial priest
and president of
the local Olympeia
festival, which is
named elsewhere in
the mosaic. Third or
fourth century AD.

dark beard. Another two represent older figures. One is shown as naked with a beard and grey hair, worn in an unusual bun on the top of his head. Another is a gymnasiarch (Fig. 3.9). He wears a tunic and cloak and has a crown on his head decorated with three busts. This seems similar to the crowns worn by imperial priests, and also to that described by Suetonius as worn by Domitian when he presided over the Capitoline games. Alföldi-Rosenbaum suggests that it depicts the figure as a flamen Augustalis acting as agonothete of a public festival.[87] A particular festival is also alluded to by the presence in another part of the mosaic of a crown inscribed in Greek ΟΛΥΜΠΕΙΑ (Olympeia), probably an allusion to a local festival given isolympic status. The athletes may then depict particular victors in the games,

[87] Suetonius, *Domitian* 4; E. Alföldi-Rosenbaum, 'A *Flamen Augustalis* on a Mosaic Pavement in the "Grandi Terme" of Aquileia', in J.-P. Darmon and A. Rebourg, eds., *La Mosaïque Gréco-Romaine IV* (Paris, 1994), 101–5.

although their specific identities would probably have been forgotten over time. The mosaic as a whole thus integrates the public world of athletic competition into the area of the baths. While the marine scenes celebrate the aquatic nature of the baths and evoke mythological figures, the bather is also surrounded by images of athletic activity and individual athletic victors. Taken as a whole, the imagery evokes a sense of beauty and celebration, while also alluding to the success of a particular local festival.

CELEBRATING ATHLETICS IN THE BATHS OF CARACALLA

Let us turn, now, to Rome and the decoration of the Baths of Caracalla. Most of the construction of the baths took place between AD 212 and 216, though some of the surrounding precinct and decoration was completed under Elagabalus and Alexander Severus.[88] The baths lie in a tradition of vast imperial *thermae*, incorporating not only bathing suites, palaestrae, and a swimming pool, but also libraries, parkland, and a stadium.[89] The whole complex was lavishly decorated with marble revetment, mosaic floors, and plentiful statuary.[90] A number of rooms were decorated with polychrome geometric mosaics, while the balconies above the palaestrae had mosaics with black and white marine scenes. The palaestrae themselves, however, areas 12E and 12W on DeLaine's map (Fig. 3.10), were decorated with athletic scenes. Two large polychrome mosaics were found in the exedrae that led from the palaestrae into the frigidarium (13E and 13W on Fig. 3.10). After their discovery in 1824 they were removed to the Lateran. They have since suffered from extensive restoration and rearrangement, though their initial composition can be seen in two watercolours made at the time of their discovery (Fig. 3.11).[91]

The mosaics are divided into a series of panels with full-length figures interspersed with busts of athletes (Pls. 1a, 1b). Amongst the full-length figures there are a number of gymnasiarchs or trainers, marked out by their dress, whereas the athletes are all naked. While a couple of figures are named, the majority are not and they are shown in a variety of poses.[92] Many carry palms and crowns as a sign of victory, whilst others are shown standing ready for the contest, often with boxing gloves. Some also wear the cirrus in their hair. Both beardless and bearded athletes appear.

The variety with which the figures are depicted suggests the desire to show a plethora of individual athletes rather than the idealized figures that we find in

---

[88] DeLaine, *Baths*, 15–16.   [89] See Nielsen, *Thermae et Balnea*, 53–5, C8.

[90] See DeLaine, *Baths*, 68–84.

[91] See Werner, *Antiker Mosaiker*, 217–51, on their restoration. The watercolours seem to be reasonably accurate, though they add loincloths to the figures for modesty!

[92] Werner, *Antiker Mosaiker*, 227, suggests that there were originally other inscriptions lost during the restoration of the mosaics.

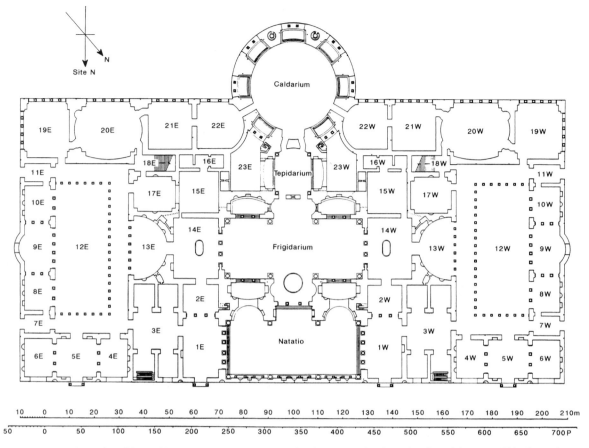

FIGURE 3.10 The Baths of Caracalla at Rome were a vast complex, incorporating into the plan of the central block two large palaestrae for exercise (12E and 12W) as well as the traditional rooms for bathing.

classicizing athletic statuary. Indeed, the faces of these athletes are given individual traits, many of them appearing rather brutal or ugly. While viewers would not necessarily have been able to identify particular individuals among the images, their treatment presents the illusion of a series of real individual athletes. There may also be an allusion to a particular athletic festival. A number of the athletes hold or carry metal crowns with protrusions. Although the manner in which these are depicted and the extensive restorations makes it hard to identify them, many seem to show the heads of flowers. Elsewhere a crown with three busts is shown at the side of the mosaic, suggesting that worn by the presiding priest of an athletic festival, possibly the Capitoline games (Pl. 1b).[93] As we have seen elsewhere, the mosaics evoke contemporary stars of the festival circuit.

[93] Rumscheid, *Kranz und Krone*, 63–4, 165–6, cats. 108a–h, identifies all those on the Baths of Caracalla mosaics as crowns of flowers, though this one does seem instead to show three busts, see Alföldi-Rosenbaum, *'Flamen Augustalis'*, 104–5, and discussion above, pp. 57–8 and 66.

FIGURE 3.11
A pair of water-
colours shows
the arrangement
of the mosaics
decorating the
palaestrae of the
Baths of Caracalla
at the time of their
excavation.

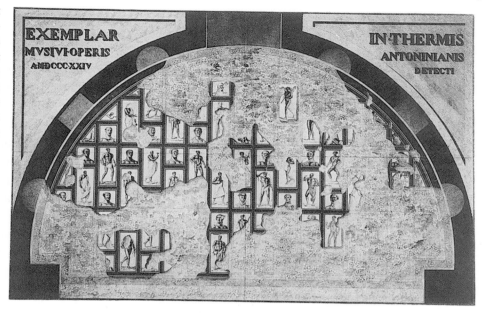

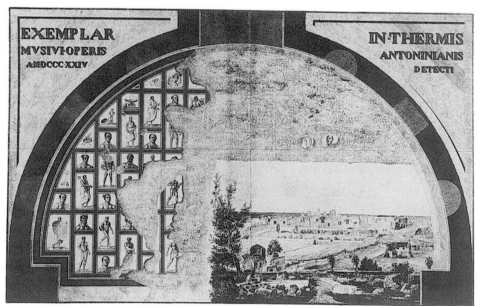

Yet they are also placed in the space between the open area of the palaestrae, where athletic activities could take place, and the frigidarium. They thus set up a connection with the bathers who viewed them, implicitly comparing these to the victorious athletes the mosaics display. The bathers may have rated themselves as good athletes, a reputation the emperor Alexander Severus is said to have enjoyed, and we have seen that mosaics elsewhere, like that of Alexander and Helix at Ostia, show an interest in contemporary athletic heroes.[94] *Aficionados* of athletic games may well have enjoyed the illusion these mosaics presented of sharing a space with their sporting heroes.

While these images evoke the world of public athletic competition, comparing those in the baths to the professional athletes shown here, they gain an extra set of associations when seen in the context of the visual display of the baths as a whole. Thus as well as these polychrome mosaics, the baths were decorated with a vast array of idealizing statuary.[95] According to Marvin, the range of sculpture displayed here was fairly traditional. Asclepius and Hygeia are present as the gods of health along with images of idealized youths suggesting beauty and exercise. Heracles is also present as the god of gymnasia and hot springs, and as a particular favourite of Caracalla. She suggests that innovation lies instead in the Baroque subjects, for example the group of Dirce and the bull.[96] The sculpture thus acts to define the space as one for beauty and bathing, and to elevate it by its decoration with *opera nobilia* and over-lifesize theatrical works. Yet if we look specifically at the athletic imagery in the baths, the mosaics and sculpture also seem to work together.

A number of athletic works are attested from the baths. A few come from the external precinct. A statue of Polycleitus' Doryphoros derives from the north-west exedra, and herms of two divinities associated with games, Apollo and Hermes, were found in the perimeter area between the library and stadium structures.[97] However, most of the athletic images were centred within the baths themselves. Within the central frigidarium there seems to have been both a copy of Myron's Discobolus and another representation of the Doryphorus.[98] There was also a representation of a naked prepubescent ephebe, which survives only in its hips and thighs.[99] Another naked male statue is indicated by the find of a male pelvis.[100] A torso of the Andros-Hermes type was found in one of the niches of the natatio and could represent the god, a hero, or an idealized portrait statue.[101] A figure of the

[94] Scriptores Historiae Augustae, *Severus Alexander* 27; see F. Castagnoli, 'Il capitello della Pigna Vaticana', *BullCom* 71 (1943–5), 1–30, at 14.

[95] See Manderscheid, *Skulpturenausstattung*, 73–6; M. Marvin, 'Freestanding Sculpture from the Baths of Caracalla', *AJA* 87 (1983), 347–83; C. Gasparri, 'Sculture provenienti dalle Terme di Caracalla e di Diocleziano', *Rivista dell' Istituto Nazionale di Archeologia e Storia dell' Arte* III.6–7 (1983–4), 133–50; DeLaine, *Baths*, 265–7.

[96] Marvin, 'Freestanding Sculpture', 378–9.

[97] All are in the Museo Nazionale Romano. The Doryphoros was probably fixed to the wall as traces of a dowel hole between the shoulders suggests.

[98] The Discobolus is attested through a thigh in the Museo Nazionale Romano and a hand with the discus in the Museo Baracco: DeLaine, *Baths*, 266, no. 8. Doryphorus: DeLaine, *Baths*, 266, no. 9.

[99] Museo Nazionale Romano 56745. Gasparri, 'Sculture', 140, fig. 9.

[100] Museo Nazionale Romano 56743. Manderscheid, *Skulpturenausstattung*, 87, no. 68; Marvin, 'Freestanding Sculpture', 365.

[101] In Museo Nazionale Romano. See DeLaine, *Baths*, 266 n. 8, on its discovery.

so-called Polycleitan Heracles type was also present, probably in the frigidarium (Fig. 3.12).[102]

A number of other images of Heracles were present. A colossal head of Heracles crowned with ivy was found in excavations in 1871–2, probably in the frigidarium, and part of an arm is recorded as coming from the south central bay of the frigidarium in 1873. DeLaine suggests that both of these may have belonged to the 'torso of Hercules with the lion's skin, it has neither head nor arms' recorded by Aldrovandi, though they are all now lost.[103] Also from this area, standing between the columns which divided the frigidarium from room 14E on DeLaine's map, come the two colossal statues of Heracles holding the Apples of the Hesperides — the Latin Hercules in Caserta and the Hercules Farnese in Naples (Fig. 3.13).[104] These images were themselves mirrored in the architectural decoration, since a number of figured capitals from the columns of the plunge pools in the frigidarium show miniature images of the larger-scale sculpture, one showing a miniature version of the Hercules Farnese type.[105]

Thus as well as figures of gods, satyrs, and portrait statues, many of which themselves showed beautifully exercised physiques, the frigidarium in particular contained a wealth of athletic male bodies. These ranged from the youthful and prepubescent to the bearded and the burly, but mostly consisted of mature adult male bodies. The male bather would see himself surrounded by images with which he could identify. As he proceeded from the palaestra into the frigidarium in the course of his bathing routine, he could imaginatively take on a series of different identities.

In the palaestra he would be, like the mosaic images beneath him, naked or at most scantily clad, and had just indulged in some sort of physical exercise.[106] He was also on the way to cleansing himself of whatever sweat he had worked up, in the same way that most of the athletes have finished their exercise and are either resting at ease or holding the marks of their triumph. The bather thus takes on these attributes of victory and contest completed as he walks over them into the frigidarium, the room towards which they point. Once within this central area, at least if approaching from the east palaestra, the bather was confronted by another burly and muscular figure, this time in marble.[107]

---

[102] On the type, see M. Marvin, 'Roman Sculptural Reproductions or Polykleitos: The Sequel', in A. Hughes and E. Ranfft, eds., *Sculpture and its Reproductions* (London, 1997), 7–28 at 17–18, who is sceptical about the identification.

[103] DeLaine, *Baths*, 267, nos. 27, 28.

[104] Their find-spots were recorded in a drawing by Antonio di Sangallo.

[105] DeLaine, *Baths*, 81. On the prominence of Heracles here and some possible interpretations, see M. Beard, 'Le mythe (grec) à Rome: Hercule aux bains', in S. Georgoudi and J.-P. Vernant, eds., *Mythes grecs au figuré* (Paris, 1996), 81–104.

[106] On nakedness in the baths, see Nielsen, *Thermae et Balnea*, 140–2, and Fagan, *Bathing in Public*, 24–9.

[107] The reference to another colossal statue of Heracles with a lionskin, DeLaine, *Baths*, 267, no. 28, may suggest that two other images of the hero at the west end balanced those to the east.

FIGURE 3.12 This idealizing statue of the Polycleitan Heracles type was found in the frigidarium of the Baths of Caracalla. Its athletic perfection draws the viewer back from the contemporary images in the palaestra to the idealized athletic forms of the fifth century BC. H: 1.24m. Second century AD.

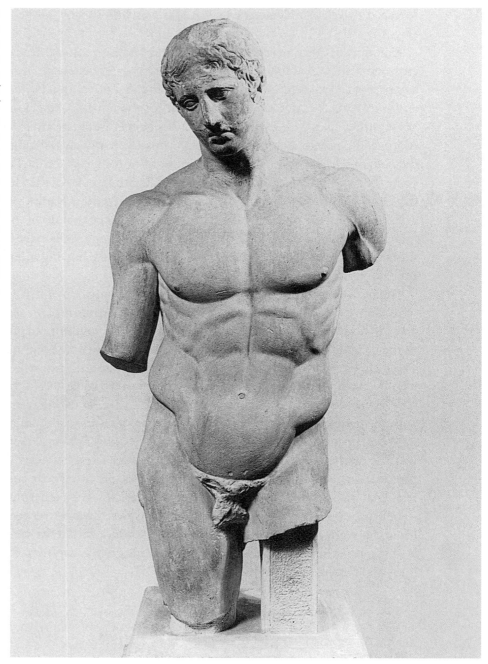

This was the image of the resting Heracles, weary after his final labour and in need of a good bath (Fig. 3.13). Along with its twin in Caserta this statue evokes a mythological world, also suggested by the Farnese Bull in the east palaestra and in the figures of Amazons and Maenads. As copies of a famous work by Lysippus the two statues are *opera nobilia*, elevating the baths by their display of artistic taste. Yet

FIGURE 3.13 The Farnese Heracles statue was found at the entrance to the frigidarium of the Baths of Caracalla at Rome, placed on the route which a bather would take from the palaestra to the frigidarium. The burly physique likens it to the mosaic images in the palaestra, forging a link between contemporary athletes and their patron deity. H: 3.17m. Severan copy of an original attributed to Lysippus.

as scholars have noted, these Severan works also stress the muscular physique of the hero. The mosaic athletes of the palaestra show a similar concentration on muscular, burly bodies. The descriptions of boxers and wrestlers which appear on inscriptions and in the epigrams of the *Greek Anthology* often stress their powerful physique, likening them to bulls and lions or the mythological super-heroes Atlas and Heracles.[108] Here Heracles' muscular body sets up a visual connection to the burly athletes on the floor of the palaestra, and indeed Heracles is the athlete *par excellence*, god of the gymnasium and a role model for wrestlers and pancratiasts. Yet the placement of the statues between the columns of the room, rather than in wall-niches, also sets up a connection between Heracles and the bathers, placing the hero firmly within the human space of the baths. Like his viewers, Heracles also rests after his exertion. While the mosaics in the palaestra suggest that bathers could see themselves in these figures of athletic prowess, Heracles too acts as an athletic role model, the brawniest and burliest of them all.

Other, classical, athletes surrounded the bather as he walked through the frigidarium, as well as images of other naked male physiques, possibly portraits set onto idealized bodies. The bather is thus led from the world of contemporary athletics, performed in the palaestra mosaics, to the muscular body of Heracles and the manly perfection of the Discobolus and the Doryphorus. We can see a link between the contemporary athletics of the palaestra and that of the classical and mythological past, with the mosaic athletes of the palaestra being the modern-day 'successors of Heracles'.[109]

The decoration of the baths suggests a keen interest in contemporary athletic spectacle and the desire of bathers to see their own activities as a reflection of those of the stars of the sporting world. The idealized statues of the frigidarium also helped to locate contemporary athletics within the Greek cultural heritage and its values. As noted above, Severan Rome seems to have witnessed an intensification of interest in Greek athletics. Septimius Severus chose to advertise one set of games on his civic coinage (Fig. 2.2), while new festivals were introduced by Elagabalus and Alexander Severus. Much of this was probably due to the interests and origins of the imperial family. While Septimius Severus himself derived from the North African city of Lepcis Magna, he had married Julia Domna from the Hellenized city of Emesa in Syria and was succeeded first by his son, Caracalla, and then by two figures from among his wife's relations, Elagabalus and Alexander Severus.[110] The dynasty thus had its roots in a Hellenized Eastern culture, helping to explain its promotion of athletic culture at Rome.

Alexander Severus appears to have played a particularly significant role. According to his biographer he was himself a keen athlete and instituted the *Agon*

---

[108] e.g. *Greek Anthology* 6.256. See L. Robert, 'Les épigrammes satiriques de Lucilius sur les athlètes: Parodie et réalités', in *L'épigramme grecque*, Entretiens sur l'Antiquité Classique 14 (1968), 181–295 at 259–73.

[109] Those who were victorious in both wrestling and the pancration at Olympia were called 'successors of Heracles' (*hoi aph Herakleous*) since Heracles himself was the first to achieve this in the Olympic games which he himself instituted. See C. A. Forbes, 'ΟΙ ΑΦ ΗΡΑΚΛΕΟΥΣ in Epictetus and Lucian', *American Journal of Philology* 60 (1939), 473–4.

[110] On the city see F. Millar, *The Roman Near East* (Cambridge, Mass., and London, 1993), 300–9.

Herculeus in Rome.[111] He is known to have restored the Baths of Nero on the Campus Martius, possibly decorating them with athletic scenes, such as the image of a victorious athlete which appears on a figured capital in the Vatican.[112] He also 'completed and decorated' the Baths of Caracalla.[113] It seems likely that at least some of the mosaic and sculptural decoration of these baths should be attributed to Alexander himself.[114] The burly figures of Heracles and the mosaic portraits of athletes, in particular, accord closely with his own interest in athletics and the institution of a festival named after Heracles at Rome. Further evidence of Alexander's interest in athletics might also be suggested by Philostratus' athletic treatise, the *Gymnasticus*.[115] Philostratus himself was closely associated with the Severan imperial family, known to have been part of the intellectual circle around Julia Domna, whom he mentions in the *Life of Apollonius of Tyana*.[116] Billault has suggested that the *Gymnasticus* was probably written in Rome between 215 and 225, when the athlete Helix (whom Philostratus mentions) was at the height of his career, though a date after Helix's victory in the Capitoline games in AD 218 might be most likely.[117] Elsewhere, Billault also suggests that Philostratus' criticism of Caracalla in *Epistle* 72 may be an implicit compliment to Alexander Severus.[118] Although Alexander himself is not mentioned in the *Gymnasticus*, Philostratus' decision to write such a work in the 220s may well have been influenced in part by a desire to compliment an emperor known for his interest in athletic pursuits.

One of Philostratus' concerns in the *Gymnasticus* is to defend the contemporary practice of athletics, and particularly the profession of athletic trainers, probably against the sorts of attacks which were made by figures like the physician Galen.[119] While doing this Philostratus also underlines its ancient Greek origins. The first part of the work concentrates on the history of athletics, arguing that ancient athletics helped to produce men like Milo, Polydamas, and Promachus, all famous athletic victors of the past, as well as heroes such as Theseus and Heracles, and

---

[111] Scriptores Historiae Augustae, *Severus Alexander* 27, 35.4.

[112] Castagnoli, 'Capitello', argues that this comes from Alexander's reconstruction of Nero's baths.

[113] Scriptores Historiae Augustae, *Severus Alexander* 25.

[114] Castagnoli, 'Capitello', 16; Insalaco, 'Mosaici', 318.

[115] I take this to be by the same author as the *Lives of the Sophists* and the *Life of Apollonius of Tyana*. On the problems of identifying the different Philostrati and their works see Anderson, *Philostratus*, 291–6; J. J. Flintermann, *Power, Paideia and Pythagoreanism* (Amsterdam, 1995), 5–14; and A. Billault, *L'Univers de Philostrate* (Brussels, 2000), 5–7.

[116] Philostratus, *Life of Apollonius of Tyana* 1.3. On Julia Domna's circle, see Bowersock, *Greek Sophists*, 101–9.

[117] Billault, *Univers*, 29. Philostratus mentions Helix at *Gymnasticus* 29.　　[118] Billault, *Univers*, 27.

[119] For a discussion setting the work in its historical context see König, *Athletics and Literature*, ch. 7, arguing that the work has a serious intent, contra the view of Anderson, *Philostratus*, 268–72, of it as a sophistic display piece. For commentaries see J. Jüthner, ed., *Philostratos über Gymnastik* (Leipzig, 1909) and A. Caretta, *Filostrato di Lemno: Il manuale dell'allenatore* (Novara, 1995).

tracing its links with military and Panhellenic activities.[120] Heracles reappears later too as embodying the ideal physique for a wrestler, where his statues seem to act as models for later athletes to follow.[121] Yet the rest of the work is firmly concerned with the contemporary world, advising trainers how to select and treat their pupils and attacking current practices of which he disapproves. The past is used to give validity to the present, to set contemporary athletics into a history going back to the classical and mythological past, in much the same way that the decorative ensemble of the Baths of Caracalla links together the victors of the present day with their classical predecessors in the frigidarium.

GREEK ATHLETICS IN GAUL AND NORTH AFRICA

The images discussed above offer strong evidence for the interest taken in athletic pursuits and spectacles in Rome and Ostia. The mosaics of Ostia show that the enthusiasms which the literary sources lament in the city of Rome also spread to her surroundings, with the Ostian public delighting in the joys of exercise in the baths and athletic spectacles just as much as the populace of Rome. While the evidence from Rome is more scattered, stray finds of athletic mosaics from the bathing rooms of elite villas suggest that this was an enthusiasm which was shared by the upper classes too, despite the hostile remarks of some intellectuals. Indeed, when we turn to the idealizing statuary which decorated elite villas around Rome we will find a similar interest in athletic themes. Before that, however, I want to look briefly at the visual evidence for Greek-style athletics in two other areas of the western empire, southern Gaul and north Africa.

The mosaic from the Great Baths of Aquileia, mentioned above, shows that cities elsewhere in Italy were also proud to celebrate the Greek-style festivals held in their own territory. A variety of visual and epigraphic evidence suggests that a number of other western provinces came to adopt Greek athletics both as a form of physical exercise and in their public festivals. The spread of festivals, in particular, has been well studied by Maria Caldelli for the area of Gallia Narbonensis.[122] Inscriptions relating to the city of Nemausus (Nîmes) suggest the presence of an artistic, and possibly also an athletic, synod here, supported by Trajan and Plotina,[123] while an earlier inscription shows that Gaius Caesar had paid for the

---

[120] Philostratus, *Gymnasticus* 1, 11. On military links, see further below, Chs. 5 and 6.

[121] *Gymnasticus* 35.

[122] M. L. Caldelli, *Gli agoni alla greca nelle regioni occidentali dell'impero: La Gallia Narbonensis* (Rome, 1997).

[123] *IG* xiv. 2496; J. H. Oliver, 'The Empress Plotina and the Sacred Thymelic Synod', *Historia* 24 (1975), 125–8; H. Lavagne, 'Rome et les associations dionysiaques en Gaule (Vienne et Nîmes)', in *L'association dionysiaque dans les sociétés anciennes* (Rome, 1986), 129–48 at 135–43; Caldelli, *Agoni alla greca*, 431–3, N16; 439–43.

building of a race track in the city.[124] Another funerary inscription honours a man for acting as agonothete (umpire of the games) in the city.[125] Notably, many of the inscriptions are written in Greek even though other public inscriptions tend to be in Latin, stressing the Greek connotations of its agonistic life.[126]

We have already seen how Naples' agonistic life, and the Greek inscriptions which commemorated it, fitted into both the city's self-perception and Roman views of her as a Greek city. A similar pattern can also be perceived in Gaul, most notably in the city of Massilia (Marseilles), founded as a Greek colony in around 600 BC. The maintenance of Massilia's Greek heritage during the Republican period is shown by references to ephebic contests and the post of gymnasiarch in Greek inscriptions of the first century BC.[127] She also seems to have exerted a Hellenizing effect over the Gauls of the surrounding area. Indeed, Strabo tells us that she had so attracted the Gauls to Greek culture that they even began to write their contracts in Greek.[128]

Yet this centre of Greek culture also seems to have attracted Roman attention, especially from the time of Augustus. Strabo notes that in his day a number of elite Romans chose to undergo their education here, rather than in Athens, and the endurance of the city as a Greek educational centre can be seen in the fact that it was here that Tacitus' father-in-law Agricola was educated. Tacitus describes the city as combining 'Greek refinement with provincial simplicity'.[129] In the second century AD Marseilles also possessed a Greek-style festival which was able to attract performers from around the Mediterranean world.[130] As in Naples, the citizens' own aware-ness of their city's roots, and the desire to maintain some form of Greek identity, probably went hand-in-hand with a Roman willingness to nurture a centre of Greek culture in the midst of a western province.

It is often difficult to trace precisely the paths by which the cultural life of cities in Gaul developed, and influences from both Marseilles and Rome have been detected.[131] When considering the influence of Greek athletic culture, in particular, both sources may have been important. While the example of Marseilles and the long-standing contact with Greek culture in this area could exert one form of influence, the example of Rome and the encouragement of the imperial family pro-vided another motivating factor. Indeed, we do not even know whether Marseilles

---

[124] *CIL* xii. 3155; Caldelli, *Agoni alla greca*, 433–5, N17.   [125] Caldelli, *Agoni alla greca*, 420–3, N7.

[126] J. Kaimio, *The Romans and the Greek Language*, Commentationes Humanarum Litterarum 64 (Helsinki, 1979), 73; Caldelli, *Agoni alla greca*, 439.

[127] *IG* xiv. 2444, 2445; Caldelli, *Agoni alla greca*, 408.

[128] Strabo 4.1.5.   [129] Strabo 4.1.5; Tacitus, *Agricola* 4.2.

[130] It is mentioned on the victory inscription of a Milesian musician, Moretti, *IAG* 74. See Caldelli, *Agoni alla greca*, 395–410, for a discussion of the evidence; this inscription is her M3.

[131] P. Gros, 'Rome ou Marseilles? Le problème de l'hellénisation de la Gaule transalpine aux deux derniers siècles de la Republique', in M. Bats, ed., *Marseilles grecque et la Gaule* (Aix, 1992), 369–79; see also G. Woolf, *Becoming Roman: The Origins of Provincial Civilization in Gaul* (Cambridge, 1998), 97 n. 51.

herself possessed a Greek festival before the second century AD, since it only then appears in the inscriptional evidence, though ephebic contests certainly took place here earlier, in the Republican period. At Naples too, however, the festival culture which was such a strong signal of the city's Greek identity was expressly encouraged by the imperial family.[132] Imperial encouragement, and the example presented from the late first century AD onwards by the Capitoline games at Rome, probably acted together with a local desire to assert southern Gaul's traditional links with Greek culture in making athletic and festival culture an appropriate means of civic self-enhancement.

The role played by the Capitoline games in encouraging Greek festival culture in Gallia Narbonensis is suggested by one of the letters of the Younger Pliny. Here Pliny applauds the abolition of a 'gymnicus agon', an athletic contest, in the city of Vienna (modern Vienne) and wishes that the games at Rome could also be stopped.[133] Pliny's concluding words strongly suggest that he sees the Capitoline games as a model encouraging the institution of other athletic contests around the empire:

the vices of the Viennenses remain amongst themselves, but ours spread far and wide. Just as in a body, so too in an empire, the most serious sickness is that which spreads from the head.   (4.22.7)

The festival at Vienna had been instituted in a bequest of a will, as a form of benefaction to the city. DeLaine has recently argued that bequests of bath buildings in towns in Italy were probably influenced by imperial munificence in Rome, and it seems likely that a similar imitation of life at Rome could lie behind the institution of local musical and athletic festivals in the cities of the western provinces.[134] Vienna was certainly a thriving and sophisticated town in the Roman empire, described as a 'most elaborate and mighty colony' by the emperor Claudius and as an eager recipient of his works by the poet Martial.[135] In the mid-first century AD it also produced the first Roman consul from Gallia Narbonensis, the senator Valerius Asiaticus. This man was a wealthy and sophisticated figure, owning the gardens of Lucullus on the Pincian Hill at Rome and showing an interest in both athletic and musical activities.[136] He shows that provincial senators could be

---

[132] See pp. 31–2 above.   [133] Pliny, *Letters* 4.22. See also p. 40 above.

[134] DeLaine, 'Benefactions'.

[135] *CIL* xiii. 1668, col. ii, l. 9 (Smallwood, *Documents*, 369); Martial, *Epigrams* 7.99. See M. Le Glay, 'Vienne Antique', in H. Stern and M. Le Glay, eds., *La Mosaïque Gréco-Romaine II* (Paris, 1975), 125–34, and A. Pelletier, *Vienne antique de la conquête romaine aux invasions alamanniques IIe siècle avant–IIIe siècle après J.-C.* (Roanne, 1982) for accounts of the city.

[136] Claudius refers to him as a 'monstrous athlete' in *CIL* xiii. 1668, col. ii, l. 15 (Smallwood, *Documents*, 369), and a group of actors known as the 'scaenici Asiatici' were probably owned by him: *CIL* xii. 1929; see M. Le Glay, 'Hercule et la *Iuuentus* Viennoise: A propos de la mosaïque des athlètes vainqueurs', in *Mosaïque: Recueil d'hommages à Henri Stern* (Paris, 1983), 265–71 at 266–7, and Lavagne, 'Rome et les associations dionysiaques en Gaule', 130–2.

cosmopolitan figures, likely to put their experience of the amusements of Rome to good use in their interactions with their home cities by introducing metropolitan attractions to the provinces.

The enduring popularity of athletic contests in the ancient city of Vienna, despite the abolition of one particular festival, can be seen in two pieces of visual evidence from the early third century AD. One is a set of wall-paintings which decorated the public latrines attached to a set of baths in St-Romain-en-Gal, just across the river from the centre of Vienne.[137] They show a series of figures of athletes, placed beneath an arcade (Pl. 2a). The paintings are now fragmentary but certainly included scenes of contests in wrestling, boxing (Pl. 2b), and the pancratium, as well as athletes preparing to throw the discus and the figure of an umpire (Pl. 2c). Like the mosaics in Ostia, they suggest that those using the baths were interested in equating their own exercises in the baths with the contests of public athletic festivals, though it is unclear whether the paintings included references to specific prizes.[138] They suggest that the athletic culture which had gradually developed in the baths of Rome and Ostia from the late first century onwards could also be seen in Gaul, serving as an indication of the cultural credentials of the inhabitants of this sophisticated town.[139]

The second piece of athletic imagery from the city is a large and impressive mosaic that was found in the Place St-Pierre.[140] The building which it decorated was not fully excavated but seems to have comprised two main quarters containing a number of small rooms as well as a large reception room in its western sector. The mosaic decorated this room (Pl. 3).[141]

The mosaic consists of a circular geometric frame divided up into a number of panels. At the centre lies an octagonal panel with a representation of Heracles wrestling with the Nemean lion, orientated towards the back of the room.[142] A circle of eight more octagons of the same size surround this central panel, all facing

---

[137] O. LeBlanc, in C. Landes, *Le stade romain et ses spectacles* (Lattes, 1994) 306–7, cat. 109; O. LeBlanc, 'Le décor des latrines des "Thermes des Lutteurs" à Saint-Romain-en-Gal (Rhône)', in *Actes des séminaires de l'association française de peintures murales antiques 1990–1991–1993 (Aix-en-Provence, Narbonne et Chartres)*, special edition, *Revue Archéologique de Picardie* 10 (1995), 239–63.

[138] One figure holds a palm and another may carry a small bag, possibly suggesting monetary prizes.

[139] On the popularity of bathing in Gaul, see G. Woolf, 'The Roman Cultural Revolution in Gaul', in S. Keay and N. Terrenato, eds., *Italy and the West: Comparative Issues in Romanization* (Oxford, 2001), 173–86 at 180–1.

[140] The excavations have never been fully published, but see the accounts given by M. Le Glay, *Gallia* 26 (1968), 586; J. Lancha, *Recueil général des mosaïques de la Gaule*, iii: *Province de Narbonnaise*, ii: *Vienne* (Paris, 1981), 54–78 (esp. 54–6 and fig. 7 on the construction of the house), and Pelletier, *Vienne*, 177–8.

[141] Detailed descriptions are given by S. Tourrenc, 'La mosaïque des "athlètes vainqueurs"', in H. Stern and M. Le Glay, eds., *La Mosaïque Gréco-Romaine II* (Paris, 1975), 135–53; Lancha, *Mosaïques de la Gaule*, 58–70, cat. 264. It is dated by Lancha (p. 70) to the end of the second or start of the third century, on grounds of style and archaeological finds, and by Tourrenc (p. 141) to *c.* AD 220.

[142] Tourrenc, 'Mosaïque', 135, with pl. 49, a view of the mosaic *in situ*.

FIGURE 3.14 Detail of an athletic mosaic from ancient Vienna in Gaul (Pl. 2a). The athlete throwing the discus is shown in a pose reminiscent of that of Myron's Discobolus. Early third century AD.

towards the centre. Small panels with theatrical masks and heads of the god Oceanus are interspersed between the octagons, and busts of the four seasons fill the corners. The most dominant features of the mosaic, however, are the athletic figures filling the octagons around Heracles.

These figures represent a spectrum of athletic activities, including boxing, running, and throwing the discus. They hold palms of victory, or stand next to vases, suggesting the prizes awarded in the contests. In one panel a herm suggests that the scene is set in a gymnasium. In two pairs of octagons, set at opposite sides of the circle, the figures are shown as if competing across the guilloche border which divides them, probably in the contests of boxing and wrestling.[143] Of the other four figures one is almost entirely destroyed while another stands in a static pose carrying a palm. The other two are shown running and throwing the discus, the latter in a pose which is reminiscent of Myron's Discobolus (Fig. 3.14).[144] Taken as a whole the figures suggest the different contests which formed part of Greek athletic competitions, including running, throwing the discus, boxing, and wrestling. The

---

[143] Lancha, *Mosaïques de la Gaule*, 64, thinks that the pair above Heracles wear boxing gloves while those below look like wrestlers.

[144] It is not an exact replica since the right arm is bent, not straight, but the position of the legs, head, and left arm are clearly reminiscent.

FIGURE 3.15 Detail of an athletic mosaic from ancient Vienna in Gaul (Pl. 2a). Two wrestlers are shown as if in competition. The one to the left has African features, suggesting an allusion to athletes from across the Roman empire. Early third century AD.

athletes are also differentiated from one another by details of their hair and faces. So, while one of the wrestlers is shown wearing a beard, his opponent wears his hair in a ponytail or *cirrus* and has African features (Fig. 3.15).[145]

The size and complexity of this mosaic and the impressive size and marble wall decoration of the room in which it was found clearly indicate that this was the most important room in the complex.[146] However, its purpose has been debated. The orientation of the mosaic towards the back of the room, and the presence of a wide geometric border on one side, suggest that it was designed to be seen by those reclining on a couch looking out at the room and that the room probably served as a triclinium or reception room.[147] Yet the complex as a whole has been interpreted either as a private house or, on the grounds of this mosaic, as some sort of guild headquarters.[148] Interpretations of the mosaic itself have also varied, with some

[145] Tourrenc, 'Mosaïque', 137. His hair is depicted in alternate lines of brown and black tesserae and appears to be plaited, though Lancha, *Mosaïques de la Gaule*, 62, interprets it as a leather cap. See pl. 16a for a detail of the head.

[146] On the wall decoration, see Lancha, *Mosaïques de la Gaule*, 68.

[147] H. Stern in the discussion of Tourrenc, 'Mosaïque', 145.

[148] House: Tourrenc, 'Mosaïque', 135; Lancha, *Mosaïques de la Gaule*, 56; Guild headquarters: Becatti in discussion of Tourrenc, 'Mosaïque', 147, expanded by M. Le Glay, 'Hercule et la *Iuuentus* Viennoise'. For a balanced discussion of the different interpretations, see Caldelli, *Agoni alla greca*, 449–50.

thinking that it alludes to a particular athletic contest while Tourrenc sees it as presenting a symbolic message about the victory of virtue over evil.[149]

The mosaic itself suggests a delight in the various contests of Greek-style athletics, set into an agonistic context by the presence of generic victory prizes such as palms and vases. Yet no specific prize or crown is shown, making it unlikely that a reference to a particular set of games is intended. Le Glay's linkage of the mosaic with a local youth association is also undermined by the presence in the mosaic of older as well as younger athletes, and of figures from around the Roman world, such as the African athlete shown in the bottom panel (Fig. 3.15).[150] Instead, the inclusion of athletes of different ages and nationalities grouped around a figure of Heracles could be an indication that it celebrates a local branch of the athletic guild, who took Heracles as their patron god, although there is no epigraphic evidence attesting to the guild here.[151] Whether the mosaic decorated a private house or a guild headquarters, however, it is a strong sign of the popularity of Greek athletic contests in Vienna in the third century AD.

Although the mosaic is dominated by the athletic figures, its inclusion of theatrical masks in the square panels around the central figure of Heracles also refers to the musical contests which formed part of Greek-style festivals. Another mosaic found at Vienne also attests to an interest in theatrical performances. It is divided into a series of panels, all of which are filled with either tragic or comic theatrical masks.[152] Other mosaics show a more general liking for athletic themes on mosaics. One found in the area of the ancient circus of Vienne and dated to the second half of the second century AD shows a pair of boxers as well as wrestling cupids while others from St-Colombe, near Vienne, and Lyons, show scenes of a wrestling match between Eros and Pan.[153] When we consider these mosaics alongside the paintings from the baths at St-Romain-en-Gal, they suggest a growing interest in Greek athletics in Vienne and its environs through the course of the second and third centuries which could be manifested both through bodily training in the baths and through spectatorship of public Greek-style festivals.

The factors motivating the local elites of cities like Vienne to institute Greek festivals or to allude to Greek athletics in their houses or public benefactions were probably many and varied. It is striking that the epigraphic and visual evidence attesting to this interest is lacking in areas further north and instead seems to be confined to the area of Gallia Narbonesis. This is precisely the area which had long

---

[149] Tourrenc, 'Mosaïque', 141–5.   [150] Le Glay, 'Hercule et la *Iuuentus* Viennoise'.

[151] Lavagne, 'Rome et les associations dionysiaques en Gaule', 131–2, argues that the guilds of both actors and athletes were accommodated here.

[152] J. Lancha, *Les mosaïques de Vienne* (Lyons, 1990), 51–6, no. 23.

[153] Lancha, *Mosaïques de la Gaule*, 136–9, no. 318, pls. 58–60; 143–5, no. 323, pl. 64a; Lancha, *Mosaïques de Vienne*, 76–9, nos. 37, 39; 91–3, no. 45; H. Stern, *Recueil général des mosaïques de la Gaule*, ii: *Province de Lyonnaise*, i: *Lyon* (Paris, 1967), 107–10, no. 138, pl. 78.

been familiar with Greek culture through the presence of Greek colonies such as Marseilles. In the Imperial period Gallia Narbonensis also seems to have witnessed an intense interest in Greek culture and learning. It had an established place on the sophistic lecture circuit and even produced the sophist and philosopher Favorinus, who rose to great fame in Rome and the Greek world.[154] Inscriptional and literary evidence also suggests a growing Greek presence throughout the second and third centuries, made up of traders and Christians as well as sophists, many of them from Asia Minor or Syria.[155] As at Rome and Ostia, then, the spread of athletic festivals and training could have been encouraged and welcomed by the area's Greek-speaking population as well as its native inhabitants. It also allowed cities like Marseilles to reassert their traditional links to Greek culture, and other non-Greek cities like Vienne to jump on the cultural bandwagon by laying claim to the area's pre-Roman, Greek, culture.

In his *Corinthian Oration* the philosopher Favorinus famously lays claim to a Hellenic identity, arguing that he deserves recognition from the Corinthians because of his struggles to fully embrace Greek culture:[156]

If someone . . . has emulated not only the voice but also the mind-set, life-style and appearance of the Greeks. . . . so that one thing should happen to him above all else, to seem Greek and to be Greek, does he not deserve to have a statue among you? And indeed in every city! Among you because, like your city, though a Roman he became Greek; in Athens because he atticizes in his speech; in Sparta because he loves the gymnasium and among all because he practises philosophy and not only has he already roused many of the Greeks to philosophize along with him, but he has also attracted more than a few barbarians.   ((Dio Chrysostom), *Or.* 37.25–6)

Like Isocrates, Favorinus here asserts the idea that Greekness lies not in birth, but in education.[157] Yet he also stresses the importance of appearance in the process of becoming Greek. It is through his adoption of Greek pursuits that he hopes to appear Greek. As Tim Whitmarsh has pointed out, Favorinus asserts the role of performance and imitation in his creation of a Greek identity.[158] Indeed, while his athletic skills are here related specifically to Sparta, just as his command of

[154] Lucian also claims that he found particular success here: *Double Indictment* 27; *Apology* 15. On Favorinus' background see Gleason, *Making Men*, 3–5.

[155] C. P. Jones, 'A Syrian in Lyon', *AJP* 99 (1978), 336–52. The persecution of the Christians of Vienne and Lyons in AD 177 included amongst the martyrs an Attalus of Pergamum and a Phrygian called Alexander. See Eusebius, *Historia Ecclesiastica* 5.1.3–63, translated as J. Stevenson, ed., *A New Eusebius: Documents Illustrating the History of the Church*, ed. W. H. C. Frend (London, 1987), 34–44, no. 23. I am grateful to Simon Swain for pointing out these references.

[156] For accounts of this speech see A. Barigazzi, ed., *Favorino di Arelate: Opere* (Florence, 1966), 298–346; Gleason, *Making Men*, 3–20; Swain, *Hellenism and Empire*, 44–5.

[157] Isocrates, *Panegyric* 50.

[158] T. Whitmarsh, '"Greece is the world": Exile and Identity in the Second Sophistic', in Goldhill, *Being Greek*, 269–305, at 296.

Atticism links him to Athens, both are crucial ways in which he asserts his identity. Through walking, talking, and exercising like a Greek, Favorinus the Gaul hopes to become one.

Favorinus is clearly a special case, and his arguments are specially tailored to his Corinthian audience.[159] Yet for the inhabitants of his native land, too, athletics might have provided a way of asserting an adherence to Greek cultural values which was in tune with the popularity of Greek performance rhetoric in Gaul itself. Here, however, the audience for these performances of Greek culture was one's fellow citizens and the desired effect might have been not to appear to be Greek but, conversely, to appear Roman. Indeed, the men who instituted festivals and funded bathing complexes in the cities of Gaul were drawn from the local elite, a group which included a number of Roman senators, familiar with the amusements of Rome and keen to introduce some of this cosmopolitan allure into their home cities. The delight which all levels of Roman society took in athletic pursuits has been clearly shown by the images discussed earlier in this chapter. This fashion for exercise *à la Grecque*, which so concerned Roman moralists, is likely to have spread, as Pliny suggests, from the capital of the Empire to its neighbouring provinces.[160]

One more factor should also be taken into account. As we will see in Chapter 8, this was a time when elites around the Mediterranean were funding bath buildings or instituting festivals. In the cosmopolitan, much-travelled world of the Roman empire, competition with other members of the elite from across the empire could have played a significant role in the motivations of individual benefactors. While the meanings with which Greek athletics was invested varied from place to place, the example set by the Capitoline games at Rome, the thriving festival culture which came to span the whole Mediterranean, and the widespread contemporary interest in Greek culture among Greeks and Romans alike, would have all helped to influence the growth of Greek athletic festivals and training in Gaul.

A further example of the impact made by Greek athletic festivals in the western part of the Roman empire can be seen in North Africa. Here a magnificent mosaic was unearthed in the 1980s in Baten Zammour on the Tahl plain in Tunisia, near the ancient city of Capsa (Gafsa; Pl. 4a).[161] While a number of other scenes of athletic competition have been found on mosaics from Roman North Africa, this one is exceptional for its size and detail.[162] Divided into four registers it shows a series of

---

[159] J. König, 'Favorinus' *Corinthian Oration* in its Corinthian context', *PCPS* 47 (2001), 141–68.

[160] Pliny, *Letters* 4.22.7.

[161] M. Khanoussi, 'Spectaculum pugilum et gymnasium: Compte rendu d'un spectacle de jeux athlétiques et de pugilat, figuré sur une mosaïque de la région de Gafsa (Tunisie)', *CRAI* (1988), 543–61; id., 'Ein römisches Mosaik aus Tunisien mit ein Darstellung eines agonistischen Wettkampfes', *Antiken Welt* 22.3 (1991), 146–53 with colour plates; R.-D. Pausz and W. Reitinger, 'Das Mosaik der gymnischen Agone von Batten Zammour, Tunisien', *Nikephoros* 5 (1992), 119–23.

[162] See M. Khanoussi, 'Les spectacles de jeux athlétiques et de pugilat dans l'Afrique romaine', *RömMitt* 98 (1991), 315–22 at 317–19, for a list of these mosaics.

contests from a Greek-style athletic festival, as well as the prizes awarded to the victors. The contests include the pentathlon, shown by a scene of a footrace in the top register and the figures of a jumper and discus-thrower in the third register, as well as matches in boxing, the pancration, and wrestling, and a torch race while wearing armour (Pl. 4c). Among these scenes of competition we see a victorious athlete being proclaimed and crowned in the second register and another victor carrying off his prize on his arm in the lower left-hand corner (Pl. 4b). A stack of other similar prize crowns are visible in the centre of this lowest register beneath a table bearing palms and bags of prize money (Pl. 4a).[163] In addition to these large metal crowns, some figures such as the trumpeters, umpire, and an athletic victor also wear floral crowns upon their heads.[164]

The presence of the prize crowns and the contests of the pentathlon as well as boxing and wrestling suggest that the mosaic records the events of a full-scale Greek athletic festival. This should be separated from the occasional spectacles of boxing and gymnastics which we also hear about in the inscriptional record, often associated with the dedication of monuments showing loyalty to the imperial house, which probably drew on an existing traditional culture of boxing as a public spectacle.[165] The cities of North Africa hosted a number of full Greek festivals, of which the most famous and prestigious were set up by the gift of the emperors and awarded sacred status. Carthage hosted the *Pythia* and *Asclepieia* festivals (the latter recorded on a mosaic floor in a private house at Althiburus),[166] while Caesarea in Mauretania held the *Commodeia* and *Severeia* festivals in honour of members of the imperial family.[167] However, the inclusion of bags of prize money on the Gafsa mosaic shows that this festival belonged to the lower category of 'prize' games (at which victors could, however, be awarded crowns in addition to their prize money) rather than to the most prestigious group of sacred 'crown' games.[168]

---

[163] On these prize crowns see Rumscheid, *Kranz und Krone*, 79–82, who clearly identifies them as crowns. In contrast, E. Specht, 'Kranz, Krone oder Korb für den Sieger', in *Altmodische Archäologie: Festschrift für Friedrich Brein* (*Forum Archaeologiae: Zeitschrift für klassische Archäologie* (14 March 2000), available via http://farch.net) has suggested that they represent baskets, but some coins show them actually being worn on the head.

[164] The floral crowns are discussed by Rumscheid, *Kranz und Krone*, 62–6, 157–8, cat. 92.

[165] These spectacles are discussed by Khanoussi, 'Spectacles de jeux athlétiques'. The idea that Africa had a separate existing tradition of boxing is suggested by the fact that spectacles are often referred to as 'spectacles of boxing and gymnastics', with boxing sometimes appearing alone without other contests, and from a reference in Suetonius, *Gaius* 18.1, to the boxing matches between Campanian and African boxers which took place between gladiatorial games.

[166] M. Ennaïfer, *Le cité d'Althiburos et l'édifice des Asclepieia* (Tunis, 1976), 130–1, fig. 153a.

[167] They are mentioned on an inscription from Ostia, *CIL* xiv. 474; Dessau, 'Due iscrizioni ostiensi'. On the Pythian festival at Carthage see also L. Robert, 'Une vision de Perpétue martyre à Carthage en 203', *CRAI* (1982), 228–76, at 231–2.

[168] On the different type of festivals see H. W. Pleket, 'Games, Prizes, Athletes and Ideology: Some Aspects of the History of Sport in the Greco-Roman World', *Stadion* (=*Arena*) 1 (1975), 49–89, at 54–71; Robert, 'Discours d'ouverture'; Spawforth, 'Agonistic Festivals', and the discussion in Ch. 8 below, pp. 246–55.

The mosaic itself comes from a small bath complex, and the area in which it was found does not seem to have been a major settlement.[169] It may have formed part of the country villa of a local notable. If so, the mosaic probably records the generosity of this man to a local town in setting up a Greek-style festival. Katherine Dunbabin has suggested that North African mosaics were often used to record past acts of euergetism, the clearest example being the Magerius mosaic from Smirat, where the central inscription tells us that Magerius had generously paid for the wild beast contests represented around the edge of the mosaic.[170] Details of clothing and the value of the prizes on the Gafsa mosaic suggest that it probably belongs to the first decades of the fourth century AD.[171] By this time athletic festivals had become commonplace across the Mediterranean world from Gaul and Italy to Asia Minor and Syria, since there had been a massive explosion in the creation of new festivals during the second and third centuries AD.[172] While many athletes would only choose to name the prestigious crown games on their victory inscriptions, smaller contests could entice athletes from around the world by their provision of cash prizes.

While we cannot know who sponsored the festival shown on the Gafsa mosaic, or for what occasion, the mosaic testifies to the spread of Greek festival culture across the Mediterranean. Yet there may also be particular resonances in the commemoration of a Greek festival in North Africa. This was an area whose elite often boasted of their familiarity with both the Greek and Latin languages, as is shown by the appearance on inscriptions of the phrase 'utraque lingua eruditus', 'learned in both languages'.[173] We have already seen how the second-century orator and philosopher Apuleius flaunted his knowledge of Greek to his audience in North Africa, and the Christian writer Tertullian also seems to have been well-versed in Greek literature.[174] Knowledge of Greek seems to have been a hallmark of the North African elite, a means of self-promotion in the competition for prestige which could still carry weight in the early fourth century.[175]

---

[169] Khanoussi, 'Spectaculum pugilum et gymnasium', 545.

[170] K. M. D. Dunbabin, *The Mosaics of Roman North Africa* (Oxford, 1978), 65–87, 117, fig. 118; and ead., *Mosaics of the Greek and Roman World*, 116–17.

[171] Khanoussi, 'Spectaculum pugilum et gymnasium', 558–60.

[172] Robert, 'Discours d'ouverture'. S. Mitchell, 'Festivals, Games and Civic Life in Roman Asia Minor', *JRS* 80 (1990), 183–93, at 190–1 puts the peak in the Severan period.

[173] e.g. *ILAlg* i. 1363, 1364. See discussion by T. Kotula, 'Utraque lingua eruditi: Une page relative à l'histoire de l'éducation dans l'Afrique romaine', in J. Bibauw, ed., *Hommage à Marcel Renard*, ii (Brussels, 1968), 386–92, though this also stresses the limitations of this education.

[174] On Apuleius, see above, p. 5; Tertullian: T. D. Barnes, *Tertullian: A Historical and Literary Study* (Oxford, 1971), 196–206.

[175] The ideological value of a Greek education is likely to have remained important, even though some scholars suggest that the standard of this education was actually declining in reality. See R. M. Ogilvie, *The Library of Lactantius* (Oxford, 1978), 109–10.

In a recent study of the presence of the Muses and literary or intellectual themes on mosaics in Gaul, Africa, and other western provinces, Janine Lancha has suggested that such features can be seen as an index of acculturation, the spread of intellectual elite culture into the western part of the empire. For her, these mosaics serve as signs of romanization.[176] Yet Greek as well as Roman motives appear on the pavements, and many of them reveal bilingualism in their choice of both Greek and Latin inscriptions. Such pavements combine Greek and Roman cultural references as part of a complete package, a sign of the host's membership of the educated classes. The Gafsa mosaic complements the interest in Greek culture that we see in other areas of elite life in North Africa. It helped to present the owner of the house as a member of the educated, cosmopolitan elite. Yet by deciding to fund and record a Greek athletic festival, the patron of this mosaic was not only presenting himself to his peers in North Africa. Like mosaics with intellectual themes, this one also shows its patron to be imbued with values which were shared more widely by the Roman imperial elite, whether they originated in Italy, Gaul, Africa, or Asia.[177]

[176] J. Lancha, *Mosaïque de culture dans l'occident Romain (Ie–IVe s.)* (Rome, 1997), especially 9–12, 377–83, 393–402.

[177] On the importance of Greek culture and education as a means of binding together the elite see P. Brown, *Power and Persuasion in Late Antiquity: Towards a Christian Empire* (Madison, Wis., 1992), 35–70.

FOUR

Idealized Statues in Roman Villas

In the last two chapters I explored the literary and visual evidence that suggests that Greek athletic festivals and training became more and more popular at Rome, and elsewhere in the western provinces, throughout the course of the first three centuries AD. The mosaic imagery of the baths, in particular, suggests that Roman bathers were keen to associate their own physical exercises with the contests that took place in public spectacles and festivals. However, in my discussion of the Baths of Caracalla at Rome, I also suggested that the portrait-like images of contemporary athletes displayed on the palaestra mosaics would have gained extra resonances when seen alongside the display of idealizing athletic statuary in the frigidarium. While these statues evoked the classical Greek past, often embodied in replicas of artworks attributed to famous sculptors like Myron, Polycleitus, and Lysippus, the mosaics suggested the competitive festival culture which was thriving in the Roman empire. Those exercising in the baths could choose to see themselves both as the heirs of the classical victor statues and as the equals of the sporting heroes so popular in the contemporary world.

In this chapter I want to turn away from the contemporary resonances presented by the mosaics to look in more detail at the idealizing athletic statuary which was produced in such quantities in imperial Rome. The production and display of statues which either directly copied or were inspired by the earlier forms of Greek art is, of course, a phenomenon which goes back to the Republican period. It is a sign of the hold which Greek culture exerted over the Roman imagination, famously encapsulated in Horace's statement that 'Captive Greece ensnared her wild conqueror'.[1] Yet from the late first century AD, the choice of athletic subjects for display in baths and villas must also be seen in the light of the contemporary interest in Greek culture and the introduction of Greek festivals and body culture to Rome.

Before turning to two imperial examples of such sculpture collections, however, I want briefly to discuss the introduction of classicizing art to Rome in the Republican period and the range of associations it could evoke. Along with gods, heroes, and mythological figures, athletes provided a central theme for the idealized sculpture (often referred to by the German term *Idealplastik*) that thronged public and private spaces in and around Rome. Such statues could include ancient

---

[1] Horace, *Letters* 2.1.156.

masterpieces transported from Greece, as well as new creations copying or inspired by works of Greek art. While earlier scholarship primarily studied these statues with a view to how they could be used to recreate lost Greek originals, recent research has focused instead on the new roles they performed within their Roman contexts.[2] In the private world of elite villas, statues were often used to articulate the identity of a space, for example by placing herms in gymnasia and animals in gardens. They can also be seen as evidence of their patrons, schooled as they were in Greek culture and rhetoric, and having served in posts in the eastern Mediterranean, placing themselves in the tradition of the Hellenistic kings, under whom the first collections of artworks were formed.[3] Such artworks thus lost some of their original significances; moved, say, from a sanctuary to a garden they took on new meanings and associations.

The Greek art found in the city of Rome itself was different yet again. Much of this entered the city as war booty, plunder from the sanctuaries of captured eastern cities and thus a sign of the power of Rome the conqueror. Many such statues were themselves then dedicated in various Roman sanctuaries, or made available to the public as the decoration of theatres and baths. One prime example is the Apoxyomenus of Lysippus, set up in front of the Baths of Agrippa on the Campus Martius, until its removal by an enamoured Tiberius provoked a public outcry.[4] Such sculpture served as a wonder to decorate the city, an *ornamentum urbis*— deemed the symbolic property of the whole Roman people to such an extent that the removal of works into private collections could be seen as a shameful act.[5] This public exhibition of a wealth of statuary, both originals and copies, led in the Imperial period to a widespread use of similar sculptural ensembles in towns all over the empire.[6]

The public display of statues in baths in Rome has already been touched on, and will be discussed further in Chapter 8, in relation to the decoration of baths and gymnasia in the east of the empire. Here, however, I wish to concentrate on the use of idealizing sculpture in Roman villas and the atmosphere such works helped to create for the owner and his guests.[7] Since the Republican period, country villas

---

[2] See most recently the essays collected in E. K. Gazda, ed., *The Ancient Art of Emulation: Studies in Artistic Originality and Tradition from the Present to Classical Antiquity* (Ann Arbor, 2002).

[3] P. Zanker, 'Zur Funktion und Bedeutung griechischer Skulptur in der Römerzeit', in H. Flashar, ed., *Le Classicisme à Rome aux Iers siècles avant et après J.-C.*, Entretiens sur l'Antiquité Classique 25 (1979), 283–314; R. Neudecker, *Die Skulpturen-Ausstattung römischer Villen in Italien* (Mainz, 1988).

[4] Pliny, *Natural History* 34.62.

[5] Note the encouragement under Augustus to make Greek originals accessible to the public. Pliny, *Natural History* 35.26 (a speech by Agrippa). See J. J. Pollitt, 'The Impact of Greek Art on Rome', *Proceedings of the American Philological Association* 108 (1978), 155–74.

[6] Zanker, 'Funktion und Bedeutung', 293–9.

[7] See especially Neudecker, *Skulpturen-Ausstattung*, building on the picture sketched in Zanker, 'Funktion und Bedeutung'.

provided elite Romans with a place for relaxation and *otium*, a space in which to indulge in activities (such as literary composition or philosophical discussion) which were inappropriate in the public world of Rome but nevertheless crucial for one's self-presentation as a member of the cultured elite.[8] Architecture and sculptural display helped to create the right sort of atmosphere for these pursuits, and to indicate the cultural leanings of the villa's owner. While literary evidence suggests that sculptural ensembles of the second and first centuries BC often contained original Greek statues,[9] the establishment of Greece and Asia as provinces of the empire removed the opportunities for the seizure of original statues from all but a few, and villa owners increasingly turned to the copies and adaptations produced by classicizing workshops.[10]

The letters of Cicero to his friend Atticus in Greece provide a particularly good example of the ways in which statues could be used to create a particular effect in this period.[11] Written between 68 and 65 BC, a series of letters shows Cicero's requests for statues to decorate his villa in Tusculum. In particular, he asks Atticus to look out for 'decoration suitable for a gymnasium (*gymnasiōdē*)'.[12] While Cicero refers to structures such as a gymnasium and a running track (*xystus*),[13] the space he envisages has much more to do with intellectual pursuits than athletics. Called his 'Academy' after the gymnasium frequented by Plato in Athens, it contains a library and is dedicated to the goddess Minerva.[14] The statues chosen by Atticus include a series of herms with bronze heads, including representations of Heracles and Athena/Minerva and some 'Megarian statues' whose appearance is not described.[15] Their main function is to evoke the setting of a Greek gymnasium and, in particular, the intellectual pursuits associated with it.[16] In other contexts Cicero could be highly critical of the athletic side of the gymnasium, agreeing with Ennius that its nakedness helped to promote pederasty and immorality.[17] Yet in the private world

---

[8] On villa life see J. D'Arms, *Romans on the Bay of Naples* (Cambridge, Mass., 1970); A. Wallace-Hadrill, 'The Villa as Cultural Symbol', in A. Frazer, ed., *The Roman Villa: Villa Urbana* (Philadelphia, Pa., 1998), 43–53.

[9] Neudecker, *Skulpturen-Ausstattung*, 5–7.

[10] On copies and new creations inspired by classical forms see P. Zanker, *Klassizistische Statuen: Studien zur Veränderung des Kunstgeschmacks in der römischen Kaiserzeit* (Mainz, 1974), xv–xx. Evidence for the direct copying of statues is provided by the casts found at Baiae: C. Landwehr, *Die antiken Gipsabgüsse aus Baiae: griechische Bronzestatuen in Abgüssen römischer Zeit* (Berlin, 1985). See also the survey of the evidence by B. S. Ridgway, *Roman Copies of Greek Sculpture: The Problem of the Originals* (Ann Arbor, 1984). Emperors could still lay their hands on Greek originals, though this is often represented as the act of a 'bad' emperor. The political significance of such thefts is discussed by S. E. Alcock, *Graecia Capta: The Landscapes of Roman Greece* (Cambridge, 1993), 175–80.

[11] Neudecker, *Skulpturen-Ausstattung*, 8–30; M. Marvin, 'Copying in Roman Sculpture: The Replica Series', in E. D'Ambra, ed., *Roman Art in Context: An Anthology* (Englewood Cliffs, NJ, 1993), 161–88.

[12] Cicero, *Ad Atticum* 1.6.2.   [13] Ibid. 1.8.2.

[14] Ibid. 1.9.2; 1.7; 1.4.3.   [15] Ibid. 1.8.2; 1.9.2; 1.10.3; 1.4.3.

[16] Neudecker, *Skulpturen-Ausstattung*, 16–17; Marvin, 'Copying', 161–7.

[17] *Tusculan Disputations* 4.70; see above, p. 40.

of his villa he could afford to ignore this aspect of the gymnasium, using it instead as a stage for his intellectual ambitions, associating him with the intellectual and philosophical aura of classical Greece.[18]

For an archaeological comparison to Cicero's gymnasium, we can turn to the Villa of the Papyri at Herculaneum. This was filled with a range of statuary which has provoked a number of different interpretations from scholars. While some seek an Epicurean theme, in line with the supposed philosophical interests of the owner, others have shown that the sculptures could also have evoked a range of other associations.[19] In particular, a number of scholars have noted that the combination of architecture and sculptural display in the large peristyle is reminiscent of the Greek gymnasium.[20] Other elements worked in harmony with this to expand the range of associations. So, Neudecker argues that while herms of Hellenistic statesmen and the bronze athletes evoked the surroundings of a Greek gymnasium, other aspects of the decoration such as a sleeping satyr suggest a divine and mythological atmosphere. Altogether, aspects of a gymnasium, sanctuary, and park were combined to create a space imbued with the aura and prestige of Greek culture.[21] As with Cicero's gymnasium, however, this was not a direct representation of any Greek building or space, but a new creation: here, the Greek gymnasium as the embodiment of all Greek culture, as seen through and for Roman eyes. Many of these Republican recreations of the gymnasium seem to concentrate on its literary and philosophical associations rather than the physical activities that took place here. These wider cultural associations of the gymnasium are likely to have remained important in the Imperial period too. Yet I want also to explore the idea that the *athleticism* of such a space became more and more important as Greek athletics gradually came to be both practised and watched in Rome.

In order to define and articulate villa spaces, a range of statue types were used, chosen according to their theme. The associations aimed at might vary depending

[18] Marvin, 'Copying', 162–4.

[19] Epicurean: G. Sauron, 'Templa Serena. A propos de la Villa des Papyri d'Herculaneum: les Champes-Elysées épicuriens', *MEFRA* 92 (1980), 277–301, though note M. R. Wojcik, *La villa dei Papyri ad Ercolano* (Rome, 1986), 275, on the possibility that the Epicurean works found were only a small proportion of the literary collection as a whole. Other interpretations include D. Pandermalis, 'Zur Programm des Statuenausstattung in der Villa dei Papyri', *AthMitt* 86 (1971), 173–209; Neudecker, *Skulpturen-Ausstattung*, 105–14, 147–57; P. G. Warden and D. G. Romano, 'The Course of Glory: Greek Art in a Roman Context at the Villa of the Papyri at Herculaneum', *Art History* 17 (1994), 228–54; S. Dillon, 'Subject Selection and Viewer Reception of Greek Portraits from Herculaneum and Tivoli', *JRA* 13 (2000), 21–40. A review of Neudecker's book and the scholarship on the villa is given by P. G. Warden, 'The Sculptural Program of the Villa of the Papyri', *JRA* 4 (1991), 257–61.

[20] Sauron, 'Templa Serena', 285–90; Wojcik, *Villa dei Papyri*, 127; Neudecker, *Skulpturen-Ausstattung*, 114. Warden and Romano, 'Course of Glory', suggest that the allusion is to a stadium and see a didactic message in the display.

[21] Neudecker, *Skulpturen-Ausstattung*, 111–13. See also Zanker, 'Funktion und Bedeutung', 286, on the multiple associations evoked by the statuary display.

on where the statues were displayed. Thus figures of Venus and Asclepius in a bath complex evoked ideas of the health and beauty associated with bathing, whereas the same statues displayed in a shrine in a garden could suggest the sacred aura of a Greek sanctuary.[22] Statues of athletes can also be seen in a similar way. Displayed in a peristyle they evoked the world of the Greek gymnasium, along with all its cultural and intellectual associations. In a bath building, by contrast, they had a functional significance, suggesting the exercise which typically formed a prelude to bathing, and the athletic beauty associated with it.[23] On a more general level, a profusion of ideal statues could also enhance a villa by adding flamboyance and luxury. When viewed alongside the marble veneer, glittering mosaics, and reflective pools of the baths, for example, marble statuary helped to elevate the bathing experience to almost divine heights.[24]

While the stress on appropriateness, *decor*, in display might seem to suggest that subject was more important than style in the choice of statuary, the two often worked together. It is significant that among the works of art decorating Roman villas, a number replicate the forms of Greek statues of the fifth or fourth centuries BC. Thus we find copies and reworkings of Praxiteles' naked Aphrodite of Cnidus, as well as copies of Myron's Discobolus and Polycleitus' Doryphorus, all of them famed works in antiquity.[25] While the tendency to see all idealizing Roman sculpture as copies of particular famous Greek originals has been rightly criticized lately, some types clearly do replicate artworks produced in the classical past.[26] This use of a famous type is likely to have evoked a *frisson* of recognition from viewers, though the original context of the image as, for example, a statue commemorating a particular athletic victory, is often lost in favour of its more generic connotations as an emblem of Greek athletic culture and beauty. In many cases, however, much idealized sculpture was only loosely linked to past Greek statues, adapting a classical pose or hairstyle rather than aiming to replicate one particular original.[27]

The decision to use particular artistic forms drawn from the Greek past is itself significant. The whole repertoire of Greek sculptural styles from the Archaic to the Hellenistic period was at times recreated in works produced during the Roman

---

[22] Neudecker, *Skulpturen-Ausstattung*, 34–6.   [23] Ibid., 61.

[24] See R. Neudecker's review of Manderscheid, *Skulpturenaausstattung* in *Gnomon* 57 (1985), 171–8 at 173–5, and DeLaine, *Baths*, 69–84.

[25] See the sources collected by A. Stewart, *Greek Sculpture: An Exploration* (New Haven and London, 1990), 255–7, T43–5; 264–6, T62–71; 277–81, T93–106.

[26] Criticism: M. Marvin, 'Roman Sculptural Reproductions or Polykleitos: The Sequel', in A. Hughes and E. Ranfft, eds., *Sculpture and its Reproductions* (London, 1997), 7–28. Ridgway, *Roman Copies*, 37–43, suggests that many originals would not actually have been available for copying, though L. Touchette, 'The Mechanics of Roman Copy Production?' in G. R. Tsetskhladze, A. J. N. W. Prag, and A. M. Snodgrass, eds., *Periplous: Papers on Classical Art and Archaeology Presented to Sir John Boardman* (London, 2000), 344–52, suggests that mechanical copying was not the only method of replication in Antiquity.

[27] Marvin, 'Roman Sculptural Reproductions', 14–26.

period. Paul Zanker has suggested that different styles were popular at different periods, with the Augustan and Hadrianic periods showing a particular delight in Polycleitan forms, though his belief that the copies themselves can be stylistically dated has been challenged by some.[28] Hölscher, however, suggests that the choice of form—Classical, Hellenistic, or Archaic—was dictated by the content and subject matter of the piece. Thus, he argues, the vividness, movement, and pathos of Hellenistic art was deemed particularly appropriate for battle narratives, whereas the calmness and gravity associated with Polycleitus' Doryphorus made it an appropriate model for Augustus' own self-image in the Prima Porta statue.[29] Latin texts suggest that particular artists, most notably those of fifth- or fourth-century Greece, were often associated with particular concepts or values; Pheidias being associated with religious themes, beauty, and majesty, Polycleitus with decorum, and Callimachus with grace. The subject matter of the work thus itself determined the choice of a particular model most associated with that type of theme.[30]

When we look at the athletic images which survive in Roman ideal sculpture it is significant that nearly all draw on classical fifth- and fourth-century models, with the styles of the sculptors Myron, Polycleitus, Praxiteles, and Lysippus being particularly popular.[31] Clearly, there were many Hellenistic models which could also have been chosen: victor statues of athletes continued being produced throughout the Hellenistic period. Glimpses of this art can be seen in the famous bronze statue of a weary boxer now in the Museo Nazionale in Rome (Fig. 4.1). Here the concentration is on the violence of the combat—blood drips down the man's battered face and he wears fierce-looking gloves on his hands. Yet, in general, sculptors of the Roman period chose to ignore these statues and concentrate instead on models from the fifth and fourth centuries BC and particularly on images of youthful beardless athletes.

We might seek to explain this by looking at artistic preferences more generally, which often tended to sideline Hellenistic art, as shown by Pliny's cutting comment 'cessavit deinde ars', 'then art ceased', when reaching the third century BC.[32] Yet Hölscher's argument would suggest that the ideological associations of these particular models must have seemed appropriate for the representation of athletic subjects. The fact that models which are associated with modesty and virtue (Polycleitus) or truth and beauty (Lysippus) are taken, rather than those suggesting

[28] Zanker, *Klassizistische Statuen* with review comments of N. Hannestad in *JRS* 67 (1977), 121–2, and C. H. Hallett, 'Kopienkritik and the Works of Polykleitos', in W. Moon, ed., *Polykleitos, the Doryphoros and Tradition* (Madison, Wis., 1995), 121–60, at 125–8.

[29] T. Hölscher, *Römische Bildsprache als semantisches System* (Heidelberg, 1987), 15–19, 32, 34. Note, however, the scepticism expressed about the idea that the Doryphorus acted as a direct model for Augustus' self-image, in R. R. R. Smith, 'Typology and Diversity in the Portraits of Augustus', *JRA* 9 (1996), 31–47, at 41–6.

[30] Hölscher, *Römische Bildsprache*, 54–60.

[31] See Zanker, *Klassizistische Statuen* for creations inspired by Polycleitan forms.

[32] Pliny, *Natural History* 34.52. He claims that it revived in the mid-second century BC.

FIGURE 4.1 This Hellenistic statue of a boxer stresses the violence and exhaustion of boxing. In contrast, the statues chosen to decorate Roman elite villas usually depict idealized images of perfectly honed bodies. From Rome. H: 1.28m. Early first century BC, possibly after a third-century BC original.

power, brutality, and exhaustion (the Boxer), suggests that athletics was seen as being about more than simply the physical acts involved.[33] Instead it is made to bear the weight of a whole set of ideals—modesty, good birth, self-restraint, education, all-round excellence. Our evidence about athletics in the contemporary Roman world suggests that growing specialization was, in fact, the trend, carried out by athletes whose bodies were tailored to a particular contest.[34] Yet the athletic figures which decorate Roman villas are perfectly proportioned—they show the bodily form which for Aristotle was the best model for youth: that of the pentathlete.[35]

ATHLETIC STATUES IN THE IMPERIAL VILLAS OF DOMITIAN AND HADRIAN

When we look at the athletic statues that come from Roman villas they usually appear in one of two contexts, the baths or a peristyle. Like those decorating public baths in Ostia and Rome, athletic statues in the baths often have a functional parallel, suggesting the exercise associated with bathing. When displayed in a peristyle, however, their combination with an architectural setting evocative of the Greek gymnasium helps to add a more general atmosphere of Greek culture and education, as we have already seen in the discussion of Cicero's Academy.[36] In the rest of this chapter I will focus on the display of athletic themes in villas of the Imperial period, to see how the resonances of this imagery had developed from the time of Cicero and the ways statues could be put to particular uses depending on the interests of the villa owner.

The first general point to notice is that a large number of athletic statues appear in the sculptural decoration of Roman villas from the late first century onwards. Their popularity should be seen not only in terms of their traditional association with Greek culture but also in the light of the contemporary interest in Greek athletics shown by the mosaic imagery. While some of the roles played by these statues in the Republican period will have continued in the later period, their nuances would also have been altered by the widespread popularity of athletic spectacles and physical training in the world beyond the confines of the villa.

Here I will look at the display of athletic statues in two particular examples, the villas of the emperors Domitian and Hadrian. These examples give us the

---

[33] On the associations of particular sculptors, see Hölscher, *Römische Bildsprache*, 54–60. The idea that statues could embody ethical qualities is also discussed by D. T. Steiner, *Images in Mind: Statues in Archaic and Classical Greek Literature and Thought* (Princeton and Oxford, 2001), 32–44.

[34] See Philostratus, *Gymnasticus* 35–6; Tacitus, *Dialogus* 10.5; and Quintilian, *Institutiones Oratoriae* 2.8. On the moral associations of athletics see the discussion of Dio Chrysostom's orations on the athlete Melancomas in König, *Athletics and Literature*, ch. 3.

[35] Aristotle, *Rhetoric* 1361b.   [36] Neudecker, *Skulpturen-Ausstattung*, 60–4.

opportunity to recreate the original architecture and display in some detail, and to set it in the light of what we know about the owners' own interests. A comparison with other villas of the period suggests that imperial villas conformed to standard patterns of elite villa display, though individual patrons certainly made different choices from the many possibilities of villa display in order to create particular individual effects.[37] Both emperors are known for their interest in Greek culture. Domitian was responsible for introducing the Greek-style Capitoline festival to Rome and Hadrian is well-known for his promotion of Greek culture both at home and abroad, though he seems to have had less of an impact on the *athletic* culture of Rome than some other emperors did.[38] The philhellenic leanings of these two emperors, expressed in their public acts, were also manifest in the decoration of their country villas. While these show continuities with the traditions of villa display established in the Republican period, their decoration would also have had more immediate resonances for the eyes of contemporary society.[39]

DOMITIAN'S VILLA AT CASTEL GANDOLFO

In the grounds of the Pope's summer palace at Castel Gandolfo in the Alban Hills, a large villa site can be confidently identified with the villa of the emperor Domitian.[40] This is mentioned by a number of ancient sources as the site for meetings of the emperor's council and his celebration of a festival in honour of Minerva.[41] Over the centuries the site has undergone a number of changes, most notably during the building of the Villa Barberini in the seventeenth century and in the laying out of the papal gardens in the 1930s. However, the basic outline of the palace can still be determined from Lugli's account, which compared his own observations of the site in 1917 with the earlier plans drawn up by Canina and Rosa (Fig. 4.2).[42]

[37] For examples of this see the catalogue in Neudecker, *Skulpturen-Ausstattung*. Not all villa-owners chose to include athletic themes, though many did.

[38] See M. T. Boatwright, *Hadrian and the City of Rome* (Princeton, 1987), 203–12, on Hadrian's promotion of Greek culture at Rome, and ead., *Hadrian and the Cities of the Roman Empire* (Princeton, 2000), 144–62, on his benefactions to Athens and Smyrna. Note, however, that the athletic synod had to wait for Antoninus to turn into reality a promise initially made by Hadrian (above, p. 35).

[39] See Raeder, *Villa Hadriana*, 289, on the continuities between Hadrian's villa and those of the Republican period.

[40] The most complete account of the villa remains that of G. Lugli, published in four parts in *BullCom* 45–8 (1917–20), here referred to as Lugli I–IV. The sources relating to the villa are collected in Lugli I and an account of the central buildings is given in Lugli II. The sculptures from the villa are collected by Neudecker, *Skulpturen-Ausstattung*, 139–44, who also gives a full bibliography.

[41] Juvenal, *Satire* 4.60–154; Suetonius, *Domitian* 4; Statius, *Silvae* 5.2.168–70; Martial, *Epigrams* 5.1.1–2.

[42] See Lugli I, 37–8; Lugli II.

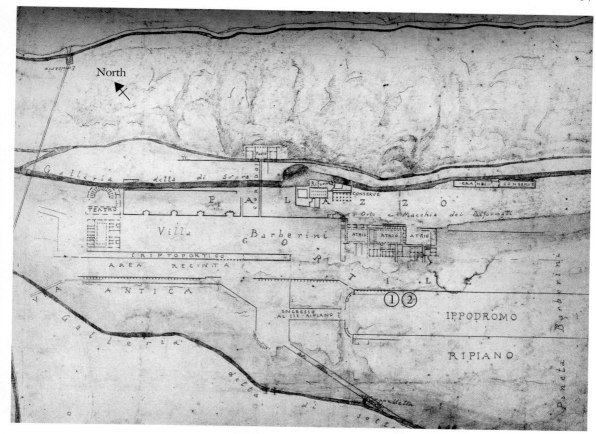

FIGURE 4.2 A map of Domitian's villa at Castel Gandolfo drawn by Rosa shows the three-court structure of the villa, with the Hippodrome lying below. The find-spots of two of the statues found in the 1930s are added showing that the athletic statues were found within the area of the Hippodrome. The basalt torso (Fig. 4.3) is marked by 1 and the Westmacott athlete type (Fig. 4.4) is marked by 2.

The central area was planned on a series of terraces with the bulk of the palace lying on the second terrace.[43] Access to the palace from the Via Appia was probably through the cryptoporticus which lies beneath this terrace and is linked to it by an internal staircase, though conclusive archaeological evidence is still lacking.[44] This central terrace supports a theatre at its north-west end, most likely the site for the events of the festival of Minerva, while the central part of the palace lay to the south-east. The rooms were arranged on a tripartite plan, consisting of a series of

[43] More recent excavations suggest that there may also have been a fourth terrace and that the villa's structures descended down to the Via Appia. See L. Crescenzi, 'La Villa di Domiziano a Castel Gandolfo', *Archeologia Laziale* 2 (1979), 99–106.

[44] Lugli II, 26. According to P. Liverani (personal communication), modern investigations have not revealed any significant remains at the top of the stairs which lead to the second terrace.

FIGURE 4.3
This basalt torso
is modelled on
the 'Ephesus
apoxyomenus' type,
showing an athlete
cleaning his strigil,
and probably
decorated the
hippodrome area of
Domitian's villa at
Castel Gandolfo.
H: 1.1m. As with
other classicizing
Roman works it is
difficult to date the
statue precisely, but
it may be Trajanic.

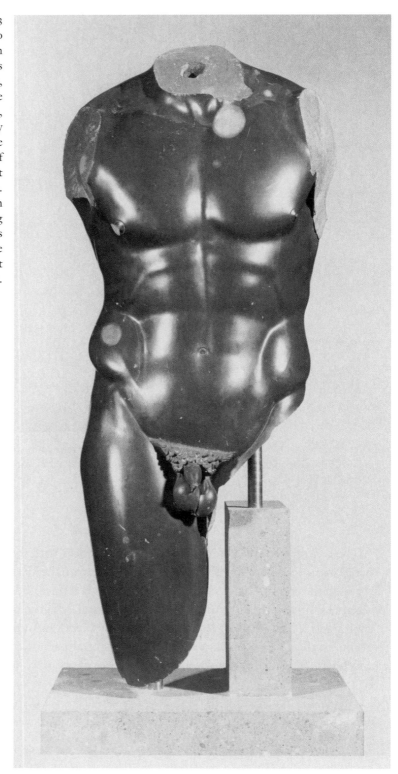

three open courtyards surrounded by reception and living rooms, in an arrangement similar to that of Domitian's palace on the Palatine.[45]

To the south-west, the villa looked out over a lower terrace which was probably occupied by parkland as well as a hippodrome. During landscaping work in the 1930s a series of athletic and other statues were found in this area, lying below the palace façade, apparently within the area of the hippodrome itself (the find-spots of two are marked on Fig. 4.2).[46] The initial report mentions a torso of Myron's Marsyas, a large female statue of a bacchante, a copy of the so-called Cyniscus of Polycleitus (also known as the Westmacott athlete type, 2 on Fig. 4.2), a basalt torso (1 on Fig. 4.2), an equestrian statue, and a mithraic monument.[47]

Other reports of the finds are provided by Nogara and Galli.[48] Nogara's report in fact refers to the discovery of eleven statues. In addition to the six mentioned above he includes three other athletic statues in addition to the Westmacott type, a torso of Eros, and a hermaphrodite Herm.[49] All the athletic statues, as well as the basalt torso, are said to have been found together in the direction of the cryptoporticus in front of the terrace supporting the palace. They were not found *in situ*, and Nogara suggests that their fragmentary state may be due to their having fallen from an initial display high up on the façade of the palace, though they might also have been abandoned here in the course of being removed by thieves or lime workers.[50]

The descriptions of these statues in the excavation reports allows them to be identified with those currently preserved in the Antiquarium of the villa.[51] In addition to the basalt torso, now recognized as a replica of the Ephesus apoxyomenus or scraper type (Fig. 4.3) and the Westmacott athlete type (Fig. 4.4), they include two replicas of the Dresden youth type (Figs 4.5, 4.6) and another statue (Fig. 4.7). This shows a male torso, leaning forwards with his arms slightly bent.[52] While no such statue is described in the excavation reports, Liverani suggests that it may be one of the four statues mentioned by Nogara in his 1933 report.[53] Another

---

[45] Lugli II, 19–22, 25, 35–6. He suggests that the architect Rabirius may have been responsible for both complexes.

[46] Lugli II, 62–8, describes the hippodrome as lying on the middle terrace. A comparison of his description with the map in L. Castelli, 'Trovamenti di antichità classica nella Villa Pontificia di Castelgandolfo', *Illustrazione Vaticana* 4 (1933), 578–80, suggests that the statues were found within this area. See also P. Liverani, *L'Antiquarium di Villa Barberini a Castel Gandolfo* (Vatican City, 1989), pl. 1.

[47] Castelli, 'Trovamenti'.

[48] B. Nogara, *AttiPontAccRomRend* 9 (1933), 70; G. Galli, 'Relazione', *AttiPontAccRomRend* 10 (1934), 68–89, at 81–7; B. Nogara, 'Recente scoperte di statuaria classica nel villa papale di Castel Gandolfo già Barberini', in C. Galassi Paluzzi, ed., *Atti del III Congresso Nazionale di Studi Romani*, i (1935), 31–88.

[49] B. Nogara, *AttiPontAccRomRend* 9 (1933), 70.   [50] Nogara, 'Recente scoperte', 34–8.

[51] See Liverani, *Antiquarium*, 55–64, nos. 21, 22, 24, 25.   [52] Liverani, *Antiquarium*, 65–6, no. 26.

[53] B. Nogara, *AttiPontAccRomRend* 9 (1933), 70, though it was not described in his 1935 article, 'Recente scoperte'.

FIGURE 4.4
This statue of the
'Westmacott athlete'
type shows an athlete
crowning himself
after victory. While it
probably copies a
classical statue set up
to commemorate
an athletic victory,
the Roman statue
stresses instead the
generic qualities of
the statue as an image
of youthful modesty
and athletic beauty.
From Domitian's
villa at Castel
Gandolfo. H: 1.62m.
Possibly Augustan.

head of an athlete conserved in the Antiquarium was found in a different area of the villa and therefore relates to a separate area of the villa's sculptural display.[54]

All five statues represent athletes. Recently scholars have expressed doubts over the identification of the Westmacott athlete type with Polycleitus' victory statue

[54] Liverani, *Antiquarium*, 62, no. 23. See also M. G. Picozzi, 'Una replica della testa dell' "Atleta Amelung" da Castel Gandolfo: Problemi ed Ipotesi', *AttiPontAccRomRend* 48 (1975–6), 95–125.

FIGURE 4.5 Two copies of the so-called 'Dresden youth' type were found at the villa, presenting images of youthful athletic beauty modelled on classical forms. This statue is treated in a slightly harder style, with the line of the rib-cage and groin clearly delineated. It is possible that the two statues were originally produced in separate periods but were united here as pendants. From Domitian's villa at Castel Gandolfo. H: 0.98m. First century AD.

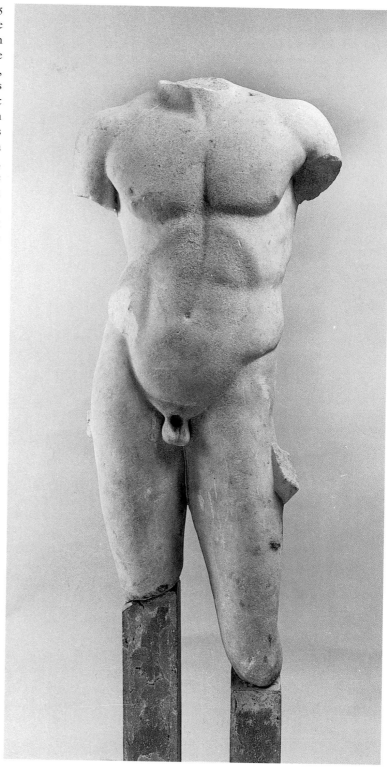

FIGURE 4.6 The second 'Dresden youth' statue shows a softer modelling of the body and a slightly more exaggerated tilt of the hips, accentuating the sensuousness of the image. From Domitian's villa at Castel Gandolfo. H: 0.98m. First century AD.

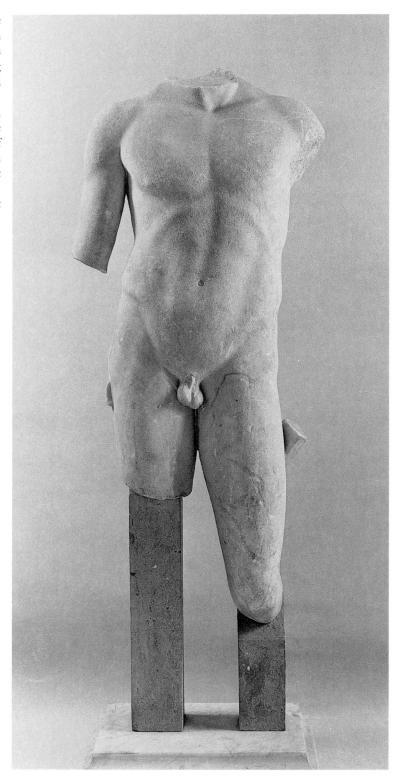

FIGURE 4.7
This statue differs from the last three in representing a mature adult athlete, shown landing after a jump. The collection of athletic statues found in Domitian's villa at Castel Gandolfo thus includes both mature images (see also Fig. 4.3) and statues of youthful prepubescent boys. They were probably displayed in the Hippodrome where they added a general classicizing aura to the space but could also remind viewers of the Greek Capitoline games set up by Domitian in Rome. H: 1.05m. First century AD?

of the boy boxer Cyniscus of Mantinea, arguing that the comparisons with the footprints on the base at Olympia are too loose to be convincing.[55] Similar doubts exist over the original model for the Ephesus apoxyomenus type, though it seems to draw on classical forms.[56] Yet both do represent athletes, the first a boy athlete placing a crown upon his head, and the second a more mature athlete cleaning his strigil after athletic activity.[57] Of the other statues, the one not mentioned in the excavation reports is interpreted by Liverani as an athlete landing after a jump.[58] The two remaining torsos are pendants, both versions of the so-called Dresden youth type, showing an athletic naked boy probably holding something in his hand. While none of the replicas preserve the hands of the youth or any attribute, one in Berlin has a depression on the nape of the neck which may have served to hold a crown.[59]

Some of the sculptures may have been produced earlier than the building of the villa and reused in its sculptural display, though it is difficult to give precise dates on purely stylistic grounds.[60] The two copies of the Dresden youth type, in particular, show notable differences in the modelling of the flesh and the exaggeration of the pose which may reflect production at two separate periods.[61] Neudecker argues that the display belongs to the post-Domitianic occupation of the villa, which is attested by the presence of some Hadrianic structures and by literary references to

[55] See D. Arnold, *Die Polykletnachfolge* (Berlin, 1969), 52–4; Zanker, *Klassizistische Statuen*, 19–21; B. S. Ridgway, 'Paene ad exemplum: Polykleitos' Other Works', in W. Moon, ed., *Polykleitos, the Doryphoros and Tradition* (Madison, Wis., 1995), 177–99, at 184. Pausanias mentions the statue in 6.4.11.

[56] See O. Benndorf, 'Erzstatuen eines griechischen Athleten', *Forschungen in Ephesos*, i (Vienna, 1906), 181–204; A. Stewart, 'Lysippan Studies 3. Not by Daedalos?', *AJA* 82 (1978), 473–82; Rausa, *Immagine*, 210–12, no. 23.

[57] The attribute which the Westmacott type held is not preserved in any copy, but the presence of a pun-tello on the head of the Castel Gandolfo statue, and of furrows at the nape of the neck in other replicas, strongly suggests that it was a crown. See Rausa, *Immagine*, 187–93, no. 8, though Ridgway, 'Paene ad exem-plum', 180, 184, is more sceptical. On the reconstruction of the Ephesus athlete as cleaning his strigil rather than using it, see F. Eichler, 'Die Bronzestatue aus Ephesos in verbesserte Wiederherstellung', *Jahrbuch der Kunsthistorischen Sammlung in Wien* 50 (1953), 15–22.

[58] P. Liverani, 'L'*Antiquarium* di Villa Barberini a Castel Gandolfo', *AttiPontAccRomRend* 61 (1988–9), 103–30 at 110–11; id., *Antiquarium*, 65–6, no. 26. See also Rausa, *Immagine*, 172–3, no. 2.

[59] Rausa, *Immagine*, 196, no. 9.14. See also Zanker, *Klassizistische Statuen*, 24–5. It has sometimes been associated with a group by Polycleitus of boys playing knucklebones: Pliny, *Natural History* 34.55–6. See A. Linfert, 'Aus Anlaß neuer Repliken des Westmacottschen Epheben und des Dresdner Knaben', in H. Beck and P. C. Bol, eds., *Polykletforschungen* (Berlin, 1993), 141–92.

[60] The Westmacott type has been dated to the second part of the first century BC: H. Lauter, *Zur Chronologie römischer Kopien nach Originalen des V. Jahrh.* (Bonn, 1966), 61–2; Zanker, *Klassizistische Statuen*, 17; while the scraper has been dated as either Flavian or Hadrianic: Rausa, *Immagine*, 210 (Flavian); G. Galli, *AttiPontAccRomRend* 10 (1934), 86 (Hadrianic—but primarily on grounds of its material which does, in fact, appear in Rome in earlier periods too).

[61] Compare the discussion of the statues found in a second-century house in Rome by E. Bartman, '*Décor et Duplicatio*: Pendants in Roman Sculptural Display', *AJA* 92 (1988), 211–25, and ead., 'Sculptural Collecting and Display in the Private Realm', in E. K. Gazda, ed., *Roman Art in the Private Sphere* (Ann Arbor, 1991), 71–88 at 81.

Marcus Aurelius' use of the villa.[62] However, it is also possible that the display was set up under Domitian himself, perhaps here using older statues while elsewhere, as in the lakeside dining grotto known as the Ninfeo Bergantino, sculptures were specially commissioned for the villa.[63]

While it is impossible to be certain precisely when the display was devised, there does seem to be a conscious programme here, perhaps originally supplemented by more statues, now lost. Nogara suggested that the fragmentary state of the statues could be due to their having fallen from a display high up on the villa façade.[64] Yet it is also possible that they decorated instead the so-called 'Hippodrome' area in which they seem to have been found. This area was bounded by two parallel walls, the upper one serving to support the terrace on which the main palace buildings were placed, while the north-western end is marked by two curved walls. Lugli notes that there do not appear to have been any steps or seats, as in a true hippodrome, and instead likens the structure to the hippodrome-shaped garden which Pliny the Younger describes in his Tuscan villa.[65] Domitian's palace on the Palatine included a similar area, surrounded by a two-storey portico and containing two fountains at either end.[66] All these gardens were probably, like that in Pliny's villa, planted with flowers and trees and used as areas for walking and talking.

We do not know the precise context in which the statues were displayed, though it is possible that they were set within a portico, similar to those which we see on some of the Campana reliefs (Fig. 4.8).[67] We could imagine a display centred around the basalt Apoxyomenus, marked out by the difference of material, and surrounded by the Dresden youths, as pendants, with perhaps the Westmacott type at one end and the jumper at the other end of the display. The presence of the athletes here, along with the general shape of the area, would perhaps suggest an allusion to a Greek stadium, rather than a hippodrome. Indeed, the Westmacott-type statue's gesture of self-crowning openly alludes to the world of Greek athletic festivals and the competitions which took place in the stadium. While this is framed within the classicizing forms of Greek sculpture, it could also remind the viewer of Domitian's own actions in introducing a musical and athletic festival to Rome and his building of Rome's first and only Greek stadium.[68] However, if the statues were displayed in a portico, the combination of statues and architecture might also have suggested a more general allusion to the Greek gymnasium in which athletic activity took

---

[62] Scriptores Historiae Augustae, *Avidius Cassius* 9.6–11; Neudecker, *Skulpturen-Ausstattung*, 143.

[63] Liverani, 'L'*Antiquarium*', 108, and id., 'Il Doriforo del Braccio Nuovo e l'Efebo tipo Westmacott di Castel Gandolfo: Nota sul restauro e sul contesto', in Beck and Bol, *Polykletforschungen*, 117–40, at 120–5, suggests that earlier statues could have been reused by Domitian.

[64] Nogara, 'Recente scoperte', 34.   [65] Pliny, *Letters* 5.6.32–40; Lugli II, 64–8.

[66] A. Claridge, *Rome: An Oxford Archaeological Guide* (Oxford, 1998), 140–1.

[67] See also Neudecker, *Skulpturen-Ausstattung*, pl. 15.4.

[68] P. Virgili, 'Le stade de Domitien', in C. Landes, ed., *Le stade romain et ses spectacles* (Lattes, 1994), 107–19.

FIGURE 4.8 This terracotta relief shows that statues of athletes were set up in porticoes along with other athletic symbols such as herms to provide an allusion to the Greek gymnasium in areas of Roman villas. H: 0.3m. First century AD.

place as part of leisure and relaxation. The provision of such sculptural decoration also celebrated the villa's role as a place for relaxation and retreat into Greek culture, increasing its luxuriousness by the evocation of classical forms and the combination of different types of marble. These statues were able to evoke both the general connotations of Greek cultural life and the specific interest in Greek athletics which was gathering pace within Roman Italy. Depending on how those viewing them wanted to see themselves, the sculptural decoration could add either the intellectual aura of the Greek gymnasium or a more specific reference to the growing trend for Greek body culture among Roman society.

HADRIAN'S VILLA AT TIVOLI

My second case study is the extensive villa of the emperor Hadrian at Tivoli. Much has been written about the villa, which has been consistently plundered for marble and statuary from the medieval period onwards, with the first serious excavations taking place in the late fifteenth century.[69] In particular, the sculptural display of the villa has received a thorough treatment by Joachim Raeder, who has sought to

[69] See M. De Franceschini, *Villa Adriana: Mosaici, Pavimenti, Edifici* (Rome, 1991), 5–11, on the excavation history. Important accounts of the villa include H. Winnefeld, *Die Villa des Hadrian bei Tivoli* (Berlin, 1895); P. Gusman, *La Villa Imperiale de Tibur* (Paris, 1904); and S. Aurigemma, *Villa Adriana* (Rome, 1961). More recently, see W. MacDonald and J. A. Pinto, *Hadrian's Villa and its Legacy* (New Haven and London, 1995) and E. Salza Prina Ricotti, *Villa Adriana: Il sogno di un imperatore* (Rome, 2001).

clarify which, among the wealth of statues attributed to the villa, have a genuine claim. He suggests that in many ways the sculptural display of the villa belongs to a pattern of villa display already developed in the Late Republic.[70]

The *Historia Augusta* famously claims that

[Hadrian] built the Tiburtine Villa marvellously, in such a way that he might inscribe there the most famous names of provinces and places and could call parts for instance, the Lyceum, the Academy, the Prytaneum, Canopus, the Poecile, Tempe. And, so that nothing should be omitted, he even made an underworld.[71]

While this might lead us to search for a specific connection with Hadrian's own life, most notably his travels around the empire, recent scholars have stressed the fact that by naming areas of his villa in this way, Hadrian was simply acting in a time-honoured tradition.[72] Rather than seeking to identify different areas of the villa with particular famous structures or places we should consider more generally the ways in which Hadrian used the conventions of villa design to accommodate his own self-representation as well as the pleasurable pursuits of villa life.[73]

I will consider here only a subsection of the vast sculptural display of the villa, and one which has until now received relatively little discussion. This is a series of statues which are attested as coming from the northern part of the villa, near the so-called 'palaestra' and 'Greek theatre' (Fig. 4.9). A number of athletic statues seem to have been found in this area of the villa, along with images of Hermes and Heracles, both gods often associated with the Greek gymnasium, leading Raeder to assert that there must have been a palaestra, or exercise ground, somewhere in this area.[74] However, the scanty remains of the area labelled as a palaestra on most maps of the villa seem more suited to a utilitarian function, causing many scholars to conclude that if a palaestra was indeed present at the villa it must have been associated with the quarters of the palace guard rather than being an area used by the emperor himself.[75]

As I have argued in detail elsewhere, however, the identification of these remains with a complex excavated by the sixteenth-century architect and antiquarian Pirro Ligorio, and named in the writings attributed to him as a palaestra, can be shown to be a mistake.[76] The identification of these remains with Ligorio's palaestra goes

[70] Raeder, *Villa Hadriana*, see especially 287–90.

[71] Scriptores Historiae Augustae, *Hadrian* 26.5–6.

[72] Raeder, *Villa Hadriana*, 289; MacDonald and Pinto, *Hadrian's Villa*, 3–6.

[73] The representational potential of imperial villas was always important since they were used as much for imperial business as for retreat. See MacDonald and Pinto, *Hadrian's Villa*, 6, for evidence of Hadrian conducting business at the villa.

[74] Raeder, *Villa Hadriana*, 298.

[75] E. Salza Prina Ricotti, 'Villa Adriana nei suoi limiti e nella sua funzionalità', *AttiPontAccRomMem* 14 (1982), 25–55, at 37; Raeder, *Villa Hadriana*, 298; MacDonald and Pinto, *Hadrian's Villa*, 41–2.

[76] See Z. Newby, 'Sculptural Display in the so-called Palaestra of Hadrian's Villa at Tivoli', *RömMitt* 109 (2002), 59–82, for a fuller account of the conclusions presented here. The authorship of the three works

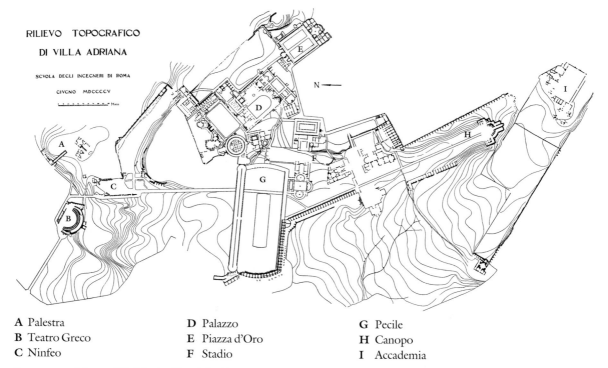

A Palestra   D Palazzo   G Pecile
B Teatro Greco   E Piazza d'Oro   H Canopo
C Ninfeo   F Stadio   I Accademia

FIGURE 4.9 Maps of Hadrian's villa at Tivoli traditionally include an area marked as a palaestra in an area of scanty ruins to the north of the site, mistakenly in my view, though a number of athletic statues do come from this northern area.

back to the map drawn by Francesco Contini in 1668. Contini's reliance on Ligorio's writings and his misidentification of the, then flooded, Greek theatre as a naumachia led him to insert another, non-existent, theatre into the northern part of the site (labelled B on Fig. 4.10).[77] Since the porticoes whose excavation was described in Ligorio's writings were close to the theatre, Contini identified them with a series of structures close to his imaginary theatre, rather than in the area around the actual Greek theatre. However, I believe that two courtyards described in these writings as a palaestra and a xystus should in fact be located close to the real northern theatre. While little remains around the area today, a large courtyard is clearly shown adjoining the western side of the theatre on the maps by Contini and Piranesi, where it is called a Hippodrome (Figs 4.10 (A), 4.11). Piranesi's map shows that this peristyle-like area had forty niches along its southern side, precisely the same number that are mentioned in Ligorio's account as decorating one of the porticoes adjoining the theatre.[78]

attributed to Ligorio is discussed by E. Salza Prina Ricotti, 'Villa Adriana in Pirro Ligorio e Francesco Contini', *Atti della Accademia Nazionale dei Lincei: Memorie* 8.17 (1973), 3–47, at 4–5, and ead., *Villa Adriana*, 29–30, who suggests that only one work was actually written by Ligorio himself.

[77] Salza Prina Ricotti, 'Villa Adriana in Pirro Ligorio', 22–5, and ead., *Villa Adriana*, 57–8.

[78] P. Ligorio, *Descrittione della superba e magnificentissima Villa Hadriana* 13c, reproduced in J. G. Graevius, ed., *Thesaurus Antiquitatum et Historiarum Italiae*, viii/4 (Leiden, 1723).

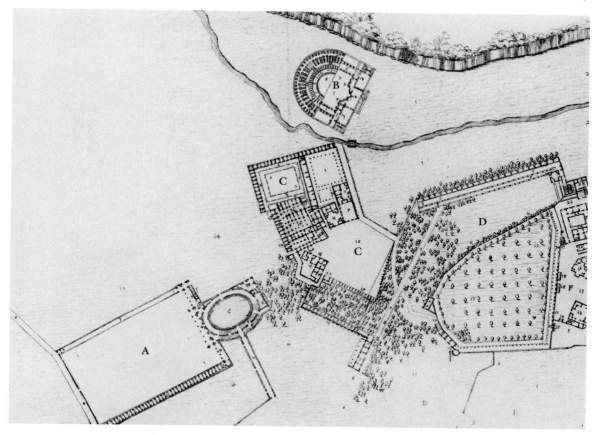

FIGURE 4.10 Contini's map of Hadrian's Villa at Tivoli (1668) labels as the palaestra an area of ruins (C) close to his invented theatre (B). Instead, the area described by Ligorio as yielding athletic statues should probably be identified with the piazza next to the real theatre, marked A, which has a series of statue niches running along its southern edge. Detail of Map of Hadrian's Villa at Tivoli by F. Contini (1668).

One of the accounts attributed to Ligorio, the *Trattato delle antichità di Tivoli et della Villa Hadriana*, lists the sculptures which were found in these porticoes. One yielded three very beautiful torsos, described as 'Herculean things', while in the other a series of statues were found, including three red marble half-figures which are identified as figures of the athlete Milo of Croton. In line with these discoveries, the author identifies the piazzas as a xystus and a palaestra respectively.[79] According to my reading of the evidence, the 'xystus' is the large courtyard to the west of the theatre, while the 'palaestra' must also have been close to the theatre, perhaps adjoining it to the north, behind the stage, like the courtyard behind the theatre at Ostia and those attached to theatres elsewhere.[80] An elaborate statuary display on athletic themes would have been much more at home here, in an area

[79] See Vatican, Vat. Lat. 5295, 14r–15r. The text is also preserved in the manuscripts in the Vatican, Barb. Lat. 4849, and the British Library, Add. MS 22001 and is quoted in Newby, 'Sculptural Display', 62–3.

[80] See Vitruvius, *De Architecture* 5.9, for this as a common feature of theatre design.

FIGURE 4.11
Piranesi's map of
this area of the
villa also shows
the remains of a
peristyle next to
the northern
theatre (labelled
here as Ipodromo
and Naumachia
respectively). The
athletic statues
that were found in
this part of the villa
were probably
displayed either in
this peristyle or in
another, perhaps
immediately to
the north of the
theatre, of which
nothing remains.

associated with the reception functions of the villa, than in the military or utilitarian building with which it has, until now, always been associated.

The descriptions of the statues are lamentably vague, and the identification of the red marble busts as portraits of a famous athlete has itself been challenged by Selena Ensoli, who suggests these were in fact figures of Isiac priests.[81] While it is possible that the *Trattato* wrongly interpreted these particular figures, the attributes which it records—olive wreaths, a lionskin, and jumping weights—do seem to point towards an athletic interpretation. The three torsos found in the portico to the west of the theatre may also have represented athletes. The vagueness of their description makes it difficult to firmly identify these torsos among the collections in modern museums, yet the lack of any attributes mentioned makes it likely that they were naked youthful figures, possibly copies of famous Greek athletic victory statues, or idealized figures of heroes. Their description as 'torsos from the knees' suggests to me that they had fallen from their niches onto the floor, in the process breaking at the vulnerable areas of the knees, neck and arms. What the 'cose Hercolee', 'Herculean things' refers to is unclear. It is possible that attributes of Hercules, such as the lionskin or club, were visible, or it may be that the account refers instead to the athletic physique of the figures.

There is, in fact, one statue, now in the Louvre and previously displayed in the Villa d'Este at Tivoli, which sounds similar to these statues (Fig. 4.12). In Del Re's description of the Villa d'Este of 1611 it is described as a 'boxer at the Fontanile dei Draghi', and Ashby suggests that it may be the sculpture described in the 1572 inventory as 'a nude Castor of marble'. It has also been known as 'Pollux'.[82] We do not have any precise information about the provenance of this statue. However, it is quite possible that it came from the excavations carried out at Hadrian's Villa by Ligorio in the 1550s and 1560s, many of the finds from which were destined for the collections of the Cardinal Ippolito d'Este.[83] As a drawing by Gusman shows, it was restored as a statue of a boxer holding both arms above his head.[84] However, only the torso of the statue, reaching from the neck down to the knees and missing the head, arms, and lower legs, is actually original, agreeing closely to the description of the torsos found in the villa as 'from the knees'. As Charbonneaux has

[81] S. Ensoli, 'Iside a Tivoli', in *Iside: Il mito, il mistero, la magia* (Milan, 1997), 418–20, and ead., 'Prêtres d'Isis en marbre rouge antique: Antinoüs dans la "Palestra" de la Villa Adriana', in J. Ch.-Gaffiot, and H. Lavagne, eds., *Hadrien: Trésors d'une villa impériale* (Paris, 1999), 79–83. She links these with three busts in Rome, Paris, and Venice which have been identified as Isiac priests. Raeder, *Villa Hadriana*, 128, accepts the attribution to the villa, though there is no documentary proof of this. For further discussion of the arguments see Newby, 'Sculptural Display', 74–8.

[82] Raeder, *Villa Hadriana*, v.17. See T. Ashby, 'The Villa d'Este at Tivoli', *Archaeologia* 61 (1908), 219–56 at 244, 253. It is Louvre, MA 889; J. Charbonneaux, *La sculpture grecque et romaine au Musée du Louvre* (Paris, 1963), 23.

[83] Salza Prina Ricotti, *Villa Adriana*, 419, fig. 158. 2, includes it among the finds from the Palaestra.

[84] Gusman, *Villa Imperiale*, 305, fig. 549.

FIGURE 4.12
Though previously
identified as a boxer,
this statue probably
showed an athlete
preparing to throw
the discus. Its exact
provenance is
uncertain, but it
might be one of the
torsos discovered
in the portico
adjoining the theatre
at Hadrian's Villa
at Tivoli. H: 1.23m.
Hadrianic.

shown, rather than being a representation of a boxer it probably showed an athlete with his arms raised, preparing to throw the discus, of a type which has been attributed to the early fifth-century sculptor Pythagoras of Rhegium, an artist renowned for his bronze statues of athletic victors.[85]

Other athletic statues attested from this northern area of the villa may also have originally been displayed in this palaestra-like area next to the theatre, set into the niches lining the southern side of the piazza. Excavations in 1928 in the cryptoporticus beneath the Casino Fede, which emerges just south of the theatre, revealed two fragments of a torso of the statue type known as the 'Amelung athlete', which showed an athlete fitting a cap to his head, probably to keep the hair out of his eyes during boxing (Fig. 4.13).[86] This type has been seen as dating back to the fifth century BC, possibly to an original by the sculptor Myron. The fragments were found with some distance between them, while a head of the same type was found nearby at the 'Ninfeo Casino Fede'.[87] The scattering of the finds suggests that the sculpture had been broken up and removed from its original display. Like the torso in the Louvre, this work too seems to evoke the style of fifth-century bronze sculpture. It too may originally have adorned one of the niches in Ligorio's 'xystus'. While such sculptural ensembles are rarely found *in situ*, the display of athletic statues between the columns of a portico is shown on a number of terracotta reliefs, suggesting that it was probably a common form of display in villa porticoes and peristyles (Fig. 4.8).

Other finds from the surrounding area reinforce this picture of a thematic display of statues on athletic subjects. While we lack a more precise provenance for them, two copies of Myron's famous Discobolus statue were found in the 'Casino Fede' area of the villa. In the eighteenth century the Conte Fede owned much of the northern part of the villa site, comprising the area around the terrace of the Doric temple, on which the Casino was built, the theatre, and the 'palaestra'.[88] It was in this general area that a replica of Myron's Discobolus was found in 1791 by Cardinal Marefoschi, now displayed in the Sala della Biga in the Vatican.[89] Another replica was also found about the same time in land belonging to the Conte Fede (Fig. 4.14),

[85] J. Charbonneaux, 'Quatre marbres antiques du Musée du Louvre', *Monuments Piots* 45 (1951), 33–51, at 42–51. On Pythagoras, see Pliny, *Natural History* 34.59.

[86] On the type, see Picozzi, 'Testa dell' "Atleta Amelung"'. The identification of this type as a boxer is supported by the presence of cylinders on the support which Raeder, *Villa Hadriana*, 82, argues are not *halteres*, but rather the cylinders carried in the hand during boxing to produce a rounded fist: B. Schröder, *Der Sport in Altertum* (Berlin, 1927), 146. See also Liverani, *Antiquarium*, 62, on the head of the same type found at Domitian's Villa at Castel Gandolfo.

[87] Raeder, *Villa Hadriana*, I.71. Villa Adriana, inv. 1060, 2746. For the discovery see R. Paribeni, 'Tivoli: Rinvenimenti di sculture a Villa Adriana', *NSc* (1932), 120–5. Picozzi, 'Testa dell' "Atleta Amelung"', 113 n. 26, suggests that the torso and head belong together.

[88] See Raeder, *Villa Hadriana*, 11.

[89] See Raeder, *Villa Hadriana*, I.127 for bibliography. Vatican, Museo Pio-Clementino, 2346.

FIGURE 4.13 A statue of the 'Amelung athlete' type showing an athlete binding up his hair in preparation for wrestling or boxing was found in pieces in a crypto-porticus near the northern theatre of Hadrian's Villa at Tivoli. Its athletic subject matter and evocation of fifth-century BC forms links it with other athletic pieces from this area of the villa. H: 1.70m. Hadrianic.

FIGURE 4.14 The 'Townley Discobolus' is one of two copies of Myron's Discobolus which were found at the villa. Its popularity in villa display can be attributed to the fact that as well as copying a famous art-work of the fifth century BC it also represented the athletic all-rounder, the pentathlete. From Hadrian's Villa at Tivoli. H: 1.65m. Hadrianic.

along with the famous Lansdowne Heracles statue now in the Getty Museum (Fig. 4.16). A letter of Zoega dated 18 February 1792 tells us that these two statues had been found in the villa, though the precise find-spot remains unclear.[90] Both were acquired by Thomas Jenkins, who then sold them to Charles Townley and Lord Shelburne respectively.[91] If originally displayed close together, the two Discobolus statues may have functioned as pendants, a method of display which seems to have been popular at the villa.[92] The fact that they, like the Amelung athlete type and the torso in the Louvre, also evoke statuary forms of the second quarter of the fifth century BC makes it possible that they were designed to be seen together with those statues in a thematic display.[93]

Other athletic statues represent a later style of art, more akin to the fourth-century feel of the Lansdowne Heracles, though it seems likely that this piece is a work of Roman eclecticism rather than a direct copy of a Greek work.[94] Two statues of the so-called 'Sandalbinder' type, a statue which has been identified both as Hermes heeding the call of Zeus and as a resting athlete, were found in the Pantanello. Excavations had been begun here by Lolli in the 1720s and were continued in 1769 by Gavin Hamilton, who drained much of the area with dramatic success. One of the sandalbinder statues, now in Copenhagen, was found here by Hamilton in 1769 (Fig. 4.15).[95] The other, now in Munich, is also said to have been found here, by Cardinal Marefoschi in 1793.[96]

Like the Lansdowne Heracles, these statues present us with a youthful idealized athletic figure. In some copies he is clearly identified as Hermes by the attributes he carries, in others the concentration is rather on his idealized physique, a snapshot image of the god pausing in the midst of his activities.[97] The same blurring of the line between idealized anonymous athletic beauty and the depiction of a particular individual occurs in the Lansdowne Heracles statue (Fig. 4.16). This shows a youthful Heracles, holding his club in one hand and the skin of the Nemean lion in

[90] H. Ellis, *The Townley Gallery* (London, 1846), 243, suggests that they were found in the 'pinacoteca' area, further to the south, though the letters from Jenkins to Townley do not specify the exact find-spot.

[91] Raeder, *Villa Hadriana* , I.127 and I.34; Zoega is cited in F. G. Welcker, *Alte Denkmäler*, i (Göttingen, 1849), 422. See also MacDonald and Pinto, *Hadrian's Villa*, 300–1, on the discovery, and S. Howard, *The Lansdowne Herakles*, 2nd edn. (Malibu, Calif., 1978), 13–15, for correspondence.

[92] F. Slavazzi, 'I programmi decorativi della villa: Temi, colori, riflessi', in *Adriano: Architettura e Progetto* (Milan, 1999), 63–7.

[93] On the popularity of this style in the villa, see Raeder, *Villa Hadriana*, 220–2. Liverani, 'L'Antiquarium', 117–20, says that the Doryphorus in the Vatican also comes from the villa, possibly found during Marefoschi's excavations. It may too have added to this athletic display.

[94] S. Lattimore, 'Two Statues of Herakles', *J. Paul Getty Museum Journal* 2 (1975), 17–26; Howard, *Lansdowne Herakles*, 22 n. 28.

[95] Raeder, *Villa Hadriana*, I. 6 gives full bibliography.   [96] Raeder, *Villa Hadriana*, I. 38.

[97] A copy in Antalya holds the *korykeion*, therefore is clearly identified as Hermes. See J. Inan, 'Der sandalenbindende Hermes', *Antike Plastik* 22 (1993), 105–16 on the type and a probable attribution to Lysippus.

FIGURE 4.15
A statue of the
'Sandalbinder' type
was also found
at the villa. It is
identified either
as the god Hermes
or as an athlete,
copying forms of
the fourth century
BC. From Hadrian's
Villa at Tivoli.
H: 1.54m.
Hadrianic.

FIGURE 4.16
The 'Lansdowne
Heracles' shows the
hero in a relaxed
pose. His well-toned
youthful body sug-
gests that he can be
seen as the model
athlete as well as a
famous hero. From
Hadrian's Villa at
Tivoli. H: 1.94m.
Hadrianic.

the other. This statue clearly recalls the hero's twelve Labours, yet its posture is also that of a resting athlete. The athletic hero relaxes after his exertions, before moving on to the next of his Labours. These statues thus exemplify the blurring between the categories of athlete, god, and hero, by showing figures of idealized youthful athletic beauty but also clearly identifying those figures as specific individuals, Heracles or Hermes, involved in particular tasks.[98] The youthful beauty of these statues is an athletic one, achieved both through the activities of the figures, and through their roles as protectors of the gymnasium and founders of athletic activity—Heracles was credited with starting the Olympic games, and Hermes with inventing wrestling.

We cannot say precisely where in the villa these statues were actually displayed, whether formally in an architectural setting, such as the piazza next to the theatre, or more informally, perhaps in the midst of a glade where viewers would see them as if accidentally coming upon the gods themselves.[99] However, what the presence of all these statues does suggest, despite our ignorance of the exact circumstances of their display, is the strong athletic theme running throughout the statuary ensemble of this area of the villa.

Some of the finds which were excavated in the Pantanello by Gavin Hamilton may also derive from the porticoes around the theatre or the nearby parkland. Hamilton records one red marble bust of a youth with an olive crown which sounds similar to those mentioned in the *Trattato*.[100] A number of other athletic subjects were found, including a bust of an athlete originally wearing a wreath or diadem; a head of an athlete, now unidentified; a head of Hermes; and a replica of the so-called Stephanos athlete.[101] A herm of Heracles wearing a wreath on his head now in the Vatican also comes from the area usually called the palaestra (Fig. 4.17).[102] The sculptural ensemble found in the northern part of the villa thus includes images of athletes in action and at rest as well as statues and busts of the two gods most closely associated with the gymnasium, Hermes and Heracles.[103] Unlike the display at Domitian's villa, which contained the boyish images of the

---

[98] On the associations between athletes and heroes, see below, Ch. 7, pp. 223–6.

[99] For the idea of statues placed in natural settings, compare Herodes Atticus' display of statues of his foster sons in his villas in the act of hunting: Philostratus, *Lives of the Sophists* 2.1 (559); Raeder, *Villa Hadriana*, 293–4; J. Tobin, *Herodes Attikos and the City of Athens: Patronage and Conflict under the Antonines* (Amsterdam, 1997), 95–111.

[100] A. H. Smith, 'Gavin Hamilton's Letters to Charles Townley', *JHS* 21 (1901), 306–21 at 310.

[101] Smith, 'Gavin Hamilton', 319–21; Raeder, *Villa Hadriana*, I.17, II.15, I.22, I.35.

[102] Raeder, *Villa Hadriana*, I.130; F. Bulgarini, *Notizie storiche, antiquarie, statistiche ed agronomiche intorno all' antichissima città di Tivoli e suo territorio* (Rome, 1848), 120, and R. Lanciani, *La Villa Adriana, guida e descrizione* (Rome, 1906), 17, record its discovery along with a red marble bust (Bulgarini) and terracotta heads (Lanciani). See De Franceschini, *Villa Adriana*, 597.

[103] Other subjects were also present. See, for example, the list of finds from Pantanello in Raeder, *Villa Hadriana*, 369–70, which included a number of Egyptianizing images.

FIGURE 4.17 This herm of Heracles wearing a wreath was found in the northern area of the villa. Both in its form and in the representation of Heracles it evoked the decoration of the Greek gymnasium. From Hadrian's Villa at Tivoli. H: 1.15m. Second century AD.

Westmacott athlete and Dresden youth types as well as two older figures, all the athlete statues found here are of adult males, sexually mature yet still youthful and at their physical peak.[104]

While we cannot be sure about the original location of the athletic statues, some at least were probably displayed in the porticoes which adjoined the northern theatre. Despite the *Trattato*'s suggestion that these porticoes or piazzas could have been used as places for wrestling and athletic activity, the lack of the necessary

[104] For a discussion of the iconography of athletes of difference ages, see N. J. Serwint, 'Greek Athletic Sculpture from the Fifth and Fourth Centuries BC: An Iconographic Study', Ph.D. thesis (Princeton, 1987), 213–43.

bathing facilities would suggest that this was the exception rather than the rule. Indeed, if athletic activity did take place here, it was probably more for entertainment, continuing the spectatorship theme of the theatre, than it was for the actual participation of the princeps himself or his guests.[105] Instead what was probably more important was the aura which these images imparted to the area they decorated.

Following Neudecker's analysis of the display of similar pieces in other villas, we can suggest that one of the intended effects of this wealth of athletic imagery was to evoke the cultural ideals of the Greek gymnasium, in particular its associations with philosophy and learning.[106] These spaces, which I suggest should be seen as part of a complex around the theatre, could have been used for the emperor and his guests to walk and talk in, perhaps during the intervals between theatrical performances. Their evocation of a Greek gymnasium is thus designed to elevate those conversations, for example by fostering an allusion to the philosophical conversations of the Platonic dialogues.

Yet the athleticism of these statues is also important. If Hadrian had wished simply to evoke the intellectual connotations of the Greek gymnasium he could have chosen instead to surround himself with portrait busts of famous writers and philosophers.[107] The choice of images like that of Myron's Discobolus is thus a deliberate one, and conjures up not only the world of the gymnasium but also Panhellenic sanctuaries like that at Olympia, which were crowded with statues of the type these images copy. Unfortunately we do not know where the original of Myron's Discobolus was actually set up, though it probably celebrated the victory of a pentathlete.[108] The statue reminds us not only of the Greek gymnasium as an educational institution, but also of the great athletic festivals of Greece which were still so popular in the Roman period and supported by imperial figures such as Hadrian himself.[109] The fact that these athletic figures are all of adult mature males, at the peak of their physical fitness, also suggests that they may have encouraged a sense of identification in their viewers, offering themselves as role models for visitors to emulate in the bathing suites elsewhere in the villa.[110] Indeed, through their balanced physiques and the fact that some are shown engaging in or

[105] We might think of performances such as those of Nero's court athletes: Suetonius, *Nero* 45.

[106] Neudecker, *Skulpturen-Ausstattung*, 60–4.

[107] For a discussion of the Roman display of images of Greek intellectuals, see P. Zanker, *The Mask of Socrates: The Image of the Intellectual in Antiquity*, trans. A. Shapiro (Berkeley, Los Angeles, and Oxford, 1995), 203–10.

[108] It has sometimes been associated with a victory statue made by Myron for display at Delphi, mentioned in Pliny, *Natural History* 34.57, though this must remain a matter for conjecture.

[109] See Boatwright, *Hadrian and the Cities of the Roman Empire*, 94–104.

[110] A copy of Polycleitus' Doryphorus was found in the small baths of the villas, suggesting that this encouragement of athletic pursuits might have been extended by the sculptural display elsewhere: Raeder, *Villa Hadriana*, I.98.

preparing for the contests of the pentathlon (which included throwing the discus and boxing), these athletic statues remind us of the ideal practice of athletics, which exercises all parts of the body rather than distorting it through over-specialization.[111] They provide a suitable model for the development of both a healthy body and a healthy mind which the villa lifestyle helped to facilitate.[112]

Another important facet of the two Discobolus statues is their evocation of a particular famous artwork. This seems to be a feature which runs throughout the villa display as a whole, with its representation of Praxiteles' statue of Aphrodite of Cnidus in the Doric temple area, and copies of the Caryatids from the Erechtheum on the Athenian Acropolis in the Canopus.[113] While these statues often have an individual significance within the area they decorate, their status as *opera nobilia* must also have been important, elevating the status of the areas they decorate. They allowed Hadrian to show his art-historical knowledge and allude to famous sights around the empire while at the same time combining these allusions with references to broader cultural values, here the educational and athletic ideals of the Greek gymnasium.

The athletic statues which decorated villas like those of Domitian and Hadrian suggested a number of allusions which drew on both their classical form and their subject matter. Their use of the forms of fifth- and fourth-century BC Greek sculpture allowed a general allusion to the cultural ideals of Classical Greece, while the particular models they copied and the subjects they represented suggested more direct messages about the education and pleasures of the villas' owners. The growing popularity of athletic pursuits in the Roman baths and the introduction of agonistic athletics as a form of public spectacle would also have expanded the associations of these classicizing images. They could thus evoke the experience of athletics in the contemporary world as well as the educational and cultural values that the Greek gymnasium had held in elite circles since the Republican period.

The multiple associations of idealized athletic statues can be shown from an examination of one particular example, Myron's Discobolus, a statue that was particularly popular in the second century AD.[114] In addition to the two statues from Hadrian's villa, another copy also comes from a villa context. This is the torso from Tor Paterno in the Museo Nazionale Romano. Although the statue itself has been dated to the Augustan period, it was found reused at the site of a small but lavishly decorated seaside villa dated to the early Antonine period.[115] The statue was

---

[111] Xenophon, *Symposium* 2.17.

[112] Cf. Pliny, *Letters* 5.6.42 on the exercise of both mind and body in his Tuscan villa, though the latter by hunting here.

[113] See Raeder, *Villa Hadriana*, 287–315, on the sculptural display of the villa.

[114] Rausa, *Immagine*, 173–7, collects the replicas of the type, including statuettes, fragments, and variants.

[115] Neudecker, *Skulpturen-Ausstattung*, 240, no. 70.1.

discovered lying slightly apart from its base, in front of a staircase leading from a side entrance of the villa into the garden.[116]

Other replicas of the type come from Rome. The Lancelloti Discobolus, the most famous and complete example, was found in 1781 in the area of the Horti Lamiani on the Esquiline hill. It has been dated to the Antonine period, a time when the Gardens were in imperial ownership.[117] Another Antonine example seems to have been reused in the Baths of Caracalla, while a torso discovered by Gavin Hamilton at Ostia came from the Baths at the Porta Marina.[118] Two other examples come from the east of the empire, from Asia Minor, where they decorated elaborately furnished marble rooms in Ephesus and Side.[119]

The identification of this type with a bronze statue by the fifth-century sculptor Myron of an athlete throwing the discus is assured by the descriptions of it in a number of imperial texts. A key example is a passage in Lucian's *Lover of Lies*, a text often evoked in discussions of Roman copies for its description of the sculpture decorating the hallway of a private house:[120]

'When you came in, did you not see', he said, 'a very beautiful statue set up in the hall, the work of Demetrius, the maker of portrait statues?' 'You don't mean the discus-thrower,' I said, 'the one bent over in the position of the throw, with his head turned back towards the hand that holds the discus, with one leg slightly bent, looking as if he would spring up at once with the cast?' 'Not that one,' said he, 'for that is one of Myron's works, the discus-thrower (*diskobolos*), you speak of. Neither do I mean the one beside it, the one binding his head with a fillet, the handsome lad, for that is Polycleitus' work. Never mind those to the right as you come in, among which stand the tyrant-slayers, modelled by Critius and Nesiotes . . .'. (*Lover of Lies* 18)[121]

The passage is illuminating for the picture it presents of a second-century sculpture collection. Sculptures of a variety of different styles, from early Classical to Hellenistic, are juxtaposed, and the description elides their status as copies, referring instead to their famous prototypes. The reader is expected to recognize them, matching the written description with a visual image inside their own heads. A similar feature also appears in Philostratus' *Imagines*, where the description of a painted image of Apollo, about to make the fatal throw of the discus which will kill his beloved Hyacinth, is described in terms strongly reminiscent of Myron's

---

[116] See R. Lanciani, 'Le antichità del territorio Laurentino nella reale tenuta di Castelporziano', *Monumenti Antichi* 16 (1906), 242–74 with pls. 1–3, esp. 246 and pl. 1.

[117] See R. Lanciani, *New Tales of Old Rome* (Boston, 1901), 219–25, whose plan is reproduced in C. C. Vermeule, *Greek Sculpture and Roman Taste* (Ann Arbor, 1977), fig. 48. Further details of the finds made in 1781 are given by C. Haüber, 'I vecchi ritrovamenti (prima del 1870)', in M. Cima and E. La Rocca, eds., *Le tranquille dimore degli dei: La residenza imperiale degli horti Lamiani* (Venice, 1986), 167–72 at 169–70.

[118] See above, pp. 56 and 70.   [119] Discussed below, pp. 244 and 262.

[120] See e.g. Bartman, 'Sculptural Collecting'.

[121] Translation A. M. Harmon (Loeb edition), modified.

statue.[122] These literary allusions reveal the statue's great fame in the second and third centuries, one reason for its inclusion in the sculptural collections of Roman villas.

While not all classicizing sculptures of the Roman period directly copied famous Greek originals, a number certainly did and their status as *opera nobilia*, famous artworks from the classical past, is likely to have been one major reason for their attraction. This aspect of Roman copies has tended to be underplayed by recent scholars. Thus Marvin argues that the letters of Cicero show that sculpture was chosen more to define the aura of a particular space than to represent great works of art, and that we may be projecting our own ideas about artistic merits back upon the ancient Romans.[123] Neudecker too seems ambivalent about the extent to which Roman choices of statuary were influenced by the fame of the originals they copied. While he suggests that the uses of Greek art by the Romans both as art and as decoration cannot be disentangled, he also asserts that the status of a work as a masterpiece is often secondary to its choice on grounds of content.[124] Yet he also presents evidence that showing one's knowledge of art was of key importance for the educated man. While this idea comes through particularly strongly in Greek texts, such as those of Lucian and Philostratus, there is also evidence of Romans attempting to use art to prove their education, knowledge, and status.[125] Thus in Petronius' *Satyricon* Trimalchio is particularly proud of his collection of bronze and silver tableware while Martial records the boasts of Vindex that he owns the very statuette by Lysippus of Heracles Epitrapezius that Alexander the Great once possessed.[126] As Koortbojian has recently suggested, Roman patrons could have been influenced in their choices of idealizing statuary by a whole range of motives, encompassing both the need to create an appropriate atmosphere and the desire to present a gallery of famous masterpieces, though some individuals may have been swayed more by one than the other.[127]

The art-historical fame of certain statues could thus add an extra prestige and glamour to the sculptural collections of Roman villas. Yet at the same time they also

[122] Philostratus, *Imagines* 1.24.2. See L. Abbonanza, 'Immagini della phantasia: Quadri di Filostrato maior tra pittura e scultura', *RömMitt* 108 (2001), 111–34, at 121–2.

[123] Marvin, 'Copying', 174–8, though Pollitt, 'Impact', discusses connoisseurship among the Romans.

[124] Neudecker, *Skulpturen-Ausstattung*, 91–104, especially 95–6. Raeder, *Villa Hadriana*, 298, also argues that the sculptures at Hadrian's villa were primarily chosen for what they represented, and that there was no line-up of famous works such as we find in Lucian.

[125] On Lucian's attitude to art see S. Maffei, *Luciano di Samosata: Descrizioni di opere d'arte* (Turin, 1994). On the cultured viewer in Greek literature see S. Goldhill, 'The Erotic Eye: Visual Stimulation and Cultural Conflict', in Goldhill, *Being Greek*, 154–94, at 157–67.

[126] Petronius, *Satyricon* 50–2; Martial, *Epigrams* 9.43.7f. Bartman, 'Décor et Duplicatio', 222–4, argues for the aesthetic interests of some Roman viewers.

[127] M. Koortbojian, 'Forms of Attention: Four Notes on Replication and Variation', in Gazda, *Ancient Art of Emulation*, 173–204, at 175–83.

functioned in the ways outlined by Marvin and Neudecker, combining with architectural features to suggest allusions to particular sorts of spaces, often those drawn from Greek civic life. In the case of the Discobolus, in addition to its art-historical prestige as an example of Myron's oeuvre, it also represented an athletic victory monument, similar to those which could still be seen at Delphi and Olympia as well as in public spaces throughout the cities of the Greek east.[128] Yet when placed in the portico of a peristyle it could also allude to the architectural setting of the Greek gymnasium, a popular choice in Roman villas for its wider intellectual and cultural values. The fact that this statue shows an athlete throwing the discus, a competition which only took place as part of the pentathlon and was therefore a mark of the athletic all-rounder, meant that it could also stand for the sort of athletic training praised by Plato and Aristotle rather than the professional specialization which these authors attacked.[129]

Not all of these associations were necessarily evoked every time the image was seen. The circumstances in which it was displayed would also affect the way it was viewed, with placement in a bathing suite suggesting an allusion to exercise in the gymnasium, while elsewhere it might appear alongside other statues as if in an art-gallery of famous works, as the passage by Lucian suggests. The sorts of images it was grouped with, the architectural setting, and its placement in a public or private space in different areas of the empire, would all have affected its interpretation. Yet the very multiplicity of its possible referents, and those of athletic images more generally, is one reason why such statues were so popular in the visual world of the Roman empire.

THE ATHLETIC BODY: YOUTH, BEAUTY, AND SEXUALITY

In its well-toned, carefully balanced physique, the Discobolus presents an ideal form of the adult male body, sexually mature yet still full of youthful energy and verve. While the sculptural collection of Hadrian's villa seems to have favoured images of adult athletes, in other villas we find more youthful images of boy athletes, most of them drawing upon fifth- and fourth-century BC sculptural forms. In this final section, I want to examine some of the other associations which these youthful images of athletic beauty might have provoked amongst their ancient viewers. In particular, I will explore the idea that idealized athletic sculpture provided the ultimate paradigm for a type of youthful male beauty that often invited an erotic response.

---

[128] See Chapter 7 below. I am convinced that Myron's original was an athletic statue, rather than a mythological figure as is sometimes suggested.

[129] Plato, *Republic* 1404a–b; Aristotle, *Rhetoric* 1.5.14; Xenophon, *Symposium* 2.17.

The question of male beauty is explored in a work by the Greek philosopher and orator Dio Chrysostom, written towards the end of the first century AD.[130] In *Oration* 21, *On Beauty*, Dio is prompted by the sight of the figure of a youth to lament the fact that true male beauty is dying out and even when it does appear is often left unrecognized and unappreciated. The dialogue shares its nostalgic tone with a number of Dio's other orations, not least the *Euboean Oration* (*Or*. 7), but it is revealing for what it suggests about the Greek view of beauty. For Dio, ideal male beauty is clearly rooted in Greek athleticism. The youth who prompts Dio's meditations is compared to the athletic victor statues set up in the past at Olympia, while the effeminacy of the Persian ideal of beauty is linked to the fact that Persian youths do not attend the gymnasium as Greeks do (1, 5). The dialogue itself also seems to be taking place in a gymnasium, since Dio's interlocutor refers to the effect of the youth's beauty on the gymnastic trainer (14).

Throughout the dialogue, however, a sense of ambiguity is created around the youth himself. He is reintroduced into the dialogue at 21.13 by the following phrase, 'about this youth (*neaniskos*), who he is and to whom he belongs'. The words pick up the opening sentence of the work: 'How majestic the youth (*neaniskos*) is, and how beautiful', leading us to assume that the same figure is being discussed in both passages. At the start we are told that the *eidos* or form of the youth is archaic, not 'of those nowadays', but rather 'of those set up at Olympia, especially the very ancient ones' (1). It is notable that we are not explicitly told here whether the youth is real or a statue. His 'form' is certainly compared to that of 'those set up at Olympia', which must refer to statues, and the omission of the actual word 'statues' suggests that he too, like them, is a statue. The use of the word *eikones*, images, in the subsequent sentence to refer to modern athletic portraits seems also to indicate that this youth is a sculpted athletic victory statue. However, this is never made explicit and the ambiguity continues when we return to the youth later (13).

Here, too, the text is evasive concerning the precise status of the youth. By asking 'who is he and to whom does he belong' the interlocutor could be asking about the person represented in the statue, in the way that an epigram inscribed on a victory statue at Olympia asks who the victor is and where he comes from.[131] However, he could also be understood as speaking about a real human youth standing before them. The ambiguities are maintained throughout the passage. The way in which the interlocutor talks about the figure's age as being about sixteen or seventeen, and his height being that of a man, could be taken as art-historical techniques of analysis. Yet he then goes on to say that the boy's modesty is such that no one can

[130] C. P. Jones, *The Roman World of Dio Chrysostom* (Cambridge, Mass., 1978), 50, 135, and J. W. Cohoon, ed., *Dio Chrysostom*, ii, Loeb Classical Library (Cambridge, Mass., 1939), 271, suggest a possible date in the late AD 80s.

[131] *IOlympia* 222, ll. 3–6.

continue looking at him unless the youth himself happens to look away, and comments on the effect which the sight of the youth has had on the trainer, all comments which suggest that this is a real youth rather than simply a statue (13–14).

Thus the youth seems both *to be* a statue, in his first appearance, and on second appearance, perhaps rather *to be like* a statue. Certainly he exerts a strong effect on those who see him—not only is Dio's interlocutor struck with admiration for the youth, but even the trainer, a man one would assume to be inured to the attractions of male beauty, is entranced (13–14).[132] The ambiguities over the youth's reality are extended when we consider Dio's answer to his interlocutor's question. Indeed, we are told, the youth does not belong to anyone, or at least he is said not to be anyone's son. The peculiarities of this statement are not followed up, since Dio then goes on to stress the Greekness of the youth's beauty (15), but it underlines his already ambiguous status. As a figure who is part real and part statue, without a father, this anonymous *neaniskos* is instead made to carry a whole weight of other associations. He stands for an ancient form of athletic Greek beauty, which carries with it not only associations with the gymnasium and athletic victory, but also the virtue of youthful modesty and shame.[133] This combination is so potent that it has the capacity to entrance its viewers, who gaze upon this paragon of beautiful, modest, athletic youth. The anonymity of this figure, who represents the ideal form of an ancient Greek beauty, is parallel to that of the idealized Roman statues of athletes discussed above. While many of these replicate the forms used in the Classical period to commemorate the specific achievements of particular individuals, the specificity of those original references is lost in favour of a generic reference to athletic prowess, turning the individual into a 'Spear-carrier' or 'Discus-thrower'.[134]

Whether Dio's youth is real or a statue he fulfils the same role, acting as a reminder of the legacy of the Greek past and serving as a symbol of an ideal type of beauty. The blurring between athletes and their statues which we find in this oration finds a number of parallels elsewhere. It is, of course, a standard trope to describe someone as being as beautiful as a statue. Already in Plato's *Charmides*, the beauty of the eponymous youth leads his admirers to look at him as though he were a statue.[135] In Dio's orations on the athlete Melancomas, too, a rival boxer who is seen exercising in the gymnasium at Naples is described as being like 'the most carefully worked statues, with a colour of well-blended bronze'.[136] For Philostratus, statues actually seem to provide the model for athletic proportions. His account of

---

[132] The same verb, the passive form of *ekplesso*, is used of both men, suggesting the astonishing effect of the boy's beauty.

[133] Similar virtues are attributed to the athlete Melancomas in Dio's *Orations* 28 and 29; on which see König, *Athletics and Literature*, ch 3.

[134] On the generalized character of such statues, see Koortbojian, 'Forms of Attention', 183–9.

[135] Plato, *Charmides* 154c.   [136] Dio Chrysostom, *Oration* 28.3.

the proper relations between ankles and wrists, forearms and shins, upper arms and thighs sounds like the strictures of an artistic canon, and in his discussion of the best physique for a wrestler, he concludes with the comment, 'and of the statues of Heracles, the more pleasing and godlike are those which are noble and without short necks'.[137] Both practical and aesthetic considerations coexist in this prescription for the best athletic physique, with athletic statues providing a standard against which real athletes can themselves be measured.

All this suggests that athletic statuary was seen as presenting the defining image of classical Greek male beauty. In Dio's *Oration* 21 this beauty is closely associated with moral qualities, in particular the youth's incredible modesty, which causes those gazing at him to feel shame. We are shown the potency of this combination of beauty and modesty—strong enough to make even grown men turn away. Yet this effect also has strong erotic overtones. In both Greek and Latin literature, the gymnasium is clearly associated with pederasty, which, in its ideal form, could be defined as a relationship involving friendship and education, as well as sexual pleasure, between an older male lover (the *erastēs*) and a beloved youth (the *erōmenos*).[138] In Greek vase painting, old comedy, and the Platonic dialogues, the gymnasium emerges as a place where lovers went to watch and converse with their beloveds, and this link between the gymnasium, erotics, and, sometimes, philosophy is still strong in Greek texts produced during the Roman period.[139] To take just one example, in the debate between the merits of boy-love and love for woman which appears in Ps.-Lucian, *Amores*, the boy-loving Athenian Callicratidas, himself a keen athlete (9), extols the simple beauty of boys in contrast to the artificial beauty of woman. For him, boys are pure, simple, and modest, occupying their days with instruments of education rather than adornment, and with their bodies toned by honest exercise on horseback and in the wrestling-schools (44–5). For Callicratidas, male love is a refinement, rather than a necessity, of life, arising at a

---

[137] Philostratus, *Gymnasticus* 35. On the idea of a canon compare *Gymnasticus* 25 with Galen, *De placitis Hippocratis et Platonis* 5.448, and A. Stewart, 'The Canon of Polykleitos: A Question of Evidence', *JHS* 98 (1978), 122–31.

[138] e.g. Plato, *Symposium* 180c–185c; *Lysis* 207d–210e. The literature on ancient sexuality, including pederasty, is extensive, much of it concerned with precisely what sorts of relationship were acceptable. See especially K. Dover, *Greek Homosexuality* (London, 1978); M. Foucault, *The History of Sexuality*, ii: *The Use of Pleasure*, trans. R. Hurley (New York, 1985); D. Cohen, 'Law, Society and Homosexuality in Classical Athens', *Past and Present* 117 (1987), 3–21; id., *Law, Sexuality and Society: The Enforcement of Morals in Ancient Athens* (Cambridge, 1991), 171–202; J. Davidson, *Courtesans and Fishcakes: The Consuming Passions of Classical Athens* (London, 1997), 167–82; id., 'Dover, Foucault and Greek Homosexuality: Penetration and the Truth of Sex', *Past and Present* 170 (2001), 3–51. On the erotics of ancient athletics, see T. F. Scanlon, *Eros and Greek Athletics* (New York, 2002), especially 199–273. See also N. Fisher, 'Gymnasia and the Democratic Values of Leisure', in P. Cartledge, P. Millett, and S. von Reden, eds., *Kosmos: Essays in Order, Conflict, and Community in Classical Athens* (Cambridge, 1998), 84–104, at 94–104.

[139] e.g. Aristophanes, *Clouds* 961–1023; Plato, *Charmides* 154a–e, 155d. The vase evidence is collected by Dover, *Greek Homosexuality*, and is also discussed by Scanlon, *Eros and Greek Athletics*, 236–49.

time when men began to live for more than just their basic needs and when the arts began to emerge. He declares it to be the inevitable outcome of a desire for virtue, virtue which is said to be *philokalos*, 'beauty-loving', leading pederasty and philosophy to blossom together (35).

While the philosophical overtones of pederastic love could also be challenged as being merely a cover in the pursuit of sexual pleasure, this nexus of ideas about athletic bodies, virtue, and sexuality remained prominent in texts written during the Roman period.[140] Taken with the concentration on athletic statues as representing the ideal form of youthful male beauty, it seems likely that naked athletic statuary could provoke an erotic response from its ancient viewers which was tied in with its more general evocation of the ideals of Greek culture and education.[141]

While Dio extols the beauty of a youth on the verge of manhood, many Romans seem to have preferred younger figures. Elizabeth Bartman has convincingly argued that the figures of youthful pre-pubescent males that often appear in the sculptural ensembles of Roman baths and villas would have elicited an erotic response.[142] In particular, she links these sensuous images with the delight in boyish beauty suggested by the epigrams of Martial and the *Greek Anthology*, and with the fact that Romans liked to surround themselves with beautiful slave boys.[143] Images of youthful naked athletes are likely to have worked in a similar way, conjuring up the pederastic culture of the Greek gymnasium (along with its associations with education and philosophy) as well as the voyeuristic erotics of the Roman baths.[144]

[140] Other examples appear in Plutarch, *Amatorius*, and Achilles Tatius, *Leucippe and Clitophon* 2.35–8. For discussions of all these texts see M. Foucault, *The History of Sexuality*, iii: *The Care of the Self*, trans. R. Hurley (London, 1986), 189–232, and S. Goldhill, *Foucault's Virginity: Ancient Erotic Fiction and the History of Sexuality* (Cambridge, 1995), 82–111, 144–61, the latter arguing for the continued relevance of these ideas.

[141] On the erotic allure of athletic statues in the Classical period see D. Steiner, 'Moving Images: Fifth-Century Victory Monuments and the Athlete's Allure', *Classical Antiquity* 17 (1998), 123–49, and ead., *Images in Mind: Statues in Archaic and Classical Greek Literature and Thought* (Princeton and Oxford, 2001), 222–34. On nakedness and its different connotations, see L. Bonfante, 'Nudity as a Costume in Classical Art', *AJA* 93 (1989), 543–70, and A. Stewart, *Art, Desire, and the Body in Ancient Greece* (Cambridge, 1997), 24–42.

[142] E. Bartman, 'Eros's Flame: Images of Sexy Boys in Roman Ideal Sculpture', in Gazda, *Ancient Art of Emulation*, 249–71, esp. 261–71.

[143] e.g. Martial, *Epigrams* 4.42, and the poems of the *Greek Anthology*, Book 12, now in a new translation by D. Hine, *Puerilities: Erotic Epigrams of the Greek Anthology* (Princeton and Oxford, 2001). On Roman sexuality see P. Veyne, 'La famille et l'amour sous le haut-empire Romain', *Annales: Économies, Sociétés, Civilisations* 33 (1978), 35–63; id., 'Homosexuality in Ancient Rome', in P. Ariès and A. Béjin, eds., *Western Sexuality*, trans A. Forster (Oxford, 1985), 26–35; E. Cantarella, *Bisexuality in the Ancient World*, trans. C. Ó Cuilleanáin (New Haven and London, 1992), 79–154; C. A. Williams, *Roman Homosexuality: Ideologies of Masculinity in Classical Antiquity* (Oxford, 1999).

[144] See Martial, *Epigrams* 1.23, 1.96, 9.27, and Petronius, *Satyricon* 92, for examples of voyeurism in the Roman baths. On the sexual opportunities of the baths see F. K. Yegül, *Baths and Bathing in Classical Antiquity* (Cambridge, Mass., 1992), 42–3; G. G. Fagan, *Bathing in Public in the Roman World* (Ann Arbor, 1999), 34–6.

In Domitian's villa at Castel Gandolfo, for example, the athletic images found in the hippodrome area may have been enjoyed for their eroticism as well as for their allusion to athletics and the Greek gymnasium. Three of the statues found here show the naked bodies of prepubescent boys—the Westmacott type and the two Dresden youth types. In the sensuous twist of the hips particularly visible in one of the Dresden types (Fig. 4.6) and in the Westmacott youth, and in the latter's coyly averted gaze (Fig. 4.4), these figures share a number of characteristics with the 'sexy boys' discussed by Bartman.[145] Their presentation of a youthful sensuous beauty is also echoed elsewhere in the villa, particularly in the four statues from the theatre of satyrs pouring wine (Fig. 4.18). These four replicas all seem to come from the same workshop and have been dated either to the first half of the first century AD or to the Flavian period.[146] According to Bartoli they were found during excavations held by Innocent X between 1644 and 1655. While he records their discovery on a 'semicircular staircase', Neudecker is undoubtably right to identify this with the cavea of the theatre.[147] Their presence in the theatre can be explained through their role as members of Dionysus' retinue. Yet the fact that four copies of the same type were shown suggests that they were also enjoyed for their own sake, for their beauty, and perhaps too their status as replicas of a famous artwork, if scholars are right to associate this type with Praxiteles' statue of a boyish satyr holding out a cup to Dionysus.[148]

The athletic statues too seem to replicate popular types of idealizing statuary. A glance at Rausa's list of the replicas of athletic types shows that the Westmacott athlete and Dresden youth are two of the most popular images.[149] While this does not prove that they go back to classical prototypes, it does suggest that these types, and their evocation of classical forms, had a certain cachet in the Roman period. When set alongside the statues from the theatre another criterion for the choice of the statues might also be revealed. Although the statues are usually seen as going back to two different sculptural styles, one characteristic of Polycleitus, the other of Praxiteles, a comparison between the figure of the Westmacott youth, in particular, and the pouring satyrs reveals a number of similarities (Figs 4.4, 4.18).[150] Both show beautiful naked boys, standing with one foot drawn back and one arm raised. Both have tender willowy bodies, curved at the waist. They look down modestly, avoiding our gaze and allowing the viewer to stare unabashed, drinking in their beauty.

---

[145] Bartman, 'Sexy Boys', 253, 256–7.   [146] Neudecker, *Skulpturen-Ausstattung*, 141, no. 9.2.

[147] P. S. Bartoli, 'Memorie di varie escavazioni fatte in Roma e nei luoghi suburbani', in C. Fea, *Miscellanea filologica critica e antiquaria*, i (Rome, 1790), 222–73, at 266–7, no. 147; Lugli II, 5; Neudecker, *Skulpturen-Ausstattung*, 140.

[148] Seen by Pausanias in a temple of Dionysus at Athens, 1.20.1–2. See Stewart, *Art, Desire*, 200.

[149] He lists 49 examples of replicas (including variants, fragments, and statuettes) of the Westmacott type, and 23 of the Dresden youth type. The only other types found in similar numbers are the Myronic Discobolus (25, discussed above, pp. 122–3) and the Discophorus (30).

[150] See Linfert, 'Anlaß neuer Repliken', 147.

FIGURE 4.18 This is one of four identical statues which were found in the theatre of Domitian's villa at Castel Gandolfo. They are probably copies of a statue of a satyr by Praxiteles but their youthful idealized physiques also link them to some of the athletic statues found in the Hippodrome and may have evoked an erotic response from ancient viewers. H: 1.45m. First century AD.

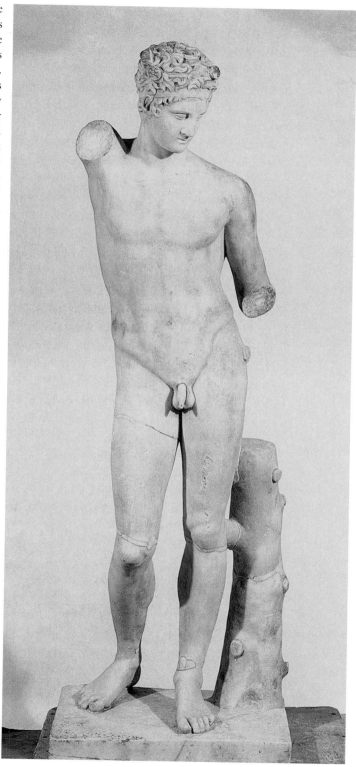

This suggests that what might be as important as the content of the statues —Dionysiac and athletic—and their status as popular images, is simply their eroticism. Indeed, the satyr-ness of the Satyrs is hardly stressed at all, only visible in their pointed ears. Otherwise the statues could show human youths, in the act of pouring wine for human masters. Their eroticism in the act of pouring wine can be paralleled in the imagery associated with the figure of Ganymede, Zeus' beloved and cup-bearer to the gods.[151]

Another eroticized boyish figure appears in the sculptural ensemble of a dining grotto in the villa, the so-called Ninfeo Bergantino on the bank of the Alban Lake.[152] The decoration of this cave seems in part to follow the programme of Tiberius' grotto at Sperlonga by representing some scenes from the life of Odysseus, including at least the escape from Polyphemus' cave and the perils posed by Scylla.[153] Among the other sculptures is a figure of a young boy, partially draped in a chlamys (Fig. 4.19). Lacking its head, and any attributes by which to firmly identify it, the statue has sometimes been identified with a figure of Paris by the sculptor Euphranor.[154] However, it is also possible that it was originally intended to represent Ganymede, cup-bearer to the gods, who was also shown at Sperlonga, though there in the midst of his abduction by the eagle.

Ganymede seems to have been a particularly popular figure in Roman art and literature, allowing Romans who were being served by their own beautiful foreign slaves to implicitly compare themselves with the king of the gods himself.[155] Indeed, Domitian's court poet Statius writes about a banquet held by the emperor to celebrate the Saturnalia in which he declares that he was served wine as if by Ganymede himself: 'these bestow pale wines; you would think them so many Idaean attendants'.[156] Ganymede returns again in a second poem, written in thanks to Domitian for hosting a banquet for senators and knights in his palace on the

---

[151] See also Stewart, *Art, Desire*, 200–2 on the erotic attractions of the original satyr statue.

[152] See Liverani, *Antiquarium*, 71.

[153] The bibliography on Sperlonga is extensive. The first detailed publication is B. Andreae and B. Continello, *Die Skulpturen von Sperlonga*, Antike Plastik 14 (Berlin, 1974). More recent studies have focused on the date of the sculptures and their place in the history of Hellenistic sculpture. See e.g. J. J. Pollitt, *Art in the Hellenistic Age* (Cambridge, 1986), 122–6; P. Moreno, *Scultura ellenistica* (Rome, 1994), 379–405; B. Andreae, in *Ulisse: il mito e la memoria* (Rome, 1996), 38, 346–53; with the analysis by B. S. Ridgway, 'The Sperlonga Sculptures: The Current State of Research', in N. T. De Grummond and B. S. Ridgway, eds., *From Pergamon to Sperlonga: Sculpture and Context* (Berkeley, Los Angeles, and London, 2000), 78–91. Other studies concentrate on the programme presented by the sculptures, first seen as an illustration of the *Odyssey*, but more recently also linked to Latin works such as the *Aeneid* and *Metamorphoses*. See Ridgway, 'Sperlonga Sculptures', 80, and H. A. Weis, 'Odysseus at Sperlonga: Hellenistic Hero or Roman Heroic Foil?', in De Grummond and Ridgway, *Pergamon to Sperlonga*, 111–65, with previous bibliography. On Sperlonga as providing a model for later imperial display, see S. Carey, 'A Tradition of Adventures in the Imperial Grotto', *Greece and Rome* 49 (2002), 44–61.

[154] Liverani, *Antiquarium*, 86–8.

[155] On the erotic attractions of Ganymede for the Romans, see Williams, *Roman Homosexuality*, 56–9.

[156] Statius, *Silvae* 1.6.33–4.

FIGURE 4.19
This statue of a
youth is notable for
its sensuality.
Found in the
Ninfeo Bergantino
of Domitian's villa
it may represent
Ganymede, though
it has also been
associated with a
statue of Paris
by the fourth-
century sculptor
Euphranor. H:
0.79m. Flavian?

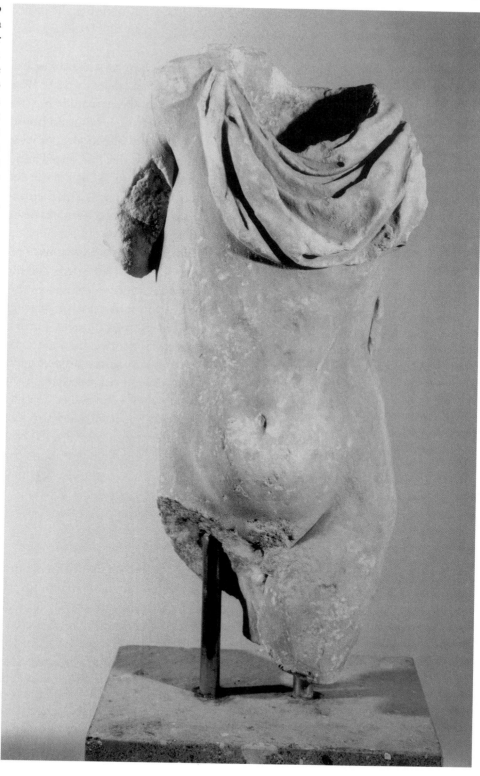

Palatine. Here Statius enthuses about the heavenly nature of the palace: 'I seem to be reclining in the midst of the stars with Jupiter and to accept immortal wine offered by an Ilian hand.'[157]

Domitian's own predilection for the eunuch Earinus was also compared by both Statius and Martial to the love between Jupiter and Ganymede.[158] Romans' sexual enjoyment of young boys, usually their own slaves, could thus be compared with Jupiter's love for Ganymede. The fact that such beautiful household slaves also often performed the function of wine-waiters at banquets provided a further point of comparison and allowed the diners the thrill of sexual anticipation. In Domitian's villa the eroticism of the youth is underlined by the way his chlamys is hitched up at the back to reveal one buttock (Fig. 4.20). This seems to be a clear statement of the sexual attractions of the boy—beautiful buttocks being one of the most-cited attributes of erotic youths.[159]

Three different areas of Domitian's villa present us with visions of prepubescent beauty: the youth in the dining grotto, the satyrs in the theatre, and the athletes in front of the villa. While all have a specific relevance in the spaces they decorate, taken together they also suggest a delight in youthful eroticism, placing the viewer in the role of a lover of young boys. While Roman morality dictated that only non-citizen boys were proper objects of erotic attention for adult males, the presentation in these statues of Greek boys, both human and mythological, elides the distinctions between slave and free. This ambiguity between free-born youth and Roman slave is particularly blurred in images of Ganymede, himself a Phrygian prince but often compared to the pretty slave-boys of Roman banquets.[160] When seen together with the eroticized images elsewhere in the villa, the boyish athletes from the hippodrome acquire an added layer of significance, evoking erotic delights which harmonize with their evocation of the world of the Greek gymnasium.

CONCLUSIONS

An examination of the athletic statues which formed part of the sculptural display of Roman villas shows that these could have a range of interconnected meanings and associations, depending upon which particular statues were chosen, and where they were displayed. When statues copying famous artworks were chosen they would have carried a certain cultural cachet, suggesting the art-historical knowledge and taste of the villa's owner. When displayed in baths, whether public or

---

[157]　Statius, *Silvae* 4.2.10–12.

[158]　Martial, *Epigrams* 8.39, 9.16, 9.36; Statius, *Silvae* 3.4.12–20. See Williams, *Roman Homosexuality*, 34.

[159]　See e.g. *Greek Anthology* 12.37–8; Bartman, 'Sexy Boys', 263–4.

[160]　For a discussion of images of Ganymede and other exotic wine-waiters on Roman table supports, see R. M. Schneider, 'Orientalische Tischdiener als römische Tischfusse', *AA* (1992), 295–305.

FIGURE 4.20
The back view
of the youth
(Fig. 4.19) reveals
one of his buttocks,
a part of the
anatomy celebrated
in homoerotic texts.

private, athletic statues of all sorts (whether copies or new creations) carried connotations of health and beauty. Elsewhere, especially if seen in an appropriate architectural context, they could suggest the wider values associated with the Greek gymnasium, defining the space they decorated as a place for philosophy and education. The idealized beauty of these statues, which rarely have portrait faces, encouraged the viewer to see their general cultural associations. If youthful prepubescent images were chosen they could also invite an erotic appreciation, while images of mature men might instead have prompted the viewer to identify himself with the figures represented.[161]

Many of these resonances suggest a continuity with the Republican period, when we see Cicero choosing statues for the atmosphere of erudition they will give to his 'gymnasium'. Yet the choice of athletic statues in villas of the late first and second centuries AD should also be seen in the context of the increasing contemporary interest in athletic pursuits both as exercise and as part of public spectacles. While Cicero seems to have been more interested in the intellectual connotations of the gymnasium, these images reassert its *athleticism*. By giving athletic activity a key place in the Hellenized atmosphere of the elite villa, they help to integrate the contemporary delight in athletic spectacles and body culture with the traditional interest shown by the Roman elite in Greek culture. They suggest that athletics could be seen as just as important a part of that culture as its literary or philosophical manifestations. In part, this may be a way of justifying elite interest in Greek athletics, against attacks such as those presented in literary record, by showing it as a logical conclusion of a long-standing interest in all areas of Greek culture.

Roman appropriations of Greek culture are often characterized by the adaptation of particular elements to fit Roman needs and desires, whether in the use of plundered sculpture to decorate the heart of Rome, or the use of Greek myths on sarcophagi to comment on Roman lives.[162] Athletic imagery is no exception. The statues which decorated Roman villas are notable for their anonymous youthful beauty. Rather than conjuring up the achievements of specific individual athletes, as did the Greek originals which they copy or evoke, these statues instead provide access to a fantasy world of idealized beauty and moral perfection. Robbed of their individuality, they serve instead as bearers of a raft of ideals and associations, Greek culture as understood and experienced by Roman eyes.

---

[161] Marvin, 'Roman Sculptural Reproductions', 23–4, suggests that athletic types were often chosen for portrait statues. On the polar responses of identification and voyeuristic objectification see L. Mulvey, 'Visual Pleasure and Narrative Cinema', in ead., *Visual and Other Pleasures* (Basingstoke, 1989), 14–26, in relation to the depiction of men and women in film. For a discussion of the application of these ideas to art history, see M. Olin, 'Gaze', in R. S. Nelson and R. Shiff, eds., *Critical Terms for Art History* (Chicago and London, 1996), 208–19; and for their application to ancient art, Stewart, *Art, Desire*, especially 13–14.

[162] P. Zanker and B. C. Ewald, *Mit Mythen leben: die Bilderwelt der römischen Sarkophage* (Munich, 2004).

While the sculptural images generally present an idealized view of Greek athletics, interested more in the past than the present, the mosaic images discussed in Chapter 3 have a more contemporary edge. With their references to real festivals and athletes, as well as to exercise within the public baths, they suggest a growing interest in Greek athletics among the bathing public of Ostia and Rome during the course of the second and third centuries AD. The earliest of the mosaics discussed comes from the Hadrianic period, though similar scenes appear earlier in the Hellenized cities of Campania. It seems logical that the appearance of these athletic scenes at this point should be linked to the consolidation of Greek festival culture in the capital, provided both by the establishment of the Capitoline games at the end of the first century and by the growing presence in the city of members of the international guild of athletes, who finally received permission to build a permanent headquarters under Antoninus Pius.

The establishment and survival of the Capitoline games seems to have been a response to a growing interest in Greek athletics, both as physical training and as a form of public spectacle. Yet the festival itself also exercised a counter influence, encouraging the growing tendency to partake in athletic activities within the baths and tempting bathers to see their own exercises as equivalent to those of their sporting heroes. These men, often figures from the Greek east with a wealth of athletic victories behind them, could also be celebrated by name in the decoration of both public and private bathing complexes. A particular spur to athletic activity can be seen in the Severan period, when emperors promoted new festivals at Rome or funded the building and decoration of bathing establishments. The imperial promotion of athletic culture in Rome is also mirrored by an increased interest in athletic imagery elsewhere, in the inn and bath complexes of Ostia and the Great Baths at Aquileia, as well as in some other areas of the western provinces.

The main frame of reference for the mosaic imagery is the world of contemporary athletic festivals. The appearance of crowns and prizes encourages bathers to think of the athletic contests taking place around them in the Graeco-Roman world. Yet when we can explore the wider decorative scheme, as in the Baths of Porta Marina at Ostia, or the Baths of Caracalla at Rome, this often expands the associations of athletic activity from the festivals of the present day to the broader associations of athletics and the Greek gymnasium with culture, education, and beauty. Idealized sculpted images of athletes from the classical past add another level of association to the activities taking place in the baths, reminding viewers of the cultural heritage of athletic imagery, as well as the popular spectacles of the contemporary world.

What was it about the contemporary cultural climate that made Greek athletic pursuits so acceptable and, indeed, popular in Rome from the late first century onwards? I have argued that this can be seen as a gradual process, beginning with the linkage of athletics and bathing in the Baths of Agrippa at Rome, and with the institution of the Greek *Sebasta* festival at Naples. While some athletic contests were introduced to Rome on an ad hoc basis in the Republican period, there does seem to have been resistance to the establishment of a permanent Greek festival here before the late first century AD, and to the idea of Romans themselves participating in athletic activity. The clearest statement of this can be found in Cornelius Nepos' observation that while in Greece it was the highest honour to be proclaimed a victor at Olympia, in Rome such an act would bring down upon one shame and dishonour (pref. 5).

The clear picture from the Republican period is that Greek athletics and the gymnasium were viewed with suspicion, blamed for encouraging immorality and effeminacy.[163] While Romans often do seem to have attended the gymnasium when spending time in the Greek cities of Sicily or the east, they could also be strongly attacked for this behaviour by those back in Rome.[164] Republican Romans certainly chose to include gymnasia and palaestrae in their villas, but the decoration of these areas seems to have concentrated on their role as places for intellectual and literary activity, firmly placed within the sphere of *otium* (leisure) and retreat from public life.[165] They knew of the centrality of athletic education and festivals in Greek culture, but these were not yet seen as appropriate for introduction into Roman civic life.

Yet during the course of the first three centuries AD Greek festivals were introduced to Rome, athletic activity encouraged within the public baths, and athletic statues introduced into the display of Roman villas. The literary sources suggest that there was still some resistance, with old-fashioned views about the pernicious influence of festivals and the gymnasium still being expressed into the second century. Yet, the literary and visual evidence also suggests that opinion on the ground, at all levels of Roman society, was increasingly in favour of Greek athletics. Certainly, this never took hold completely. Traditional reservations about the appearance of Roman citizens in public spectacles seem to have prevented any but a few taking part in competitions like those of the Capitoline games. In any case, physical training in the baths was probably never intensive enough to produce professional athletes like those nurtured from childhood in the cities of the eastern Mediterranean, though Rome's literary culture could produce figures like the child poet Q. Sulpicius Maximus, who won the contest in Greek poetry in the *Capitolia* of AD 94.[166] Athletic training in the gymnasium also never became part of the

---

[163] Cicero, *De republica* 4.4.4. For a good discussion of attitudes to athletic festivals and the gymnasium in the Republican period, see J.-L. Ferrary, *Philhellénisme et Impérialisme: Aspects idéologiques de la conquête romaine du monde Hellénistique* (Rome, 1988), 517–26.

[164] A good example is P. Scipio Africanus, who was attacked in the Roman senate for attending the gymnasium in Sicily in Greek dress: Livy 29.19.11; Plutarch, *Cato the Elder* 3.7.

[165] P. Grimal, *Les jardins romains*, 3rd edn. (Paris, 1984), 249–52, 361–3.

[166] Caldelli, *Agon*, 126, with bibliography.

educational system in Rome in the way that it continued to be an essential part of the Greek *ephēbeia*, though the scenes of athletic activity which appear on some Roman child sarcophagi suggest that athletic pursuits were popular among children as well as adults.[167] When such activities did take place, it was generally within the area of the baths and their attached palaestrae, while the 'gymnasium' structures attached to elite villas seem to have served instead for gentle walking and discussion rather than serious athletic activity.

Yet as a form of entertainment and as a leisure activity within the Roman baths, athletic pursuits were clearly incredibly popular, with visual imagery encouraging bathers to see their activities as equivalent to those of their sporting heroes, mostly figures from the Greek east. Why was it that this aspect of Greek culture, received with such hostility before, became so widespread? It seems likely to me that this must be largely due to the increasingly cosmopolitan, multicultural, nature of Roman society. The influx of figures from the eastern part of the Empire into the city of Rome, and the influences they brought with them, are powerfully illustrated by Juvenal's *Satire* 3 and Lucian's comments in *On Salaried Posts in Great Houses* as well as in the inscriptional record.[168]

Yet it was not only Greeks of the lower social scale who infiltrated Roman society. Studies of the composition of the Roman senate show that the number of eastern senators gradually increased from the late first century onwards, with a peak in the mid-second century.[169] A number of these reached the consulship, as did the Sardian notable Ti. Julius Celsus Polemaeanus in AD 92 and the Athenian sophist Herodes Atticus in 143.[170] The promotion of such figures seems to begin with Domitian, who first appointed them as governors of praetorian provinces and elevated them to the consulship.[171] As the number of eastern men in the senate rose, so would have their visibility within Roman elite society. Such men were required to reside in Italy, and many acquired houses and villas at Rome, like those of Herodes Atticus and the Quintilii brothers from Alexandria Troas along the Via Appia.[172] While many must have spent their time commuting between Rome and their home cities, they would have become part of Roman elite society, mingling with the other members of the elite from across the Roman empire who might come to Rome as sophists or ambassadors. Within this cosmopolitan society, old Republic values about what was or was not appropriate for a Roman citizen

---

[167] On the *ephēbeia* see below, Chapters 5 and 6.   [168] See above, p. 62, n. 75.

[169] H. Halfmann, *Die Senatoren aus dem östlichen Teil des Imperium Romanum bis zum Ende des 2. Jahrhunderts n. Chr* (Göttingen, 1979); A. Chastagnol, *Le sénat romain à l'époque impériale: Recherches sur la composition de l'Assemblée et le statut de ses membres* (Paris, 1992), 159–68, esp. 161–2.

[170] Halfmann, *Senatoren*, 111–12, no. 16; 155–60, no. 68.

[171] B. W. Jones, *Domitian and the Senatorial Order: A Prosopographical Study of Domitian's Relationship with the Senate, AD 81–96* (Philadelphia, 1979), 70–1.

[172] Tobin, *Herodes Attikos*, 355–71; A. Ricci, *La villa dei Quintilii* (Rome, 1998). On the need to reside in Italy, see Chastagnol, *Sénat romain*, 164–8.

yielded as a new sort of elite culture was created, one which was heavily based on a common education and, in particular, knowledge of Greek culture.[173] Of course, the correct use of Greek culture had been a marker of the Roman elite since the Republican period.[174] Now, however, with the creation of an imperial, rather than a more narrowly defined Roman or Italian, elite at Rome, where senators came from across the Mediterranean and emperors could derive from Spain, Gaul, or North Africa, elements of Greek culture which had previously jarred with Roman values gradually became less of a threat and could be enjoyed instead for the sense of luxury and exoticism which they provided.

The spread of festivals and athletic training into other areas of the western provinces, such as Gaul and North Africa, was influenced both by the experiences of their elites in Rome and other provinces and by the individual histories of particular places. So southern Gaul was already heavily influenced by Greek culture through the presence of Greek colonies, and individual cities seem to have enjoyed presenting themselves as centres of Greek culture, a trend which was actively encouraged by some Roman emperors. In North Africa too, an interest in Greek athletics can be tied in with the long-standing use of Greek culture for purposes of self-promotion in intra-elite rivalries. The spread of Greek athletics into the western provinces seems to have been patchy, with the evidence pointing to areas which had long been part of the Mediterranean world, rather than to the northern provinces such as Britain. Even if the example of Rome provided a major spur to the residents of some areas to enjoy and promote Greek athletic festivals, it seems that an interest in and predisposition towards Greek culture was also an essential factor.

It is impossible to unpick precisely the ways in which Greek athletics was understood by any one resident of the western Roman empire. Depending on background, education, and audience, it could have appeared to be one of the bonuses of being part of a multicultural empire, a sign of belonging to an elite marked by its knowledge of and adherence to Greek cultural values, or, occasionally, a statement of the claims to a Greek identity of one's home city. Yet in the majority of cases athletic pursuits seem to have been kept within the leisure or spectacle culture of these cities, a sign of the benefits of Rome's empire, and another example of the ways that Greek culture could be put to the service of Roman needs.

---

[173] On the role of *paideia* in Late Antiquity see P. Brown, *Power and Persuasion in Late Antiquity: Towards a Christian Empire* (Madison, Wis., 1992); R. A. Kaster, *Guardians of Language: The Grammarian and Society in Late Antiquity* (Berkeley, Los Angeles, and London, 1998). Schmitz, *Bildung und Macht*, discusses the earlier period, though with a focus on the Greek elite, rather than the role of *paideia* in linking members of the elite from across the empire.

[174] Among his many works on this theme (above, p. 3, n. 8), see A. Wallace-Hadrill, 'Vivere alla greca per essere Romani', in S. Settis, ed., *I Greci*, II/3 (Torino, 1998), 938–63.

PART II

Athletics and Identity in the Greek East

Training Warriors
The Merits of a Physical Education

In the first half of this book I have shown how Greek athletic culture gradually took an increasing hold over the spectacle and bathing culture of Roman life. Both literary and visual evidence suggest a keen interest in the athletic contests which took place within public spectacles, and the desire to see one's own exercises in the baths as in some ways parallel to those of the empire's great sporting heroes. While contemporary athletic festivals were thriving, athletics could also be associated with the classical past, and in particular with the cultural ideals of the Greek gymnasium. The idealized images that decorated elite villas had a number of continuities with villa display in earlier periods too, except that the contemporary interest in athletics seems to have encouraged reference to the athletic, as well as the intellectual, associations of the gymnasium.

However, this interest in Greek athletics, even when it spilled over into the public festivals of Rome, was still essentially confined to the world of leisure, entertainment, and relaxation. Greek festivals added to the range of Roman spectacles but they never seriously impinged on Rome's civic self-identity, except as a way of showing her place at the centre of a great empire, able to call upon new and exotic forms of entertainment. Similarly, while exercising in the Greek manner or decorating one's home with athletic statues could show one to be a man of the world, familiar with cosmopolitan culture or fully versed in the Greek heritage, if done with care it could also be fully compatible with one's Roman identity, a matter of absorbing what was best from the Greek world without losing the sense of Rome's own superior position in the imperial hierarchy. In the west, then, with the exception of towns like Naples or Marseilles, which had more of a vested interest in claiming a serious Greek identity, Greek athletics was primarily part of the world of entertainment and leisure, deeply popular, but never a crucial part of Roman identity.

Some of these characteristics were shared by the Greek world. Here too athletic contests in civic festivals were an important form of spectacle and entertainment, and classicizing statues may well have been chosen as much for their art-historical prestige as for ideological reasons, as indeed Lucian suggests.[1] The evidence of

---

[1] Lucian, *Lover of Lies* 18; see above, p. 123.

Dio's Oration *On Beauty* as well as a number of other texts also suggests that Greeks as well as Romans could appreciate the erotic attractions of young athletes and their statues.[2] Yet here athletics also seems to have played a deeper, more crucial, role in the formulation of both individual and civic senses of identity. While Romans could use Greek athletics as a sign of their knowledge of Greek culture, for the Greeks themselves that knowledge and appreciation was a crucial way of proving their claims to a true Greek identity. Such claims took on an increasing importance within the world of the Second Sophistic, where rhetoric and literature, as well as civic life, were saturated with references to the culture of the Greek past.[3]

In the second half of this book, I intend to explore the meanings which athletic activity had for the residents of the cities of the Greek east. I will concentrate in particular on the ways that it continued to play a crucial role in civic life, especially in constructing relationships with the past and with the traditions of Greek culture. Alongside the visual remains I will also consider the textual evidence relating to Greek athletics and the values and ideals with which athletic activity is associated there.[4] Whereas in Rome the elite literary evidence is usually hostile to athletic activity, though at the same time attesting to its popularity, the Greek texts clearly assert the central position which athletics held within Greek culture, although they could also sometimes question this position and contemporary sporting practice.

In the chapters that follow I will focus on three different aspects of athletics in the Greek east of the empire. I discuss firstly the role which athletics played within Greek education, particularly as manifested through Solon's words in the *Anacharsis* and in the visual monuments produced by the *ephēbeia* in Sparta and Athens. I will then turn to the importance of Olympia and athletic victory monuments in the construction of Greek civic identities, as revealed by Pausanias' discussion of Olympia and by the archaeological evidence. Finally, I will turn to contemporary euergetic practices in the Greek east, looking at the buildings and festivals set up by members of local elites and at the ways their decoration or commemoration in visual form asserted the values associated with athletic activity.

For any study of the role which athletic pursuits played within the formation and negotiation of Greek cultural identities in the Roman empire, Lucian's *Anacharsis* is a key text.[5] Framed as a pseudo-Platonic dialogue between the Athenian sage Solon and the wise barbarian Anacharsis, this ambiguous and amusing text presents us with Solon's defence of Greek athletics to the sceptical Scythian. The

---

[2] See above, pp. 126–9.   [3] For further discussion, see pp. 7–11.

[4] For a recent discussion, see König, *Athletics and Literature*. He concentrates on the variety of representations of athletics found in the literature, whereas I will be more concerned with the overlaps and continuities.

[5] See R. B. Branham, *Unruly Eloquence: Lucian and the Comedy of Traditions* (Cambridge, Mass., and London, 1989), 82–104; S. Goldhill, 'Introduction: Setting an Agenda: "Everything is Greece to the Wise" ', in id., *Being Greek*, 1–25 at 1–4; and König, 'Athletic Training', 97–117.

dialogue's fictional setting is sixth-century Athens, within the shady grounds of the Lyceum to which the pair retire when Anacharsis begins to tire of the heat of the sun.[6] Yet Solon's defence of athletics as playing a crucial role within the formation of good citizen soldiers and Anacharsis' rejection of his claims also have powerful resonances in the contemporary world of the mid-second century AD.[7]

The dialogue starts with Anacharsis questioning Solon about the unfamiliar activities he sees before him:

'Why then, Solon, do your young men do these things? Some of them are throwing each other down, clinging to them, while others are strangling and twisting and fastening themselves together, rolling in the mud like pigs.' (1)

After a long description of the different activities he sees, of pairs of youths grappling together in the mud or sand, and of others kicking or hitting one another while a man in a purple cloak urges them on, Anacharsis concludes with a question, 'So I want to know what good it can be to do this; since it seems to me more like madness' (5).

As Branham has shown in his sensitive analysis of this piece, the un-athletic vocabulary put into the mouth of Anacharsis presents traditional time-honoured pursuits of the Greek gymnasium, such as wrestling and the pancratium, as they might be seen through non-Greek eyes.[8] From this starting-point, a view of athletics as bizarre and irrational, seen through the uncomprehending eyes of a foreigner, we move on to Solon's explanation of these acts and the roles that they play within Greek culture, none of which appears ultimately to be accepted by Anacharsis. Scholars have sought to identify both Cynic and Epicurean ideas in this piece, and have argued over which figure, if either, presents the views of Lucian himself.[9] Yet Branham is surely right to point out that Lucian seems less concerned to argue for one particular view of Greek athletics (as a crucial component of traditional Greek culture or a ridiculous waste of energy) than to indicate, with a great deal of humour, the instability of cultural norms. The ways in which Lucian's dialogue engages with the different contemporary constructions of Hellenic identity have been well analysed by both Branham and König.[10] Yet Lucian's choice

[6] On this humorous reworking of the Platonic setting, see Goldhill, 'Introduction', 3.

[7] On Lucian's dates see J. Schwartz, *Biographie de Lucien de Samosata* (Brussels, 1965), 9–21, and C. P. Jones, *Culture and Society in Lucian* (Cambridge, Mass., 1986), 8. On the Anacharsis, see Schwartz, *Lucien de Samosata*, 47, and Jones, *Culture and Society*, 167.

[8] Branham, *Unruly Eloquence*, 88–90.

[9] R. Heinze, 'Anacharsis', *Philologus* 50 (1891), 458–68, and J. Bompaire, *Lucien Écrivain: Imitation et création* (Paris, 1958), 678–82, see Anacharsis as expressing Cynic views, while G. Anderson, *Lucian: Theme and Variation in the Second Sophistic* (Leiden, 1976), 114–16, suggests that Lucian himself shares the Cynics' disapproval of athletics. Jones, *Culture and Society*, 28, notes that the dialogue can also be seen as Epicurean. See J. F. Kindstrand, *Anacharsis: The Legend and the Apophthegmata* (Uppsala, 1981), especially 65–7, and Branham, *Unruly Eloquence*, 101, for further analysis of the debate.

[10] Branham, *Unruly Eloquence*, 89–91, 101–4; see also König, *Athletics and Literature*, ch. 2.

of athletics as the focus for his investigation into cultural values itself assumes and relies upon the central position which athletics still held within second-century Greek culture.[11] This status could be challenged, but it was also continually reasserted by the athletic activities that took place in gymnasia and stadia throughout the Greek world, and by the representation of these activities in inscriptions, statues, and reliefs.[12]

I want to concentrate here on the ways in which Solon's defence of athletics engages with the pursuits which were actually practised in the gymnasium at the time Lucian was writing. One area that Solon discusses at length is the place of athletics within the education of Athenian youths, a role which is likely to have had resonances with the *ephēbeia* as it was still practised and experienced within second-century Athens and other Greek cities. In order to explore these associations further, it is worth going through the dialogue in some detail.

As we have seen, it starts without an introductory framework, with an initially anonymous speaker questioning Solon over the bizarre activities he sees taking place before him, described in language which highlights their incomprehensibility to the speaker. It is only when Solon replies (6) that we learn that the questioner is the Scythian Anacharsis, renowned in Greek literature as a wise barbarian who came to Athens to learn of Greek customs.[13] Solon's initial response to Anacharsis' amazement is simply to declare that this is due to his ignorance of Greek customs, which he will soon come to understand and even to adopt. Anacharsis, unwilling to be brushed off so easily, disagrees and demands to be told more.

At this point Solon tells him that the place in which they stand is a gymnasium, dedicated to Apollo Lycius, and that the youths are competing in wrestling and the pancratium. Anacharsis asks what the prizes might be for victory in these (to his mind) shameful contests. At this point Solon brings in Panhellenic games, moving from the simple contests of the gymnasium which they are currently observing to those of prestigious international festivals—the *periodos* circuit of Olympia, Delphi, Isthmia, and Nemea, to which he adds, in a gesture of patriotism, the Panathenaea.[14] If Solon hoped that this allusion to the wider world of Greek festivals would reinforce his claim that athletics is both useful and pleasant (as at 6), however, he is sadly amiss. Anacharsis laughs at the prospect of competing for apples or a crown of parsley, and remains unconvinced by Solon's assertion that the

---

[11]   e.g. Branham, *Unruly Eloquence*, 101. See also Jones, *Culture and Society*, 28.

[12]   On challenges, see Branham, *Unruly Eloquence*, 86–8. The long-standing tradition of intellectual opposition to athletics is discussed by B. Bilinski, *L'agonistica sportiva nella Grecia antica: aspetti sociali e ispirazioni letterarie* (Rome, 1959), 74–87, and S. Müller, *Das Volk der Athleten: Untersuchungen zur Ideologie und Kritik des Sports in der griechisch-römischen Antike* (Trier, 1995).

[13]   See Kindstrand, *Anacharsis*, for full details of the traditions surrounding him.

[14]   In Lucian's own day the status of this festival had recently been elevated by Hadrian; see S. Follet, *Athènes au IIe et au IIIe siècle: Études chronologiques et prosopographiques* (Paris, 1976), 331.

real prize is not the crown itself but the reputation (*doxa*) which accompanies it. Indeed, to Solon's assertion that he will understand once he sees the crowds such contests attract (10), he replies that the fact that there are so many witnesses to such contests in fact makes them worse (11).

Having failed to convince Anacharsis of the attraction of athletic festivals, Solon seems to recognize that a fuller and more detailed exposition is needed (14). A true recognition of the worth of athletics lies within an overall picture of the best way to conduct a state, he says, the very matter in which Anacharsis declares himself to be primarily interested. Solon reveals that the true goal of athletic activity is not inconsequential prizes—indeed, he acknowledges that few of the youths so educated will indeed win success at Nemea or Olympia. Rather, what these exercises train one for is a competition whose prize is truly magnificent. This wreath, we are told, embodies 'all human happiness, by which I mean freedom for each man individually and for the state in general, wealth, reputation, enjoyment of ancestral feasts, safety for one's family and, in short, the best things which one might pray to receive from the gods' (15). Athletics, then, is made the bedrock of the entire Hellenic way of life.

Solon begins with an explanation of the Greek city, whose identity lies not in its buildings but its citizens (20). The education of these citizens is therefore of crucial importance for the well-being of the city, and all precautions are taken to ensure that they are both 'virtuous in soul and strong (*ischuroi*) in body'. He then explains the details of an Athenian education:

Then having received them (from their mothers and nurses) we teach them, setting lessons and exercises for their souls and in other ways accustoming their bodies to hardships (*tous ponous*). (20)

For the formation of their souls youths are taught reading, writing, music, and arithmetic, as well as the moral lessons of Homer and Hesiod.[15] Solon proposes to pass over the continuation of this moral instruction into adulthood but is encouraged to by Anacharsis' request. He explains how they learn the laws of the community through public inscriptions and are encouraged to converse with sophists and philosophers—a comment which must surely have had contemporary resonances for Lucian's readership! Finally, they learn from the comedies and tragedies performed in the theatre how to emulate virtue and avoid vice (22). Anacharsis, alas, is unimpressed, mocking the ridiculous clothing worn by comic and tragic actors and misinterpreting the reactions of the audience as showing scorn or pity for the actors themselves, rather than the deeds represented on stage.

Hurrying past Anacharsis' mockery of Greek drama, Solon turns to athletic training, the aims of which he sets out at length in 24–30. Chief among these is to

---

[15] On Greek education, see H. I. Marrou, *A History of Education in Antiquity*, trans. G. Lamb, 2nd edn. (London, 1977).

make youths' bodies strong and supple and to train them to receive blows and endure hardships. So, for example, training in boxing and the pancration is given 'so that they are accustomed to endure toils/hardships (*tous ponous karterein*) and to meet blows and not recoil for fear of injuries' (24). This training is explicitly said to train men for warfare. It gives them a stamina which is set in powerful contrast to the weak, pale bodies of those who have not trained in this way and therefore wilt in battle under the heat of the sun (a clear reference, of course, to Anacharsis himself, who has previously complained about the sun). While such training may give one added endurance, aesthetic motivations also seem to be at work here. The athlete's body is bronzed and lean, imbued with symmetry. They glow with good condition (*euexia*). These are not only effective, but also beautiful bodies.[16] Indeed, competitions in physical beauty appear to have been a regular part of ephebic and civic festivals, especially in the Hellenistic period. So we hear of contests in *euexia* (good condition) and *eutaxia* (good discipline) as well as *euandria* (manliness).[17] The precise nature of these contests is unclear, but they seem to have combined reward for good discipline with an appreciation of physical beauty. Indeed, Athenaeus explicitly describes the *euandria* as a contest in beauty.[18] Solon's description would seem to coincide with the ideal of the Hellenic gymnasium, where the well-trained, obedient body is also a beautiful one. It also evokes the well-proportioned bronze statues which were set up to successful athletes, creating a link between athletes and their statues which can also be seen in Dio Chrysostom's description of an athlete at Naples and in Philostratus' *Gymnasticus*.[19]

Solon, however, is keen to stress the usefulness of all athletic pursuits as a training for warfare. Jumping practice helps when one needs to jump over ditches, training in throwing the javelin and the discus have a direct military link, and wrestling whilst covered in mud helps prepare one for the need to carry the body of a wounded friend off the battlefield (27–8). While some of these claims are exaggerated for comic effect, Solon's aim is clear—to prove his argument that athletic

---

[16] See also *Anacharsis* 29, where Solon again praises the appearance of the athletes.

[17] e.g. *IG* ii². 2311, l. 75 (the *euandria* at the Panathenaic games) and *SEG* 27.261, ll. 45–8 (Contests in *euexia*, *eutaxia*, and *philoponia* held during the Hermaia festival in the gymnasium at Beroea, Macedonia). The evidence is discussed by N. B. Crowther, 'Male "Beauty" Contests in Greece', *AC* 54 (1985), 285–91, and id., 'Euexia, Eutaxia, Philoponia: Three Contests of the Greek Gymnasium', *ZPE* 85 (1991), 301–4. On the *euandria* at Athens, see also N. B. Reed, 'The *Euandria* Competition Reconsidered', *Ancient World* 15 (1987), 59–64; J. Neils, 'The Panathenaia and Kleisthenic Ideology', in W. D. E. Coulson, O. Palagia, T. L. Shear Jr., H. A. Shapiro, and F. J. Frost, eds., *The Archaeology of Athens and Attica under the Democracy* (Oxford, 1994), 151–60; A. L. Boegehold, 'Group and Single Competitions at the Panathenaia', in J. Neils, ed., *Worshipping Athena: Panathenaia and Parthenon* (Madison, Wis., 1996), 95–105, at 97–103; N. Fisher, 'Gymnasia and the Democratic Values of Leisure', in P. Cartledge, P. Millett, and S. von Reden, eds., *Kosmos: Essays in Order, Conflict, and Community in Classical Athens* (Cambridge, 1998), 84–104, at 90–3; and P. Wilson, *The Athenian Institution of the Khoregia: The Chorus, the City and the Stage* (Cambridge, 2000), 38.

[18] Athenaeus 13.565f–566a.

[19] Dio Chrysostom, *Oration* 28.3; Philostratus, *Gymnasticus* 35; discussed above, pp. 127–8.

training plays a crucial role in preparing the city's youth to become 'noble guardians of the city' and protectors of its freedom (*eleutheria*) (30). Despite this long and ingenious exegesis, Anacharsis remains unconvinced, pointing out that naked bodies are no defence against weapons and dismissing athletic exercises as childish amusements. He suggests that Athens has fallen into such a state of peace that it is no longer capable of resisting any serious military attack (31–3).

Anacharsis' rejection of Solon's link between athletics and warfare may well have contemporary significance, evoking traditional Roman claims that the gymnasium in fact induces weakness and effeminacy rather than military strength.[20] On the one hand, then, Anacharsis seems to represent a sceptical voice, pointing out the irrelevance of this training in late sixth-century BC Athens, and, by inference, the province of Achaia in the *pax romana* of the second century.[21] In contrast to this, Solon's determined assertion of this link might also tap into contemporary claims about the continued relevance of traditional forms of education, and particularly the athletic training in the gymnasium, even within the generally peaceful circumstances of the second century. While Anacharsis suggests that such pursuits are pointless, Solon's claims may instead have found an echo in the ideological significance which an ephebic education continued to have in the Roman period.

One example of this continuing relevance can be seen in Pausanias' description of the Achaean town of Pellene.[22] He tells us that no one may be enrolled as a citizen here until he has first served as an ephebe. These ephebes train in the ancient gymnasium at Pellene, where Pausanias also sees a stone statue of the Olympic victor Promachus whose victories took place in the late fifth century BC.[23] As well as being a successful athlete, with victories in the pancratium at Olympia, Isthmia, and Nemea, Promachus was also a military figure. His defeat of numerous enemies in battle during a war with Corinth is paired with his athletic defeat of the famous athlete Polydamas of Scotoussa. For Pausanias, Promachus' athletic and military successes go together, and his example continues to stand before the ephebes of the second century through the statue in their training ground. The idea that Promachus' statue here stands as an incitement to emulation is reinforced by Pausanias' discussion of the Olympic wrestler Chaeron in the following passage. This athlete was even more successful than Promachus at the Olympics, winning four victories to Promachus' one. However, Pausanias tells us that the Pelleneans will not even mention his name, a slur he attributes to the fact that Chaeron had overthrown the city's constitution and, in the reign of Alexander the Great, set himself up as tyrant of the city.[24]

---

[20] See above, p. 40.   [21] See König, 'Athletic Training', 112–13.   [22] Pausanias 7.27.5–7.
[23] Pausanias 7.27.5. See Moretti, *Olympionikai*, 111, no. 355, 404 BC.
[24] 7.27.7–8. On the links between athletic victory and tyranny in the Archaic and early Classical periods, see C. Mann, *Athlet und Polis im archaischen und frühklassischen Griechenland* (Göttingen, 2001), 64–9 and *passim*.

Much of Pausanias' discussion here can be paralleled with his attitudes to Greek freedom and the link between athletic and military victories expressed elsewhere within the work.[25] Yet it also finds echoes in the ideas expressed by Solon in Lucian's *Anacharsis*, a work probably written a decade or so earlier than Pausanias' *Description of Greece*.[26] For both, athletics is part of the traditional education of good citizens. For Solon, these citizens are precisely trained to protect the city, to preserve its freedom (*eleutheria*). No wonder, then, that by becoming tyrant of his own city Chaeron has forfeited his claims to be honoured as a victorious athlete and a suitable role model for the city's youth. It is instead the patriotic Promachus, who fights to protect his city from a neighbour, as well as winning her prestige through his athletic victories, whose statue inspires the youth of the Roman period. This correspondence in ideas found in the works of Lucian and Pausanias suggests that Solon's view of the role of athletics in the Athenian educational system may have found a number of adherents in second-century Greece. While ideas about the link between athletics and warfare may well have seemed anachronistic to some in the world of the *pax romana*, where cities had forfeited their claims to independent military policy, their ideological power was still alive and kicking.

In the rest of this chapter and the next, I propose to look at how the ideological associations of the Greek *ephēbeia* in mainland Greece were represented in the visual arts of the second and early third centuries. As my analysis of Pausanias suggests, the setting of ephebic activities often within ancient buildings and before honorific statues of famous predecessors must have created an awareness of the continuity between the *ephēbeia* as practised in Roman times and the classical past. Here I shall concentrate on the ephebic rituals at Sparta, which have been well discussed in Kennell's recent book, as well as the rather lesser known but equally interesting evidence of the *ephēbeia* at Athens in the Imperial period, discussed in Chapter 6.[27] For both cities, I will suggest, the *ephēbeia* was one of the key ways in which to assert the continuing importance of traditional Hellenic values within the Roman empire.

SPARTAN STRENGTHS: THE *AGŌGĒ* AND ITS CONTESTS

Solon's defence of athletic pursuits to Anacharsis ends on a strange note. After failing to convince the Scythian that unarmed exercises in the gymnasium are indeed a good training for war, Solon deals again, briefly, with the question of athletic festivals, arguing that they encourage their spectators towards athletic

---

[25] See discussion in Chapter 7.

[26] For the dates of these works (*Anacharsis* mid-second century, Pausanias *c.* 160–80) see n. 7 above and Ch. 7, n. 1.

[27] N. M. Kennell, *The Gymnasium of Virtue: Education and Culture in Ancient Sparta* (Chapel Hill, 1995).

pursuits and the love of glory (36). He rejects Anacharsis' suggestion that youths should be tested in armed combat with one another as brutal and unprofitable, but he turns to a practice which seems equally useless to Anacharsis—the violent contests of the Spartan *agōgē*.[28] So he warns Anacharsis not to laugh if he visits Sparta and witnesses the contests of its distinctive educational system. Here Anacharsis can expect to see ball games in the theatre, team games between 'Heraclids' and 'Lycurgids' on an island, and, above all, the famous whipping contest at the altar of Artemis Orthia. During this, Spartan youths are urged to endure the strokes of the whip as long as possible, to the extent that, Solon claims, some have even died rather than give in (38). Solon's attitude to the Spartan whipping contest is confusing and ambiguous. He proffers it to Anacharsis as an example of a practice which he should accept rather than mock, since, he claims, Lycurgus instituted such contests to inculcate courage and endurance. Yet when Anacharsis asks why the Athenians themselves do not copy this admirable practice Solon can only weakly reply that they prefer their own traditions (39). As Branham suggests, the overriding effect of the dialogue as a whole is not to argue in favour of one or other side of the question, but rather to create humour out of the mismatch between figures with different cultural backgrounds.[29]

Yet while the dialogue as a whole questions cultural norms—the alleged links between the activities of the gymnasium, Panhellenic victories, military prowess and Hellenic freedom—Solon himself appears firmly convinced of these, albeit unable to fully explain them to Anacharsis. For him, an athletic education as practised at Sparta or Athens lies at the heart of the Greek way of life. Two themes which consistently reappear in his defence of athletics are freedom and endurance. It is athletics which develops the military skills to preserve Greek freedom and independence (30) and it is contests such as those at Sparta which give youths the power to endure all manner of privations. In Solon's account we repeatedly find phrases suggesting the link between athletics and endurance. So, boxing and the pancratium encourage youths 'to endure toils/hardships' (*tous ponous karterein*, 24) while later the same terminology reappears in relation to the whipping contest, when the boys' parents urge them 'to hold out against the toil as long as possible and to endure the sufferings' (38). Indeed the notorious contest at Sparta, which is named in some sources as 'the flagellation' (*diamastigōsis*), also seems to have been known as 'the endurance contest' (*agōn tēs karterias*).[30]

[28] Anacharsis' suggestion may have evoked thoughts of gladiatorial games, which were popular in Roman Athens and are often attacked by Greek intellectuals; see Dio Chrysostom, *Oration* 31.131, and Philostratus, *Life of Apollonius of Tyana* 4.22.

[29] Branham, *Unruly Eloquence*, 101–4.

[30] *Diamastigōsis*: [Plutarch] *Laconian Institutions* 40.239d; Tertullian, *Ad Martyras* 4.8. *Agōn tēs karterias*: Philostratus, *Life of Apollonius of Tyana* 6.20. On the naming of the contest, see Kennell, *Gymnasium of Virtue*, 26.

For Lucian's Solon, the chief contest in the Spartan educational system is the whipping contest, where powers of endurance are tested to the utmost degree. Solon claims that some prefer to die rather than admit defeat and that Anacharsis would be able to see the honours given to the statues set up to them at public expense. The statues commemorate their victories, acting as prizes as well as a focus for cultic honours in the same way that statues erected to victorious athletes also often invited cultic attention.[31] To our eyes the whipping contest might seem to have very little to do with athletics, yet a detailed look at the ways in which the ritual is treated in literary texts suggests that it was regarded as the ultimate test of athletic courage.

The literary sources, and particularly the detailed accounts given by Lucian, Pausanias, and Philostratus, allow us to draw up a detailed picture of the scene.[32] A row of boys line up before the Altar of Artemis Orthia with their hands above their heads, waiting to be whipped so that the blood from their wounds drips onto the Altar itself. For some of our sources the religious implications of the ritual seem dominant. Both Pausanias and Philostratus describe the contest as an amelioration of the earlier practice of human sacrifice to the bloodthirsty Artemis Orthia, a goddess imported to Greece from Scythia.[33] Yet, while the goddess demands the sacrifice of blood on her altar, this is also shown as being accomplished within the framework and ideals of the Spartan educational system, as a further way to encourage Spartan youths to develop powers of endurance. In fact, it now seems certain that the ritual as practised in the Roman period was almost entirely invention, while being presented and exalted as proof of the continuity of traditional Spartan values.[34]

While Pausanias and Apollonius describe the whipping ritual's religious aspects, for Lucian's Solon, these are completely ignored. It is grouped instead with other examples of the contests that took place in the Spartan educational system as simply the most extreme example in a system of education that produces strong, hardened, courageous bodies. For Philostratus too, elsewhere, the whipping contest is firmly associated with athletic pursuits. In the *Gymnasticus*, a treatise that attempts to draw together contemporary athletic training with its traditional place in Greek culture, Philostratus ends, like Lucian, with the whipping ritual. After discussion of the Spartan custom of training in boxing and the pancratium he continues as follows:

---

[31] See discussion below, pp. 224–6.

[32] The testimonia are collected by Kennell, *Gymnasium of Virtue*, 149–61, and discussed at 70–83.

[33] Pausanias 3.16.10; Philostratus, *Life of Apollonius of Tyana* 6.20. For a discussion of the power of the cult image in Pausanias' passage see J. Elsner, 'Image and Ritual: Reflections on the Religious Appreciation of Classical Art', *Classical Quarterly* 46 (1996), 515–31, at 524–5.

[34] See P. Cartledge and A. Spawforth, *Hellenistic and Roman Sparta: A Tale of Two Cities* (London, 1989), 207; and especially Kennell, *Gymnasium of Virtue*, 78–84.

They say that the Spartans themselves exercise in this way, not for the sake of competition but only for endurance, which is a quality of those who are going to be whipped, since the law is for them to be lacerated on the altar.   (*Gym.* 58)[35]

While much of the rest of the treatise has been concerned to outline the history of various athletic contests, and the best ways of training athletes for these, Philostratus ends with our focus on the Spartan altar. This might seem strange to a modern reader, but when viewed in the light of other writings about athletics and endurance it makes sense. The endurance contest at Sparta is the ultimate test of athletic training, a training that fitted the body to endure physical pain in the hope of renown.

The violence of the whipping contest is emphasized in many of these passages, as is the danger of death. Kennell has suggested that few, if any, boys actually did die, yet the possibility that they might do is clearly important.[36] Both Cicero and Plutarch refer to boys being whipped 'to the point of death' while Lucian's Solon explicitly says that some actually have died.[37] The idea that boys could be led by their courage and love of renown to die rather than admit defeat finds a number of parallels in stories about famous athletes. One notorious example is an athlete from Phigalia in Arcadia whose story is told by both Pausanias and Philostratus. This man, named Arrachion by Pausanias and Arrichion by Philostratus, was a pancratiast of the sixth century BC. Pausanias tells his story after seeing a stone statue of the athlete in the agora of Phigalia, which Frazer sought to identify with an archaic kouros statue found in the area and seen by him in 1890.[38] After two previous Olympic victories Arrachion was competing at Olympia in the fifty-fourth festival (564 BC) in the pancratium. While being held around the neck by his opponent, Arrachion managed to dislocate his opponent's toe, forcing him by the pain to admit defeat at the very moment that he himself expired. He was thus declared the victor.

Philostratus too tells the story in both the *Gymnasticus* and the *Imagines*.[39] In the *Gymnasticus* it is told as part of a series of anecdotes about the role of athletic trainers in encouraging their athletes. So, we are told, Arrichion was just at the point of giving up in the contest when his trainer Erucias spurred him on by shouting. 'How great a funeral honour not to have given up at Olympia' (21). Philostratus tells the stories of other trainers of famous athletes, including Promachus of Pellene, before ending with an example from his own time. 'I myself heard of the

---

[35] Trans. Kennell, *Gymnasium of Virtue*, 158.   [36] Ibid., 73–4.

[37] Cicero, *Tusculan Disputations* 2.34; Plutarch, *Life of Lycurgus* 18.2; Lucian, *Anacharsis* 38.

[38] Pausanias 8.40.1–2. J. G. Frazer, *Pausanias's Description of Greece* (London, 1898), iii. 40–1 (on 2.5.4) and iv. 391–2 (on 8.40.1); Hyde, *OVM*, 326–8. The statue is now in the Olympia museum.

[39] Philostratus, *Gymnasticus* 21, Philostratus the Elder, *Imagines* 2.7.5. Though it is impossible to say for certain that these two works are by the same author it seems likely to me that they are. On the question of authorship see the bibliography collected on p. 75, n. 115.

endurance (*karterian*) of Mandrogenes the Magnesian, which served him in his youth in the pancratium, and which he attributed to his trainer.[40] This man had apparently written to the athlete's mother telling her to believe it if she received reports that her son was dead, but not to believe any reports that he had been defeated. On learning this Mandrogenes was filled with the courage to ensure that his trainer should not be proved a liar or his mother be deceived (23). The reference to the athlete's mother resonates with accounts of the Spartan whipping contest, where we are explicitly told that parents urge their sons on to endurance, preferring them to die in victory than live in defeat.[41] The acts of figures like Mandrogenes and the Spartan youths proclaim the possibility that the courage and endurance possessed by figures from the past could still be found in the contemporary world.

Violence and the risk of death are clearly shown in these sources to be integral parts of Greek athletics. Indeed, Pausanias follows his discussion of Arrachion with the story of the boxer Creugas, who was awarded victory at the Nemean games after his opponent Damoxenus killed him by piercing his ribs and pulling out his entrails.[42] Such stories prove the lie to modern idealists who wish to see the Greek games as honourable, fair competitions in contrast to the bloody violence of the Roman gladiatorial contests.[43] While Greek intellectuals too could attack the violence of the amphitheatre, stories such as these suggest that violence and danger could also be seen as an inherent element of Greek athletics even from earliest periods.

This aspect of athletic training certainly seems to have found full expression in the contests which took place at Sparta. Solon's description of these at the end of the *Anacharsis* suggests their violence. As well as the endurance contest itself, he mentions two other contests:

Do not think they are exerting themselves in vain when rushing together they strike one another in the theatre over a ball or, going away into a place surrounded by water, divided into companies, they treat one another as enemies, naked like these are, until one lot drive the other contingent out of the enclosure, either the Heraclids driving the Lycurgans or the opposite, pushing them into the water.   (38)

This contest is also described by Pausanias in his account of the area known as the Platanistas:[44]

---

[40] He can be identified with L. Silcius Firmus Mandrogenes of Magnesia on the Maeander who is named in a Magnesian inscription as a circuit victor (*periodonikēs*) in the pancratium (*Inschriften von Magnesia* 199). Moretti, *Olympionikai*, 171, no. 912, tentatively places his Olympic victory in AD 213.

[41] Lucian, *Anacharsis* 38; Seneca the younger, *De providentia* 4.11; Statius, *Thebaid* 4.231–3.

[42] Pausanias 8.40.3–5. Damoxenus forfeited his victory because of cheating, rather than his violence.

[43] e.g. E. N. Gardiner, *Athletics of the Ancient World* (Oxford, 1930), 49.

[44] On this contest, see Cartledge and Spawforth, *Hellenistic and Roman Sparta*, 205, and Kennell, *Gymnasium of Virtue*, 55–9.

There is a place called Platanistas from the unbroken ring of tall plane trees growing round it. The place itself, where it is customary for the ephebes to fight, is surrounded by a moat just like an island in the sea; you enter it by bridges. On each of the two bridges stand images; on one side an image of Heracles, on the other a likeness of Lycurgus. Among the laws Lycurgus laid down for the constitution are those regulating the battle of the ephebes . . . Before the battle they sacrifice in the Phoebaeum which is outside the city, not far distant from Therapne. Here each company sacrifices a puppy to Enyalius . . . At the sacrifice the ephebes set trained boars to fight; the company whose boar wins generally gains the victory in the Platanistas. Such are the performances in the Phoebaeum. A little before the middle of the next day they enter by the bridges into the place I have mentioned. They cast lots during the night to decide by which entrance each band is to go in. In fighting they use their hands, kick with their feet, bite, and gouge out the eyes of their opponents. Man to man they fight in the way I have described, but in the melee they charge violently and push one another into the water.   (3.14.8–10)[45]

This account stresses the violence of the encounter. While without arms, the ephebes use all their natural weapons, including teeth and nails, to defeat their opponents. If we see this in athletic terms, it sounds as though they are practising the most extreme form of the pancratium in this contest. In his description of the painting of Arrichion in *Imagines* 2.6, Philostratus describes this contest: 'for these things are all permissible in the pancratium—anything except biting and gouging. The Lacedaemonians, indeed, allow even these, because, I suppose, they are train-ing themselves for battle' (2.6.3). In the *Gymnasticus* too we repeatedly hear of how the Spartans use athletic techniques for warlike ends, resorting to the pancratium when they lost their weapons at Thermopylae (11), and requiring their athletic trainers to teach skills for war (20). In his description of the contest at the Platanistas Pausanias repeatedly uses the words for battle (*machē*) and fighting (*machomai*).[46] Through this battle, then, the ephebes reveal themselves to be the rightful heirs of Sparta's warlike past.

Indeed, ephebic education in general, as well as the whole Spartan way of life, seems always to have been associated with training for warfare. Some scholars have suggested that ephebic education gradually lost its military purpose during the Hellenistic and Roman periods, when professional armies were developed and individual cities had little scope for independent military policy.[47] However, while involvement in the *ephēbeia* does seem, by the Roman period, to have become primarily a matter for elite youths rather than all young male citizens, there is powerful evidence that its military connotations still played an important part. We

---

[45] Trans. Jones (Loeb edition) with some changes.

[46] On the parallel use of athletic terminology to describe warfare, see T. F. Scanlon, 'Combat and Contest: Athletic Metaphors for Warfare in Greek Literature', in S. J. Bandy, ed., *Coroebus Triumphs: The Alliance of Sport and the Arts* (San Diego, 1988), 230–44.

[47] A. Dumont, *L'Essai sur l'éphébie attique* (Paris, 1876), 36, 234–9; Marrou, *A History of Education*, 107–8.

have already seen the link between athletics and warfare expressed by Solon in the *Anacharsis*. The visual and epigraphic evidence discussed here and in the next chapter also suggests that the military associations of ephebic education remained strong.[48]

We have evidence that soldiers from Greek cities did indeed take part in some military activities during this period.[49] Herodian tells us that troops from both Macedonia and Sparta took part in Caracalla's campaign against the Parthians in AD 214–17.[50] The Spartan contingent was called the 'Pitanate lochos', a term which clearly recalls Herodotus' account of the Persian war, but also had resonances with the ephebic divisions into which Spartan ephebes were organized.[51] The tombstone of one of these soldiers was found at Sparta. Its inscription proudly proclaims that he had fought 'against the Persians' and it shows the deceased dressed in military costume.[52] The Spartans had also taken part in the earlier Parthian campaign led by Lucius Verus in 163–6.[53] As Spawforth has argued, it was clearly important to maintain the image of Roman Sparta as a worthy heir to her classical past.[54] The violent contests of the *agōgē*, and the knowledge that ex-ephebes could indeed fulfil this training by taking part in military activities, were one way of proving this.

When seen in this climate, the battle of the ephebes at the Platanistas continually reasserts the traditional warlike nature of the Spartans, denying claims that they have sunk into luxury. Such accusations were common in the contemporary world. After a passage in the *Gymnasticus* where he asserts the ancient connection between athletics and warfare, Philostratus attacks the later slide into luxury: 'After that things changed. They became unwarlike rather than warlike, lazy after active, self-indulgent instead of austere' (44). A century or so earlier, too, Dio Chrysostom lamented the sight of a gymnasium turned into a cornfield in Euboea.[55] As Alcock has shown, these complaints fit into a rhetoric of decline which bemoans the extent to which Greece has fallen from her erstwhile heights.[56] Yet at the same time this is paired with a struggle to return her to those heights, to re-experience the cultural

---

[48] Indeed Nigel Kennell suggests that military training continued to play a crucial part in the Roman *ephēbeia* with ex-ephebes acting as a form of civic police force. I am very grateful to him for sharing with me his ideas, which will be presented in a forthcoming book on the *ephēbeia* in the Hellenistic and Roman periods.

[49] In addition to the discussion below, see C. P. Jones, 'The Levy at Thespiae under Marcus Aurelius', *Greek, Roman and Byzantine Studies* 12 (1971), 45–8.

[50] Herodian 4.8.3. See A. J. S. Spawforth, 'Notes on the Third Century AD in Spartan Epigraphy', *ABSA* 79 (1984), 263–88, esp. 267–9.

[51] Herodotus 9.53. See Cartledge and Spawforth, *Hellenistic and Roman Sparta*, 118, and Kennell, *Gymnasium of Virtue*, 95.

[52] Spawforth, 'Notes', 268–9; P. Wolters, 'Ein Denkmal der Partherkriege', *AthMitt* 28 (1903), 291–300, with drawing.

[53] Cartledge and Spawforth, *Hellenistic and Roman Sparta*, 115.

[54] Ibid., 115–19, 190–211.   [55] Dio Chrysostom, *Oration* 7.38–9.

[56] S. E. Alcock, *Graecia Capta: The Landscapes of Roman Greece* (Cambridge, 1993), 24–32.

greatness of Greece. This is the professed aim of Philostratus in the *Gymnasticus*, a work which seeks to reassert the value of traditional athletic training and continually tries to revive the greatness of the past in the present.[57] It is also the aim of Apollonius in Philostratus' recreation of his life.[58]

Indeed, in this work Apollonius is expressly credited with helping to re-establish ancestral values in Sparta.[59] While travelling to Olympia, the sage was met by some Spartan envoys who asked him to visit their city. Noting their un-Spartan effeminate appearance—smooth legs, sleek hair, and no beards—he sent a letter to the Ephors urging them to forbid hot baths and depilation and restore the ancient regime. Upon this, we are told, the palaestrae were again frequented, common meals resumed, and 'Lacedaemon became like herself' (4.27). Since Philostratus is describing the activities of a man who had lived over one hundred years before, this story has a nice twist. For the third-century visitor to Sparta, who could see all around him evidence of the enduring impact of the Lycurgan customs, particularly in events such as the whipping contest, the present reality serves as living proof of Apollonius' impact on the city.

The archaism of these rituals, expressly shown by Apollonius' command to restore 'the ancient customs' (*to archaion*), can also be seen in the epigraphical record. Excavations in the Sanctuary of Artemis Orthia to the east of the city at the start of the twentieth century revealed a number of votive dedications incorporated into the foundations of the third-century theatre built here to accommodate spectators to the rituals (Fig. 5.1).[60] These commemorate the victories of Spartan ephebes in various contests associated with the *agōgē*, such as the *mōa* and *keloia*, both musical contests, and the *katthēratorion*, probably a type of hunting dance.[61] The dedications take the form of a stele, usually with a pediment and acroteria above, and with an inset where a bronze sickle, the prize for victory, would have been inserted. Sometimes other symbols of victory are also depicted, such as a crown or palm branch (Fig. 5.2).[62] The inscriptions are fairly brief, identifying the victor, his ephebic position, and his contest. The date of the victory is given according to the presiding official (*patronomos*) and the inscription ends with the victor's dedication of his sickle to Artemis Orthia.

---

[57] See discussion above, pp. 75–6.

[58] A number of recent studies have shown that Philostratus adjusts the biographical tradition to present Apollonius as the embodiment of his own Hellenic values. See especially J. J. Flintermann, *Power, Paideia and Pythagoreanism* (Amsterdam, 1995), which builds on E. L. Bowie, 'Apollonios of Tyana: Tradition and Reality', *ANRW* II.16.2 (Berlin and New York, 1978), 1652–99. J. Elsner, 'Hagiographic Geography: Travel and Allegory in the *Life of Apollonius of Tyana*', *JHS* 117 (1997), 22–37, discusses the importance of religion in this portrayal. Most recently see S. Swain, 'Defending Hellenism: Philostratus, *In Honour of Apollonius*', in M. Edwards, M. Goodman, and S. Price, eds., *Apologetics in the Roman Empire* (Oxford, 1999), 157–96.

[59] Also discussed in Cartledge and Spawforth, *Hellenistic and Roman Sparta*, 106–7.

[60] They are collected in A. M. Woodward, 'Inscriptions', in R. M. Dawkins, ed., *The Sanctuary of Artemis Orthia at Sparta* (London, 1929), 285–377.

[61] Kennell, *Gymnasium of Virtue*, 51–5.   [62] Woodward, 'Inscriptions', 324, no. 51.

FIGURE 5.1 View of the Sanctuary of Artemis Orthia, Sparta, from the south. This shows the view from the foundations of the third-century AD Roman theatre towards the temple, with the altar where the whipping contest took place in the foreground.

While a couple of earlier dedications have been found, the majority date to the Roman period, especially the second century AD.[63] On a number of these, mostly dating between 130 and the early third century, we find an archaizing Laconian dialect replacing the usual *koinē*. The unfamiliar words, different to those which we find on other civic inscriptions, would have been an instant visual sign of the antiquity of the rituals commemorated here (Fig. 5.3).[64] The stelae usually have a protruding section at the base, for insertion into a base. They would have been crowded around the Sanctuary of Artemis Orthia before they were reused in the third century in the building of the theatre. This then provided a more permanent structure to accommodate the crowds who came to view the whipping ritual taking place at the altar before them.[65]

Only one of the stelae found mentions this ritual, called, as in the *Life of Apollonius*, the *agōn karterias*, though Woodward suggested that three earlier stelae

[63] Woodward, 'Inscriptions', 292–3.

[64] Ibid., 323–4, no. 50. See Kennell, *Gymnasium of Virtue*, 87–9, for a full account, from which this is drawn. The most notable features are the replacement of a final sigma by rho and the elimination of the intervocal sigma. Thus we find *neikaar* instead of *nikēsas*, *Ioulir* instead of *Ioulios*, etc.

[65] On the theatre, see R. M. Dawkins, 'The Sanctuary', in id., ed., *The Sanctuary of Artemis Orthia at Sparta* (London, 1929), 1–51, at 36–49.

FIGURE 5.2 Sickle dedications set up in the sanctuary of Artemis Orthia at Sparta recorded the victories of the ephebes. This one has an inset where the sickle awarded as a prize would have been fixed, and is incised with a crown and palm, proclaiming the idea of victory. Found built into the third-century theatre, Sanctuary of Artemis Orthia, Sparta. H: 0.65m. *c*.150 AD. *IG* v. 1. 293.

mentioning the *eubalkēs* might also refer to this contest.[66] It seems likely that the majority of the victors in the whipping contests were rewarded instead with the greater honour of a public statue, as indeed Lucian suggests.[67] Three statue bases have been found, again built into the theatre foundations (Fig. 5.4). While granted by the city, they often appear to have been funded by a family member or member of the victor's own ephebic tribe.[68] On these the victor is referred to as 'altar victor'

---

[66] Woodward, 'Inscriptions', 316–17, no. 37. The others are nos. 16, 18, and 84, discussed on pp. 288–9.

[67] *Anacharsis* 38.

[68] Woodward, 'Inscriptions', no. 142 (*IG* v. i. 653a): funded by the victor's bouagoi (team leaders); no. 143 (*IG* v. i. 653b, Fig. 5.4 here): funded by the bouagos' mother; no. 144: funded by victor's brother.

FIGURE 5.3
The archaizing Laconian
dialect used on this
sickle dedication
immediately asserted
the supposed antiquity
of the contests it
commemorates. Found
built into the third-
century theatre,
Sanctuary of Artemis
Orthia, Sparta.
H: 0.54m. *c.*150 AD.
IG v. 1. 292.

(*bōmoneikēn*)[69] or 'having endured illustriously' (*epiphanōr kartereanta*)[70] and is praised for his courage (*andreias charin*).[71] Another base in Sparta Museum, whose provenance is not recorded, was set up by the victor's brothers (Fig. 5.5). It reads as follows:

[The Polis honours] Epigonus son of Philostratus, altar victor, for the sake of his courage. His brothers Phoibion and Epictetes bore the cost.   (*IG* v. 1. 652)

---

[69] Woodward, 'Inscriptions', no. 143 (*IG* v. i. 653b); 144.
[70] Ibid., no. 142 (*IG* v. i. 653a), in the Laconian dialect.   [71] Ibid., no. 143 (*IG* v. i. 653b).

FIGURE 5.4 Altar victors could be honoured with a public statue set up in the sanctuary itself as well as elsewhere around the city, showing the importance of the Spartan *agōgē*, and especially the whipping contest, in the Roman period. This statue base, now partially buried, bears an inscription informing us that the statue was dedicated by the city to the altar victor Marcus Aurelius Cleonymus. Total height: 1.45m. Early third century AD. *IG* v. 1. 653b.

While the bronze statues which decorated these bases are long lost, the cuttings on this particular base suggest that the victor was shown standing in a relaxed position with his left foot slightly forward. He shares this pose with a number of honorific statues where the honorand is often clothed in a chiton and himation.[72] While we cannot tell whether the statue which was placed here was clothed or naked, it does seem to have shown the victor standing at ease rather than in any sort of 'action'

[72] On the conventions of honorific portrait statues, see R. R. R. Smith, 'Cultural Choice and Political Identity in Honorific Portrait Statues in the Greek East in the Second Century AD', *JRS* 88 (1998), 56–93, esp. 65–8.

FIGURE 5.5 This marble base bore a statue of the altar victor Epigonus, who is praised here for his courage. The statue seems to have been shown standing in a relaxed pose. W: 0.48m. *IG* v. 1. 652.

pose. In addition to those set up at the sanctuary itself, other statues were probably set up around the city in sites such as the agora and theatre.

From all these scattered pieces of evidence we can draw up a partial picture of the visual scene in Sparta at the time of ephebic festivals. These dominated the city from east to west, taking place in the Sanctuary of Artemis Orthia, the city's theatre and the Platanistas. The Sanctuary of Artemis Orthia with its long altar running in front of the Doric temple must have been surrounded with honorific stelae, bristling with the sickles won by victorious ephebes. Even before the rearrangement of the sanctuary in the third century there seems to have been some honorific seating to accommodate those who came to watch the rituals of the Spartan *agōgē*.[73] Later dedications probably also replaced those reused in the construction of the theatre here. The link to the past, visually expressed by the archaic dialect on some of the stelae, was also continually reasserted through Sparta's own distinctive contests, and the traditional hardiness of her people reinforced by the crowds of proud parents urging on their sons to greater feats of endurance. These feats were then also publicly declared through honorific statues set up around the city.

[73] Dawkins, 'Sanctuary', 36–7, fig. 20.

Other contests, such as the ball game in the city's theatre and the battle fought at the Platanistas, again presented the hardy products of Sparta's distinctive educational system to public view. In many of these contests, such as the ball game and the whipping contest, the ephebes were divided into teams called *obae*, named according to the ancient wards of Sparta—Mesoa, Pitane, Limnae, Cynosura, and Neopolitae.[74] Non-Spartans were occasionally admitted to the Spartan *agōgē*, such as the Athenian Tib. Claudius Atticus Herodes, and his son, the famous sophist Herodes Atticus.[75] Yet despite this, a strong link with Sparta's own land and people was preserved through these divisions. In the battle at the Platanistas two teams, probably those who had survived a number of heats, were set against one another. They were linked with either Heracles or Lycurgus, the legendary founder of the Spartan constitution, each team entering the battle ground by a bridge on which a statue of their patron was placed. Heracles also appears elsewhere in Sparta as a patron for ephebic contests. According to Pausanias there was an ancient statue of the hero placed on the Dromos (racecourse) where the teams in the ball game were accustomed to sacrifice.[76] Throughout the Greek world we find Heracles appearing in contexts associated with athletics and the gymnasium, therefore his appearance here comes as no surprise. However, the fact that he is given equal status with Lycurgus in the Platanistas grove suggests a Spartan appropriation of him, to make him particularly associated with their own brand of athletic toughness. Indeed, Heracles was particularly renowned for his success in heavy athletics—credited with winning both the wrestling and pancratium on the same day at Olympia, with the result that all athletes who achieved the same result subsequently gained the title 'After Heracles' (*ho aph' Heracleous*).[77] He was therefore a particularly appropriate choice as a role-model for athletes trained to endure violent combat sports.

As well as the statues of the hero which Pausanias describes seeing on the Dromos and the Platanistas at Sparta, a number of hip herms of the hero have also been found in this same general area to the west of the Acropolis (Fig. 5.6). They were found during the excavation of a bath complex in the early twentieth century where they had been reused in a later wall.[78] Stylistically dated to the Severan period, these show half-length figures of a bearded Heracles draped in a mantle and holding his lionskin and club. Seven herms exist in total, the majority coming from the baths or the surrounding fields, though one was found behind the stage of the

[74] Cartledge and Spawforth, *Hellenistic and Roman Sparta*, 203; Kennell, *Gymnasium of Virtue*, 40–1.

[75] See A. J. S. Spawforth, 'Sparta and the Family of Herodes Atticus: A Reconsideration of the Evidence', *ABSA* 75 (1980), 203–20, esp. 203–7; and Cartledge and Spawforth, *Hellenistic and Roman Sparta*, 113, 167 n. 10.

[76] Pausanias 3.14.6.

[77] C. A. Forbes, '"ΟΙ ΑΦ' ΗΡΑΚΛΕΟΥΣ in Epictetus and Lucian', *American Journal of Philology* 60 (1939), 473–4.

[78] A. J. B. Wace, 'Excavations at Sparta: The Roman Baths (Arapissa)', *ABSA* 12 (1905–6), 407–14.

FIGURE 5.6 This hip herm of Heracles was found in the so-called Baths of Arapissa at Sparta, where it probably featured in the original display. Heracles played an important role in the contests of the Spartan *agōgē* and his representation in a bath complex would have helped to link together physical relaxation in the baths with the ideological associations of the Spartan educational system. H: 2.3m. Severan.

theatre.[79] The nature of the building in which they were found has been debated, and it seems to have seen a number of different phases of building activity, though its association with bathing seems assured. Only a collection of scanty ruins currently remain of the complex (Fig. 5.7).[80]

While Spawforth has suggested that it could be the Gymnasium of Eurycles mentioned by Pausanias as lying in this general area, Torelli has sought to identify

---

[79] For a fuller description see O. Palagia, 'Seven Pilasters of Heracles from Sparta', in S. Walker and A. Cameron, eds., *The Greek Renaissance in the Roman Empire*, BICS Supplement 55 (London, 1989), 122–9. The herms can be divided into three variant types.

[80] See Wace, 'Excavations', 409, 413.

FIGURE 5.7 View of part of the remains of the so-called 'Arapissa' bath complex, Sparta. The identity of the complex has been debated, but should probably be seen as a bathing complex located in the same general area as the Platanistas and Dromos, both of which were used for ephebic activities.

this area with the Platanistas itself.[81] He suggests that the semicircular room shown on the excavation plan was originally a circular space, and should be identified with the Platanistas as described by Pausanias (Fig. 5.8). He also suggests that the so-called Teatro Marritimo of Hadrian's Villa at Tivoli was itself a copy of this structure. While tempting, it is hard to be convinced by this identification. In particular, the rooms which surround this circular area do not seem to find any correspondence in Pausanias' account and there is no obvious place to accommodate the spectators who must have attended the contest. It seems more reasonable to identify the ruins as a bathing complex set in the same general areas as the Platanistas itself.

Regardless of the precise identification of this complex, it seems likely that the herms found reused here originally decorated this area, possible in a palaestra attached to the baths.[82] Set up in an area to the west of the theatre, in the part of the

<hr />

[81] Cartledge and Spawforth, *Hellenistic and Roman Sparta*, 129–30; M. Torelli, 'Da Sparta a Villa Adriana: le terme d'Arapissa, il ginnasio del Platanistas e il Teatro Marittimo', in M. Gnade, ed., *Stips Votiva: Papers presented to C. M. Stibbe* (Amsterdam, 1991), 225–32.

[82] Palagia, 'Seven Pilasters', 127–8, suggests that they may instead have decorated the theatre, but since the majority were found here this seems a more likely spot for their original display.

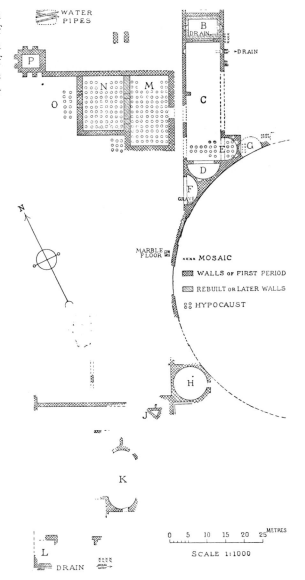

FIGURE 5.8 The excavation plan of the baths shows a series of heated rooms to the north with a semi-circular area at the centre of the complex. The Heracles herms were discovered built into a later wall in room M.

city where we know the Platanistas and Dromos both also lay, they would have evoked those other statues of Heracles which played a part in the contests of the ephebes. Heracles here, then, does not just stand for athletics in general, but links those frequenting this bath complex to the ideals of endurance embedded in the contests of the Spartan *agōgē*. While Apollonius would no doubt have disapproved heartily of such luxurious warm baths, those exercising here could both have their cake and eat it—indulge in the ideal that they were following the model of Heracles while simultaneously enjoying the luxury of Roman-style bathing.

Indeed, the presence of these herms in a bathing complex is indicative of the way in which the associations of the *agōgē* must have spread out beyond the narrow confines of the ephebes themselves. Other Spartan men who exercised in the civic gymnasia or won athletic victories around the Greek world would also have been able to associate themselves with the traditional virtues of a Spartan education. Through their status as ex-ephebes, or simply through their identity as Spartan citizens, they could associate themselves with the endurance rituals for which their city was widely famed. I now wish to turn to the Athenian *ephēbeia*, to see whether this too embodied the virtues and values for which Athens wished to be known.

SIX

The Athenian *Ephēbeia*
Performing the Past

The Athenian *ephēbeia* in the Roman period has not received much attention, despite the fact that most of our epigraphic evidence dates to the first to third centuries AD. So, Pelekides' 1962 study ends with 31 BC, with only minimal discussion of the later evidence.[1] Where the inscriptions have received attention, it has been primarily in the interests of prosopography and chronology, though Graindor also looked at ephebic festivals and the honorific portraits.[2] This is perhaps due to the lack of attention paid to the Athenian *ephēbeia* in the literary sources of the Roman period. While the ephebes of Athens do find occasional mention, particularly in Philostratus' account of Herodes Atticus in *The Lives of the Sophists*, their pursuits do not appear to have excited the same literary interest as those of Sparta. However, the epigraphic record suggests that the *ephēbeia* was indeed thriving in Roman Athens and that ephebes would have been prominent in both ephebic and civic festivals. While the literary sources are relatively quiet here, inscriptions, reliefs, and portraits present persuasive material evidence of the importance of the *ephēbeia* in Athenian cultural life.

Much of this evidence comes from a series of inscribed stelae and herms, some with portrait heads, which were found in the mid-nineteenth century in the area of

---

[1] C. Pelekides, *Histoire de l'éphébie attique des origines à 31 avant Jésus-Christ* (Paris, 1962). The nineteenth-century study by A. Dumont, *L'Essai sur l'éphébie attique* (Paris, 1876), does also consider the Roman evidence, but clearly views the history of the institution as one of decline, see e.g. 35–6. Other studies are primarily interested in the origins of the *ephēbeia*, e.g. A. Brenot, *Recherches sur l'éphébie attique et en particulier sur la date de l'institution* (Paris, 1920). The arguments over the date of its initiation are reviewed in Pelekides, *Histoire*, 7–17, and H. V. De Marcellus, 'The Origins and Nature of the Attic Ephebeia to 200 BC', D.Phil. thesis (Oxford, 1994). The same bias appears in Delorme's study of the gymnasium: J. Delorme, *Gymnasion: Étude sur les monuments consacrés à l'éducation en Grèce* (Paris, 1960). Nigel Kennell's forthcoming book on the *ephēbeia* will be a welcome corrective to this and I am grateful to him for discussing the subject with me.

[2] See especially S. Follet, *Athènes au IIe et au IIIe siècle: Études chronologiques et prosopographiques* (Paris, 1976). Graindor's many works on Athenian chronology are collected by Follet, *Athènes*, 2 n. 7. Those dealing with the *ephēbeia* include 'Les cosmètes du Musée d'Athènes', *BCH* 39 (1915), 241–401, and 'Études sur l'éphébie attique sous l'Empire', *Musée Belge* 26 (1922), 165–228.

the church of St Demetrius Katephoris to the east of the Roman agora.[3] They had been reused as building material in a wall whose construction should probably be dated to around AD 280, according to the evidence of a coin hoard found beneath it.[4] Some of the inscriptions mention 'those around/attending the Diogenium' (*hoi peri to Diogeneion*) while one mentions the erection of three stelae, one at Eleusis and two at Athens, in the Eleusinium and the Diogenium.[5] It seems reasonable to assume, therefore, that these stelae were originally set up in the Diogenium gymnasium, which must have served as the seat of the *ephēbeia* in the Roman period and probably lay nearby in the area to the east of the Roman agora and Tower of the Winds.[6]

It may be noted that Solon's discussion with Anacharsis, which relates the athletic activities around them to the physical education of Athenian youths, is set in the Lyceum. It might, then, be questioned whether Solon's words should be seen as relating especially to the Athenian ephebic system, rather than more generally to exercise in the gymnasium as a whole. I believe that there are several reasons for the choice of the Lyceum here. On the most prosaic level, at the dramatic date of the dialogue in the sixth century BC, the Diogenium did not yet exist; it was only built in the third century BC. However, Solon's defence of athletics through a discussion of Athenian education, and the association of physical athletics with training for war, would surely have evoked thoughts of the Athenian *ephēbeia*. This was the most formal example of this education and one which was traditionally associated with military training.[7] Yet by setting the dialogue in the Lyceum, Lucian allows his readers to project the ephebic system of education back into the Archaic period, giving it an antiquity equal to that of the Spartan *agōgē* which was credited to the lawgiver Lycurgus. Here, then, Athens' educational system is given a similar pedigree through its eulogy by the Athenian lawgiver Solon. At the same time, it allows the associations of athletic education with warfare to spill over into other types of athletic activity, such as those practised in the many gymnasia of Greek cities outside the formal bounds of the *ephēbeia*.[8] On a literary level, of course, it also

---

[3] They can be found in *IG* ii². 1962–2291 and 3730–3773. On their discovery see Graindor, 'Cosmètes', 241, and E. Lattanzi, *I ritratti dei cosmeti nel museo nazionale di Atene* (Rome, 1968), 15–17. The ephebic inscriptions have recently been re-examined by P. Wilson, 'A Corpus of Ephebic Inscriptions from Roman Athens 31 BC–267 AD', Ph.D. thesis (Monash, 1992), with a concentration on datings and readings. I am grateful to Sean Byrne for drawing my attention to this study.

[4] T. L. Shear, *AJA* 42 (1938), 1–16, at 4; Lattanzi, *Ritratti*, 31.   [5] *IG* ii². 1078.

[6] Graindor, 'Cosmètes', 242–4; Lattanzi, *Ritratti*, 21–3; J. Travlos, *A Pictorial Dictionary of Ancient Athens* (London, 1971), 576–7, U on fig. 722. For a more sceptical view see Delorme, *Gymnasion*, 143–6. On the relationship between the ephebes and 'those around the Diogenium', possibly future ephebes, see Dumont, *Essai*, 45–50.

[7] Aristotle, *Athenian Constitution* 42.

[8] The athletic activities of ex-ephebes, organized into bands of 'Neoi', may also be important here. See C. A. Forbes, *Neoi: A Contribution to the Study of Greek Associations* (Middletown, Conn., 1913).

allows for an allusion to the Platonic dialogues, which are often set in gymnasia or palaestrae.[9]

It is appropriate, then, to see whether the ideas which Solon associates with athletic education in the *Anacharsis* find any parallels in the *ephēbeia* as it was practised at the time Lucian was writing, the High Roman empire. Key among these ideas, as we have seen above, are the link with military training and the desire to produce good citizens who will act as defenders of the city and its freedom. The linkage of athletics to the ability to secure personal, civic, or Greek freedom through military prowess also appears in other literary texts of the period. So, when describing early athletes like Polymestor, Glaucon, and Polydamas, Philostratus declares:

They fought on account of their walls and nor did they fail but, thought worthy of memorials and trophies, they made a warlike training from gymnastics and did gymnastic deeds in war. (*Gymnasticus* 43)

Elsewhere in the work too Philostratus makes the link between athletic competition and military training. When describing the invention of various types of contests he claims that wrestling and the pancratium were devised specifically for use in warfare, by the Athenians at Marathon and the Spartans at Thermopylae (11), a statement which echoes Solon's claims that athletic contests prepare one for battle. It is significant here that the battles he mentions are both Panhellenic ones against a foreign foe, the Persians. Indeed when describing the race in armour Philostratus says that the most famous example is that held at Plataea, which commemorates the victory against the Persians and has the severe penalty that any man who runs a second time and loses must forfeit his life.[10] We know from Pausanias that this festival was called the 'Eleutheria' in commemoration of the Greek freedom won here in 479 BC, and inscriptions also reveal that the victor of the race in armour won the title 'Best of the Hellenes' (*aristos Hellēnōn*).[11] The link between athletics and warfare is thus made in explicitly Panhellenic contexts, where the battles fought are those for the freedom of Greece against the barbarians. The same linkage between athletics, citizenship, and defence of freedom occurs in Pausanias, where the victorious athletes whose statues he sees are often remembered for military as well

---

[9] On Lucian's literary pretensions see J. Bompaire, *Lucien Écrivain: Imitation et création* (Paris, 1958), especially 547–735. On Lucian's representation of Athens in his works see S. Follet, 'Lucien et l'Athènes des Antonins', in A. Billault, ed., *Lucien de Samosata: Actes du colloque international de Lyon organisé au Centre d'Études Romaines et Gallo-Romaines les 30 septembre–1er octobre 1993* (Paris, 1994), 131–9, and E. Oudot-Lutz, 'La représentation des Athéniens dans l'oeuvre de Lucien', also in Billault, *Lucien*, 141–8; though neither discusses the *Anacharsis* in any detail.

[10] Philostratus, *Gymnasticus* 8. This law appears nowhere else. See J. Jüthner, ed., *Philostratos über Gymnastik* (Leipzig, 1909), 201.

[11] Pausanias 9.2.6. *Inschriften von Milet*, 369. See L. Robert, 'Recherches Épigraphiques, 1: Aristos Hellēnōn', *REA* 31 (1929), 13–20.

as athletic victories. One example is the athlete Promachus of Pellene, discussed above, whose statue stood in the gymnasium used by the ephebes.[12]

All this suggests, then, that athletic pursuits in civic gymnasia could be seen as part of an education which produced loyal, courageous, citizen soldiers, ready to defend their homeland or even the whole of Greece against the barbarian. I now want to look at the activities which Athenian ephebes took part in and recorded, in both inscriptions and visual images, to see whether the idea of the ephebe as a future soldier and defender of his country was indeed present in Roman Athens. Just as at Sparta, where Pausanias records the involvement of ephebes in a number of festivals such as the Hyacinthia and Gymnopaidia, as well as the contests discussed above, Athenian ephebes also took part in both ephebic and civic festivals that expressed the ideals associated with the city and its youth.

Allusions to these festivals can be found in a number of ephebic inscriptions. As well as the inscriptions put up by individual ephebes in commemoration of a particular victory, references to athletic contests can also be found in the ephebic lists. These consist of a list of the ephebes enrolled in a particular year, put up at the expense of the *cosmētēs*, the magistrate responsible for the *ephēbeia* during that year. It is these officials, primarily, who are honoured in the portrait herms found along with the ephebic lists in the area of St Demetrius Katephoris, though only a few of the heads survive intact with their inscribed herms, and a couple show beardless figures who may be ephebes.[13] The inscriptions which survive show that these portraits were set up by the ephebes themselves to the *cosmētēs*, with the permission of the Areopagus and sometimes the Boule.[14] Scenes of ephebes honouring their *cosmētēs* also appear at the top of some ephebic lists. These usually show the *cosmētēs* standing in the centre, often bearded and wearing a himation. Around him stand two ephebes, naked except for the chlamys hung from the right shoulder, who are shown in the act of crowning him.

While the composition is fairly standardized, individual reliefs introduce some variety into the depiction.[15] So in the earliest example, dated to the reign of Trajan, four rather than two figures surround the *cosmētēs*, though only the central two actually crown him (Fig. 6.1).[16] From the name labels above them we can identify them as the two sons of the *cosmētēs*, Aristoboulus and Lucius. The two outer

[12] See above, p. 149. This aspect of Pausanias' narrative is discussed further in Chapter 7.

[13] See Graindor, 'Cosmètes', and Lattanzi, *Ritratti*, for a fuller discussion. The portraits are on display in the National Museum in Athens, along with a few ephebic lists showing relief decoration. See K. Rhomiopoulou, *Hellenoromaika glypta tou ethnikou archaiologikou mouseiou* (Athens, 1997), 46–67. Other ephebic lists and many headless inscribed herms are kept in the Epigraphical Museum in Athens.

[14] Lattanzi, *Ritratti*, 23–30.

[15] See discussions by Graindor, 'Cosmètes', 251–64, and Lattanzi, *Ritratti*, 80–3.

[16] Athens, National Museum, inv. 1469, *IG* iii. 1092; *IG* ii². 2017; J. N. Svoronos, *Das Athener National Museum*, German trans. (Athens, 1937), 615–16, cat. 250.

FIGURE 6.1 Upper part of an ephebic relief showing the crowning of the cosmetes by his sons and two other ephebes. The presence of symbols such as palm branches, strigils and amphoras alludes to the athletic activities and contests in which the ephebes took part. H: 0.76m. Trajanic. *IG* ii². 2017.

ephebes, Dionysius and Glaucias, both hold palm branches while amphorae stand at the feet of all four ephebes. The one to the far left, Dionysius, also holds a strigil in his right hand. Here, then, the honorific crowning of the *cosmētēs* by his sons is coupled with indications of the athletic prowess of the athletes, indicated by their palms. The strigil also acts as another sign of the athletic pursuits of the gymnasium. Indeed, in another relief which decorates a blank stele, whose original inscription was either painted or never inscribed, only one of the ephebes crowns the *cosmētēs* while the other stands crowning himself next to a prominent displayed vase, presumably his prize (Fig. 6.2).[17]

[17] Athens, National Museum, inv. 1468; Svoronos, *Athener National Museum*, 618, cat. 255; Rhomiopoulou, *Hellenoromaika glypta*, 46, cat. 35.

FIGURE 6.2
Uninscribed
ephebic relief
showing the
crowning of the
cosmetes at the top
and rowers in a
boat race at the
bottom. At the top
one of the ephebes
is shown crowning
himself and stand-
ing next to a large
vase, alluding to an
athletic victory.
H: 1.06m.
Hadrianic.

Elsewhere a stele of AD 139/140 shows a *cosmētēs* being crowned by two figures of whom one may be not an ephebe but another official of the gymnasium, given that he is dressed in a himation rather than the usual ephebic chlamys (Fig. 6.3).[18] In a later relief, dating to AD 212/13, both ephebes crown the *cosmētēs* while also holding palms in their left hands, and a small vase stands by the feet of the one to the right (Fig. 6.4).[19] The *cosmētēs* himself here is shown standing by a group of bookrolls, a clear allusion to his intellectual *paideia*. In some herm portraits too, attributes such as a himation around the shoulders and certain details of hair and beard evoked the traditional iconography of the intellectual.[20] So, the portrait of a *cosmētēs* of the early third century AD shares a number of similarities with portraits of Thucydides and Euripides, especially in the short beard, receding hairline, and furrowed brow, as well as the himation around his shoulders (Fig. 6.5).[21]

The relief scenes of the honouring of the *cosmētēs* by his ephebes show the many associations of the *ephēbeia*. While the *cosmētēs* is shown as a decorous mature man, a man of *paideia*, the youthful ephebes are often associated with athletic pursuits. They hold palms of victory and stand next to vases which evoke both the prizes offered in the games and the oil which was used in the gymnasium.[22] Yet so far these images do not give any specific details of festivals or contests in which the athletes had been successful. For this, I shall turn to the epigraphical evidence that we have for ephebic contests and the visual representations of them which appear on a few reliefs.

As well as listing the names of the ephebes enrolled in a given year, the ephebic lists also name those who held particular posts within the *ephēbeia*. In addition to the posts undertaken by adult Athenian citizens, such as the post of *cosmētēs* and *paidotribēs*, or trainer, a number of positions were filled by the ephebes themselves. This is particularly true of positions with a financial obligation, many of which mimicked civic magistracies at the level of the *ephēbeia*. So we find ephebes acting

---

[18] Athens, National Museum inv. 1484, *IG* iii. 1112, *IG* ii². 2044; Svoronos, *Athener National Museum*, 619, cat. 257; Rhomiopoulou, *Hellenoromaika glypta*, 47, cat. 36. Svoronos and Rhomiopoulou identify both outer figures as ephebes without commenting on the differences in dress, though see Lattanzi, *Ritratti*, 83.

[19] Athens, National Museum, inv. 1465, *IG* iii. 1177, *IG* ii². 2208; Svoronos, *Athener National Museum*, 617–18, cat. 254; Rhomiopoulou, *Hellenoromaika glypta*, 49, cat. 38.

[20] See Lattanzi, *Ritratti*, 67–74; P. Zanker, *The Mask of Socrates: The Image of the Intellectual in Antiquity*, trans. A. Shapiro (Berkeley, Los Angeles, and Oxford, 1995), 220–8. Note, however, the reservations expressed by R. R. R. Smith, 'Cultural Choice and Political Identity in Honorific Portrait Statues in the Greek East in the Second Century AD', *JRS* 88 (1998), 56–93, at 79–81.

[21] Athens National Museum, inv. 388, Lattanzi, *Ritratti*, 55–6, no. 22. Compare especially with a portrait identified as Thucydides in Holkham Hall; Zanker, *Mask*, 72, fig. 42.

[22] P. Graindor, *Athènes de Tibère à Trajan* (Cairo, 1931), 198, and Follet, *Athènes*, 339–40, discuss the identification of these vessels. I would argue, however, that there does not always need to be a direct reference to either the gymnasiarchy or a specific contest, but that they can serve as more genenal allusions to athletic activity, prizes in the games, and the generosity of individual ephebes.

FIGURE 6.3
Ephebic relief
showing the crown-
ing of the cosmetes
by an ephebe and
another ephebic
official. H: 1.32m.
AD 139/40. *IG* ii².
2044.

FIGURE 6.4 Ephebic relief showing the crowning of the cosmetes. The intellectual prowess of the cosmetes is alluded to through the bookrolls at his feet, while the ephebes hold palms, suggesting athletic victories. H: 1.42m. AD 212/13. *IG* ii². 2208.

FIGURE 6.5 This herm portrait of a cosmetes shows him with the attributes of an intellectual: a furrowed brow, receding hairline, and himation. H: 0.70m. First half of third century AD.

as the *gymnasiarchēs*, responsible for providing oil for the ephebes in the gymnasium, usually for a month at a time, or named as the *agōnothetēs* (director of the games) of a particular ephebic festival. Many of these festivals were set up in honour of the imperial family, such as the Germaniceia, Hadrianeia, and two festivals in honour of Antinous, the Antinoia in the City and in Eleusis, while others are presented as continuations or revivals of older Attic festivals, such as the Theseia and Athenaea.[23] The different contests which took place during the festivals are spelt out in one inscription, which lists the various victors.[24] After the introduction, 'these were victorious in the games of the ephebes', the victors are listed according to festival and contest. For the majority of festivals, the contests consisted of the following: heraldry, encomium, poetry, long-distance race (*dolichos*), three categories of the stade foot race, double stade race, three categories of wrestling, three categories of the pancratium, and the race in armour (*hoplos*).[25]

In addition, the inscription mentions that all the ephebes were victorious in the race to Agras, presumably in a contest with non-ephebes. After the list of victors in the ephebic contests the inscription lists other victors in the naval battle (*naumachia*), torch race (*lampadia*), and oratorical contests.[26] It then ends with a list of ephebes divided into two groups, the Theseidae and Heracleidae. The festivals to which these contests relate are not very clear. One of the torch race victories is linked with a festival 'to the Heroes' while another seems to have been part of a festival honouring someone whose name begins 'Gaius'. Orations, referred to simply as '*logoi*', are mentioned at the 'Haloia of the ephebes' while we are told that Aurelius Alcamenes performed at the *peri alkēs* festival ('contest of strength'). Both these references probably refer to an exhortatory speech (*logos protreptikos*) given at the occasion of the festival to spur on the contestants.[27] Of these festivals, only the *peri alkēs* contest appears in the list of ephebic *agōnothetai*. Indeed, Aurelius Alcamenes, named in line 238, also acted as *agōnothetēs* for this festival.[28] It does not appear in the other list of victories, however, unlike other ephebic festivals, such as the Antinoia, which appear in both lists.

I will return to this contest's mysterious identity a little later. The other festivals mentioned here are equally shady. The 'Haloa of the ephebes' is mentioned only here, and would seem to be separate from the Haloa festival celebrated by the city.[29]

---

[23] e.g. *IG* ii². 2094, col. A, ll. 43–55; 2119, ll. 8–23. Full details are given by Dumont, *Essai*, 260–305; Graindor, 'Études'; Pelekides, *Histoire*, 211–56 (though concentrating on the earlier period); and Follet, *Athènes*, 317–50. The Athenaea seems to have been introduced in 189/190 by Commodus, see Follet, *Athènes*, 320. The Athenaea was supposed to have been renamed the Panathenaea by Theseus (Pausanias 8.2.1) and there is no evidence that it ever existed as a separate festival in Antiquity. This 'revival' should probably be seen as an archaizing invention. I am grateful to Nigel Kennell for drawing my attention to this point.

[24] *IG* ii². 2119, ll. 126–222. This is the fullest list of contests. Note, however, that it may not list all contests since another inscription, *IG* ii². 2024, ll. 135, records a victory in the torch race at the Germaniceia which does not appear here.

[25] See Graindor, 'Études', 168–9, commenting on the presence of three groups (*taxeis*) in the stade, wrestling, and pancratium.

[26] *IG* ii². 2119, ll. 223–38. See the discussion by Graindor, 'Études', 216–19.

[27] *Logous protreptikous* (restored from *ptikous*) are mentioned in line 232 just above these references.

[28] *IG* ii². 2119, l. 18.   [29] Graindor, 'Études', 212–13.

Plate 1a. The mosaic from the exedra of the western palaestra of the Baths of Caracalla shows a combination of full-scale athletes with busts of individual figures. Many of the athletes carry attributes of victory and their contemporary appearance links them to the festivals taking place in Rome during the early third century AD. First half of the third century AD, possibly 220s. Vatican, Museo Gregoriano Profano.

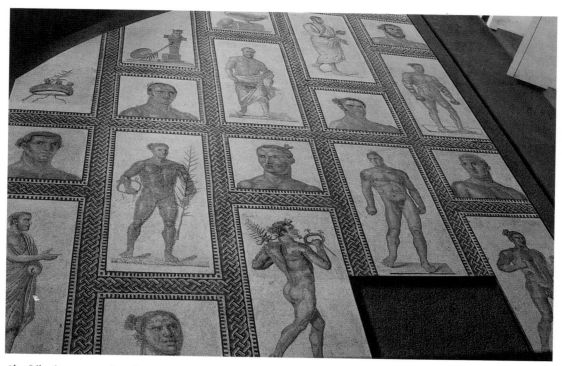

Plate 1b. Like its companion from the western palaestra, this mosaic from the exedra of the eastern palaestra of the Baths of Caracalla serves to link contemporary athletic festivals with the exercises that took place in this area of the baths. Included at the edge of the mosaic is a crown with three busts similar to that worn by the chief magistrate at the Capitoline games in Rome. First half of the third century AD, possibly 220s. Vatican, Museo Gregoriano Profano.

Plate 2a (*above*). The latrines of a bath complex in ancient Vienna in Gaul were decorated with paintings showing athletes boxing, throwing the discus and wrestling. The images attest to the spread of interest in Greek-style athletics from Rome and Italy into other western provinces. H:1.1m. Early third century AD. Musée Gallo-Romain de Saint-Romain-en-Gal.

Plate 2b (*far left*). Detail showing one of the boxers.

Plate 2c (*left*). Detail showing the umpire of the games

Plate 3. This large mosaic decorated a building in ancient Vienna in Gaul and shows athletes competing in a variety of events surrounding the athletic patron deity, Heracles. It may have decorated the headquarters of a local athletic guild. L: 7.5m. Early third century AD. Musée Gallo-Romain de Saint-Romain-en-Gal.

Plate 4a (*above*). This mosaic found at Baten Zammour in Tunisia shows in detail the different contests of a Greek-style athletic festival. The prize table in the foreground is laden with moneybags showing that cash prizes were granted to the victors. The mosaic probably alludes to a benefaction by a member of the local elite, showing the impact of Greek athletic festivals even in Latin-speaking provinces such as North Africa. Early fourth century AD. Gafsa Museum.

Plate 4b (*far left*). Detail showing a victorious athlete carrying off his prize crown.

Plate 4c (*left*). Detail showing the wrestling match and a torch race.

Two of the other contests mentioned, the race to Agras and torch race 'to the heroes', may, however, be evidence of ephebes competing in festivals organized by the city as a whole. Thus Graindor suggests that the torch race to the heroes might have been part of the Epitaphia festival, and the race to Agras part of the celebrations in honour of Artemis Agrotera, which involved a procession of armed ephebes.[30] While it is impossible to be certain of which festivals these contests formed a part, the fact that they do not appear in the list of ephebic *agōnothetai* seems to suggest that they are examples of the ephebes participating in civic festivals held by the city of Athens. Indeed, the role of the ephebes in civic cults seems to have been extensive throughout the Hellenistic and Roman periods. For example, we know of their involvement in the cult of Demeter and Persephone at Eleusis, where the ephebes marched in armour, crowned with myrtle, to accompany the sacred objects at the time of the mysteries.[31]

NAVAL BATTLES AND THE TRADITIONS OF ATHENS' PANHELLENIC PAST

The reference in *IG* ii². 2119 to a *naumachia* or naval battle is particularly interesting since this contest features both in the ephebic inscriptions and in the reliefs decorating some of the stelae. Follet has suggested that a reference to the *naumachia* in either words or images should be seen as a reference to the regattas which were held during the Panathenaic festival and thus as an indication that the stele gives the ephebic list for a Panathenaic year.[32] Her starting-point is a third-century stele explicitly dated to the 35th Panathenaea (AD 255/6). This shows a helmeted head of Athena in a shield between two amphorae in the pediment and, at the bottom of the stele, a draped figure standing in a boat holding a palm and an oar. He is labelled beneath as 'naumachus Herennius Dexippus'.[33] She thus suggests that images of boats and amphorae can both be associated with years when the great Panathenaea was held, and presents a number of examples when these features do indeed appear in a Panathenaic year.[34] However, there are a number of objections to her assumption that all references to *naumachiae* in these reliefs necessarily refer to a naval victory at the Panathenaea.

[30] Ibid., 214–15. See also Pelekides, *Histoire*, 219–20.

[31] *IG* ii². 1078, dated to the third century AD. See discussions by Dumont, *Essai*, 260–7, and Pelekides, *Histoire*, 220–3.

[32] Follet, *Athènes*, 339–43.

[33] *IG* ii². 2245, Athens Epigraphical Museum, inv. 10038. See P. Graindor, *Album d'inscriptions attiques d'époque impériale* (Gand, 1924), pl. 82.

[34] Follet, *Athènes*, 341–2.

Indeed, we know of a number of other festivals held in Athens which included naval contests attended by the ephebes.[35] A series of ephebic decrees from the late second and early first centuries BC provide detailed accounts of ephebic activities throughout the year.[36] A few of these may be particularly significant in view of the images we find appearing on later stelae. So, on 16 Munichion the ephebes participated in the festival of Artemis Munichia at Munichia before celebrating the Aianteia at Salamis.[37] Both festivals involved ephebic processions, sacrifices, and naval contests, while the ephebes also voyaged around the coast of Munichia in sacred ships and took part in a torch race and long race at Salamis, the latter against the local inhabitants.[38] The naval contest is called a 'contest of the boats' (*hamillan tōn ploiōn*), which may refer to a race or a mock battle. The regattas which took place on the final day of the Panathenaea are referred to in similar terms in the fourth-century BC decree which lists the prizes awarded at the festival.[39]

It is likely that the *naumachiai* which appear on inscriptions of the Imperial period are the later successors to these *hamillai*.[40] The reliefs which appear on the ephebic lists suggest that these contests were mock battles rather than races. The exception is an uninscribed relief discussed above (Fig. 6.2).[41] At the bottom of this we see a boat in which eight figures sit as though they have been rowing while the one at the rear holds a palm of victory. This could well record a victory in a ship race.

Elsewhere, however, we see instead scenes of one or more boats where some of the figures are standing up, brandishing oars, as if keeping a lookout while the others row. This can be seen most clearly on a relief set up by two team captains (*systremmatarchai*) to record the members of their team (Fig. 6.6).[42] The carving of the inscription is extremely haphazard here, but the relief decoration is one of the most vibrant examples (Fig. 6.7). Five figures are shown in a trireme, all naked

---

[35] On Athenian festivals the crucial accounts, still followed by later scholars, are those of A. Mommsen, *Feste der Stadt Athen in Altertum* (Leipzig, 1898), and L. Deubner, *Attische Feste* (Berlin, 1932). More recent studies include H. W. Parke, *Festivals of the Athenians* (London, 1977); R. Parker, *Athenian Religion: A History* (Oxford, 1996); and, on the archaeological evidence, E. Simon, *Festivals of Attica: An Archaeological Commentary* (Madison, Wis., 1983). For discussions of ephebic involvement see Graindor, 'Études'; Pelekides, *Histoire*, 211–56; and Follet, *Athènes*, 317–50.

[36] e.g. *IG* ii². 1006, 1008, 1011, 1029, and 1030.

[37] See Deubner, *Attische Feste*, 204–5, 228; and Pelekides, *Histoire*, 247–9.

[38] *IG* ii². 1006, ll. 29–31; 1008, ll. 21–3; 1011, ll. 16–17 (references to sacred ships and long race at Salamis) and l. 54 (torch race); 1028, ll. 21–4.

[39] *IG* ii². 2311, l. 78 (*hamilla neōn*). See Mommsen, *Feste*, 145–8.

[40] Graindor, 'Études', 217; Deubner, *Attische Feste*, 205.

[41] Athens National Museum, inv. 1468; Svoronos, *Athener National Museum*, 618, cat. 255; Rhomiopoulou, *Hellenoromaika glypta*, 46, cat. 35.

[42] *IG* ii². 2087; Athens National Museum, inv. 1466; Rhomiopoulou, *Hellenoromaika glypta*, 48, cat. 37. On the roles of these ephebic team captains, see J. H. Oliver, 'Athenian Lists of Ephebic Teams', *Archaiologike Ephemeris* (1971), 66–74. This is his no. 4.

FIGURE 6.6
Ephebic relief
dedicated by two
systremmatarchai
(team leaders)
showing figures
involved in a naval
contest. Like a num-
ber of other reliefs
this attests to the
enduring import-
ance of Athens'
naval past in the
Imperial period.
H: 0.79m.
AD 163/4. *IG* ii².
2087.

except for a chlamys attached at the right shoulder, the usual form of ephebic
dress. The central three figures are rowing but two others stand at either end of the
boat holding oars over their shoulders. While the one at the front moves to the
right, that at the rear is stationary, looking over his shoulder as if to watch out for

FIGURE 6.7
Detail of Fig. 6.6,
showing the relief
decoration.

opponents. The whole scene has a feel of movement and narrative as if we see a snapshot of the middle of the battle. It is unclear whether one of the teams has in fact won a victory in the *naumachia* since none is mentioned in the inscription, and no crowns or palms appear in the relief. Rather, the image perhaps sums up the solidarity of the team in a contest in which they had to work together. While elsewhere it is the leader of the team, the *systremmatarchēs*, who is named as victor, this relief notes the involvement of the whole team in such contests.[43]

While naval contests certainly took place in the Panathenaea as well as at Munichia and Salamis, I see no reason to associate all representations of boats on ephebic lists as relating to the Panathenaea rather than one of the other festivals. Indeed, in two cases we are explicitly told that the victories took place at Munichia and Salamis.[44] Both stelae include a relief depiction of a boat, although in the case of the victory at Salamis it is lightly sketched at the bottom of the stele rather than being properly carved.[45] In the second inscription the association between the imagery and the victory recorded is made more explicit (Fig. 6.8).[46] The stele as preserved in the Athens National Museum only represents the left half of the original block, the right side being in Oxford.[47] At the top of the inscription is a pediment

---

[43]   For systremmatarchs as victors see *IG* ii². 2208 and 2245; Oliver, 'Athenian Lists', 74.

[44]   *IG* ii². 1996, l. 9; 2130, after l. 46. Follet, *Athènes*, 340–1, wrongly describes it as 2119 and rejects an association with the festivals of Munichia and Salamis, unreasonably in my view.

[45]   *IG* ii². 1996; Athens, Epigraphical Museum, inv. 10343; Graindor, *Album*, pl. 18.

[46]   *IG* ii². 2130; Athens, National Museum, inv. 1470; Svoronos, *Athener National Museum*, 617, cat. 253.

[47]   Graindor, *Album*, pl. 65.

FIGURE 6.8 Only the left half of this ephebic inscription is shown here. At the top a figure of Heracles stood in the centre of a group of athletes. The bottom of the stele is dominated by the carving of a boat, illustrating a victory in the naval contest at Munichia. H: 1.71m. AD 192/3. *IG* ii². 2130.

FIGURE 6.9 Detail of
Fig. 6.8, showing relief
scene of athletes and
Hercules.

FIGURE 6.9 Detail of Fig. 6.8, showing relief scene of athletes and Hercules.

with the remains of a flying figure, probably a Nike, above whom was written 'To Good Fortune'. Beneath her is a recessed panel showing four figures (Fig. 6.9). To the far left an athlete runs to the left holding a lighted torch, a lit altar by his right knee.[48] Next come a pair of wrestlers or pancratiasts. The final figure, partly lost, is a representation of Heracles, standing in the Farnese pose with his right hand behind his back, and resting on his club which is draped with the lionskin and stands on a rock. The remains of a spear tip held by another figure can just be seen next to the club. As it stands half the panel is missing, allowing space for another

---

[48] Another representation of a torch race appeared on a relief now lost, *IG* ii². 1992 (III. 1275). See Graindor, 'Études', 217 n. 1.

FIGURE 6.10
Detail of Fig. 6.8,
showing the relief
scene at the base of
the stele, the victors
in a naval contest.

two or three figures. While Heracles would appear to be standing just to the left of centre, he was probably the central figure in the original composition.[49] The scene as a whole alludes to the activities typically associated with the *ephēbeia* under the patron of the gymnasium, Heracles.

At the bottom of the slab the left half is entirely dominated by the image of a ship with three figures (Fig. 6.10). The one to the left is draped and seated, steering the boat, while the other two are naked. One holds a crown and palm, the other an oar. They are clearly the two ephebes named in the lines immediately above as Philistides of Piraeus and Publius Aelius Cornelius of Pallene, competitors in a naval battle at Munichia. These two figures reappear elsewhere in the inscription. Philistides is listed as archon and gymnasiarch for the whole year—a sign of his wealth since this post was usually held monthly, while Cornelius acted as *stratēgos* and *agonothetēs* of the *peri alkēs* contest.[50] It would seem as though this image was included as a special request from the man commissioning the stele. The surface of the slab had to be carved away in order to accommodate the image, showing that the decision to include it was made after the slab had already been prepared for inscription. While we do not know the identity of the *cosmētēs* (magistrate) who set up the stele, the name of his deputy, the *anticosmētēs*, is significant. He is Publius Aelius Isochrysus from Pallene, surely the father of the victor Cornelius and also of

[49] Alternatively he may have shared this privileged position with the figure holding the spear, possibly another god or hero, who is now completely lost.

[50] *IG* ii². 2130, ll. 50–4, 81–2.

Publius Aelius Pheidimus of Pallene. The latter is praised on the inscription for his lavish presidency of the Lenaea and Epinicia festivals, where he feasted his fellow ephebes and those attending the Diogeneum.[51] The victors celebrated are thus two particularly wealthy and elite ephebes, one of them the son of an ephebic official.

Indeed, elsewhere too the figural decoration of these lists often celebrates the deeds or victories of the wealthiest ephebes. So, in the relief showing the crowning of the *cosmētēs* Eireneus, discussed above (Fig. 6.1), Graindor suggested that the vases which stand by the ephebes' feet allude to their actions as gymnasiarchs, while the two ephebes actually crowning the *cosmētēs* are his sons.[52] A desire on the part of those setting up the stelae to celebrate the deeds of themselves or their families also seems to lie behind the depiction on the stele of 255/6 of the naval victor Herennius Dexippus.[53] The introductory preface to the list tells us that it was set up by the systremmatarchs, who are listed elsewhere, starting with Herennius Ptolemaeus and then Herennius Dexippus himself.[54] These two brothers were the sons of the Athenian orator and writer P. Herennius Dexippus who acted as agono-thete of the Panathenaic festival, which probably explains why the Panathenaic symbols and date appear in the pediment.[55] They can be seen as a way for two of the ephebes funding the stele to draw attention to the acts of their father as well as to the success of one of them in the *naumachia*, possibly that of the Panathenaea itself. Another inscription records their father's dedication of a new prow ornament for the Panathenaic ship, and a reference to a victory of one of the sons at this festival would be appropriate.[56] While this reading of the stele would suggest that Follet was right here to see the Panathenaic date, symbolism, and ship race as all connected, I would argue that it was the personal motivations of the dedicators which played the key role. Where representations of ships appear elsewhere, then, there is no reason to assume that they must represent the Panathenaic contest.

In addition to the reliefs already discussed, another representation of the *naumachia* can be seen on the ephebic list of AD 212/13, set up by the *cosmētēs* Aurelius Dositheus, also known as Thales, who is shown being crowned at the top of the slab (Fig. 6.4).[57] After the lists of ephebes comes a heading which stands out because of the size of the lettering: 'those competing in the naval battle' (*hoi [na]u[mach]ēsante[s]*). Beneath this are listed three names, with a fourth probably

---

[51] *IG* ii². 2130, ll. 60–3, 87–93.   [52] Graindor, 'Cosmètes', 253–5.

[53] *IG* ii². 2245; Athens, Epigraphic Museum, 10038; Graindor, *Album*, pl. 82.

[54] *IG* ii². 2245, ll. 7, 301f.

[55] Follet, *Athènes*, 334–5. On Dexippus see F. Millar, 'P. Herennius Dexippus: The Greek World and the Third-Century Invasions', *JRS* 59 (1969), 12–29.

[56] *IG* ii². 3198. Note, however, that no imperial inscription specifically mentions the *naumachia* at the Panathenaea.

[57] *IG* ii². 2208; Athens, National Museum, inv. 1465; Svoronos, *Athener National Museum*, 617–18, cat. 254; Rhomiopoulou, *Hellenoromaika glypta*, 49, cat. 38.

FIGURE 6.11 Detail of Fig. 6.4. Relief scene of two boats at the base of the stele, illustrating the victories in a naval battle that are recorded in the inscription immediately above.

lost: Aurelius Dositheus, son of Thales; Aurelius Heracleides, son of Thales and Aurelius Anthus, son of Teimon. The named ephebes thus include the two sons of the *cosmētēs*. Beneath their names can be seen two ships, each manned by two figures, a seated naked rower and a standing draped figure who holds an oar and probably represents the ephebe named above (Fig. 6.11). The lower right part of the stele is lost but two more ships and the name of a fourth figure were probably shown here. The three ephebes whose names survive all took an active part in the running of the *ephēbeia*. All three are listed as gymnasiarchs while Aurelius Heracleides and Aurelius Anthus both acted as systremmatarchs and the sons of the *cosmētēs* also acted as agonothetes of various festivals.[58] Again, the figures whose activities are recorded on the stele seem to be those from the most prominent families.

Yet the motives of self-representation do not explain everything about these reliefs. It is notable that it is the *naumachia* in particular which received attention in these reliefs rather than one of the many other contests in which ephebes took part.[59] In fact, I will argue, these reliefs suggest the continuing importance of Athens' military history in the Roman period and the ideological link between ephebic training and military prowess.

[58] ll. 80–2, 95–6, 103–5.
[59] The torch race does also appear, as on *IG* ii². 1992 and 2130, but does not seem to have been as popular as the naval contest.

In particular, the festivals which were held in honour of Artemis and Ajax at Munichia and Salamis were both associated with the victory won over the Persians at Salamis in 480 BC. In a list of the military victories celebrated in Athenian festivals, Plutarch tells us that 16 Munichion was dedicated to the goddess Artemis because it was on that day that she shone on the Greeks as they were conquering at Salamis.[60] The festival of Ajax at Salamis seems to follow immediately after that at Munichia, and would also appear to be associated with the victory at Salamis. Indeed, it took place in the very area where the victory was won, and honoured a hero who was believed to have given his support to the Athenians on the day of the battle.[61] During this festival the ephebes also stopped at the trophy on Salamis and sacrificed to Zeus Tropaeus.[62] It is unclear precisely what form the *naumachiai* referred to actually took. They probably involved the display of naval skills and manoeuvring, rather than actual fighting. Yet these displays of naval skills during festivals associated with the victory over the Persians, and the fact that they are explicitly called 'battles' in the inscriptions, suggests that they were designed to evoke the memory of the battle of Salamis. Through these ephebic contests, the city of Athens re-enacted her traditional claims to naval prowess.[63]

In the decrees of the second and first centuries BC, the activities of the ephebes at the festivals of Artemis and Ajax are closely linked with other actions in which they celebrated Athens' military past. So, they paraded in armour at both the Epitaphia and the Theseia festivals, and also ran a race in armour from the military tomb in the Cerameicus in honour of those fallen in warfare.[64] Both festivals also seem to have included torch races.[65] The ephebes also sacrificed to 'those who died on behalf of freedom' at the tomb at Marathon.[66] In the last centuries before Christ, then, the ephebes seem to have played a key part in festivals which commemorated Athens' military history. The military qualities of the ephebes themselves also seem to have been under scrutiny since they paraded in armour

---

[60] Plutarch, *On the Fame of the Athenians* 349f. Mommsen, *Feste*, 462, notes that the victory at Salamis actually took place on 20 Boedromion, but this was clearly forgotten or obscured by Plutarch's time.

[61] Herodotus 8.64. See Mommsen, *Feste*, 452–3, and Deubner, *Attische Feste*, 228.

[62] *IG* ii². 1028, l. 27. See Pelekides, *Histoire*, 248 n. 4, on references to this sacrifice in other decrees, with a different order of events.

[63] Graindor, 'Études', 217, suggests that these ephebic contests may also have inspired the mock naval battle of Salamis held by Augustus in 2 BC; *Res Gestae* 23. On the popularity of these contests as spectacles at Rome, see K. Coleman, 'Launching into History: Aquatic Displays in the Early Empire', *JRS* 83 (1993), 48–74. Other cities in the Greek East also seem to have put on aquatic displays, to judge from the archaeological evidence: G. Traversari, *Gli Spettacoli in Acqua nel Teatro Tardo-Antico* (Rome, 1960), esp. 21–53. I am grateful to Hazel Dodge for information on this.

[64] *IG* ii². 1006, ll. 22–3; Aristotle, *Athenian Constitution* 58; Diodorus 11.33. See Thalheim, 'Epitaphia', in A. Pauly, G. Wissowa, and W. Kroll, *Real-Enzyklopädie der klassischen Altertumswissenschaft*, vi (1907), 218–19.

[65] *IG* ii². 2998 commemorates victories in the torch race at both festivals at the end of the first century BC.

[66] *IG* ii². 1006, ll. 26–30; 1008, l. 21.

and are praised on a number of decrees for their discipline and decorum during the procession to Salamis.[67]

The lack of similarly detailed decrees for the Imperial period makes it difficult to know what changes had occurred to the ephebes' role in these festivals. Yet the associations of the festivals with the Persian wars still seem to be of great importance. Plutarch declares that Athens celebrates festivals in memory of the victories at Marathon and Salamis, while Pausanias tells us that in his day the Athenians still paid honours to Ajax on Salamis and also mentions the trophy erected there after the victory in 480.[68] Indeed, such victories also seem to have provided much of the material for contemporary orators.[69] The naval battles in which the ephebes took part at Munichia and Salamis would have helped to reassert the memory of this most famous naval victory over the Persians in 480 BC.[70] The enduring importance of this victory, as well as the land victory at Marathon in 490, can be seen in the many references to it throughout Athenian literature and especially in the orations which were delivered each year in honour of those fallen in war.[71] One such oration, that contained within Plato's *Menexenus*, seems to have been repeatedly delivered each year at the Epitaphia by the time of Cicero and perhaps also later.[72]

I would suggest, therefore, that a number of the representations of ships on ephebic stelae refer to naval victories at Salamis and Munichia, where the mock battles were held as part of festivals celebrating the Athenian victory over the Persians and reminding Athens of the successes in her military past. As we have seen above, athletics are often linked with the Panhellenic victories of the Greeks against barbarians in the writings of Philostratus and Pausanias. Solon in Lucian's *Anacharsis* also specifically identifies the role of athletics in Athenian education as being to create good citizen soldiers who will protect the freedom of the city. While he mentions athletic contests such as wrestling and the pentathlon, activities which

---

[67] *IG* ii². 1006, ll. 31–2; cf. 1008, l. 24 and 1028, l. 26.

[68] Plutarch, *On the Fame of the Athenians* 349d–f; Pausanias 1.35.3; 1.36.1.

[69] Plutarch, *Precepts of Statecraft* 17.814c, cautions statesmen against stirring up people with such themes and urges them to leave them to the orators. Philostratus, *Lives of the Sophists* 2.15 (595), tells us that the sophist Proclus of Naucratis was nicknamed Marathon, perhaps because of his liking of this theme. D. A. Russell, *Greek Declamation* (Cambridge, 1983), 107, records 43 known examples of speeches on this topic. On the enduring importance of the Persian Wars in later Greek and Roman history, see A. J. S. Spawforth, 'Symbol of Unity? The Persian-Wars Tradition in the Roman Empire', in S. Hornblower, ed., *Greek Historiography* (Oxford, 1994), 233–47, and S. E. Alcock, *Archaeologies of the Greek Past: Landscape, Monuments, and Memories* (Cambridge, 2002), 74–86.

[70] Note that the scene of Greeks fighting Persians also appears on a few Attic sarcophagi produced during this period, as a variant of the more common scene of the Battle at the Ships in *Iliad* 15. See G. Koch and H. Sichtermann, *Römische Sarkophage: Handbuch der Archäologie* (Munich, 1982), 410–14.

[71] The most famous is Pericles' funeral speech in Thucydides 2.35–46, which, however, skirts over Athens' military victories. However, these are made much of in later speeches: Plato, *Menexenos* 240e–241c; Lysias, *Funeral Oration* 20–6; Demosthenes, *Funeral Oration* 10–11. On these see N. Loraux, *L'invention d'Athènes: Histoire de l'oration funèbre dans la 'cité classique'* (Paris and New York, 1981), esp. 157–73.

[72] Cicero, *Orator* 44 (154); Thalheim, 'Epitaphia', in *Real-Enzyklopädie*, vi (1907), 218–19.

FIGURE 6.12
Detail of an
ephebic relief
showing figures in
military costume,
underscoring the
link between the
ephēbeia and
military training.
AD 143/4. *IG* ii².
2050. Athens,
Epigraphical
Museum, inv. 12554
(previously
National Museum,
inv. 1483).

ephebes across the Greek world participated in, the ephebic reliefs concentrate on one particular example of ephebic contests, the *naumachia*. They suggest that in the Athens of the second and third centuries, the naval contests of the ephebes were an important way of re-experiencing the city's glorious military past.

The ephebes also seem to have played a part in other events commemorating Athenian warriors and Panhellenic victories. A reference to the military associations of the ephebes appears on an ephebic list of 143/4, where we find a scene of the crowning of the *cosmētēs* which differs from those seen so far (Fig. 6.12).[73] Here the *cosmētēs*, standing in the centre as usual, is dressed in military costume, carrying a spear in his right hand and a sword in the left. A naked ephebe with a chlamys and a shield stands to the left crowning him while to the right stands another figure dressed, like the *cosmētēs*, in military costume. This figure holds a phiale in his lowered right hand and both he and the *cosmētēs* wear crowns. The presence of the crowns and phiale suggests that this probably reflects a religious festival where the ephebes processed in armour, rather than a specific military victory; however, it is striking for the explicit stress here on the military connotations of the *ephēbeia*.[74]

[73] *IG* ii². 2050 (iii. 1124), Athens, Epigraphical Museum, inv. 12554; previously National Museum, inv. 1483, see P. Castriotes, *Glypta tou Ethnikou Mouseiou* (Athens, 1908), 265–6, no. 1483, and Svoronos, *Athener National Museum*, 618–19, cat. 256 (with incorrect inventory number). See Follet, *Athènes*, 208–9, on the date.

[74] Lattanzi, *Ritratti*, 82, suggests that it may show the costume worn by the *cosmētēs* when he accompanied the ephebic procession to Eleusis.

The ephebes may also have continued to compete at the Epitaphia festival and certainly also played a role in a festival at Plataea.[75] Some inscriptions refer to a distribution of money made to the ephebes on the occasion of the 'dialogue at Plataea'.[76] Noel Robertson has convincingly argued that this *dialogos* was a debate between the Athenians and Spartans over who should lead the Eleutheria procession, at which the ephebes were in attendance.[77] The involvement of the ephebes in the Eleutheria festival commemorating the victory over the Persians in 479 BC fits in well with the role they played elsewhere in commemorating military victories of the past.[78]

Thus the *ephēbeia* seems to have had a continuing association with military pursuits into the Roman period, and to have played an important role in the festivals which celebrated military victories of the past. Yet it is specifically naval contests which are commemorated on the ephebic reliefs, with other contests such as torch races and wrestling appearing only rarely. This is in contrast to ephebic reliefs elsewhere, such as those from Varna on the Black Sea, which show instead scenes of wrestling and boxing.[79] It would seem that the ephebes of second- and third-century Athens wanted to stress instead their prowess in one particular contest, the *naumachia*.

While Follet would explain this as being due to the importance of the Panathenaic ship as a symbol of one of Athens' most important festivals, I would suggest that the significance of naval power in Athens' military history, and particularly in the battle against the Persians at Salamis, was the decisive factor. Indeed, the use during the Panathenaea of a mechanized ship to carry the peplos dedicated to Athena may also have first begun in the second century AD, since the first explicit description of it comes in Philostratus' account of the stadium dedicated by the sophist Herodes Atticus in AD 143.[80] In both the Panathenaic procession and the ephebic contests, the prominence of ships can be attributed to the importance of keeping alive the memory of Athens' naval history, evoking the city's heyday in

---

[75] See Graindor, 'Études', 214–15, on the Epitaphia, though the evidence is slight and rests on an identification of this festival with that referred to in *IG* ii². 2119 as 'to the heroes'.

[76] *IG* ii². 2113, ll. 142–5; 2089, ll. 14–17; 2130, ll. 37–40.

[77] N. Robertson, 'A Point of Precedence at Plataia: The Dispute between Athens and Sparta over Leading the Procession', *Hesperia* 55 (1986), 88–102.

[78] Though Graindor, 'Études', 219, thinks that they attended the yearly rather than the penteric Eleutheria.

[79] On these see L. Robert, 'Un relief inscrit au musée de Stamboul', in id., *Hellenica* 11–12 (Paris, 1960), 369–80; J-C. Moretti, in C. Landes, ed., *Le Stade romain et ses spectacles* (Lattes, 1994), 269–75, 288–93, cats. 94–5.

[80] Philostratus, *Lives of the Sophists* 2.1 (550); J. Tobin, *Herodes Attikos and the City of Athens: Patronage and Conflict under the Antonines* (Amsterdam, 1997), 87–8. See J. L. Shear, 'Polis and Panathenaia: The History and Development of Athena's Festival', Ph.D. thesis (Pennsylvania, 2001), 143–55, for the argument that the use of a ship float to carry the peplos only began in the Roman period.

the fifth century at the head of a naval empire.[81] By identifying themselves with *naval* supremacy, the ephebes could also define themselves against other cities which could not claim such a past. In particular, it could distinguish them clearly from Sparta, a city whose own ephebic system, the *agōgē*, attracted so much attention in the Roman period.[82] The laws of Iphitus and Lycurgus were said to have banned the Spartans from naval trade, allowing their later involvement in such matters to be seen as a sign of decline from their previous heights. While Sparta too had a number of naval victories in her past, their status would appear to have been rather more ambiguous in the Roman period.[83] In Athens, by contrast, such victories could clearly evoke the city's golden period in the fifth century BC.

The ephebic contests and festivals of both Athens and Sparta, as experienced in the High Roman Empire, are characterized by an allusion to the past, and the desire to re-experience and revitalize that past through the activities of the present. The images decorating the stelae of the Athenian *ephēbeia* were clearly chosen with care. They are a manifest sign of the enduring importance to Athens of her naval past and the crucial role which she had played in the Panhellenic struggle against the Persians.

HERODES ATTICUS AND THE *PERI ALKĒS* CONTEST

While the Athenian *ephēbeia* did not attract literary attention to the degree that the Spartan *agōgē* did, it must nevertheless have been a conspicuous feature of Athenian life. The ephebes continued to play a visible role in both ephebic and civic festivals through their processions, contests, and displays. Inscribed stelae and honorific herm portraits of their magistrates thronged the gymnasium in which they met, in the very heart of the city. Their victories were also recorded on private dedications, some inscribed with scenes of crowns or palms.[84] Occasionally they were scratched into the side of existing monuments, such as herm portraits (Fig. 6.13).[85] This rich visual and epigraphical evidence asserts the continuing importance of the *ephēbeia* in Roman Athens.

[81] On the Panathenaic ship, see Shear, 'Polis and Panathenaia', 154–5.

[82] Like Athens, she also received the attention of the emperor Hadrian, who elevated both by his institution of the Panhellenion, though Athens clearly got the better deal. See P. Cartledge and A. Spawforth, *Hellenistic and Roman Sparta: A Tale of Two Cities* (London, 1989), 108–10, and M. T. Boatwright, *Hadrian and the Cities of the Roman Empire* (Princeton, 2000), 58, 65, 84, 147–57.

[83] See especially Philostratus, *Life of Apollonius*, 4.32 and 6.20, where even Sparta's naval successes are viewed in a hostile light as being contrary to the laws of Lycurgus and Iphitus, and maritime trade is especially frowned upon.

[84] See *IG* ii². 2980–3016 for a collection of such dedications; 3015 has the names of festivals written in crowns, with a palm branch between.

[85] *IG* ii². 2026; Athens, Epigraphic Museum, inv. 10323.

FIGURE 6.13 Later inscription added to a herm portrait, recording victories in the Philadelphia, Epinicia, and Theseia festivals. Such inscriptions reveal the pride which Athenian ephebes took in their athletic victories. Total H: 0.84m. The later inscriptions date to the end of the second century AD. *IG* ii². 2026.

In order to explore further the role played by the ephebes within Athenian civic culture we can look at their interactions with the great Athenian sophist and benefactor Herodes Atticus.[86] In his discussion of Herodes' many benefactions Philostratus tells us that he was responsible for changing the customary dress of the ephebes:

He also changed the dress of the Athenian ephebes to the current form, being the first to clothe them in white cloaks (*chlamydas*), for before this they were clad in black whenever they sat in assembly or escorted a procession, for the public mourning of the Athenians of

[86] On Herodes, see P. Graindor, *Un milliardaire antique: Hérode Atticus et sa famille* (Cairo, 1930); W. Ameling, *Herodes Atticus* (Hildesheim, 1983); and Tobin, *Herodes Attikos*.

the herald Copreus whom they themselves had killed when he was dragging the sons of Heracles away from the altar.   (*Lives of the Sophists* 2.1, 550)

An inscription from Eleusis which lists the ephebes for the year 165/6 also refers to this gift. Here the ephebes are called 'the first to wear white' (*tous protous leukophorēsantas*). We are told that the president of the ephebes asked whether anyone had any objections to the ephebes wearing white on the day they marched to Eleusis and that no one spoke up. So Herodes declared, 'O ephebes, in my presence you shall never lack for white cloaks.'[87]

The justification for this change is somewhat unclear. In Philostratus' account the black cloaks are linked with Athenian mourning for the herald Copreus. Graindor had suggested that Herodes, as a member of the Ceryces *genos* and hence a descendant of the herald, undertook to remove this bloodguilt from them and thus provided the white cloaks.[88] However, another interpretation is provided by an inscription at Herodes' own estate at Marathon. This records a poem in celebration of Herodes' safe return from Sirmium after he had been indicted before the emperor Marcus Aurelius. It describes the pomp with which the Athenians escorted Herodes from Eleusis to the city, attended by 'ephebes gleaming in bronze, youths whom he himself, when they were still mourning (Theseus') forgetfulness of father Aegeus, separated from the black raiment of atonement and clothed in shining garb at his own expense'.[89] Whether the ephebes' black clothing was due to Theseus' forgetfulness, when he omitted to change his black sails to white and thus inadvertently caused his father's suicide, or to the Athenians' murder of Copreus, could obviously be debated at this period, in much the same way as the topics which form the content of Plutarch's *Greek and Roman Questions*.[90]

What is certain, however, is that Herodes persuaded the ephebes to relinquish these signs of mourning and guilt, undoubtably in an erudite sophistic speech, and promised to reclothe them himself. The change of clothing thus marks a change in focus, from guilt to innocence, from the past to the present and future. The inscription recording this gift at Eleusis is topped by a dedication to the co-emperors Marcus Aurelius and Lucius Verus, acknowledging their victories in the East.[91] The association between this dedication and the rest of the inscription makes it possible that these victories were seen as initiating a new era in Athens, an era in

---

[87] *IG* ii². 2090. For date, see Follet, *Athènes*, 206–7.

[88] P. Graindor, *Musée Belge* (1912), 88.

[89] *IG* ii². 3606; trans. J. H. Oliver, *Marcus Aurelius: Aspects of Civic and Cultural Policy in the East*, Hesperia Supplement 13 (Princeton, 1970), 34. For the interpretation of the text see P. Roussel, 'Les chlamydes noires des éphèbes Athéniens', *REA* 43 (1941), 163–5; Tobin, *Herodes Atticus*, 202–4, 272–5.

[90] On the ritual significance of the black cloaks see P. Vidal-Naquet, 'The Black Hunter and the Origin of the Athenian Ephebia', in id., *The Black Hunter: Forms of Thought and Forms of Society in the Greek World*, trans. A. Szegedy-Maszak (Baltimore and London, 1986), 106–28, at 112.

[91] *IG* ii². 2090, ll. 2–3.

which past sins could be forgiven and the Athenian ephebe restored to his former purity. The procession of the ephebes in armour and shining white cloaks to Eleusis would thus be symbolic of the new life given to the city by the imperial victories. While this scenario cannot be proven, it would be in keeping with the ways in which victories over the east were seen as analogous to the traditional Greek struggle over the barbarian.[92] Elsewhere too we find the widespread use of civic festivals to honour the emperors as well as civic gods, and the emperors themselves equated to ancient civic heroes.[93] Just as Hadrian's building activities in Athens could present him as a new founder of the city, the victories of Marcus and Lucius were perhaps here seen as ushering in a new era of Athenian history, one which wiped away the sins of the previous founder, Theseus.[94]

Herodes would be the pivotal figure in this plan. Responsible for finding both antiquarian and contemporary reasons for the change, through his benefaction he would always be associated with this renewal in ephebic dress. Indeed, elsewhere too Herodes preserves an association with the ephebes. After his death the Athenians removed his body from his estate at Marathon (Herodes' choice of resting-place) and brought it to Athens to be buried in the Panathenaic stadium he had built. Just as they had previously escorted the living Herodes from Eleusis to Athens, the ephebes now escorted his body to Athens, in the traditional manner of an honorific funeral.[95]

Herodes also seems to have been honoured in an ephebic festival held at Eleusis, though the precise details are somewhat unclear. This festival is referred to on an ephebic inscription. A list of the agonothetes of various ephebic festivals is followed thus:

The team leaders (*taxiarchoi*) of the contest of strength (*peri alkēs*): Lucius Cydathenaeus and Heracon . . . sius. The victors over the *pareutaktous* in the contest first held at Eleusis in honour of Claudius Herodes: in the wrestling Eirenius of Phaleron, in the pancratium Zoilos of Phaleron. (*IG* ii². 2094, ll. 50–5)[96]

---

[92] See above, p. 156.

[93] On the integration of the imperial family into civic life, see Price, *Rituals and Power*, esp. 101–32, and G. M. Rogers, *The Sacred Identity of Ephesos: Foundation Myths of a Roman City* (London and New York, 1991), 80–126, esp. 91–5. For their role in festivals see also below, pp. 249–51.

[94] On Hadrian's building programme see D. Willers, *Hadrians panhellenisches Programm: archäologische Beiträge zur Neugestaltung Athens durch Hadrian* (Basel, 1990). On the representation of him as the new founder of Athens, most cogently expressed in the inscription on the Arch of Hadrian, see A. J. S. Spawforth and S. Walker, 'The World of the Panhellenion I: Athens and Eleusis', *JRS* 75 (1985), 78–104, at 92–100, esp. 93; and Boatwright, *Hadrian and the Cities*, 144–57, esp. 147.

[95] Philostratus, *Lives of the Sophists* 2.1 (565–6). For opposing views on the exact placement of Herodes' tomb see J. Tobin, 'Some New Thoughts on Herodes Atticus's Tomb, His Stadium of 143/4, and Philostratus *VS* 2.550', *AJA* 97 (1993), 81–9; ead., *Herodes Attikos*, 177–85; and K. Welch, 'Greek Stadia and Roman Spectacles: Asia, Athens and the Tomb of Herodes Atticus', *JRA* 11 (1998), 117–45, at 138–45.

[96] On the meaning of *pareutaktous*, possibly a term for the oldest ephebes, see Graindor, 'Études', 203.

Graindor interpreted this inscription as proof that the *peri alkēs* contest, which also occurs in other ephebic lists, was instituted in honour of Herodes Atticus and held at Eleusis. Since only taxiarchs are named here, he suggests that Herodes himself acted as agonothete on this first occasion. He also suggests that the only contests involved were the wrestling and pancratium, a concentration on heavy athletics which would be in line with the title of the contest as 'about strength'. He dates the inscription to *c.* 145.[97] Follet, however, shows that the inscription must date to around 166/7 since it features the same undersecretary as *IG* ii². 2090, the inscription which mentions Herodes' gift of cloaks where the presence of imperial titles allows the date to be ascertained.[98] Therefore, she asserts that Graindor was wrong to associate the festival in honour of Herodes at Eleusis with the *peri alkēs*, which is found mentioned in earlier lists too.[99] She thinks that the festival at Eleusis was instituted in recognition of Herodes' gift of the cloaks, and that the *peri alkēs* contest was a separate event. However, she also asserts that the *peri alkēs* contest only included the wrestling and pancratium, a statement which relies on maintaining the link in this inscription between the contest at Eleusis and the *peri alkēs* contest, which she herself rejects.[100]

So, were there two festivals, one in honour of Herodes Atticus instituted in around 166/7 AD including contests in wrestling and the pancratium, and another, attested from 143/4, which was called the *peri alkēs* and for which the only activity we can be sure of was a *logos protreptikos*? The argument for separating the two has been made by Follet and rests on the fact that the *peri alkēs* appears in inscriptions earlier than that referring to the contest first held in honour of Herodes. Yet there are also arguments against this separation. The festival in honour of Herodes does not appear in any list of agonothetes. In the disputed inscription the two contests do seem to be closely linked. Although it could be argued that the text moves from agonothetes (including the taxiarchs of the *peri alkēs*) to victors, the only victors recorded here are those in the festival to Herodes. They might, therefore, be seen as comment on the previous two lines, an indication of the successful athletes in the games. Indeed, one possible solution to this problem would be to see the reference to the 'contest first held at Eleusis in honour of Herodes' not as a separate event but as a special version of the *peri alkēs* festival dedicated to Herodes because of his benefactions to the Athenian *ephēbeia*. Eleusis is clearly important in this context. The initial gift of cloaks to the ephebes seems to have taken place on the occasion of their procession to Eleusis. When they meet Herodes to escort him back after his

---

[97] Graindor, 'Études', 201–6.   [98] Follet, *Athènes*, 57, 225.   [99] Ibid., 319.

[100] She footnotes Graindor here, but his evidence comes from this very inscription. I have not been able to find any reference to the contests of the *peri alkēs* in any other inscription. Where it is mentioned it is usually in association with a list of agonothetes, or in relation to a *logos proptreptikos* as in *IG* ii². 2119, ll. 237–8, discussed above.

FIGURE 6.14 This votive relief was set up by an ephebic official to commemorate an ephebic victory at Eleusis. The depiction here of Heracles reclining on his lionskin suggests a possible connection between the contest in which they were victorious and the god. H: 0.67m. Mid-second century AD.

trip to Sirmium, the parade also goes from Eleusis to Athens, in what Jennifer Tobin has described as 'a sort of reverse Eleusinian procession'.[101] A contest which took place at Eleusis would therefore be an appropriate occasion on which to honour Herodes for his gift.

There is some evidence that the god Heracles might have been associated with a contest held at Eleusis. Follet suggests that a slab from Athens now in Oxford might be associated with the *peri alkēs* contest (Fig. 6.14).[102] It shows Heracles lying on a lionskin beneath a tree. The inscription describes it as a dedication by the *sōphronistēs* (ephebic official) Athenaeus son of Spendon of Eleusis, for the ephebes after the victory in Eleusis. Athletic dedications to Heracles are common, and the reference to a victory at Eleusis may simply be due to the dedicator's origins, yet there may also be a stronger connection between Heracles, Eleusis, and the *peri*

---

[101] Tobin, *Herodes Attikos*, 203–4.

[102] *IG* ii². 3012; R. Chandler, *Marmora Oxoniensia* (Oxford, 1763), pt. ii, p. 105, no. 57 with pl. 8; A. Michaelis, *Ancient Marbles in Great Britain*, trans. C. A. M. Fennell (Cambridge, 1882), 573, no. 135. Follet, *Athènes*, 319.

alkēs contest (which is not, however, explicitly named here). Another inscription seems to honour the victory of one Heracleides, a descendant of Heracles, in the *peri alkēs* contest.[103]

A link between Heracles and the *peri alkēs* contest would certainly make sense. The name of the contest suggests that it involved trials of strength and force, the very qualities for which Heracles was renowned.[104] If the *peri alkēs* contest did consist of trials in wrestling and the pancratium, these were precisely the two sports at which Heracles was said to have excelled at Olympia.[105] Another piece in the jigsaw is suggested by *IG* ii². 2119, an inscription discussed above.[106] As already noted, the inscription gives a list of victors in the contests of the ephebes, followed by the names of victors in the naval contest (*naumachia*), torch race (*lampadia*) and speeches (*logoi*). The final victor mentioned is Aurelius Alcamenes, agonothete of the *peri alkēs* contest and apparently credited with giving a *logos protreptikos* (exhortatory speech) at this very contest. Below this are two lists of ephebes, identified as either Thesiadae (followers of Theseus) or Heracleidae (followers of Heracles).[107]

Graindor suggests that these two divisions might be related to the *peri alkēs* contests, as the divisions (*taxeis*) whose leaders (*taxiarchoi*) are referred to in *IG* ii². 2094. He also notes that Herodes Atticus himself was said to be descended from both Heracles and Theseus.[108] If followed, this would suggest that both Theseus and Heracles were important figures in the *peri alkēs* contest. We have already seen that Heracles would be an appropriate patron for this contest of strength. Yet Theseus too seems to have been used as a role model in the contest. A fragmentary inscription starts with the note that the ephebes have decided to inscribe on a stele the *logos protreptikos* spoken by Isochrysus of Phleious, the archon of the ephebes and agonothete of the *peri alkēs* contest.[109] It seems reasonable to assume that, like Aurelius Alcamenes in *IG* ii². 2119, Isochrysus delivered this speech at the *peri alkēs* contest over which he presided. Much of the content of his speech is lost. However, it seems to have used Theseus as an example for Isochrysus' fellow ephebes to follow. So we find references to Theseus' toils (*ponous*) and particularly to his activities as an ephebe: 'Being an ephebe . . . he sailed to Crete and freed from tribute his homeland, citizens and ephebes.' He then suggests that the ephebes, seeing such things, should be encouraged to imitate them, though they themselves will

---

[103] W. Peek, 'Zu einem Epheben-Epigramm aus Athen', *Athens Annals of Archaeology* 6 (1973), 125–7; Follet, *Athènes*, 319.

[104] Athenaeus 13.561d, describing the presence of Eros, Hermes, and Heracles in the gymnasium, explicitly says that Heracles is associated with strength (*alkē*).

[105] See discussion above, p. 163.   [106] p. 178.   [107] *IG* ii². 2119, ll. 237–62.

[108] Graindor, 'Études', 205. See *IG* xiv. 1389, ll. 30–3, and Tobin, *Herodes Attikos*, 13.

[109] *IG* ii². 2291. For advice on composing such speeches of encouragement to athletes, see Ps.-Dionysius, *On Epideictic Speeches* 7, conveniently translated in D. A. Russell and N. G. Wilson, eds., *Menander Rhetor* (Oxford, 1981), 377–81.

struggle not with beasts but with one another.[110] Here Theseus is clearly used as a model ephebe for the Athenian youths to imitate.

Putting all these pieces together, we gain a picture fully in keeping with the archaistic tenor of second-century Athenian society, and the interests of its famous intellectuals. The *peri alkēs* was a contest held at Eleusis, under the auspices of both Heracles and Theseus, with the ephebes divided into two groups under these two patrons, just as the Spartans at the Platanistas were associated with either Heracles or Lycurgus.[111] Here Theseus' presence is due to his status as the founder of Athens, whose labours could be equated with those of Heracles himself, as they had been in the fifth century BC on the Athenian treasury at Delphi and, closer to home, on the metopes of the Temple of Hephaestus in the Athenian agora.[112] Heracles, of course, is the heavy athlete *par excellence*, a worthy patron for a contest which made a test of strength and may have focused on the two athletic specialities particularly associated with him. This contest, held at Eleusis since the 140s, was later, in *c.* 166/7, dedicated as a special honour to Herodes Atticus, probably in thanks for his benefactions. Indeed, Herodes' gift of new white cloaks removed from the Athenian ephebes a stain of guilt associated either with Theseus himself, or with the defence of the sons of Heracles. Both these heroes thus find a mention in the rationale for the traditional ephebic costume and its renewal.

In some ways the *peri alkēs* contest seems tantalizingly similar to the ephebic contests at Sparta, its name suggesting a concentration on strength similar to that of the endurance contest, while the presence of two taxiarchs and troops possibly named after Heracles and Theseus find parallels in the battle at the Platanistas. Unlike them, however, it never seems to have found literary fame, unless Solon's references to toils (*ponoi*) in the *Anacharsis* are a veiled allusion. The relative quietness of the literary sources can be explained as due to the many other claims Athens could present as a repository of Greek culture. Sparta's fame rested specifically on the harshness of her military training, with the result that the contests here found a great deal of attention. Athens, in contrast, had a number of other competing attractions to beguile the tourist, not least her splendid art and architecture and her status as a major centre of the Second Sophistic.[113] The visual and epigraphic

---

[110] *IG* ii². 2291, ll. 45–8, 50–1.

[111] Graindor, 'Études', 205, suggests that one division competed in the wrestling, the other in the pancratium, but they could equally be seen as teams whose members competed in both events.

[112] Treasury: A. Stewart, *Greek Sculpture: An Exploration* (New Haven and London, 1990), 132–3; Temple of Hephaestus: H. Koch, *Studien zum Theseustempel in Athen* (Berlin, 1955). On the importance of Theseus in fifth-century Athens, see D. Castriota, *Myth, Ethos and Actuality: Official Art in Fifth-Century BC Athens* (Madison, Wis., 1992), 33–63.

[113] On the importance of Athens in the Second Sophistic, as both a centre and an inspiration, see Bowersock, *Greek Sophists*, 4–6, 17–18; Bowie, 'Greeks and their Past', 168–74; Anderson, *Second Sophistic*, 24–5, 119–21. See also the papers in M. C. Hoff and S. I. Rotroff, eds., *The Romanization of Athens: Proceedings of a Conference held at Lincoln, Nebraska*, Oxbow Monograph 94 (Oxford, 1997) on the impact of Roman rule on the city.

evidence, however, presents a convincing picture of the enduring importance of the activities of the *ephēbeia* in constructions of Athens' civic identity in the second and third centuries AD.

The evidence discussed in the last two chapters clearly shows the ways in which the athletic training given to ephebes in Sparta and Athens set up a series of associations with traditional, especially military, values. In both cases the contests and festivals in which the ephebes took part, and the representation of these in statues, reliefs, and inscriptions, reaffirmed the continued relevance of the archaic and classical Greek past in the second and third centuries AD. This adoption of practices implying continuity with the past, even if they are in fact relatively recent products, can be likened to what Hobsbawm calls 'the invention of tradition', a means by which communities adopt archaizing rituals or practices in order to legitimize their status or advertise membership in a group.[114] In imperial Greece the prominence of the violent contests of the Spartan *agōgē* and the visual commemoration of Athenian *naumachia* victories on ephebic reliefs helped to present Sparta and Athens as worthy heirs to the Greek past while also defining their own individual characteristics.

This validation works on both a civic and an individual level. While the city's identity and status is asserted through the activities of its youth, participation in such activities was also a way for individual members of the civic elite to proclaim their adherence to traditional values. Herodes Atticus' decision to donate new cloaks to the ephebes should be seen alongside his other acts of euergetism to the city of Athens, most notably his dedication of a new marble stadium for the Panathenaic games of AD 143.[115] Such acts helped to reaffirm the crucial importance of Athens' civic institutions, and to raise her profile throughout the Greek world.[116]

Ephebic activities should not be seen in isolation. The contests of the youths at Sparta or Athens had a wider significance for the identity of the city as a whole, and would have set up resonances with the activities of adult citizens. The Spartan soldiers who accompanied Caracalla's Eastern campaign can be seen as fulfilling the military training they had received as youths, while other figures can be seen playing important roles in the protection of their home cities against the incursions of foreign tribes.[117] As one example, the Athenian orator and writer P. Herennius

---

[114] E. Hobsbawm, 'Introduction: Inventing Tradition', in E. Hobsbawm and T. Ranger, eds., *The Invention of Tradition* (Cambridge, 1983), 1–14.

[115] Philostratus, *Lives of the Sophists* 2.1 (550); Pausanias 1.19.6. On the stadium see C. Gasparri, 'Lo stadio Panatenaico', *Annuario della Scuola Archeologica di Atene* 52–3 (1974–5), 313–93; D. G. Romano, 'The Panathenaic Stadium and Theatre of Lykourgos: An Examination of the Facilities on the Pnyx Hill', *AJA* 89 (1985), 441–54, at 444–5, arguing that Herodes' structure was a new undertaking and not built on the site of an earlier Lycurgan stadium; Tobin, *Herodes Attikos*, 162–85.

[116] On Herodes' motives see Tobin, *Herodes Attikos*, 58–65, 161–210.

[117] See above, p. 156, and below, pp. 227–8.

Dexippus, agonothete of the Panathenaic festival in 255/6 and father of the ephebes who appear in the ephebic list for that year, was also credited later in life with leading the Athenian resistance to the Herulian raids of AD 267.[118] As we will see in the next chapter, the linkage between athletics, warfare, and Greek freedom went wider than the *ephēbeia*, to incorporate the activities of past and present victors in Panhellenic contests. However, the activities of the ephebes played a crucial role in asserting the continuity in values between the cities of the Greek world in the Roman period and their classical pasts. The epigraphic, visual, and literary evidence discussed here clearly suggests the enduring importance of this nexus of ideas about education, athletics, and warfare within Greek civic ideology during the Roman empire.

[118] Scriptores Historiae Augustae, *The Two Gallieni*, 13.8; F. Millar, 'P. Herennius Dexippus: The Greek World and the Third-Century Invasions', *JRS* 59 (1969), 12–29, though the evidence of the *Historia Augusta* has been questioned, see G. Fowden, 'City and Mountain in Late Roman Attica', *JHS* 108 (1988), 48–59, at 51 n. 13.

SEVEN

Olympia and Pausanias' Construction of Greece

The previous two chapters have shown the enduring importance of the ephebic institutions of Athens and Sparta in the creation of civic identities during the Roman period. It is likely that an exploration of the educational systems of other Greek cities would reveal a similar picture, though tailored to the specific representational needs of individual cities. In the next two chapters, I wish to turn from athletic education to the commemoration of athletic victories won in public festivals, and the importance of these in civic self-representation. Some of the themes raised above, particularly concerning the linkage between athletic and military victories, also reappear here, yet I will also show the crucial importance which agonistic festivals had as a symbol of Greek culture. First, I will focus upon the Olympic games, central to any discussion of athletics in the Roman world, just as they are to sport today. This can be clearly seen in Philostratus' treatise on athletics, the *Gymnasticus*, which explicitly takes Olympia as its model: 'in all this the customs of the Eleans lie at hand, for it is necessary to describe such things from the most accurate sources' (*Gym.* 2). While the previous two chapters have focused on the ways in which the values of the past were re-experienced through contemporary ephebic activities, I will here concentrate instead on the enduring impact that past Olympic victories continued to play in assertions of civic identity and prestige.

In order to evaluate the significance that the games at Olympia continued to hold in the Roman period, and especially the role of statues and monuments which commemorated Olympic victories, I propose to take as my guide the second-century travel writer Pausanias. In recent years, Pausanias' *Guide to Greece* has come to be seen as a work firmly enmeshed in the cultural concerns of its time, the second half of the second century AD.[1] In this work Pausanias, an educated

---

[1] On the dating of Pausanias' work see C. Habicht, *Pausanias' Guide to Ancient Greece*, 2nd edn. (Berkeley, Los Angeles, and London, 1988), 9–12; K. W. Arafat, *Pausanias' Greece: Ancient Artists and Roman Rulers* (Cambridge, 1996), 8; and, most recently, E. Bowie, 'Inspiration and Aspiration: Date, Genre, and Readership', in S. E. Alcock, J. F. Cherry, and J. Elsner, eds., *Pausanias: Travel and Memory in Roman Greece* (New York, 2001), 21–32. Book 1 was probably written *c.*160 and the whole work finished before Marcus Aurelius' death in 180 (though cf. Arafat, *Pausanias' Greece*, 8, for an earlier start).

Greek from Asia Minor, describes the sights, monuments, rituals, and history of mainland Greece as he experienced them during his travels over a period of about thirty years.[2] As has been argued by recent scholars, Pausanias' work is no mere *Baedeker* or *Blue Guide* for the ancient traveller, but a carefully constructed literary work that presents a very particular image of Greece and its monuments.[3]

In this chapter I will look at Pausanias' treatment of Olympia and of the statues and monuments to athletic victors which he describes seeing on his travels. For Pausanias, Olympia and Olympic victories hold a key place in the conception of what it is to be Greek. The monuments and statues which he describes, mostly honouring athletes of the archaic or classical past, show the enduring legacy of those figures even within the Roman present and clearly fit into Pausanias' overall approach to ancient Greece and its monuments. Yet while this account may well have a particular Pausanian spin, an examination of other contemporary accounts suggests that Pausanias was not alone in seeing Olympia as the symbolic heart of Greece. Pausanias' account is certainly a unique account of an individual's experience of Greece, but it is also, I will argue, representative of the cultural concerns of his age.[4]

Pausanias provides us with an experiential account of Greece, describing its cities, rites, and monuments as one would approach them on a journey which starts in Attica and then moves in a roughly clockwise direction through the Peloponnese before re-entering central Greece and finishing in Locris. As his narrative travels through these regions he describes their histories—reaching back to their mythical founders as well as retelling key moments in their pasts. Susan Alcock has described Pausanias' account as a 'landscape of memory' where the author depicts particular memories of the past as being preserved and re-enacted through rites, oral histories, and monuments.[5] As she notes, a key theme in Pausanias' account is Greece's Panhellenic past, particularly the events and monuments associated with the Persian Wars, but also other struggles of Greeks against barbarians such as the Trojan War or the Gallic invasion of Greece.[6]

---

[2] On Pausanias' hometown, probably Magnesia ad Sipylum in Lydia, see Habicht, *Pausanias' Guide*, 13–15. Recent research has shown conclusively that Pausanias was an eyewitness of the sites he describes, against the view of earlier scholars such as Wilamowitz: Habicht, *Pausanias' Guide*, 3–4, 165–75.

[3] See especially P. Veyne, *Did the Greeks Believe in their Myths? An Essay on the Constitutive Imagination*, trans. P. Wissing (Chicago, 1988), 3; J. Elsner, *Art and the Roman Viewer* (Cambridge, 1995), 127–9; and J. Elsner, 'Structuring "Greece". Pausanias' *Periegesis* as a Literary Construct', in Alcock, Cherry, and Elsner, *Pausanias*, 3–20. For the comparison of Pausanias' work to a guide book, see J. G. Frazer, *Pausanias' Description of Greece* (London, 1898), xxiv.

[4] On the way Pausanias relates to the general characteristics of his age, see E. Bowie, 'Past and Present in Pausanias', in *Pausanias Historien*, Entretiens sur l'Antiquité Classique 41 (Geneva, 1994), 207–30.

[5] See S. Alcock, 'Landscapes of Memory and the Authority of Pausanias', in *Pausanias Historien*, 241–67.

[6] Alcock, 'Landscapes of Memory', 248–60.

Pausanias espouses the ideal of a free and unified Greece, praising as Panhellenic heroes men who strove to defend the freedom of Greece, from Themistocles to Philopoemen, but berating those who brought honour to their own cities at the cost of Greece as a whole.[7] Indeed, he describes those who took part in the Peloponnesian War, even the most distinguished among them, as 'the murderers, almost wreckers, of Greece' (8.52.3). Yet while Pausanias declares his admiration for Panhellenic unity, his descriptions of individual cities and regions often revel in their distinctiveness and describe monuments which attest to past victories, often over neighbouring cities. He also records the rival claims made by different cities, sometimes adjudicating between them.[8] Objects and monuments play a key role in proving the inhabitants' accounts of their past significance. Thus the Temple of Athena Alea at Tegea is said to contain the hide of the legendary Calydonian boar (its tusks having been taken away by Augustus) and the fetters worn by Spartan prisoners when they dug the plain of Tegea (8.36.1, 37.2).[9] Bizarre rituals or unusual deities also serve to single out specific areas, such as the whipping ritual in honour of Artemis Orthia at Sparta (3.16.10–11) or the horse-headed Black Demeter of the Phigalians (8.52.1–5). While other features serve to bind these communities to the rest of Greece, myth, rituals, and monuments can also define their individuality, asserting their claims to a specific importance within the wider Greek world.[10]

Pausanias' construction of a Greece which is both unified by a shared history and culture, but also made up of cities with discrete and individual traditions and peculiarities, seems to express the realities of Greece at this time. In other texts too we hear about local guides keen to share and discuss the histories of their individual towns, and Lucian jokingly suggests that they find a ready market in tourists eager for outlandish tales.[11] In constructing both a shared Panhellenic identity and an individual civic one, monuments play a crucial role in Pausanias' account and, it would seem, in the cities he visits, whose inhabitants provided him with much of his information. It is within this context of the construction of senses of identity that I will explore the role of athletic statues.

---

[7] Pausanias, 8.52.1–6. On this aspect of Pausanias see Habicht, *Pausanias' Guide*, 104–16.

[8] On civic rivalries in Pausanias, see Alcock, 'Landscapes of Memory', 262–5. On rivalries in Asia Minor see C. P. Jones, *The Roman World of Dio Chrysostom* (Cambridge, Mass., 1978), 83–94.

[9] See M. Pretzler, 'Myth and History at Tegea: Local Tradition and Community Identity', in T. H. Nielsen and J. Roy, eds., *Defining Ancient Arcadia* (Copenhagen, 1999), 89–129.

[10] On monuments as confirming local traditions in Pausanias, see C. Jacob, 'The Greek Traveler's Areas of Knowledge: Myth and other Discourses in Pausanias' Description of Greece', *Yale French Studies* 59 (1980), 65–85, at 77–82. For a discussion of this in Asia Minor, see Z. Newby, 'Art and Identity in Asia Minor', in S. Scott and J. Webster, eds., *Roman Imperialism and Provincial Art* (Cambridge, 2003), 192–213.

[11] Lucian, *Lover of Lies* 4. Compare Pausanias 2.23.6. For other references and a discussion of exegetes, see C. P. Jones, 'Pausanias and His Guides', in Alcock, Cherry, and Elsner, *Pausanias*, 33–9.

OLYMPIA

In 1.26.4, during his account of the Athenian Acropolis, Pausanias breaks off to declare the objective of his work—to give a description of 'panta ta hellēnika', all Greece, and all things relating to Greece.[12] At the very centre of this Greece lies Olympia, the central focus of the work with Elis uniquely occupying two books to every other region's one. Within these two books, Olympia dominates. After an account of the history and territory of the Eleans, which itself contains a number of references to Olympia (e.g. 5.2.5, 5.4.5–6, 5.6.7), Pausanias turns to the sanctuary itself. First he gives a history of the development of the games, arguing that they can be traced back to the Golden Age (5.7.6) and describing the additions, through time, of various different contests.

Then, at 5.10.1, he starts his physical description of the sanctuary, the Altis, with an account of the Temple of Olympian Zeus (5.10.2–12.8). Next he describes the Pelopium and the Great Altar of Zeus (5.13.1–14.3) before beginning the first of four tours of the Altis, dividing up its monuments into thematic categories.[13] The first tour describes the altars in the sanctuary, approaching them, as Pausanias tells us at 5.14.4 and again at 5.14.7, in the order in which the Eleans sacrifice to them.[14] Next we are given a description of the temple of Hera and the objects displayed there, especially the Chest of Cypselus, and the nearby pillar of Oenomaus and the Metroum (5.16.1–20.10) before embarking on another tour of the Altis, this time looking at the votive offerings (5.21.1).[15] This description is itself divided into two: first, an account of the statues of Zeus, including those made from the fines imposed on corrupt athletes (the Zanes: 5.21.2–18), then later an account of other offerings set up in the Altis (5.25.1–27.12).

The final tour of the Altis is the longest, the account of the statues set up to honour Olympic victors, which dominates Book 6 (6.1.1–18.7). This has been carefully foreshadowed by Pausanias' comments at 5.21.1 and 5.25.1 where he outlines his divisions between votive and honorific statues. His discussion of the Zanes in Book 5 can also be seen as a negative version of the account of the victor statues which follows. Pausanias gives a detailed description of the Zanes statues, telling us the names, dates, and specialities of the athletes whose fines paid for them, and

---

[12] On this phrase see Elsner, *Art and the Roman Viewer*, 128, though note also the caveat in Pausanias 3.11.1 and the discussion by J. I. Porter, 'Ideals and Ruins: Pausanias, Longinus and the Second Sophistic', in Alcock, Cherry, and Elsner, *Pausanias*, 63–92 at 67–76.

[13] For an analysis of Pausanias' account of Olympia, to which the following is indebted, see Elsner, 'Structuring "Greece"'.

[14] On this see Elsner, *Art and the Roman Viewer*, 136.

[15] On the Temple of Hera and the possibility that it was being used as a storehouse in Pausanias' day, see K. W. Arafat, 'Pausanias and the Temple of Hera', *ABSA* 90 (1995), 461–73. On the Chest of Cypselus, see A. N. Snodgrass, 'Pausanias and the Chest of Kypselos', in Alcock, Cherry, and Elsner, *Pausanias*, 127–41.

FIGURE 7.1 This view of the entrance to the stadium at Olympia shows on the left the bases of the Zanes statues set up from the fines imposed on corrupt athletes. These acted as warnings against cheating to all athletes entering the stadium.

describing the inscriptions on the statues themselves (5.21.4, 6–7). The inscriptions state that the images act as warnings to other athletes not to take bribes, a warning which was given added point by the prominent placement of these statues at the entrance to the stadium itself (Fig. 7.1). They also honour the Eleans for taking action against corrupt athletes. These statues, in Pausanias' account of them, thus serve as the mirror image of the victor statues described in Book 6. Rather than celebrating the victories of a particular athlete, they praise the Elean organizers of the games, and when Pausanias lists the athletes and their opponents it brings shame, rather than glory, upon them. Through this negative version, we are thus prepared for the true glories of the athletes celebrated in the victor statues of Book 6 (6.1.1–18.7). At the end of his account of the victor statues, Pausanias describes the treasuries (6.19.1–15) and Mount Cronius, the stadium, racecourse, and gymnasium (6.20.1–21.3). The rest of Book 6 is occupied by a description of the territory around Olympia and the city of Elis itself.

Pausanias' description of the victory statues displayed at Olympia has been discussed by Hans-Volkmar Herrmann.[16] His path through the Altis can be

---

[16] H.-V. Herrmann, 'Die Siegerstatuen von Olympia', *Nikephoros* 1 (1988), 119–83.

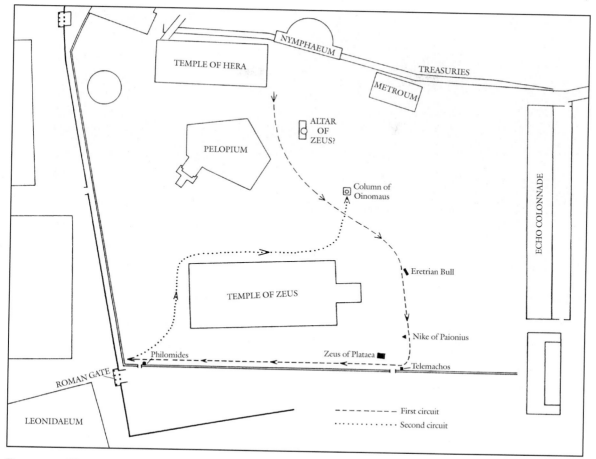

FIGURE 7.2 Herrmann's plan recreates the path taken by Pausanias in his tour of the victor statues in the Altis at Olympia.

reconstructed by comparison of the account with the remaining statue bases.[17] Having begun in front of the temple of Hera he travelled south-east, passing between the Pelopium and the Altar of Zeus and then in front of the Temple of Zeus before turning westwards at the statue of the athlete Telemachus (Figs. 7.2, 7.3). A second tour took him from the Roman gate near the Leonidaeum, behind the temple of Zeus towards the column of Oenomaus. The texture of his narrative varies. Some statues receive only a brief mention, listing the victor, his city, and his speciality as well as, sometimes, the sculptor of the statue, information probably derived from the inscription on the statue base.[18] Others are treated at length, with

[17] A. Trendelenburg, *Pausanias in Olympia* (1914), 54–9; Herrmann, 'Siegerstatuen', 132–4. For an account of archaeologists' use of Pausanias' account and of Pausanias' omissions, see A. Jacquemin, 'Pausanias, le sanctuaire d'Olympie et les archéologues', in D. Knoepfler and M. Piérart, eds., *Éditer, traduire, commenter: Pausanias en l'an 2000* (Geneva, 2001), 283–300.

[18] See H. Whittaker, 'Pausanias and His Use of Inscriptions', *Symbolae Osloenses* 66 (1991), 171–86.

FIGURE 7.3 View along Pausanias' route through the Altis at Olympia, going south-west from the Temple of Hera. The statue bases crowding the route can be clearly seen.

Pausanias providing us with anecdotes relating to the life and career of the athlete, such as he provides for the boxer Glaucus at 6.10.1–3. The boxer's success at Olympia was achieved when his father reminded him to use 'the plough stroke', a reference to a time in his youth when he had driven a loose ploughshare back into the plough with his bare hand. His ensuing prowess as a boxer was then enshrined in his statue, which, Pausanias tells us, showed a figure shadow-boxing.

As Herrmann has noted, Pausanias' account of the victor statues shows a clear preference for archaic or classical statues over late Hellenistic or Roman ones, despite the fact that the surviving statue bases show that statues continued to be erected here in later periods.[19] His account corresponds to his general artistic taste in the work towards archaic and classical works as opposed to Roman ones.[20] Yet the concentration on the victory monuments of athletes from the sixth and fifth centuries BC also has ideological implications. Pausanias' Olympia is saturated with the memory of the classical past, whose continuing relevance is constantly reasserted

---

[19] Herrmann, 'Siegerstatuen', 123–4. More detailed accounts of the epigraphic evidence are given by A. Farrington, 'Olympic Victors and the Popularity of the Olympic Games in the Imperial Period', *Tyche* 12 (1997), 15–46, and T. F. Scanlon, *Eros and Greek Athletics* (New York, 2002), 40–63.

[20] See K. W. Arafat, 'Pausanias' Attitude to Antiquities', *ABSA* 87 (1992), 387–409.

by the statues that throng the Altis. The antiquity of this site is made especially clear at the end of Pausanias' discussion of the victor statues, where he focuses on the very first victor statues, two wooden statues placed near the pillar of Oenomaus (6.18.7). At 5.20.6 Pausanias had told us of the discovery in his own time of ancient remains here, found during the erection of a victory monument for a Roman senator. Here, however, this ancient remnant of Olympia's distant past is associated instead with the very earliest victory monuments, putting the emphasis again on the antiquity of this key Hellenic site.

Pausanias' account of Olympia stresses its importance on a number of levels. The antiquity of the site and its festival is shown through his account of its history, and the importance of the festival itself is clearly shown through the many statues set up to commemorate victories here. Olympia is also shown as a central religious and Panhellenic site. Pausanias' account of the many altars in the Altis stresses the sanctity of the place, while his discussion of the votive offerings made here also indicates Olympia's role as a showcase for all of Greece, a place where cities chose to celebrate and commemorate their military, as well as their athletic, victories. Thus, among the votives which Pausanias describes, we hear about monuments commemorating important Panhellenic achievements, such as the statue of Zeus dedicated by the Greeks who fought the Persians at Plataea, inscribed with the names of all those cities which took part (5.23.1–3). Other votives, however, commemorate victories over fellow Greek cities, or even, in the case of the Zeus dedicated by the Roman general Mummius, of a non-Greek over the Greeks themselves (5.24.4).

A similar representation of Olympia's antiquity and its role as a Panhellenic meeting-place can be found in Philostratus' *Life of Apollonius of Tyana*. There, Olympia is represented as a meeting-place for Greece, a centre to which people flock to see the sage Apollonius of Tyana after he has mysteriously escaped persecution at the hands of Domitian (8.15). In a discussion about what constitutes a festival, Apollonius suggests that Olympia is naturally fitted for its purpose. While its gymnasia, stoas, fountains, and houses have been constructed by human arts, the area was already topographically suited to its role. The river Alpheius provided water for drinking and bathing, the hippodrome was a natural place for horses to run, the valley served as a stadium for athletes, and the groves supplied the wreaths for the winners (8.18). Rather than being purely the product of human construction, then, the festival at Olympia is shown as the natural consequence of the landscape itself.

The antiquity of Olympia is clearly of crucial importance for both Pausanias and Philostratus. Yet this is not to say that Olympia was merely a showcase for the past during the Imperial period. The archaeological remains of the site show that it continued to be adorned with new buildings throughout the Imperial period. A recently discovered bronze plaque shows that athletic victories continued at least into the late fourth century, recording the victories of two Athenian brothers in

AD 381 and 385, though evidence for victories in the earlier fourth century is more scanty.[21] However, the inscriptional evidence does seem to suggest that the majority of these imperial athletic victors came from the cities of Asia Minor and Egypt, rather than the cities of mainland Greece.[22] For those cities described by Pausanias, the prestige they gained by having produced Olympic victors may well have rested largely on the achievements of those in the past.

The sheer space given by Pausanias to Olympia, its history, and its monuments, suggests that conceptually as well as physically it lies at the very heart of his construction of Greece. While scholars have commented on the rather abrupt start and end to Pausanias' work, most suggest that it is substantially complete, though perhaps lacking a dedicatory preface. The complex webs of interconnections that run throughout the ten books suggest that we should see this work as a carefully planned literary work. The decision to place Olympia at its very heart, uniquely treated in two books, is highly significant.[23] Other prominent parts of any narrative are its beginning and end, and here too we find discussions of key areas within the Greek world. So Book 1 is dominated by the discussion of Athens, while Book 10 includes the description of the important Panhellenic sanctuary of Delphi, though without the lavish detail which Pausanias expends on Olympia.

Each of these sites could have asserted an equal claim to be seen as the heart of Greece—Athens as the centre of the new Panhellenion and a focal city in the world of the Second Sophistic, and Delphi as the key oracular sanctuary of the ancient world, fount of the many oracles which pepper the narrative.[24] Yet Pausanias chooses instead to place Olympia at the centre of his vision of Greece. We can perhaps see this as an indication of a Greek view of Greece, as opposed to the imperial view suggested by the activities of some Roman emperors. The Panhellenion is a key institution to consider here. Founded in AD 131/2, this body had its headquarters at Athens and included amongst its members cities from mainland Greece, Asia Minor, and Crete and Cyrene who could lay claim (albeit sometimes a tenuous one) to Greek descent.[25] While some Greek cities certainly welcomed this proposal, the initiative for this body seems to have arisen with Hadrian himself, and

---

[21] U. Sinn, G. Ladstätter, A. Martin, and T. Völlig, 'Bericht über das Forschungsprojekt "Olympia während der römischen Kaiserzeit und in der Spätantike" III. Die Arbeiten im Jahr 1994', *Nikephoros* 7 (1994), 229–50. J. Ebert discusses the inscription at 238–41.

[22] Farrington, 'Olympic Victors', 16–19; Scanlon, *Eros*, 56.

[23] On the text see Habicht, *Pausanias' Guide*, 4–8, and Bowie, 'Inspiration and Aspiration', especially 28. See also Elsner, 'Structuring "Greece"', on the work as a careful literary construct.

[24] e.g. 3.3.6–7; 4.9.4; 8.11.10.

[25] On membership and admission see A. J. S. Spawforth and S. Walker, 'The World of the Panhellenion I: Athens and Eleusis', *JRS* 75 (1985), 78–104, and 'The World of the Panhellenion II: Three Dorian Cities', *JRS* 76 (1986), 88–105; I. Romeo, 'The Panhellenion and Ethnic Identity in Hadrianic Greece', *Classical Philology* 97 (2002), 21–40.

can be seen as a continuation of his earlier policies to create a unified body of Greek states which privileged the ancient cities of the Greek mainland.[26] A recently discovered decree from Thyatira in Lycia certainly seems to stress the centrality of Athens within the Panhellenion, calling her a Benefactress to all, suggesting that the body acted in part as a homage to the city.[27] This pre-eminence may have been resented by some, such as the most prestigious cities of Roman Asia Minor, Ephesus, Smyrna, and Pergamum, which do not appear amongst the members of the body. Its eponymous festival, the Panhellenia, also seems to have had some trouble attracting competitors, at least in the later second century.[28] All this suggests that the Hadrianic construction of a Greece centred around the ancient city of Athens could be challenged or resisted by some in the Greek world. Pausanias' decision to place Olympia at the centre of his work is a clear sign that he had a very different vision of Greece. For him, it is Olympia which is central to Panhellenic identity.

This is not to say that Pausanias ignores Athens. Indeed, he chooses to start his work with Attica and also links his discussion of Olympia with Athens at 5.10.1. Here he makes the following declaration:

Many are the sights to be seen in Greece, and many are the wonders to be heard; but most especially do the rites at Eleusis and the Games at Olympia partake of the divine mind.

Olympia and Eleusis, itself within the territory of Athens, are thus singled out as the sites of the most sacred activity in the whole of Greece.

Olympia is also linked with Delphi in Pausanias' account. Thus in 6.19.1, when Pausanias turns away from his discussion of athletic victor statues to describe the terrace to the north of the Heraeum, he starts as follows: 'On this terrace are treasuries, just as in Delphi certain of the Greeks have made treasuries to Apollo.' Just as his words at 5.10.1 looked back to the discussion of Eleusis in Book 1, this comment foreshadows the later discussion of the Delphic treasuries which Pausanias will give in Book 10, again situating Olympia at the centre of a triad of great Greek sanctuaries.[29] The comparison to Delphi also reminds us that Olympia was at the centre of another group of sanctuaries, the four centres of the ancient *periodos* or festival circuit which also included the Crown Games at Nemea, Isthmia, and

---

[26] See A. J. S. Spawforth, 'The Panhellenion Again', *Chiron* 29 (1999), 339–52, contra C. P. Jones, 'The Panhellenion', *Chiron* 26 (1996), 29–56, arguing for an initiative amongst the Greeks themselves, modified in id., 'A Decree of Thyatira in Lycia', *Chiron* 29 (1999), 1–21 at 15.

[27] Jones, 'Decree', 2, at line 15; see Spawforth, 'Panhellenion Again', 343.

[28] J. H. Oliver, *Greek Constitutions of Early Roman Emperors from Inscriptions and Papyri*, Memoirs of the American Philosophical Society 178 (Philadelphia, 1989), nos. 188, 245. See also Spawforth, 'Panhellenion Again', 351 with n. 64.

[29] 10.11.1–5. On Pausanias' references to Eleusis and Delphi here and his placement of Olympia at the centre, see also Elsner, 'Structuring "Greece"', 6, 11.

Delphi. While all these centres continued to be popular in the Roman world, Pausanias treats both Nemea and Isthmia in a rather cursory fashion.[30]

There were probably both literary and ideological reasons for this. The fact that both Isthmia and Nemea fall within the same general area, the subject of his second book, would have made a detailed account of both cumbersome and repetitive. Yet both festivals could also be seen as lacking the necessary connection with the past which made Olympia so attractive. Imperial Corinth was in fact a Roman colony, founded after the destruction of the Greek city by Mummius in 146 BC and hence lacking the continuity with the classical past which is so important throughout Pausanias' narrative.[31] The Nemean festival had also by now been transferred to Argos.[32] Neither was an appropriate choice for Pausanias' construction of a Panhellenic Greece whose glorious Greek past could still be re-experienced within its sites, monuments, and rituals.

Delphi, however, was another matter. Contemporary sources suggest that the games held here drew extensive crowds in the Roman period.[33] It forms the backdrop to Plutarch's dialogue *On the Decline of Oracles* as well as for *On the Pythian Oracle* and, like Athens, had received the attention of the emperor Hadrian. He had served as eponymous magistrate here, as at Athens and Sparta, and seems to have considered it as a possible candidate for the centre of the Panhellenion before deciding on Athens.[34] Pausanias does provide a detailed account of the sanctuary and its festival which in some ways mirrors that of Olympia. Thus he describes the evolution of the festival from the oldest contest, singing a hymn to the god, through all the other contests which were gradually added, just as he had done at Olympia (10.7.2–8). A discussion of the membership of the Amphictyonic League establishes the Panhellenic credentials of the sanctuary, before we move onto the sanctuary itself (10.8.1–5). In his introductory remarks Pausanias makes it clear that he will only discuss a few of the votive offerings and makes a direct reference back to his account of Olympia:

Concerning the votive offerings (*anathēmata*) I will mention those which seem to me most worthy of mention. Those athletes and competitors in music whom the majority of mankind have neglected, I hardly consider to be worthy of attention. The athletes who have left a reputation behind them I have indicated in my account of Elis. Phaylus of Croton,

---

[30] This popularity is suggested by their appearance at the top of many victor inscriptions. See, Moretti, *IAG*, 174, no. 65; 183, no. 67; and Caldelli, *Agon*, 54.

[31] On constructions of Corinth's civic identity in the Roman period see J. König, 'Favorinus' *Corinthian Oration* in its Corinthian context', *PCPS* 47 (2001), 141–68.

[32] On the movement of the games and the site at Nemea, see S. G. Millar, 'Excavations at the Panhellenic Site of Nemea: Cults, Politics and Games', in W. J. Raschke, ed., *The Archaeology of the Olympics: The Olympics and Other Festivals in Antiquity* (Madison, Wis., 1988), 141–51.

[33] Aulus Gellius, *Noctes Atticae* 12.5.1.

[34] See M. R. Flacelière, 'Hadrien et Delphes', *CRAI* (1971), 175–85, and D. Willers, *Hadrians panhellenisches Programm: archäologische Beiträge zur Neugestaltung Athens durch Hadrian* (Basel, 1990), 99–100.

who won no victory at Olympia, won at the Pythia two victories in the pentathlon and a third in the stade race. He also fought at sea against the Persians in his own ship, having fitted it out himself and manned it with citizens of Croton who were in Greece. The statue of this man is at Delphi. (10.9.2)

Here Pausanias first declares that he will be selective in his account of the votives at Delphi, declaring that all the most worthy athletes have already been discussed by him in his account of their statues at Elis. The clear assumption is that any athlete worth his salt must have been victorious at Olympia as well as Delphi—Olympia, the oldest of the Greek festivals, is also pre-eminent in reputation. However, he then goes on to mention one athlete who had not been successful at Olympia, Phaylus of Croton. As well as learning of Phaylus' Pythian victories, however, we also find that he had taken part in one of the most famous Panhellenic battles of all time—the sea battle against the Persians at Salamis in 480 BC. While Pausanias' previous remarks would suggest that he was not one of the most prestigious athletes of his time, his Panhellenic actions win him mention in his account. Pausanias' reference to the man's statue comes only at the end of this account. While it was presumably erected to commemorate his Delphic victory, it seems in Pausanias' eyes to be a memorial of his military actions as well.

With Delphi running a close second, Olympia is still clearly presented as the most important centre of all, with her victorious athletes being the most prestigious of mortals and Delphi's musical victors earning barely a glance. Athletics, rather than simply festivals, lie at the heart of Pausanias' Greece. Pausanias' lengthy account of the statues and dedications in the Altis also suggests that the past significance of the sanctuary and the continuing vitality of that past lies in the very monuments which adorn it. This is made particularly clear when we look at Pausanias' treatment of other, abandoned, festivals. In Book 8 Pausanias describes a sanctuary of Pan on Mount Lycaeus in Arcadia, the very mountain on which Zeus was said to have been reared. Here, we are told, are a stadium and hippodrome, where the Lycaean games used to be held in the olden days. Here too there are statue bases, with no statues on them, though one still preserves its inscription (8.38.5). The overall tone of the description is melancholic, the lapsing of the festival mirrored in the absence of the statues, with only a few signs of its past importance. At Olympia, in contrast, the enduring vitality of Greek culture is embodied through the numerous statues and monuments Pausanias describes.

Yet Olympia's vitality does not only lie in the sanctuary itself. It shows itself also in the many allusions to Olympic victory which are scattered throughout Pausanias' narrative as he describes the histories and monuments of different Greek states. In the next section I will examine how past monuments to Olympic victories, which were still displayed in the cities of mainland Greece to be seen by Pausanias and his contemporaries, forged a link with Olympia and helped to assert a city's status within the Panhellenic world.

CELEBRATING ATHLETIC VICTORIES IN THE CITIES OF GREECE

Throughout Pausanias' narrative he mentions statues or monuments associated with athletic victors, many of them Olympic victors whose statues in their home cities help to set up a connection between the city and the Panhellenic centre of Greece. The ways in which Pausanias discusses these statues reveals the associations that past athletic victories still held in the world of the Roman empire, both for Pausanias and for the cities in which these statues were erected. Here I will discuss just a few of the examples described by Pausanias, as well as the archaeological evidence that suggests that the memory of past victories was still important in the contemporary world.

In his discussion of the statues and offerings on the Athenian Acropolis Pausanias mentions three which commemorate athletes.[35] Only one of these is explicitly said to have been an Olympic victor, the seventh-century victor Cylon. Pausanias actually expresses surprise at the presence of Cylon's bronze statue on the Acropolis since he had plotted to become tyrant of Athens.[36] He decides that it must be due to Cylon's good looks and fame, both as an Olympic victor and as the son-in-law of Theagenes, tyrant of Megara (1.28.1).[37] Two other athletes also seem to have had statues. Pausanias mentions one of Epicharinus, 'who practised the race in armour' (*hoplitodromein askēantos*), made by the sculptor Critias.[38] He also mentions 'Hermolycus the pancratiast' and says that he will pass over him since he has been discussed by others (1.23.9–10). While Pausanias does not explicitly say that a statue of Hermolycus was present, its existence can be surmised by this passing reference.[39] The reference to other writers must refer to Herodotus' discussion of the battle between the Greeks and Persians at Mycale in 479 BC. Herodotus declares that of all those who fought at the battle, the Athenians fought best and that among them the best fighter was Hermolycus the pancratiast.[40] Pausanias'

---

[35] Pausanias also describes a painting showing the Nemean victories of Alcibiades displayed in a room to the left of the Propylaia, 1.22.7. Another athletic statue, of the pancratiast Autolycus, was in the prytaneion, 1.18.3.

[36] Compare Pausanias 7.27.7 on Chaeron, discussed above, pp. 149–50.

[37] Moretti, *Olympionikai*, 65, no. 56, gives the date of his victory as 640 BC. The statue must, therefore, have been set up posthumously. On Cylon, see D. G. Kyle, *Athletics in Ancient Athens* (Leiden, 1987), 50–1, and C. Mann, *Athlet und Polis im archaischen und frühklassischen Griechenland* (Göttingen, 2001) 64–8.

[38] Hyde, *OVM*, 204 and n. 3, suggests that the statue was shown in action. The base of Epicharinus' statue has been found and names the artists as Critius and Nesiotes: *CIA* i. 376. On Pausanias' spelling of the name here, see Hyde, *OVM*, 372.

[39] In his discussion of the statues at Olympia Pausanias refers to other figures in a similar way. See Herrmann, 'Siegerstatuen', 135.

[40] Herodotus 9.105. For discussion of this and the previous statue, see Hyde, *OVM*, 372–3.

motive for mentioning Hermolycus, albeit briefly, then, was probably his involvement in a major Panhellenic victory as much as his athletic success.[41]

Pausanias' attitudes here can be tied in with those shown elsewhere. As seen above, in his description of the gymnasium at Pellene, the sight of a statue of the Olympic victor Promachus prompts Pausanias to recall both his military and athletic victories, while the tyrannical activities of another citizen, Chaeron, preclude his commemoration, Olympic victories not withstanding (7.27.5–8).[42] Here too, Pausanias is surprised at the commemoration of a would-be tyrant, albeit one who was an Olympic victor, while his passing reference to Hermolycus prompts his reader to recall that man's famous military victories. Indeed, other statues set up on the Acropolis may also have been designed to evoke military victories. As Marco Romano has shown, a statue base found close to those of Hermolycus and Epicharinus contains an inscription recording the dedicatee as Phaylus of Croton.[43] As restored by Moretti, it would seem to have mentioned both his athletic victories at Delphi and his involvement in the battle of Salamis against the Persians.[44] Romano suggests that the erection in the fifth century BC of three athletic statues, those of Epicharinus, Hermolycus, and Phaylus, was specifically designed to evoke both their athletic achievements and their involvement in the various battles of the Persian wars, presenting the men as examples of virtue.[45]

Pausanias' text does not mention the statue of Phaylus. It is possible that this is due to a lacuna in the text at this point, or that Pausanias was more interested here in the commemoration of Athenian figures.[46] Yet the motivations which Romano suggests for the erection of this group in the fifth century BC could still have been strong for their second-century viewers. Pausanias recalls Phaylus' involvement in the Persian wars in 10.9.2 and also alludes here to Herodotus' praise of Hermolycus. Phaylus' statue seems to have shown the athlete in an active pose.[47] The iconography of the image and the fame of the figure would have worked together to assert the link between athletic prowess and military activity that we have already seen expressed by Solon in the *Anacharsis* and by the images of the Spartan and Athenian *ephēbeia*.

This connection between athletics and warfare can also be found elsewhere in Pausanias' text. At the very end of Book 1, we hear of the grave of one of the most famous Olympic victors, Orsippus of Megara. While in the agora at Megara Pausanias records seeing the grave of this man. He tells us that Orsippus won the

---

[41] Pausanias does not mention Phaylus' statue, which seems to have been displayed nearby, though this may be due to damage to the text. See M. Romano, 'L'epigrafe ateniese a Phayllos (IG, I³, 2, 823)', *ZPE* 123 (1998), 105–16, at 109 n. 15.

[42] See above, pp. 149–50.   [43] Romano, 'L'epigrafe ateniese a Phayllos'.

[44] Moretti, *IAG*, 24–9, no. 11.   [45] Romano, 'L'epigrafe ateniese a Phayllos', 107–12.

[46] On possibility of a lacuna see Romano, 'L'epigrafe ateniese a Phayllos', 109 n. 15.

[47] Romano, 'L'epigrafe ateniese a Phayllos', 106, 111–12.

stade race at Olympia running naked while all his competitors were wearing loin-cloths, a decision which Pausanias thinks was probably deliberate. He also notes that Orsippus later annexed some neighbouring territory for Megara. Orsippus' fame thus rests both on his victory at Olympia as the first naked runner and on his military prowess, again repeating the combination we have seen elsewhere.[48]

Indeed, the discovery of an inscription at Megara reveals that both these facts were celebrated on Orsippus' tomb. This inscription celebrates the 'warlike' Orrhippus (probably the Megarian form of the name) both for his success in winning back territory and for being the first Greek to be crowned at Olympia naked, when all previous stade runners had worn loincloths.[49] It also reveals that the Megarians had set up a memorial to him at the prompting of the Delphic oracle, which elsewhere too often features in accounts of the posthumous honours granted to earlier Greek athletes.

The overlap between Pausanias' account and the inscription suggests that Pausanias was drawing his information from this inscription or its predecessor.[50] It is significant, then, that Pausanias actually seems to have changed the order of the inscription, putting Orsippus' athletic success first, and then telling us of his military acts, whereas the inscription describes Orsippus as 'warlike' (*daiphrōn*) and details his military acts first and athletic ones second. Pausanias, it seems, deliber-ately highlights Orsippus' athletic victory and his place within the historical devel-opment of Greek athletics.[51] Yet the enduring importance to the Megarians of Orsippus' victory as the first naked athlete at Olympia is also clearly underscored by the content of the inscription and the fact that it seems to have been reinscribed during the Roman period.[52] The combination of Pausanias' account and the epi-graphic evidence suggests that the Olympic victory of an eighth-century athlete was still a matter of public pride in the second century AD.

While the majority of the athletes mentioned by Pausanias come from the clas-sical past, a more contemporary figure appears in Book 2. In his description of the territory of Sicyon, Pausanias mentions a bronze statue set in the enclosure of

---

[48] On the issue of athletic nakedness, see J. A. Arieti, 'Nudity in Greek Athletics', *Classical World* 68 (1974–5), 431–6; N. B. Crowther, 'Athletic Dress and Nudity in Greek Athletics', *Eranos* 80 (1982), 163–8; J.-P. Thuillier, 'La nudité athlétique (Grèce, Etrurie, Rome)', *Nikephoros* 1 (1988), 29–48; M. MacDonnell, 'The Introduction of Athletic Nudity: Thucydides, Plato and the Vases', *JHS* 111 (1991), 182–93; and, with further bibliography and discussion, A. Stewart, *Art, Desire and the Body in Ancient Greece* (Cambridge, 1997), 27, 239.

[49] *IG* vii. 52.

[50] On Pausanias' use of inscriptions in general see Habicht, *Pausanias' Guide*, 64–94; Whittaker, 'Pausanias and Inscriptions'.

[51] There were other, rival, claimants to the title of the first naked athlete at Olympia, against which Orsippus' status is upheld by both Pausanias and the Megarians, see above, n. 48.

[52] The inscription itself seems to be a later copy of an earlier inscription. *IG* vii. 52 dates it to between the second and fifth centuries AD, while Moretti, *Olympionikai*, 61–2, no. 16, suggests a date in the fifth century AD. His victory is usually dated to 720 BC.

the sanctuary of Asclepius at Titane. This commemorated a Sicyonian named Granianus, who had won victories in the pentathlon, stade race, and diaulos race at Olympia (2.11.8). Pausanias gives no further information about the athlete or the dates of his victories, but Moretti has identified him with the Aelius Granianus who appears on an inscription relating to a prize game at Sparta, dated to between AD 120 and 180.[53]

Harry Sidebottom has recently argued that Pausanias often juxtaposes events from many different time periods, conflating historical divisions and encouraging the reader to think of the contemporary Greeks as not so different to those of the ancient past.[54] The mention here of a contemporary figure acts in precisely this way, reminding us that athletic victory statues continued to be produced in the Roman period. Their display alongside statues from the ancient past helped to reassert the idea that the values of that past were still current in the contemporary world.

In his description of the city of Argos, however, we return to the past. Two victory statues are mentioned in Pausanias' description of 'the most illustrious (*epiphanestaton*) sight in Argos', the sanctuary of Apollo Lycius (2.19.3). Within the temple of the god, Pausanias mentions a statue of Ladas, 'the swiftest runner of his time' and then later refers in passing to a statue of the boxer Creugas outside (2.19.7, 20.1). Neither is described in much detail, but both are figures who will reappear elsewhere in Pausanias' narrative. Ladas is mentioned again in Book 3, when Pausanias describes his tomb on the road between Sparta and Arcadia. There too Pausanias describes him as 'the swiftest runner of his time', using exactly the same words as in this passage. He also mentions a namesake of this famous Ladas who had won a victory in the stade race at Olympia and, according to the Olympic records, came from Aegium in Achaea (3.21.1).[55] Of Ladas himself, he tells us that he seems to have died on his way home after he had been crowned for a victory in the long race (*dolichos*) at Olympia.

Pausanias' references to Ladas have caused some confusion to scholars who debate whether the athlete was a citizen of Sparta, as the reference to him falling ill on the way home seems to suggest, or of Argos, where his statue stood in the Sanctuary of Apollo.[56] Elsewhere too Ladas appears in Pausanias' text. In Book 8 Pausanias describes seeing a stadium named after Ladas on the road between Mantinea and Orchomenus, where the athlete practised his running (8.12.5).

[53] *SEG* xi. 838, ll. 10–11. See A. M. Woodward, 'Excavations at Sparta. III. The Inscriptions', *ABSA* 26 (1923–5), 159–239 at 213–19, and Moretti, *Olympionikai*, 163, no. 848.

[54] H. Sidebottom, 'Pausanias: Past, Present, and Closure', *CQ* 52.2 (2002), 494–9.

[55] Pausanias tells us that he has his information from the Olympic records, a comment which foreshadows his later discussion of Olympia. In 10.23.14 we learn that this victory was in the 125th Olympiad, that is 280 BC.

[56] See Hyde, *OVM*, 364–5, who favours Sparta, and Moretti, *Olympionikai*, 96, no. 160, favouring Argos and suggesting a victory in 460 BC or shortly after.

Whatever his homeland, however, Ladas was certainly one of the most famous athletes of the classical past. He appears in much Latin literature as emblematic for speed and had a bronze statue made of him by the fifth-century sculptor Myron, which seems to have been famous in Antiquity.[57] Pausanias does not, however, refer to the artist of Ladas' statue at Argos, nor does he mention any statue to him at Olympia, therefore it is possible that the statue by Myron originally stood at Olympia but had been taken to Rome by Pausanias' day.[58]

Creugas, likewise, is not mentioned in any detail here, but appears again in Book 8 where the story of his boxing contest with the Syracusan Damoxenus is told as a comparison to the famous story of the Phigalian athlete Arrachion (8.40.3–5).[59] The two athletes were boxing at the Nemean games, when Damoxenus killed his opponent by striking him under the ribs with outstretched fingers, piercing his skin and pulling out his entrails. Creugas died on the spot but was awarded the victory by the judges and had his statue set up in Argos, where Pausanias himself had seen it, a clear reference back to the passage in Book 2.

Such cross-references to other parts of Pausanias' narrative are also an important feature of the references to Olympic victors in Book 3 on Laconia. Pausanias refers to eight Olympic victors in this book, a number which perhaps reflects the general dominance of the Laconians at Olympia in the early days of the festival.[60] Those whom Pausanias mentions as being honoured at Sparta for Olympic victories include three figures who had won athletic victories in the seventh century BC, in addition to two Spartan women who had won victories in the chariot races, Cynisca and Euryleonis.[61] At 3.13.9 he describes seeing a statue of the wrestler Heteomocles, who had won five Olympic victories. Pausanias also mentions Heteomocles' father Hipposthenes here, who had won six Olympic victories for wrestling, and who reappears a little later in the narrative at 3.15.7.[62] There he tells us about a temple of Hipposthenes, who is worshipped here as Poseidon, in accordance with an oracle. While some modern scholars believe that Pausanias has confused the worship of Poseidon Hippios with that of Hipposthenes, the fact that

---

[57] References in Latin literature: Catullus 55.25; Martial 2.86, 10.100. Myron's statue: *Greek Anthology* 16.53, 54 (only the latter explicitly identifies the sculptor as Myron).

[58] On the statue see Hyde, *OVM*, 196–7.   [59] Arrachion's story is discussed above, p. 153.

[60] On this dominance see Delorme, *Gymnasion: Étude sur les monuments consacrés à l'éducation en Grèce* (Paris, 1960), 21–2; H. Pleket, 'Zur Soziologie des antiken Sports', *Mededelingen van het Nederlands Instituut te Rome* 36 (1974), 57–87 at 59–60; and Mann, *Athlet und Polis*, 121–39.

[61] These women are mentioned at 3.15.1 and 3.17.6 and their victories date to the fourth century BC. Cynisca also reappears in the description of Olympia, at 5.12.5 (bronze horses dedicated in the temple of Zeus) and 6.1.6 (her victory monument). See Moretti, *Olympionikai*, nos. 373, 381 (Cynisca) and no. 418 (Euryleonis).

[62] See Moretti, *Olympionikai*, 66–8, nos. 61, 66, 68, 70, 73, 75, 82–6, for the dates of their victories. Pausanias also tells us at 5.8.9 that Hipposthenes won the boys' wrestling match when it was first introduced at Olympia in the 37th Olympiad, i.e. 632 BC.

Pausanias believes it possible that Hipposthenes was worshipped in Sparta with divine honours is itself significant.[63] Indeed, Hipposthenes fits into a pattern of athletic victors who are honoured after their deaths with heroic or divine honours, often at the prompting of the Delphic oracle. We have already encountered Orsippus of Megara, whose tomb, according to the inscription, was set up at the order of Delphi. Later too we will hear of Oebotas of Dyme and Theagenes of Thasos, who also receive cultic worship at the order of the Delphic oracle.[64]

The third Olympic athletic victor honoured at Sparta is even earlier than Heteomocles and Hipposthenes. The runner Chionis is honoured with a stele set up near the tombs of the Agiad kings and the running course, which was inscribed with his victories at Olympia and elsewhere (3.14.3). These victories included seven Olympic victories, four in the stade race and three in the double stade (*diaulos*). The race in armour, we are told, was not yet practised at Olympia when Chionis competed there, a fact that dates his victories before its introduction in 520 BC.[65] In fact, Chionis seems to have been victorious in the mid-seventh century BC, and is also said to have helped in the founding of Cyrene.[66] Chionis reappears in Pausanias' discussion of the statues at Olympia itself, where we are told that a stele here too recorded his victories. Pausanias states that the stele must have been erected by the Lacedaemonians rather than Chionis himself since it refers to the fact that the race in armour had not yet been instituted at Olympia, a comment which clearly suggests that the stele was erected once the contest *had* been instituted (6.13.2).

The correspondences between Pausanias' descriptions of the two stelae suggest that they probably contained the same text and were set up at the same time. Pausanias says that there was also a statue at Olympia next to the stele, though he argues that it cannot be a portrait image (*eikōn*) of Chionis since it was made by Myron, a sculptor active much later. It was probably, however, set up along with the stele by the Spartans in order to promote the fame of their runner Chionis in rivalry with the Crotonian runner Astylus, whose statue stood next to that of Chionis at Olympia.[67] Pausanias only refers to Astylus' victories in the stade and diaulos, but he also seems to have been victorious in the race in armour, allowing

[63] See Hyde, *OVM*, 362, and Moretti, *Olympionikai*, 66–7, no. 61.

[64] Orsippus: *IG* vii. 52, though Pausanias 1.44.1 does not mention the oracle; Oebotas: 6.3.8, 7.17.6–7; Theagenes: 6.11.2–9. On athletes as heroes, see J. Fontenrose, 'The Hero as Athlete', *California Studies in Classical Antiquity* 1 (1968), 73–104. The role of statues in these cults is discussed further below, pp. 223–6.

[65] At 5.8.10 Pausanias dates the introduction of this contest to the 65th Olympic games.

[66] He is Moretti, *Olympionikai*, 64, nos. 42–7, with victories in 664, 660, and 656 BC. Pausanias (4.23.4) gives his first Olympic victory to Olympiad 28, in 668 BC. Moretti, however, thinks that this is a mistake and instead follows Africanus in giving Charmis of Sparta as victor that year (*Olympionikai*, 63–4, no. 40).

[67] Hyde, *OVM*, 362, and Rausa, *Immagine*, 19, 80, both think that the statue was commissioned by the Spartans in around 470 BC to celebrate Chionis' victory, though neither specifically mention Pausanias' comments.

him to assume the title of *triastēs*—as a victor in three separate foot races.[68] It seems likely, then, that Chionis' statue and stelae were set up in the 470s or 460s and that the reference to the race in armour should be seen as a direct rebuttal to any suggestion that Astylus' victories in this as well made him superior.[69]

In the case of Hipposthenes and Chionis, then, their monuments at Sparta pave the way for their mention in Book 6 and indeed Chionis is physically represented in both Sparta and Olympia by these two apparently identical inscribed stelae. Another case of a Spartan honoured in a similar way appears in Book 6, where Pausanias records the dedication of a stele at Olympia by the runner Deinosthenes of Lacedaemonia next to his statue. He also tells us that the inscription on the stele recorded the distance between this stele and another at Olympia.[70] The stelae of Chionis and Deinosthenes thus show the relationship set up between individual Greek cities, here Sparta, and the sanctuary at Olympia.

Elsewhere, Pausanias' descriptions of relatively small towns suggest that a city's claim to have produced an Olympic victor, even at some time in the distant past, could still draw attention in the Roman period. Pausanias' description of the city of Acriae on the coast is very brief. The city's main claim to fame is its temple to the Mother of the Gods, which the inhabitants claim to be the oldest sanctuary to the goddess in the Peloponnese. He also says that the city once produced an Olympic victor, the runner Nicocles, who in two festivals won five prizes for running and has a monument set up to him between the gymnasium and the harbour wall (3.22.5). Pausanias then turns to the next city. The mention of Nicocles in this brief account of what appears to be a relatively insignificant city shows the importance to all cities, small as well as large, of being able to claim an Olympic victor. Acriae may be small and insignificant, but through its sanctuary and Olympic victor it wins a place in Pausanias' account.

Other similar instances where an Olympic victor proves the importance of an otherwise marginal town appear in the later books. In 8.36.1 Pausanias describes the city of Methydrium. While this was later absorbed into the city of Megalopolis, Pausanias tells us that it had produced Olympic victors. These victors prove that Methydrium did once have an individual civic identity. A similar use of Panhellenic victors to prove the existence of a city occurs in 10.33.8. Here Pausanias asserts that the existence of a city called Parapotamii is proved not only by a reference in

---

[68] See Moretti, *Olympionikai*, 82–3, nos. 178–9, 186–7, 196–9, 219. His victories were in 488, 484, 480, and possibly 476 BC. Oxyrhynchus Papyri 222 also gives him as a victor in the race in armour, and Moretti thinks it likely that Pausanias' text is lacunose at this point.

[69] Hyde, *OVM*, 362, agrees that the stelae were erected at the same time as the statue. Rausa, *Immagine*, 19, 80, thinks that the stelae were set up immediately after the victory but, as Pausanias notes, this is disproved by their mention of the race in armour.

[70] 6.16.8. The slab has been found, *IOlympia* 171, and agrees with Pausanias' account except for a minor discrepancy in the figures.

Herodotus, but also by the fact that it produced an athlete who won the boys' boxing match at the Pythian festival.[71] Victories at the Panhellenic festivals are thus one of the ways in which even obscure or lost cities preserve their memory in Pausanias' account.

The examination of Pausanias' treatment of athletic victors suggests a number of conclusions. The references to Olympic victors, particularly numerous in Book 3, help to signal the importance to individual cities of having produced a victor at Olympia, and prepare the reader for the detailed discussion of Olympia in Books 5 and 6. Yet these victors are not only important as athletes. Men of the ancient past, like Orsippus and Hipposthenes, could later receive public memorials in the centre of their towns, with honours equating them to heroes or even gods. Others are renowned as much for their military as for their athletic successes—such as the pancratiast Hermolycus at Athens.

Among these figures are a number of men who will reappear later in the course of the narrative, such as the Spartan runner Chionis, who reappears in Book 4, when his victories in the stade race are used for dating purposes, and again in Book 6. Another such figure is the runner Ladas, so famous in later literature for his speed and bronze statue by Myron that he seems to have lost his civic identity. Instead he has become a figure who belongs to all of Greece, represented and remembered in Argos, Laconia, and Arcadia through different monuments. Ladas seems to be the exception, however. Other athletes are clearly tied to particular towns, one of the many ways in which the cities Pausanias visits recorded their own individual importance within the wider Greek world, whether they were as small as Acriae, or as important, historically, as Sparta. In the Roman world of the second century AD, the memory of past Olympic victories, asserted through the presence of ancient statues or monuments, was one of the ways in which cities continued to assert their Hellenic identity.

Epigraphic evidence suggests that Olympic victors were actually relatively scarce in the cities of mainland Greece in the Imperial period, when the majority of Olympic victors come instead from Asia or Egypt.[72] The statues and monuments set up to past victors were thus one of the ways these cities could continue to assert their place within the Hellenic world. Yet some new victors did emerge and their victories could be commemorated both at home and in Olympia. One example comes from the third century AD in the figure of the runner P. Aelius Alcandridas of Sparta. This man twice achieved victories in the foot race at all four of the major Panhellenic festivals, and was also given the title 'best of the Hellenes' (*aristos Hellēnōn*) for his victory in the race in armour at Plataea. Evidence of his victories comes from a statue base at Olympia and from three inscriptions at Sparta.[73] One

[71] Herodotus 8.33.   [72] Farrington, 'Olympic Victors'; Scanlon, *Eros*, 40–63.
[73] *IOlympia* 238. See Moretti, *Olympionikai*, 917, 920, for details.

of these is a statue base, later built into a wall on the north side of the Spartan acropolis.[74] Alcandridas was thus honoured with victory statues at both Sparta and Olympia, following a model laid down in the classical past and through these new statues asserting the continuity between ancient and Roman Sparta.

The monuments that Pausanias describes play an essential role in communicating the link between individual cities and their victors and the Panhellenic centre of Olympia. His descriptions of monuments in various cities, such as Chionis' stele at Sparta, point towards the account of Olympia which dominates the centre of the work. Within the discussion of Olympia, however, the description of statues, stelae, and the athletes they commemorate also points backwards and forwards to other parts of the narrative. Pausanias' literary web of careful cross-references thus replicates the patterns established on the ground by the objects themselves. This web of connections and referents conforms to a centre–periphery model, where Olympia is like the centre of a wheel, extending its spokes out to all the individual cities of Greece. Monuments commemorating Olympic victories in these cities thus indicate the centrality of Olympia and, through Olympia's status as a Panhellenic centre, the city's own claims to be seen as part of the Greek world. In turn, however, the monuments at Olympia, with their inscriptions naming the victor's *patria*, also attest to the importance of local identity and citizenship within the world of Panhellenic success.

This close interconnection between local identity and Olympic success is made explicit at various points throughout Pausanias' narrative. Thus, we are told in Book 6 that it is only when the Messenians returned to the Peloponnese after their long exile that they again began to win Olympic victories, starting with the victory of one Damiscus in the boys' footrace of 368 BC (6.2.10).[75] Indeed, Book 4, which contains a long account of the Messenians' struggles and exile from the Peloponnese, is entirely lacking in any reference to Olympic victors, except when these are used, like Chionis, for dating purposes.[76] However, these references to the Spartan Chionis' victories in 668 (4.23.4) and 664 BC (4.23.10), while ostensibly used for dating purposes, also mirror the political events Pausanias describes. The defeat of the Messenians by the Spartans in warfare is mirrored by the victory of a

---

[74] Woodward, 'Excavations at Sparta', 89, no. 6; *SEG* xi. 831.

[75] He is Moretti, *Olympionikai*, no. 417. The importance of this argument for Pausanias' view of the link between civic identity and Olympic victory is shown by the fact that he is careful to discount any victories which might seem to disprove it, such as those of Leontiscus and Symmachus.

[76] On Book 4, where the relatively short discussion of monuments at the end of the book perhaps replicates the banishment of the Messenians, see S. E. Alcock, 'The Peculiar Book Four and the Problem of the Messenian Past', in Alcock, Cherry, and Elsner, *Pausanias*, 142–53. For further discussion of Messene see S. E. Alcock, *Archaeologies of the Greek Past: Landscape, Monuments, and Memories* (Cambridge, 2002), 132–75.

Spartan runner at the Olympics. As elsewhere, athletic and military success go together.[77] We are told, however, that the Messenians managed to keep their local customs and Doric dialect during their long 300-year exile (4.27.11). When it comes to Olympic success, keeping to local customs and language is clearly not enough. It is only when the Messenians are also topographically Greek, back on their home soil, that they can begin again to win at Olympia.[78]

This concentration on the physical importance of one's homeland is reinforced by the placement of victory monuments in key places in the victor's city as well as at Olympia. Indeed, in some cases there also seems to be a direct connection made between athletic success and the preservation of a city's territory. In his discussion of Arcadia in Book 8, Pausanias records the Arcadian claim that the boundary between their land and that of Elis is the river Erymanthus, while the Eleans claim that the boundary is marked by the tomb of Coroebus. The tomb itself has an inscription, he tells us, which declares that Coroebus was the first man to win at Olympia and that his grave was made at the end of Elean territory (8.26.3–4). The Olympic victor Coroebus seems here also to have a continuing active role in preserving the boundaries of Elean territory. Orsippus' tomb too, though placed in the agora of Megara, also signified the extent of civic territory through its inscription recording his additions to Megarian land. Civic territory and Olympic victory, then, seem to be closely entwined in Pausanias' vision of Greece.[79]

Statues set up to a victor in his hometown also indicate the reciprocal relationship between the athlete and his city. Several stories in Pausanias alert us to the importance both for cities to commemorate their victors properly, and for the victors themselves to give credit to their city. Thus, in the story of the athlete Oebotas of Dyme, which is told in Book 7, it is only when the Achaeans give proper recognition to their Olympic victor that they begin again to be successful at Olympia. The statue of Oebotas at Olympia is mentioned in 6.3.8, where Pausanias tells us that it was set up by the Achaeans at the prompting of a Delphic oracle in the eightieth Olympiad (460 BC), in commemoration of a victory won at the sixth festival in 756 BC. Pausanias also records here the story that Oebotas took part in the battle against the Persians in Plataea in 479 BC. He rejects the story, on the grounds that

---

[77] This link is especially close for the Spartans, who are said to have used athletics primarily as a training for war: see Philostratus, *Gymnasticus* 11, 19.

[78] On this passage see Elsner 'Structuring "Greece"', 17.

[79] The practice of setting up victory monuments on the borders of a city's territory seems to have been long-established practice. Thus an inscription from a sanctuary of Athena in the territory of Sybaris commemorated the Olympic victory of the pancratiast Cleombrotus (see J. Ebert, *Griechische Epigramme auf Sieger an gymnischen und hippischen Agonen* (Berlin, 1972), 251–4 with other bibliography) and a statue of Astylus was set up in the Sanctuary of Hera Lacinia in Croton: Pausanias 6.13.1. I am grateful to James Davidson for discussion of this phenomenon.

Oebotas was well and truly dead by this time, and says that he will tell the full story of Oebotas in his account of Achaea.[80]

This he does when he reaches the town of Dyme, previously called Paleia, as is shown by the inscription on Oebotas' statue at Olympia (7.17.6–7). Oebotas' statue and inscription at Olympia are here used by Pausanias as a source for information on Oebotas' home town. A little later he records Oebotas' grave in the territory of Dyme, and explains his story. Although Oebotas was the first Achaean to win a victory at Olympia, he received no recognition of this from the Achaeans and promptly put a curse on them that no other Achaean in future should win an Olympic victory. Finally the Achaeans asked the god at Delphi why they had been so unsuccessful, and on learning the reason started to honour Oebotas and set up a statue to him at Olympia, whereupon an Achaean athlete, Sostratus of Pellene, promptly won the stade race for boys. Even in his own time, Pausanias states, it is the custom for Achaean athletes going to compete at Olympia to sacrifice to Oebotas as a hero and, if they win, to crown his statue at Olympia (7.17.13–14).[81]

Here the monuments commemorating the athlete are actively involved in ensuring subsequent Olympic victories, and the passage from home town to Olympia is repeated in the attention they receive: the sacrifices at Oebotas' tomb before the contest are followed by the crowning of his statue in Olympia afterwards. In a number of other cases too, the athlete's statue serves as his double after his death, and is often endowed with magical properties. This link between athletes and their statues is most clearly shown by the famous fifth-century athlete Theagenes of Thasos, whose statue at Olympia provokes a long discussion by Pausanias (6.11.2–9).[82] Theagenes' fame rests both on his numerous athletic victories in boxing, running, and the pancration (1,400 according to Pausanias, including many at Olympia, Delphi, Isthmia, and Nemea—6.11.4–6) and on his involvement with statues. As a boy, Theagenes is said to have picked up a bronze statue from the agora and carried it home, a feat which showed his superhuman strength but nearly earned him death at the hands of his fellow-citizens (6.11.2–3). Pausanias also recalls the Thasian claim that Theagenes was the son of Heracles, a parentage which would explain his immense strength. After Theagenes' death he seems to have lived

[80] Note, however, that other Olympic athletes who afterwards received heroic honours are also often said to have been involved in important battles: Fontenrose, 'The Hero as Athlete', 79, suggests that Oebotas was present as a phantom. See also L. Kurke, 'The Economy of Kudos', in C. Dougherty and L. Kurke, eds., *Cultural Poetics in Archaic Greece: Cult, Performance, Politics* (Cambridge, 1993), 131–63, especially 133–7 on the talismanic powers of crown victors.

[81] Note, however, that there do seem to have been Achaean victors between Oebotas and Sostratus, including those Pausanias himself records at 4.15.1 (688 BC) and 5.9.1 (496 BC). See W. K. Pritchett, *Pausanias Periegetes*, ii (Amsterdam, 1999), 119. His omission of them here suggests the importance of this story for Pausanias' view of athletes and their statues.

[82] This passage is also discussed by Fontenrose, 'The Hero as Athlete', and J. Elsner, 'Image and Ritual: Reflections on the Religious Appreciation of Classical Art', *CQ* 46 (1996), 515–31, especially 526–8.

on through his own portrait statue, set up in his home city. Pausanias tells us that after Theagenes' death an enemy of his used to come and flog the statue, as if he were flogging the athlete himself. The statue took its revenge by falling on the man and killing him, with the result that it was accused of murder by the Thasians and dropped into the sea (6.11.6). All through these events the statue acts, and is treated, like a living being, standing in for Theagenes himself. When famine falls upon the city and envoys are sent to Delphi, the oracle too treats the statue as a living figure, urging the Thasians to recall their exiles, a command which is finally understood to mean Theagenes (6.11.7–8). With his statue retrieved and honoured with sacrifices by the Thasians, Theagenes finally receives his due recognition. Indeed, Pausanias tells us that he has seen statues of the athlete all over the Greek and Barbarian world, honoured with sacrifices and credited with healing powers (6.11.9). Aspects of this story reappear in other literary sources too, attesting to Theagenes' fame as both an athlete and a hero in the second century AD.[83]

As Fontenrose has shown in his discussion of athletic heroes, the stories of Oebotas and Theagenes share a number of similarities.[84] Both are successful athletes who fail to receive the correct honours from their homelands. While Oebotas is not initially granted a statue at all, Theagenes' statue is actually removed and thrown into the sea. This dishonour brings deprivation (of athletic success or food) upon the home cities until the Delphic oracle explains the problem. With their statues (re)erected and honoured with sacrifices the athletes are re-established as important civic heroes, providing athletic or healing remedies to those who worship them.[85]

This heroization of athletic victors appears to be a phenomenon linked specifically to archaic and early classical Greece and to times of civic crisis.[86] However, much of our evidence in fact comes from literary sources of the second and third centuries AD, suggesting a continuing contemporary belief in the powers of ancient athletes and their statues. So, in Lucian's *Parliament of the Gods*, the figure of Momus suggests that Apollo has lost his powers now that other lesser figures can give oracles and that statues of Polydamas at Olympia and of Theagenes at Thasos have the power to heal fevers. He also complains that the heroes Hector and

---

[83] Compare Dio Chrysostom, *Oration* 31.95–9 (mistreatment of the statue) and Lucian, *The Parliament of the Gods* 12 (healing powers).

[84] Fontenrose, 'The Hero as Athlete', 76–7. For other accounts of tales relating to athletes and their statues see F. Bohringer, 'Cultes d'athlètes en Grèce classique: propos politiques, discours mythiques', *REA* 81 (1979), 5–18; S. Lattimore, 'The Nature of Early Greek Victor Statues', in S. J. Bandy, ed., *Coroebus Triumphs: The Alliance of Sport and the Arts* (San Diego, 1988), 245–56; Kurke, 'Economy of Kudos'; D. T. Steiner, *Images in Mind: Statues in Archaic and Classical Greek Literature and Thought* (Princeton and Oxford, 2001), 5–11.

[85] Kurke, 'Economy of Kudos', 149–53, stresses the importance of *statues* in these stories, underplayed by Fontenrose.

[86] Bohringer, 'Cultes d'athlètes'.

Protesilaus receive sacrifice in Troy and the Chersonnese.[87] Protesilaus appears again in Philostratus' *Heroicus* as a particularly athletic hero. The wine-grower in whose territory the hero's ghost resides recounts his athletic prowess—in shadow-boxing, throwing the discus, and especially running.[88] This hero embodies the powers of both Oebotas and Theagenes. He acts as a source of oracular advice to the athletes who consult him, many of them apparently contemporary figures, such as the early-third-century athlete Helix, as well as curing diseases.[89] These texts suggest that statues of ancient heroic athletes or athletic heroes continued to play an important religious role in the second and third centuries AD, when they could be consulted and honoured by aspiring athletes as well as by the sick.[90]

Yet as well as showing the religious and healing powers of some athletic victor statues, Pausanias also indicates the significance of the statue as a sign of respect from a city to its athletes, a testament to the honour which the athlete has brought, through his victory, onto his home town.[91] The stories of Theagenes and Oebotas show the dangers when a city fails to honour its athletes appropriately. Yet the reverse of this is the duty which the Olympic athlete also owes to his own community. This is most clearly shown in Pausanias' discussion of the athlete Astylus of Croton, mentioned above as famous for victories in the foot races at three separate Olympic festivals of the early fifth century BC and honoured with a statue at Olympia. When Astylus decided in his second two victories to announce himself as a Syracusan, rather than a Crotonian, to curry favour with Hiero, the tyrant of Syracuse, his home city took revenge. They turned his house into a prison and took down the statue of him in the sanctuary of Hera Lacinia (6.13.1). Astylus' obliteration of Croton through choosing to be heralded as a citizen of a different city, was punished by the obliteration of his images back at home.

This nexus of stories suggests the importance which statues and monuments played in recording athletic victories both for the athlete himself and for his city. The honour which the athlete brought to his city was rightly recognized and rewarded by the erection of an honorific statue at home, as well as with other

---

[87] Lucian, *The Parliament of the Gods* 12.   [88] Philostratus, *Heroicus* 13.

[89] Philostratus, *Heroicus* 14–15 (oracles), 126 (healing). Philostratus names five athletes: the Cilician pancratiast nicknamed Halter, 'Jumping-Weight'; three boxers, Plutarch, Hermesias of Egypt, and Eudaimon of Egypt; and the pancratiast Helix. Of these only Helix and Eudaimon can be identified. Helix was victorious at Olympia in 213 and 217 and then at the Capitoline games in Rome in AD 218, not mentioned here (Moretti, *Olympionikai*, 889). Eudaimon won at Olympia in AD 169 (Moretti, *Olympionikai*, 874). See V. Rossi, ed., *Filostrato, 'Eroico'* (Venice, 1997), 208 n. 56.

[90] Archaeological evidence for this cultic worship is provided by an offering box found at Thasos, dated to around AD 100: S. G. Miller, *Arete: Greek Sports from Ancient Sources*, 2nd edn. (Berkeley and Los Angeles, 1991), no. 110b.

[91] On the importance of victor statues in this exchange of honour, see Kurke, 'Economy of Kudos', 141–9. On the relationship between an athlete and his home town in the Archaic and Classical periods see Mann, *Athlet und Polis*, highlighting the possible tensions.

honours such as a triumphal entrance into the city and meals at public expense. When these honours were not awarded, as in the case of Oebotas, all further members of his community were deprived of athletic victories until the wrong was righted. In contrast, when the victories of Astylus were removed from Croton by his announcement of himself as a Syracusan, his honours too must come down. Victory and statues thus echo one another.

The enduring importance of such monuments in Pausanias' own day is shown by the fact that honours to Oebotas are said to continue into his own day. Other literary references elsewhere suggest a similar view of the importance of honorific statues. Thus Dio Chrysostom in his *Oration* 31 rebukes the Rhodians for their practice of reinscribing old portrait statues to reuse them to honour contemporary figures, many of them Roman officials. This, he says, is the worst of all fates which could befall those commemorated in the statues, to remove an honour once granted to them when they have not done anything to deserve such dishonour.[92] He draws a direct comparison with the case of Olympic victors, arguing that no one would be willing to compete for the Olympic crown if they knew that their victor statues could easily be appropriated by someone else.[93] In Rhodes, however, such terrible things have indeed happened, leading to the preposterous situation where the name of a young man is inscribed on the statue of an old man, or that of a weakling on a statue of a boxer.[94]

Pausanias' account of Olympia and the network of statues which bind individual communities to the centre of Greece is firmly concerned with the past. The statues which he singles out for mention are predominantly those of the fifth and fourth centuries BC. Yet in some cases the associations which Pausanias asserts between athletics and military prowess are also shown as being still valid in his contemporary world. This is especially clear in a story told towards the very end of the work, in Book 10. Here Pausanias is describing the city of Elataea in Phocis. As elsewhere, he describes the history of the city, ending with her experiences in the struggle against the Costobocian tribes which overran Greece in his own day:

Then a certain Mnesibulus gathered a company of men around him and having killed many of the barbarians he himself fell in the battle. This Mnesibulus had won many victories in running, among them victories in the footrace and the double race with shield in the two hundred and thirty-fifth Olympics. A bronze statue of Mnesibulus stands in the street of the runner at Elataea.   (10.34.5)

---

[92] Dio Chrysostom, *Oration* 31.27–9, 71–2.   [93] Dio Chrysostom, *Oration* 31.21.

[94] Dio Chrysostom, *Oration* 31.156. The practice of reinscribing statues is discussed in J. Shear, 'Reusing Statues, Rewriting Inscriptions, and Bestowing Honours in Roman Athens', and V. Platt, '"Honour Takes Wing": Deceptive Inscriptions in Imperial Greece', both in R. Leader-Newby and Z. Newby, eds., *Art and Inscriptions in the Ancient World* (forthcoming).

Mnesibulus' victories against the barbarians are coupled with a recollection of his Olympic victories in AD 161.[95] An inscription from Elataea itself also tells us that Mnesibulus was twice circuit-victor (*periodonikēs*) and 'best of the Hellenes', a title awarded for a victory in the race in armour at Plataea.[96] This successful athlete was also a military figure, bringing renown to his city through his athletic victories while also defending her in warfare. The city's recognition of its citizen is itself embodied in the bronze statue memorializing him and in the street named after it. As with the statue of Granianus mentioned in Book 2 (2.11.7), Pausanias here describes a contemporary athlete whose statue could be seen alongside those of figures from the classical past. This juxtaposition of ancient and modern, and Pausanias' praise of Mnesibulus' military victories, acts as a clear sign that Greece could still produce athletic and military heroes in the late second century AD.

Pausanias' account strongly suggests that the numerous old athletic statues which could still be seen at Olympia and scattered throughout the cities of Greece helped to assert the continuing relevance of past athletic victories for constructions of civic identity in the Roman period. While Olympic victories may in fact have declined among athletes from the cities of mainland Greece, in favour of those from Egypt or the east, when they did occur their commemoration in statues and inscriptions helped to assert the link with the past and the continuing importance of athletic victories and festivals as a sign of Greek identity. While Hadrian had sought to put Athens at the centre of Greece, Pausanias presents us with a different construction of Greece. As for Apollonius in Philostratus' biography of the sage, this Greece is centred upon the athletic, Panhellenic festival at Olympia.[97] While this looks back to the ancient past, the continuing presence and visiblity of athletic statues throughout the cities and sanctuaries of Greece also acts as a continual reminder of the centrality of athletic success as an emblem of Hellenic identity, and the potential for Greece to continue producing athletic and military heroes even into the Roman empire.

[95] Moretti, *Olympionikai*, 54, nos. 868–9. On this raid, see F. Millar, 'P. Herennius Dexippus and the Third-Century Invasions', *JRS* 59 (1969), 12–29 at 28.

[96] *SIG* 871. On the title see above, p. 170, n. 11.   [97] Philostratus, *Life of Apollonius of Tyana* 8.15.

EIGHT

Gymnasia, Festivals, and Euergetism in Asia Minor

In Chapters 5 and 6 above, I explored the associations attaching to an athletic education in the second and third centuries AD, particularly as experienced at the two great centres of Athens and Sparta in mainland Greece. The *ephēbeia* continued to be practised in other Greek cities too, as attested by the epigraphical dossiers of cities as geographically disparate as Odessus (modern-day Varna in Bulgaria), Alexandria, and Termessus in Pisidia (south-west Turkey).[1] Throughout these cities the ephebes, mostly the sons of wealthy local elites, continued to train in athletic pursuits and to take part in both ephebic and local festivals. Both before and after the formal *ephēbeia* too, Greek men would have continued to attend the gymnasium for education (in intellectual as well as physical pursuits) and for general social relaxation.[2]

As we have seen, the youths of Greek cities could take part in athletic contests both in specifically ephebic festivals and in local festivals such as the Munichia and Aianteia at Athens. However, as we have seen in the last chapter, another important side of athletics was expressed through victories at international festivals such as that at Olympia. The gymnasium acted as the intersection between these two aspects of Greek athletics. As the main area for athletic training it produced the athletes who would go on to win important public victories, yet through its association with military training, and both physical and intellectual education, it also carried wider associations with the whole of Greek culture. In this chapter I propose to look at the sculptural display of new gymnasia in the second century AD, examining the

---

[1] Odessus: G. Mihailov, *Inscriptiones Graecae in Bulgaria repertae*, i² (Sofia, 1970), 106–18, nos. 47–51; L. Robert, 'Un relief inscrit au musée de Stamboul', in id., *Hellenica* 11–12 (Paris, 1960), 369–80; J-C. Moretti, in C. Landes, ed., *Le Stade romain et ses spectacles* (Lattes, 1994), 272–5, 291–3, cat. 95. Egypt: see B. Legras, *Néotēs: Recherches sur les jeunes grecs dans l'Égypte Ptolémaïque et Romaine* (Paris, 1999). Termessus: *Tituli Asiae Minoris*, iii. i, nos. 199–213; O. van Nijf, 'Inscriptions and Civic Memory in the Roman East', in A. E. Cooley, ed., *The Afterlife of Inscriptions* (London, 2000), 21–36 at 30–1.

[2] On the different roles played by the gymnasium, see J. Delorme, *Gymnasion: Étude sur les monuments consacrés à l'éducation en Grèce* (Paris, 1960), 272–361. His study stops at the end of the first century BC, when we see the introduction of Roman-style bathing suites into gymnasium complexes. While Delorme claims that this put an end to the traditional role of the gymnasium (e.g. 243–50) I will argue that its associations with athleticism and education continued to be strong throughout the Roman period.

ways in which this decoration articulated the place of the gymnasium, and its benefactors, within civic society. I will then turn to consider the impact of athletic festivals in these cities, considering their place in the self-representation of cities, donors, and victorious athletes. While the previous chapters have concentrated primarily on mainland Greece, here I turn to Asia Minor, whose thriving civic life during the Roman period has left plentiful remains in the archaeological and epigraphic record.

ATHLETICS AND EUERGETISM IN EPHESUS

The relationship between Greek athletic festivals and the world of the gymnasium in archaic and classical Greece has exercised a number of scholars. Certainly the gymnasium served as the major place of preparation for the athletes who competed in Panhellenic festivals. However, it also seems to have developed independently as a place for everyday physical exercise and, later, for both military training and intellectual pursuits.[3] All these associations seem to have remained strong in the Roman period too. The athletes whose victories are recorded on plentiful inscriptions throughout the Roman world would have continued to exercise in civic gymnasia, yet these spaces were also places for general athletic activity and carried with them all the multiple associations of the Greek gymnasium. Here I will explore the ways in which these associations were conveyed by the sculptural decoration of gymnasia in Ephesus, a major metropolitan centre in the first three centuries AD.[4]

By the end of the second century AD the city of Ephesus could boast a lavishly decorated public centre, including no fewer than four gymnasium complexes.[5] All were linked with Roman-style bathing suites, as became usual in the eastern provinces during the Roman empire.[6] The introduction of hot baths to gymnasium

---

[3] On the development of the gymnasium and its links with military training and competitive athletics see Delorme, *Gymnasion*, 9–30, and H. W. Pleket, 'Zur Soziologie des antiken Sports', *Mededelingen van het Nederlands Instituut te Rome* 36 (1974), 57–87 at 61–2.

[4] L. M. White, 'Urban Development and Social Change in Imperial Ephesos', in H. Koester, ed., *Ephesos: Metropolis of Asia* (Valley Forge, Pa., 1995), 27–79, at 34–49.

[5] See I. Nielsen, *Thermae et Balnea*, ii. 36–7, cats. 295, 297–8, 300. There were also two other bathing complexes without associated palaestrae. For an account of the general development of the city, see P. Scherrer, 'The City of Ephesos from the Roman Period to Late Antiquity', in Koester, *Ephesos*, 1–25; and id., 'The Historical Topography of Ephesos', in D. Parrish, ed., *Urbanism in Western Asia Minor: New Studies on Aphrodisias, Ephesos, Hierapolis, Pergamon, Perge and Xanthos*, JRA Supplement 45 (Portsmouth, RI, 2001), 57–87.

[6] See A. Farrington, 'Imperial Bath Buildings in South-West Asia Minor', in S. Macready and F. H. Thompson, eds., *Roman Architecture in the Greek World*, Society of Antiquaries Occasional Papers 10 (London, 1987), 50–9; F. K. Yegül, *Baths and Bathing in Classical Antiquity* (Cambridge, Mass., 1992), 250–313; Nielsen, *Thermae et Balnea*, i. 105–8. For a comparison with the situation in mainland Greece, see A. Farrington, 'The Introduction and Spread of Roman Bathing in Greece', in J. DeLaine and D. E. Johnston, eds., *Roman Baths and Bathing*, i, JRA Supplement 37 (Portsmouth, RI, 1999), 57–65.

complexes seems to have first become popular during the Hellenistic period, and was continued with a new impetus under the Roman empire, often using Roman construction techniques.[7] Lavish bathing establishments became a civic necessity, reflecting the empire-wide adoption of Roman-style bathing habits that could occasionally be attacked by austere idealists but was nevertheless an essential part of civilized life.[8] Yet in the eastern provinces this culture of public bathing was incorporated into the existing culture of the gymnasium, which remained strong. As Trajan (rather patronizingly) commented to Pliny, 'these little Greeks love their gymnasia'.[9]

The provision of bath-gymnasium complexes can be seen as one of the ways in which Greek cities of the Roman world continued to exercise their traditional culture at the same time as adopting the advantages of much Roman material culture. In Greg Woolf's words, 'Greeks of all sorts, then, remained Greeks while using Roman things.'[10] The traditional associations of the gymnasium seem to have remained strong, even when the physical layout of the gymnasium was altered. My interest here is in the intersection between cultural associations and material display. The physical layout of these complexes often seems to derive from Roman techniques and models. Like major bath buildings in Rome, too, those in Ephesus were lavishly decorated with sculptural displays.[11] My aim is to investigate how these displays presented an individualized view of the associations of the Ephesian gymnasium, while also conforming to cosmopolitan styles. I will concentrate particularly on the sculptural display of the palestrae in the Harbour Baths, the Baths of Vedius, and the East Bath-Gymnasium.[12]

These three bath-gymnasia were all built between the late first and the end of the second century AD. The Harbour baths appear to be the earliest, dated to the late first century AD, while the Baths of Vedius belong to the reign of Antoninus Pius, to whom, along with Artemis Ephesia and the city, they were dedicated.[13] The East Baths seem to have been built in the middle of the second century with the palaestra and its decoration added at the end of the century.[14] In all three, the sculptural

---

[7] Yegül, *Baths and Bathing*, 21–4.

[8] Philostratus, *Life of Apollonius of Tyana* 4.27 (Apollonius attacks Spartans), 4.42 (Demetrius criticizes Nero's baths in Rome).

[9] Pliny, *Letters* 10.40.

[10] G. Woolf, 'Becoming Roman, Staying Greek: Culture, Identity and the Civilising Process in the Roman East', *PCPS* 40 (1994), 116–43, at 128.

[11] On this see Manderscheid, *Skulpturenausstattung*, and the review by R. Neudecker in *Gnomon* 57 (1985), 171–8. For the distribution of baths with sculptural display see Manderscheid, *Skulpturenausstattung*, 5. Three of the five decorated baths he records in the province of Asia are in Ephesus.

[12] For full bibliographies on these, see H. Manderscheid, *Bibliographie zum römischen Badewesen unter besonderer Berücksichtigung der öffentlichen Thermen* (Munich, 1988), 108–10.

[13] Harbour baths: O. Benndorf, 'Erzstatue eines griechischen Athleten', *Forschungen in Ephesos*, i (Vienna, 1906), 181–204, at 182–3. Vedius Baths: *IEphesos* ii. 438.

[14] J. Keil, *JÖAI* 27 (1932), supplement, 5–72, at 33–4; Manderscheid, *Skulpturenausstattung*, 91.

displays combine features which we have also seen in Rome, the display of idealized statues of gods, goddesses, and athletes, along with portrait statues of particular individuals. Yet here, unlike in the Baths of Caracalla, for example, the donors were members of the local elite. While the choice of sculptural decoration may have been influenced by the decorative schemes of bath buildings in the capital, their display within the context of the gymnasium in a Greek city of the eastern half of the empire would also have set up resonances with the traditional associations of the gymnasium in Greek culture.[15]

Our knowledge of the sculptural display of the Harbour Baths is only partial.[16] Some of the building seems to have been destroyed by fire, possibly during the Gothic invasion of 263, and the bathing rooms were rebuilt in the fourth century AD.[17] However, we do have a firm provenance for the most famous piece of sculpture found here, the bronze statue of an athlete cleaning his strigil, now in Vienna (Fig. 8.1).[18] This was found in fragments lying in front of the aedicula where it had originally stood, flanking the entrance to the lavishly decorated 'marble room' on the southern side of the palaestra (Fig. 8.2, c outside Room AI).[19] Fragments of the inscribed base on which it stood were also found and suggest that it was dedicated by a private individual during the gymnasiarchy of L. Claudius Phrygianus.[20] The marble room itself would also have been decorated with statues set into the niches on its three walls. Of these only the marble heads of a goddess and a philosopher survive.[21]

More sculptures seem to have been displayed in the passageway leading from the palaestra eastwards to the so-called Verulanus Hall, a large open space surrounded by porticoes which was decorated by one C. Claudius Verulanus during the reign of Hadrian.[22] The decoration of this passageway (D on Fig. 8.2) included the figures of a satyr and Mercury, as well as a group known only from its inscribed base where it is referred to as a 'statue group' (*symplēgma tōn andriantōn*) possibly showing a

---

[15] For the argument that extensive sculptural displays in baths began in Rome, see Manderscheid, *Skulpturenausstattung*, 16–20. P. Zanker, 'Zur Funktion und Bedeutung griechischer Skulptur in der Römerzeit', in H. Flashar, ed., *Le Classicisme à Rome aux Iers siècles avant et après J.-C.*, Entretiens sur l'Antiquité Classique 25 (Geneva, 1979), 283–314, at 293–9, also argues that Rome provided a model to be followed by the rest of the empire.

[16] See Manderscheid, *Skulpturenausstattung*, 86–8, cats. 155–72, for a list of finds.

[17] Benndorf, 'Erzstatue', 181–4.

[18] Vienna, Kunsthistorisches Museum, inv. 3168 (restored from 234 pieces). See Benndorf, 'Erzstatue'; S. Lattimore, 'The Bronze Apoxyomenos from Ephesos', *AJA* 76 (1972), 13–16; A. Stewart, 'Lysippan Studies 3. Not by Daedalos?', *AJA* 82 (1978), 473–82. On the motif, see F. Eichler, 'Die Bronzestatue aus Ephesos in verbesserte Wiederherstellung', *Jahrbuch der Kunsthistorischen Sammlung in Wien* 50 (1953), 15–22. Most recently see C. O. Pavese, 'L'atleta di Ephesos', in H. Friesinger and F. Krinzinger, eds., *100 Jahre Österreichische Forschungen in Ephesos: Akten des Symposions Wien 1995*, Archäologisches Forschungen 1 (Vienna, 1999), 579–84.

[19] Benndorf, 'Erzstatue', 184–6.   [20] Ibid., 186, 202–4.

[21] Manderscheid, *Skulpturenausstattung*, 86–7, cats. 159, 162.   [22] *IEphesos* ii. 430.

FIGURE 8.1 This classicizing bronze statue of an athlete cleaning his strigil decorated the palaestra of the Harbour Baths at Ephesus, evoking the traditional values of Greek athletics. H: 1.92m. First century AD evoking fourth-century BC forms.

FIGURE 8.2
This excavation
plan shows the
palaestra of
the Harbour
Bath-Gymnasium
at Ephesus, which was
lavishly decorated with
sculpture in the
'marble rooms', AI and
A2, and in the passage-
way leading to the
Verulanus Hall, D.
The bronze athlete was
found at the spot
marked c, flanking the
entrance to room AI.
Trajanic. Harbour
Bath-Gymnasium,
Ephesus; excavation
plan.

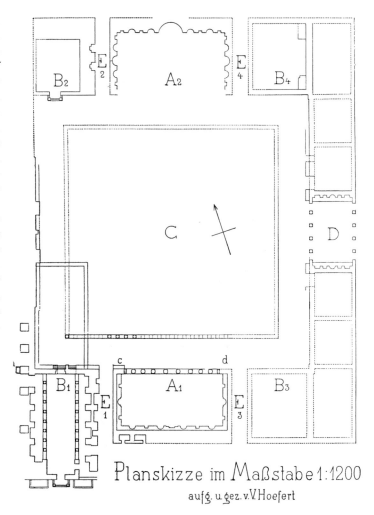

pair of wrestlers or other athletes.[23] Four other similar statue bases also refer to statue groups. These bases were reused in the fourth century rebuilding of the baths and all bear bilingual inscriptions describing the dedication of the statues to Artemis Ephesia, the emperor Trajan, and the city of Ephesus. The dedicators all differ and included freedmen as well as free citizens. The statues which stood on the bases are described as follows: 'a group of Theseus', 'a group of Athamas' (probably shown killing his son, Learchos), 'Daedalus and Icarus' and, simply, 'statue group'.[24]

[23] Manderscheid, *Skulpturenausstattung*, 86–7, cats. 155, 157, 164. On the possible subject of this group, see J. Keil, 'Skulpturengruppen in Ephesos', *JÖAI* 39 (1952), 42–6, at 43.

[24] See Keil, 'Skulpturengruppen', and A. Betz, 'Ephesia', *Klio* 52 (1970), 27–32, for further details. Manderscheid, *Skulpturenausstattung*, 87, suggests an original display in the frigidarium, where the bases were later reused, but the fact that another similar base was found between the palaestra and Verulanus Hall may suggest an original display in this area of the complex.

As far as we can reconstruct it, this bath-gymnasium complex appears to have been started in the reign of Domitian. Its decoration continued over the next few decades with some of the sculptural display added by generous individuals in the reign of Trajan and the large open court to the east embellished in marble veneer under Hadrian. The bathing part of the complex was then rebuilt in the fourth century and called the 'baths of Constantius'.[25] The dedications on the statue groups mentioned above show that they were dedicated to the city, its patron goddess, and the ruling emperor, a combination of honorands which can be paralleled elsewhere in the dedicatory inscriptions on public buildings.[26] The use of bilingual inscriptions suggests the cosmopolitan standing of the donors—Greeks who were also fully versed in Roman culture and the Latin language. They also advertise the benefactions of these figures to both Greek- and Latin-speaking visitors, suggesting the status of Ephesus as a city that could attract people from all around the empire.

While we cannot build up a complete picture of the sculptural display of these baths, certain images displayed in the palaestra do seem to have stressed the connection with Greek athletics and the cultural associations of the gymnasium. The bronze image of the athlete with the strigil links together the two aspects of the complex, both the athletic exercises which took place here and the bodily cleansing which succeeded them. Physical exertion may also have been evoked in the mythological *exempla* presented in the statue-groups mentioned above, particularly in the case of Theseus where we can expect a scene of one of the hero's labours, and possibly in the two, otherwise unspecified, *symplēgmata*, which may have shown groups of struggling athletes. On the other hand, the intellectual credentials of the gymnasium were also evoked through the statue of a philosopher. These intellectual and athletic associations of the space were then placed under the wider auspices of the Greek pantheon, whose statues also graced the walls of the marble rooms, the Verulanus Hall and the propylon.

Many of these associations reappear in the other two bath-gymnasium complexes, whose sculptural displays can be studied in greater detail. Like the Harbour Baths, both the Baths of Vedius and the East Baths-Gymnasium combine Roman-style bathing rooms with a palaestra surrounded with various rooms. Among these rooms both complexes possess a lavishly decorated room equivalent to the 'marble rooms' in the Harbour Baths (marked A on Figs 8.2, 8.3, 8.4). These rooms all share the following characteristics: they are placed in the centre of one of the sides of the palaestra and are open to the palaestra with only a screen of columns separating them from the portico. On the other three sides the walls are adorned with a two-storeyed aediculated façade of statue niches separated by columns. In both

---

[25] J. Keil, *JÖAI* 28 (1933), supplement, 14–23, S. J. Friesen, *Twice Neokoros: Ephesus, Asia and the Cult of the Flavian Imperial Family* (Leiden, 1993), 121–3.

[26] e.g. the Vedius Baths, discussed below (*IEphesos* ii. 438).

FIGURE 8.3
The Vedius
Bath-Gymnasium
at Ephesus incor-
porated rooms
for bathing to the
west and, in its
eastern part, a
palaestra for
physical exercise.
On one of the
main axes of this
palaestra lies a
lavishly decorated
marble room,
marked here as A,
which yielded
both portrait
statues and
idealized sculp-
ture. Antonine.
Vedius Bath-
Gymnasium,
Ephesus;
excavation plan.

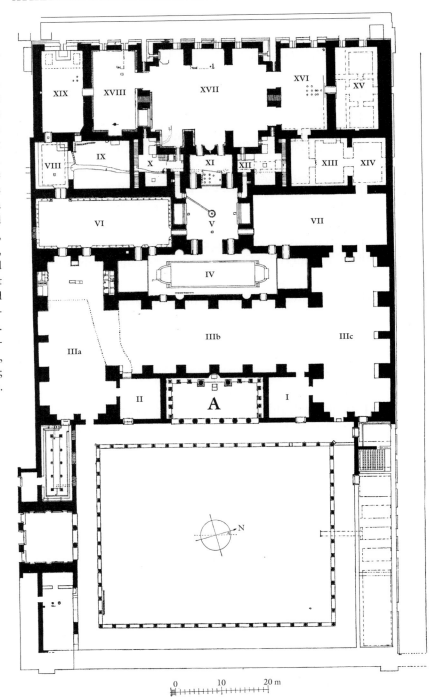

FIGURE 8.4 Like the Vedius Bath-Gymnasium, the East Bath-Gymnasium at Ephesus also incorporated a palaestra with a magnificently decorated display room on one of its axes (A). Opposite this lay a room equipped with seating which probably served as a lecture hall (B). Mid-second century with additions to gymnasium in late second century AD. East Bath-Gymnasium, Ephesus; excavation plan.

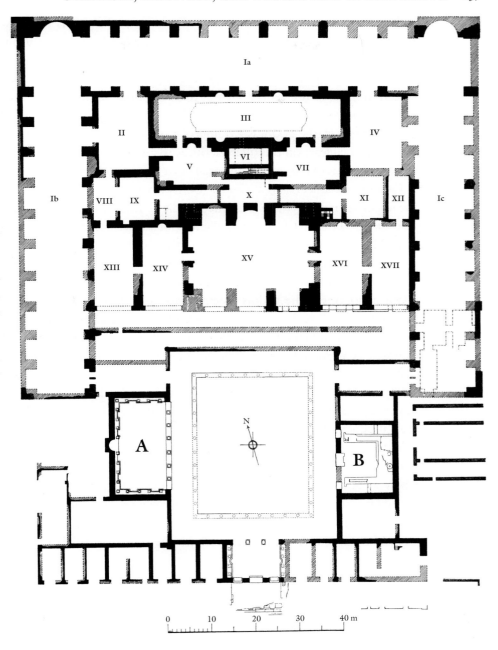

the Baths of Vedius and the East Baths the central niche is larger than those surrounding it. This style of decoration, the so-called 'marble style', finds a number of parallels in other monuments within Ephesus itself, such as the Library of Celsus and Nymphaeum of Trajan.[27]

[27] 'Marble style': see J. B. Ward-Perkins, *Roman Architecture* (New York, 1977), 284.

These rooms have often been referred to as 'imperial rooms' or 'Kaisersäle' due to their supposed role as places for the imperial cult, an association discussed by Yegül.[28] The term was first coined in relation to the central room in the bath-gymnasium complex of Vedius (A on Fig. 8.3). Here the excavators found an altar placed in front of the central niche. An inscription running along the architrave outside this room identified the complex as a dedication to the emperor Antoninus Pius, along with the goddess Artemis of Ephesus and the city itself.[29] The lesson seemed to be clear: on this altar sacrifices would have been made to the imperial cult and a statue of the emperor himself must have stood in the large central niche.[30]

Other gymnasia also have similar rooms where inscriptions suggest a link with the imperial family. So a room in the Middle Gymnasium at Pergamum yielded an inscribed dedication to the imperial gods (*theoi sebastoi*) Augustus and Livia as well as to Hermes and Heracles, suggesting that both new and old gods were worshipped here together.[31] This particular room does not share the lavish appearance of the rooms at Ephesus, yet in the bath-gymnasium complex at Sardis we find a room analogous to the Vedius Gymnasium room in both appearance and dedication (Fig. 8.5). Here the inscription carved along the architrave dedicates the room to Caracalla and Geta along with their mother Julia Domna as 'mother of the camps'.[32] While no altar or imperial image was found in this room, Yegül suggests that a table found in the synagogue to the south of the gymnasium may have originally served as its altar table.[33] He also points out the discovery of the statue of an imperial priest in the marble room in the East Baths at Ephesus as further evidence that cultic activities took place in such rooms.[34]

Yet there are a number of problems with seeing all such rooms as places for worship of the imperial family. The room in the Vedius Gymnasium is the only one where an altar has actually been found, and even here no image of the emperor himself was discovered.[35] Indeed, even when statues of emperors and a dedication to the emperor are both present, there is no need to assume that all such places served for cultic activity. As we saw with the statue bases in the Harbour Baths

---

[28] F. K. Yegül, 'A Study in Architectural Iconography: Kaisersaal and the Imperial Cult', *Art Bulletin* 64 (1982), 7–31.

[29] *IEphesos* ii. 431. A comparison with *IEphesos* ii. 438, found in the frigidarium, shows that the dedicator was Publius Vedius Antoninus and the complex as a whole was referred to as a gymnasium. See J. Keil, *JÖAI* 24 (1929), supplement, 20–52, at 27, and *JÖAI* 25 (1929), supplement, 5–52, at 26. The site is currently being re-excavated. For a report and history of previous excavations see M. Steskal and M. La Torre, 'Das Vediusgymnasium in Ephesos', *JÖAI* 70 (2001), 221–44.

[30] J. Keil, *JÖAI* 24 (1929), supplement, 36.

[31] *Inscriptiones Graecae ad res Romanas pertinentes*, iv (1908), no. 318. It is room 57 on Delorme, *Gymnasion*, fig. 48. See Yegül, 'Kaisersaal', 12.

[32] C. Foss, 'Appendix: Inscriptions Related to the Complex', in F. K. Yegül, *The Bath-Gymnasium Complex at Sardis* (Cambridge, Mass., 1986), 167–72, at 170, no. 3.

[33] Yegül, 'Kaisersaal', 12.   [34] Ibid., 11–12.   [35] Price, *Rituals and Power*, 144.

FIGURE 8.5 The Bath-Gymnasium at Sardis included a marble room similar to those at Ephesus, though here with an entrance in its rear wall into the baths. This view of it after restoration gives an idea of how those elsewhere would also have appeared. Severan.

(which bore statues of non-imperial subjects) an object could be dedicated to the reigning emperor without there being any suggestion of actual worship. As Simon Price has shown, the imperial family was accommodated into civic life in a variety of different ways, not all of them involving actual cultic activities.[36] The imperial image was certainly omnipresent in the cities of the Roman empire and may well have been present in these marble rooms, though no imperial images have, in fact, been found in the rooms in Ephesus. Yet to call them 'imperial rooms' presupposes the dominance of their imperial function which underplays the impact of other aspects of their decorative programmes.

It is these decorative programmes which I now wish to examine. Excavations in the marble room of Vedius' gymnasium revealed a series of statues.[37] They include a number of draped figures, probably to be seen as portrait statues, including one of a bearded man which Keil suggested represented the donor of the complex,

[36] Price, *Rituals and Power*. See 136–46 on the impact of the imperial cult on civic architecture.
[37] See Keil, *JÖAI* 24 (1929), supplement, 38–51, figs 19–27; Manderscheid, *Skulpturenausstattung*, 88–91, cats. 173–91 (including pieces found elsewhere in the complex).

Publius Vedius Antoninus (Fig. 8.6).[38] As Sheila Dillon has shown, the distinctive hairstyle shared by this piece and the statue of an imperial priest found in the East Bath-Gymnasium (Fig. 8.7) indicates that they represent the same individual.[39] While Keil had suggested that the imperial priest in the East Bath-Gymnasium was the Ephesian sophist Flavius Damianus, there is no evidence that he ever held this role.[40] Instead, it seems more likely that the man represented in both statues was a member of the Vedii family, perhaps the donor of the Vedius Gymnasium or his father. Both are known to have acted as imperial priests and to have been important benefactors to the city.[41]

The identity of the donor of the East Bath-Gymnasium remains unknown, though the presence of a portrait of one of the Vedii within this complex suggests that it may have been funded by a member of the same family. While Keil's identification of the imperial priest as Flavius Damianus is untenable, his suggestion that this complex was funded by Damianus or his wife, Vedia Phaedrina, the daughter of Vedius Antoninus, is still attractive.[42] The decoration of the East Gymnasium seems to belong to the late second century, whereas the Vedius Gymnasium was dedicated to Antoninus Pius.[43] The same donor is therefore unlikely. However, it was common practice for individual benefactors to set up portraits of their wider families as well as themselves and their spouses.[44] If Damianus was responsible for embellishing the palaestra he may well have wanted to advertise his relationship, through marriage, to one of the most prominent Ephesian families.[45] Alternatively a donation by Vedia Phaedrina herself is also possible, and we know of a number of female benefactors in this period. In this case she would be celebrating the achievements of her father or grandfather just as the

---

[38] *IEphesos* ii. 431, 438. Keil, *JÖAI* 24 (1929), supplement, 39, no. 3; Manderscheid, *Skulpturenausstattung*, 44–5. This is Vedius Antoninus (III) as listed in the stemma in *IEphesos* viii. i. 88–9.

[39] S. Dillon, 'The Portraits of a Civic Benefactor in 2nd-c. Ephesos', *JRA* 9 (1996), 261–74.

[40] Keil, *JÖAI* 27 (1932), supplement, 5–72, at 40–2. His identification rested on the restoration of a fragment of the inscribed architrave (*IEphesos* ii. 439) as referring to Vedia Phaedrina, Damianus' wife. See Dillon, 'Portraits', 272; R. R. R. Smith, 'Cultural Choice and Political Identity in Honorific Portrait Statues in the Greek East in the Second Century AD', *JRS* 88 (1998), 56–93, at 81–2.

[41] Dillon, 'Portraits', 272–4.

[42] Note, however, that the fragmentary architrave, discussed above, cannot be conclusive.

[43] Manderscheid, *Skulpturenausstattung*, 14–15. For more bibliography on the dating see Dillon, 'Portraits', 272 n. 36.

[44] The best example is the sculptural display of the nymphaeum set up by Herodes Atticus and his wife at Olympia, where portraits of the donors' family are paired with those of the imperial family. See R. Bol, *Das Statuenprogramm des Herodes-Atticus-Nymphäums*, Olympischen Forschungen 15 (Berlin, 1984); Smith, 'Honorific Portrait Statues', 75–7.

[45] On the status of this family see Dillon, 'Portraits', 272–3. The inscriptions relating to them are listed in the stemma given in *IEphesos* vii.1, 88–9. It is also possible that another descendant of the Vedii embellished the gymnasium, such as Vedius Antoninus (III)'s son, M. Cl. P. Vedius Papianus Antoninus, who is also named as a benefactor of the city, *IEphesos* iii. 730.

FIGURE 8.6 This portrait statue was found in the marble room in the Bath-Gymnasium of Vedius at Ephesus and probably represents the donor of the building, M. Claudius P. Vedius Antoninus Phaedrus Sabinianus, or his father. H: 1.16m. Antonine.

FIGURE 8.7 A portrait statue found in the marble room in the East Bath-Gymnasium at Ephesus represents the same individual as the statue in Fig. 8.6, probably one of the Vedii Antonini and a relative of the donor. H: 2.32m. Severan.

benefactress Plancia Magna set up statues of her father and brother in the gateway she funded at Perge.[46] The room opposite the marble room in the palaestra of these baths was equipped with rows of seating (B on Fig. 8.4). It seems deliberately designed to act as an auditorium or lecture hall.[47] This accommodation of the intellectual side of the gymnasium would seem to be fully in keeping with the interests of a teacher and sophist like Damianus.[48] Through the embellishment of a gymnasium at the eastern end of the city, the heirs of Vedius Antoninus also asserted the dominance of the family throughout the city, from the Coressian gate at the north to the Magnesian gate at the east.

The decorative programme of the palaestra of the East Bath-Gymnasium seems not to have stressed the particularly athletic aspects of the complex. In addition to a number of male and female portrait statues, the marble room was also decorated with the figures of Fortune, Venus, Cupid, and a Muse.[49] A head identified by Keil as that of Septimius Severus probably instead represents the god Asclepius.[50] The display thus combines references to the Greek pantheon with exaltation of the donor's own family. The figure of a muse also hints at the intellectual aspects of the complex, which find a space in the room opposite. This concentration on the intellectual side of gymnasium education can be seen elsewhere too, as in the Baths of Faustina at Miletus which was equipped with a room decorated with the statues of the Muses, Apollo, and an imperial couple, probably Marcus Aurelius and Faustina.[51]

In the Baths of Vedius, however, the sculptural display of the marble room integrates the athletic side of the gymnasium into a display which also honours the donor and the Greek gods.[52] In addition to the statue identified as one of the Vedii Antonini, three other portrait statues were found here, two female and one male, all lacking heads. Among the other statues were images of the gods traditionally associated with health, bathing, and beauty: Hygeia, Asclepius, and Aphrodite. Another statue shows a young hunter with a dog, identified as a representation of

[46] See M. T. Boatwright, 'The City Gate of Plancia Magna in Perge', in E. D'Ambra, ed., *Roman Art in Context: An Anthology* (Englewood Cliffs, NJ, 1993), 189–207.

[47] J. Keil, *JÖAI* 28 (1933), supplement, 5–44, at 9–10.

[48] On Damianus see Philostratus, *Lives of the Sophists* 2.23 (605–6). He also served as *grammateus* in Ephesus: *IEphesos* iii. 811, ll. 22–3.

[49] Sculptural finds: Keil, *JÖAI* 27 (1932), supplement, 34–51; Manderscheid, *Skulpturenausstattung*, 91–3, cats. 192–206.

[50] J. Keil, *JÖAI* 27 (1932), supplement, 43–4; M. Aurenhammer, *Die Skulpturen von Ephesos: Bildwerke aus Stein: Idealplastik I*, Forschungen in Ephesos 10/1 (Vienna, 1990), 137–8, cat. 115.

[51] Manderscheid, *Skulpturenausstattung*, 43–4, 93–6, cats. 207–28. On the history of the complex see A. von Gerkan and F. Krischen, eds., *Milet 1:9: Thermen und Palaestren* (Berlin, 1928), 54–100, and G. Kleiner, *Die Ruinen von Milet* (Berlin, 1968), 101–9.

[52] Statues: Keil, *JÖAI* 24 (1929), supplement, 38–45 with figs 19–31; Manderscheid, *Skulpturenausstattung*, 86–91, cats. 155–72. A number of reliefs were found in addition to sculptures in the round.

the founder of the city, Androclus, who was said to have received an oracle that he would found the city where he killed a boar.[53] Among the other fragments found in the room are a hand holding a discus, belonging to a copy of Myron's discobolus,[54] and a foot and shin on a base, positioned in such a way that the statue seems to have depicted a running man.[55] Here, then, we find two athletic images inserted among a group of Greek gods, portrait statues, and the founder of the city. All of these work together to stress the Greek identity and culture of the city, and draw a line from its first founder to its most current benefactor.

All these buildings are the products of euergetism. Sometimes the whole building and its decoration were funded by one wealthy individual, as Vedius proudly boasts on the inscription in his gymnasium.[56] At others, the sculptural display was acquired piecemeal through individual donations by different individuals, as in the Harbour Baths. Yet in all cases these individuals must have thought the erection and decoration of a bath-gymnasium complex a worthwhile expenditure of their resources. They had deliberately chosen this particular form of donation.[57] Buildings were always a popular choice, since they would survive as an enduring monument to the prestige and patriotism of the donor, leaving his name imprinted across the city.[58] Yet the function of the buildings is also important.

This can be seen particular clearly in the sophist Herodes Atticus' donations in mainland Greece. At Athens he donated a Panathenaic stadium, for use in the four-yearly Panathenaic festival, and also an odeum, constructed in the memory of his wife, both of which remain. He funded another odeum in Corinth, statues of Poseidon and Amphitrite in the temple at the Isthmus and a stadium at Delphi.[59] In Olympia his construction (in Regilla's name) of a monumental nymphaeum led Lucian to refer to him in the *Passing of Peregrinus* as 'a benefactor to Greece who had brought water to Olympia and put a stop to the thirst of those at the festival'.[60]

---

[53] Izmir, Archaeological Museum, inv. 45. The face has portrait features. See Manderscheid, *Skulpturenausstattung*, 65 nn. 478–9, and Aurenhammer, *Skulpturen*, 126–9, no. 105. On Androclus see H. Thür, 'The Processional Way in Ephesos as a Place of Cult and Burial', in Koester, *Ephesos*, 157–99, at 171–3.

[54] Izmir, Archaeological Museum, inv. 473; Aurenhammer, *Skulpturen*, 156, cat. 138.

[55] Keil, *JÖAI* 24 (1929), supplement, 40, cat. 8, fig. 30. Its current location is unclear: see Manderscheid, *Skulpturenausstattung*, 90, cat. 190 and Aurenhammer, *Skulpturen*, 156.

[56] *IEphesos* ii. 438.

[57] See P. Veyne, *Bread and Circuses: Historical Sociology and Political Pluralism*, trans. B. Pearce (London, 1990), 70–200, on the factors influencing Greek civic euergetism.

[58] P. Vedius Antoninus' building projects also included the Bouleuterion (also known as the odeum), where a letter from the emperor Antoninus Pius praising him was found: *IEphesos*, ii. 460; *SIG* 850. See J. Keil, 'Inschriften', *Forschungen von Ephesos* 3 (Vienna, 1923), 91–168, at 168 n. 5, and E. L. Bowie, 'The Vedii Antonini and the Temple of Hadrian', *Proceedings of the Tenth International Congress of Classical Archaeology* (Ankara, 1973), 866–74, at 871.

[59] Philostratus, *Lives of the Sophists* 2.1 (550–1); Pausanias 1.19.6 (stadium at Athens), 2.1.7–9 (statues at Isthmus), 7.20.6 (odeum at Athens), 10.32.1 (stadium at Delphi).

[60] Lucian, *The Passing of Peregrinus* 19; J. Tobin, *Herodes Attikos and the City of Athens: Patronage and Conflict under the Antonines* (Amsterdam, 1997), 301, 306–7; Smith, 'Honorific Portrait Statues', 75–7.

Herodes' benefactions can be seen as specifically designed not only to exalt himself and his family, as Tobin shows, but also to stress his keen appreciation and support of all the trappings of Greek culture.[61] It is significant that in addition to Athens, his home town, Herodes' benefactions concentrate around three of the sites of the four great Panhellenic festivals: Olympia, the Isthmus at Corinth, and Delphi. Donors like Herodes and Vedius, sophists or statesmen, chose to build gymnasia, stadia, or odea because of the importance of these buildings, and the activities associated with them, within traditional classical Greek culture as it was esteemed and experienced in the second century AD.

It is also significant here that the majority of the sculptural display in the bath-gymnasia of Asia Minor comes from the gymnasium part of the complex rather than the bathing suites, as was more usual in Rome and North Africa.[62] Indeed, the 'marble rooms' or 'imperial rooms' seem to have played a particularly important role as display areas. Rather than being seen as areas for the imperial cult, it seems more likely that the imperial dedications and images which sometimes appear in these rooms were motivated instead by the adoption of these prominently placed rooms as showpieces for the complex as a whole. In Ephesus all the rooms are placed on a prominent axis of the building, at right angles to the main propylon. While the sculptural display of the Harbour Baths can only be partially reconstructed, the displays in both the Vedius and East Bath-Gymnasia show a carefully formulated combination of private portraits, images of the gods, and references to the cultural associations of the gymnasium. Such displays may have been influenced by the trend at Rome for filling bathing spaces with a combination of ideal statuary and portraiture and, as in Rome, they help to articulate the nature of the space as one for relaxation, health, and exercise.[63] Yet each individual collection of statues also helped to create specific connotations for the complex they decorated.

In the East Baths at Ephesus we seem to find a dominance of female figures (perhaps an indication of a female patron for the Baths) as well as references to the intellectual role of the gymnasium. In the Vedius Baths, by contrast, we find statues of the heroic founder of the city and athletic statues, one at least a copy of a famous fifth-century bronze. The reference here to the athletic activities of the gymnasium may have been influenced by the placement of this complex next to the stadium, where public athletic competitions would have taken place.[64] Athletes competing in these competitions are likely to have used this adjoining gymnasium

[61] Tobin, *Herodes Attikos*, 58–65, 161–210. [62] Manderscheid, *Skulpturenausstattung*, 23.

[63] On the associations of these programmes see Manderscheid, *Skulpturenausstattung*, 28–45.

[64] For athletic festivals held at Ephesus see Moretti, *IAG*, cat. 76 (the Hadrianeia, Balbilleia, and Epineicia) and 184–5, 212–14. Friesen, *Twice Neokoros*, 121–37, argues that the earliest set of baths in Ephesus, the Harbour Baths, were built to accommodate the Ephesian Olympics founded in honour of Domitian. The palaestra in the Theatre Baths also has a series of steps running along one side which could have accommodated spectators, see J. Keil, *JÖAI* 27 (1932), supplement, 16–25, fig. 10.

before and after their contests. The world of contemporary athletic competitions is thus linked with the ideals of classical athletic beauty, as expressed through the Discobolus statue. The overall impression of the ensemble is to show the patronage of classical Greek culture, expressed through these idealizing statue types, by one of the most influential figures of second-century Ephesus. While the statue types are drawn from the world of classical art, this is not merely an antiquarian display. Indeed, the intellectual and athletic activities to which these idealized statues of muses and athletes alluded were continually re-experienced in the rooms around them. The present is thus presented as a legitimate successor to the past, stressing the continuity of Greek culture. This is emphatically not a culture that excludes present realities. The sculptural ensembles of these bath-gymnasium complexes revel in performing Greek culture in the presence and under the auspices of Roman power. This is particularly clear in the Hall of the Muses in the Baths of Faustina at Miletus. While the Muse statues allude to the intellectual aspect of the Greek gymnasium, the imperial statues standing in the apse of the room are a clear expression that the emperors themselves value and endorse Greek *paideia*.

CIVIC FESTIVALS AND CIVIC IDENTITY

The imperial family was also accommodated within Greek civic culture in the numerous festivals which sprang up around the Greek east.[65] While some of these were the result of benefactions by the emperors themselves, many were acts of euergetism by members of the local civic elite. They provided an alternative means of self-enhancement to the erection of impressive public buildings and, like those buildings, could be dedicated to the ruling power.[66] Even when a festival did not explicitly bear the name of the emperor, the imperial presence was ubiquitous, from the imperial rescripts appended to inscriptions about the festival, to the prayers on behalf of the imperial family and the statues carried in processions.[67]

---

[65] On the growth of festivals during the Roman period see Robert, 'Discours d'ouverture'; Spawforth, 'Agonistic Festivals'; S. Mitchell, 'Festivals, Games and Civic Life in Roman Asia Minor', *JRS* 80 (1990), 183–93; M. T. Boatwright, *Hadrian and the Cities of the Roman Empire* (Princeton, 2000), 94–104; O. van Nijf, 'Local Heroes: Athletics, Festivals and Elite Self-Fashioning in the Roman East', in S. Goldhill, ed., *Being Greek under Rome: Cultural Identity, the Second Sophistic and the Development of Empire* (Cambridge, 2001), 306–34, at 307–14. On the integration of the imperial cult, see Price, *Rituals and Power*, 101–32.

[66] See Pliny, *Letters* 10.75, for an example of a benefactor wishing to fund either a building or a festival in honour of the emperor Trajan.

[67] See van Nijf, 'Local Heroes', 318–20, commenting on the institution of the Demostheneia at Oenoanda; M. Wörrle, *Stadt und Fest in kaiserzeitliche Kleinasien* (Munich, 1988). For the role of imperial statues in these processions see especially the Salutaris inscription from Ephesus: G. M. Rogers, *The Sacred Identity of Ephesos: Foundation Myths of a Roman City* (London, 1991), 80–126.

Festivals came in a wide range of sizes, from small games with a purely local or regional catchment area to larger and more prestigious Panhellenic affairs.[68] They are usually divided into two categories as either games where prize money was awarded to the victors (*agōnes thematikoi*) or crown games, often also called sacred games (*agōnes hieroi kai stephaneitai*).[69] At these the prize was a symbolic one, a crown made out of the foliage of a tree associated with the festival—for example the olive at Olympia and the laurel at Delphi.[70] Some sacred games outside mainland Greece were also called 'Olympian' or 'Pythian', a sign that they were run according to those rules. Sacred games were the most prestigious and victory in them could bring an athlete valuable benefits from his home city, including an honorific statue, freedom from taxation, meals at public expense, and the right to a ceremonial procession on his return (*eiselasis*). As the numbers of festivals increased, however, the financial burden of these benefits also gradually increased. As a result sacred or eiselastic status had to be specifically granted by the emperor himself.[71] While small local festivals may have provided an opportunity to assert civic or local identity, larger festivals could bring both symbolic and financial rewards, allowing a city to present itself to a wider audience, vie with its neighbours, and reap the benefits of external attention.[72]

Cities were keen to advertise their festivals, as can be seen on the many agonistic motives that appear on civic coinage.[73] Ziegler shows that many of the festivals celebrated on coins from Cilicia are in honour of the emperors and reflect grants of neocorate (imperial cult) status to the cities involved. He associates these honours with the increased presence of imperial troops in this area, epecially during the third century. Emperors could use grants of neocorate or metropolitan status to reward the loyalty of certain cities, while for the cities themselves such titles were

---

[68] For an example of regional games, see the pan-Lycian games set up in Oenoanda by Julius Lucius Pilius Euarestus in the 220s: A. S. Hall and N. P. Milner, 'Education and Athletics: Documents Illustrating the Festivals of Oenoanda', in D. French, ed., *Studies in the History and Topography of Lycia and Pisidia: In Memoriam A. S. Hall*, British Institute of Archaeology at Ankara Monograph 19 (London, 1994), 7–47, at 8–29.

[69] H. Pleket, 'Games, Prizes, Athletes and Ideology: Some Aspects of the History of Sport in the Greco-Roman World', *Stadion* (= *Arena*) 1 (1975), 49–89, at 54–71; Robert, 'Discours d'ouverture'; Spawforth 'Agonistic Festivals'.

[70] On victory crowns, and especially that at Isthmia, see O. Broneer, 'The Isthmian Victory Crown', *AJA* 66 (1962), 259–63. Apples were also given as a prize at Pythian games: Lucian, *Anacharsis* 9. See L. Robert, 'Les boules dans les types monétaires agonistiques', *Hellenica* 7 (1949), 93–104.

[71] See F. Millar, *The Emperor in the Roman World*, 2nd edn. (London, 1992), 449–52. For a study of imperial involvement in the festivals of Cilicia, see R. Ziegler, *Städtisches Prestige und kaiserliche Politik: Studien zum Festwesen in Ostkilikien im 2. und 3. Jahrhundert n. Chr.* (Düsseldorf, 1985). Not all sacred games were also eiselastic.

[72] On the impact of festivals see Spawforth, 'Agonistic Festivals', 196.

[73] See Ziegler, *Städtisches Prestige*; K. Harl, *Civic Coins and Civic Politics in the Roman East AD 180–275* (Berkeley, Los Angeles, and London, 1987), 63–70.

FIGURE 8.8 Civic festivals were often commemorated on civic coinage. The reverse of a bronze coin minted by Hierapolis in Phrygia shows a laurel wreath inscribed ΠΥΘΙΑ (Pythia), advertising the city's most prestigious festival. Diameter: 0.95 cm. Severan.

keenly sought after both as a sign of loyalty to Rome and as a weapon in inter-city rivalries over status.[74] While neocorate status is usually celebrated on earlier coins through images of new imperial temples, in late second-century and third-century Cilicia it seems to have been primarily expressed through reference to imperial festivals bearing names such as Commodeia, Severeia, and Epinicia.[75]

The imagery used to advertise festivals varies. Often the name of the festival is written inside a crown or a wreath (Fig. 8.8). Usually this is the wreath of foliage which was offered as a prize at the games, though sometimes a crown with imperial busts appears, such as that worn by the presiding priest.[76] Elsewhere the coins show the athletes who competed at the games, or the prizes awarded (Fig. 8.9).[77] Often they depict a table bearing one or more large cylindrical crowns, sometimes with palm branches emerging from the top.[78] Similar crowns also advertised civic festivals on public architecture.

FIGURE 8.9 Another coin minted by Hierapolis shows a prize table with two crowns inscribed ΠΥΘΙΑ and AKTIA (Pythia, Actia) advertising two local festivals. Diameter: 1.15cm. Severan.

[74] Ziegler, *Städtisches Prestige*, 67–123. See also Harl, *Civic Coins*, 66–7. Inter-city rivalries are dramatically revealed in Dio Chrysostom, *Orations* 34, 38. See L. Robert, 'La titulature de Nicée et de Nicomédie: la gloire et la haine', *Harvard Studies in Classical Philology* 81 (1977) 1–39; C. P. Jones, *The Roman World of Dio Chrysostom* (Cambridge, Mass., 1978), 71–94.

[75] Ziegler, *Städtisches Prestige*, 58–66, 124–6, with the review comments of Mitchell, 'Festivals', 192–3. On the role of festivals in the imperial cult see Price, *Rituals and Power*, 101–32. On the representation of temples on coins see Price, *Rituals and Power*, 180 and pls. 2–3; Friesen, *Twice Neokoros*, 65–6, pls. 8–9.

[76] On these crowns compare the relief published by M. Wörrle, 'Neue Inschriftenfunde aus Aizanoi I', *Chiron* 22 (1992), 337–76, at 349–68 with pl. 5. Rumscheid, *Kranz und Krone*, 7–51, suggests that such crowns were a mark of the presidency of public games. See pp. 24–31 on the coins.

[77] For other examples, see Harl, *Civic Coins*, pls. 28–9.

[78] I follow Rumscheid, *Kranz und Krone*, 79–82, in identifying these cylindrical objects as crowns, contra E. Specht, 'Kranz, Krone oder Korb für den Sieger', in *Altmodische Archäologie: Festschrift für Friedrich Brein* (*Forum Archaeologiae: Zeitschrift für klassische Archäologie* (14 March 2000), available via http://farch.net), who suggests that they represent baskets.

An examination of the civic coinage and architecture of Hierapolis in Phrygia shows the importance with which a particular city viewed its public festivals. Among the festivals celebrated here one of the most important seems to have been that in honour of the patron deity of the city, Apollo Archegetes, which was given status equal to the Pythian games and is often referred to on the coins simply as Pythia (Figs 8.8, 8.9).[79] While it is primarily known through documents of the third century AD, it may also have been held in the second century.[80]

As well as advertising the festival on their civic coinage, the Hierapolitans gave it pride of place on the decoration of a new stage building for the theatre. The inscription shows that the theatre was dedicated to Apollo Archegetes, the other civic gods, and the imperial family, Septimius Severus, Caracalla, Geta, and Julia Domna, dating it to AD 206–8.[81] The stage building was lavishly decorated with marble columns and reliefs. At the base of the building these showed the myths and cult of Apollo and his sister goddess, Artemis of Ephesus, while the upper storeys featured scenes of the rape of Persephone and the cult of Dionysus. At the focal point of the decoration, however, the reliefs situated above the main entrance onto the stage (the *porta regia*) proudly proclaim the importance of Hierapolis' chief civic festival (Fig. 8.10).[82]

In the central panel, positioned immediately above the doorway, is a scene of the Severan imperial family accompanied by various gods and personifications. The scene is dominated by a large decorated metallic crown placed on a table, an exaggerated version of the crown awarded to victorious athletes in a public festival.[83] In front of the table lies a river god, while to the left are a series of personifications, labelled by inscriptions above, though these are now fragmentary. From the left are shown a seated male figure next to a tripod, possibly symbolizing *Agōn* (competition), a female figure labelled *Agōnothesia* (presidency of the games) and the personification of the city of Hierapolis, originally holding a statuette of the patron god Apollo.[84] On the far side of the table stand the imperial family. Septimius Severus is seated in the centre, with a winged Nike (Victory) behind him. Flanking him to the left stands Caracalla, while Geta (later partially erased) and Julia Domna stand to the right. To the far right stand the figures of Tyche (Fortune) and the

[79] *BMC Phrygia*, Hierapolis 66, 71. On the numismatic evidence for festivals see F. G. von Papen, 'Die Spiele von Hierapolis', *Zeitschrift für Numismatik* 26 (1908), 161–82, and A. Johnston, 'Hierapolis Revisited', *The Numismatic Chronicle* 144 (1984), 52–80.

[80] For a review of the evidence for this and other festivals see T. Ritti, *Hierapolis Scavi e Ricerche*, i: *Fonti Letterarie ed Epigrafiche*, Archeologica 53 (Rome, 1985), 57–97.

[81] F. D'Andria and T. Ritti, *Hierapolis Scavi e Ricerche*, ii: *Le Sculture del Teatro*, Archeologica 55 (Rome, 1985), 9–10.

[82] The reliefs are described in detail by Ritti, *Hierapolis*, i. 57–77.

[83] Harl, *Civic Coins*, pl. 8.7, illustrates a coin showing an athlete wearing such a crown. See also n. 78 above.

[84] See Ritti, *Hierapolis*, i. 60–2. Hierapolis is identified through comparison with another relief from the orchestra of the theatre; ibid., pl. 7a.

FIGURE 8.10 The first-storey relief decoration of the *scaenae frons* of the theatre at Hierapolis also commemorated its major festival, the Pythia. In the centre of the stage the emperor Septimius Severus is shown along with his family next to personifications of the city and a table with a prize crown, indicating that the festival takes place under the patronage of the imperial family. Length of central block: 3.7m. AD 206–8.

goddess Roma. Again, all the figures were originally identified by inscriptions above their heads.

More personifications appear on the side reliefs. To the left are shown the figures of *Sunthusia* (Joint Sacrifice), *Oikoumenē* (the inhabited world), and *Aiōn* (time) while to the right appear *Andreia* (courage) and *Sunodos* (the guild of actors) along with a priestess and an athlete crowning himself.[85] The back of the left side panel shows a young boy being crowned victor, labelled above with the epithet Pythian (*Pythikos*) (Fig. 8.11), while the back of the right side panel shows a scene of sacrifice.[86] The short ends of these projecting side panels show, on the left, the president of the games (*agōnothetēs*) with a female figure and, on the right, another athlete being crowned.[87]

The overall message is clear. The Hierapolitans celebrate their major civic festival, held in honour of Apollo Archegetes (whose statue was probably held by Hierapolis in the central relief) and bearing the title Pythian. The personifications

[85] See Ritti, *Hierapolis*, i. 60–2. Hierapolis is identified through comparison with another relief from the orchestra of the theatre; ibid., pls. 4b, 5a.

[86] Ibid., pl. 6a.   [87] Ibid., pls. 4a, 5b.

FIGURE 8.11 On the back of the panel flanking the central scene to the left a naked boy athlete, labelled above as
ΠΥΘΙΚΟΣ (Pythian), is shown being crowned. To the right an adult athlete crowns himself. Both figures assert the
role that athletic contests played within the festival. L: 1.65m. AD 206–8.

stress the connection between the festival and the city (represented by the figures
of Hierapolis and a river god) and also show its wider impact through the
personifications of worldwide sacrifice and time. To the right both the athletic and
artistic sides of the festival are stressed through the martial figure of courage and
the personification of the guild of actors, who holds a tragic mask. Athletic victories, in particular, are shown through the representation of a number of naked male
figures either crowning themselves or being crowned. At the centre of all this
sits Septimius Severus, a clear sign that the festival itself is held under the auspices
of the imperial power, by whom its status had perhaps been increased.[88]

Through coins and the decoration of public monuments cities advertised both
their religious festivals and the favour of the imperial house. Festivals provided a
way of interacting with the imperial power while also maintaining a sense of Greek
civic identity. Their importance can be shown not only through the images on
coins and buildings, but also in the fact that many wealthy individuals chose
to spend their money on festivals as a way of enhancing their own prestige and
benefiting their cities.

[88] Ibid., 73–4, suggests that he may have given the festival 'sacred' status, perhaps influenced by the
Hierapolitan sophist Antipater who acted as imperial secretary at the Severan court.

The rivalry of individual benefactors can be clearly seen in the epigraphical record of the Lycian city of Oenoanda, where the wealthy elite seem to have vied to outdo their predecessors in setting up athletic festivals.[89] Statues seem to have played an important part in the festivals at Oenoanda. This emerges particularly clearly in the poem carved on the base of a statue of the benefactor Julius Lucius Pilius Euarestus, composed either by Euarestus himself or by his brother-in-law Fronto, whose statue stood nearby.[90] This man had initally set up a penteric athletic contest for the city, called the Severeia Alexandreia Euaresteia, some time in the AD 220s.[91] The inscription on his statue records his decision, at the fifth meeting of the festival, to add artistic contests as well:

Agonothete for life I have put up prizes for the strong in the famous stadia of athletic Heracles. But one who has earned his living from the Muses ought to have provided gifts for his own Muses; therefore, having celebrated myself this fifth festival, I have put up prizes welcome to Muses for artistic performances.[92]

Here Euarestus refers to his position as grammaticus for the city. Since he himself was responsible for literary education in the city he has decided to add musical contests to the purely athletic festival he had previously set up. In the second stanza he also draws attention to the victory statues which he had funded as part of his benefaction:

This is the fifth festival, o sweet fatherland, I, Euarestus, have myself celebrated for you, rejoicing, and these are the fifth statues that I am again erecting in bronze, symbols of virtue and wisdom (*aretēs sumbola kai sophiēs*). Many have put up fair prizes for cities, after they were dead, but, in his own life, no mortal man. I alone dared to do this and it rejoices my heart to delight in the brazen images. So, abating your criticism, all those who have dread Envy, look upon my statue with emulous eyes.[93]

As well as the fact that Euarestus instituted this festival while still alive, rather than in his will, he also draws attention to the fact that he has funded bronze statues for the victors. These statues thus celebrated not only the athletes themselves, but also Euarestus, whose name appears on their bases.[94] According to his own statement, they are also meant to serve as symbols of virtue and wisdom, an assertion, then, of the moral qualities associated with athletic prowess. Another example of this can be seen on a statue base commemorating the athlete Aurelius Achilles which was found in the Hadrianic baths at Aphrodisias. In the inscription the city of Ephesus

---

[89] See Hall and Milner, 'Education and Athletics', esp. 30, 33, commenting on the extra inclusion of Termessus and Cibyra in the pan-Lycian festival funded by M. Aurelius Artemon and his wife ('Education and Athletics', no. 22). All the translations which follow are theirs, occasionally with minor adjustments.

[90] See Hall and Milner, 'Education and Athletics', 25, commenting on lines 11–12. Fronto's name is mentioned either in the nominative, indicating that he himself wrote the verses, or in the vocative, in which case Euarestus wrote them. Either way the poem is written in the first person, as if spoken by Euarestus himself.

[91] Hall and Milner, 'Education and Athletics', esp. 29.   [92] Ibid., 24, no. 18b, ll. 1–6.

[93] Ibid., 24, no. 18b, ll. 15–22.   [94] Ibid., 9–18, nos. 1–7.

honours the athlete for his victories at the Olympeia in Ephesus as well as for his moral virtue, attributing to him 'complete virtue of both body and soul'.[95] This suggests that the statues of victorious athletes which were set up in cities around the Greek east did not just serve as memorials of physical prowess but could also carry wider connotations of ethical qualities.

The successful athlete is not the only one to reap the benefits of his victory. His home city also shares in the associated glory and often honours the athlete with a crown and statue. The reciprocal relationship between the athlete and his city is clearly expressed in an epigram appended to the statue of Euarestus' brother-in-law, P. Sthenius Fronto. The inscription declares that Fronto was victorious in the men's pancratium in the fifth contest funded by Euarestus. In the epigram below, the victor speaks in the first person:

First my fatherland crowned me for the boys' wrestling and honoured me with a glorious statue in bronze; later, having carried off for my fatherland the men's pancratium (in the festival) open to all Lycians, I set up a lovely statue.[96]

Fronto's early victory as a boy is rewarded with a public statue. He then returns the honour by winning another victory against stronger competition in the men's pancratium. Statues fulfil a key role in this reciprocal relationship, both honouring the victor and serving to adorn the city. We saw in the previous chapter how statues commemorating past athletic victories continued to play an important role in the Roman period, asserting a city's status and her place in the Hellenic world. Fronto's statue shows that new athletic statues continued to play a similar role.

The status of the athletes honoured in these bronze statues seems to be high. In Oenoanda the statue of Fronto the pancratiast stood next to that of his brother-in-law, the wealthy benefactor, in a conspicuous position at the entrance to the agora.[97] Elsewhere in the city too, the family lineage carved onto the tomb of the aristocratic Licinnia Flavilla proudly announced the athletic successes of her nephew L. Septimius Flavianus Flavillianus.[98] In cities across Asia Minor, an athletic victor was a trump card in games of self-representation. A series of inscriptions from the stadium at Aezanoi celebrate the notable M. Ulpius Appuleius Eurycles. Among these is a block carved with a series of wreaths inscribed with various titles.

[95] L. Robert, 'Inscriptions grecques d'Asie Mineure', in W. M. Calder and J. Keil, eds., *Anatolian Studies presented to W. H. Buckler* (Manchester, 1939), 227–48; reprinted in id., *Opera Minora Selecta*, i. 611–32, see esp. 619–20; C. P. Jones, 'Two Inscriptions from Aphrodisias', *Harvard Studies in Classical Philology* 85 (1981), 107–29; C. Roueché, *Performers and Partisans at Aphrodisias in the Roman and Late Roman periods*, JRS Monograph 6 (London, 1993), 202–6, no. 72. For a discussion linking such inscriptions to Dio Chrysostom's orations for the athlete Melancomas, see König, *Athletics and Literature*, ch. 3.

[96] Hall and Milner, 'Education and Athletics', 9–11, no. 1.

[97] Ibid., 14, fig. 2.4, shows their location (nos. 1E, 18E).

[98] *Inscriptiones Graecae ad res Romanas pertinentes*, iii. 500, col. v, ll. 1–3. See A. S. Hall, N. P. Milner, and J. J. Coulton, 'The Mausoleum of Licinnia Flavilla and Flavianus Diogenes of Oinoanda: Epigraphy and Architecture', *Anatolian Studies* 46 (1996), 111–44, esp. 122–3.

In addition to the imperial priesthoods held by Eurycles and his relatives, an olive wreath contains the following inscription: 'Antonius Asclepiades having won the boys' boxing at the Olympia in Pisa'.[99] Another inscription identifies this man as the grandfather of Eurycles' wife and gives the date of his victory as the 218th Olympics, that is, AD 93.[100]

There are many more such examples. Indeed, a number of recent studies of this evidence have shown the flaws in earlier histories of athletics in the Roman empire.[101] While older scholars used to assert that athletics in the Roman period was a debased activity, peopled by mindless, muscle-bound professionals rather than educated, elite amateurs, more recent scholarship has shown both the ideological concerns which produced those views and the prolific evidence against them.[102] We certainly cannot say that all victorious athletes of the Roman period came from the upper classes. However, a large proportion do seem to have been from wealthy elite families, and those who came from poorer backgrounds could gain both wealth and status from their athletic victories.[103] As we saw with the victories in the *naumachia* depicted on Attic ephebic reliefs, victors from wealthy and elite families were most likely to find their exploits celebrated in public statues and inscriptions. Yet Euarestus' view of these statues as symbols of virtue and wisdom suggests that athletic victories in public festivals could also be seen as a key sign of the *paideia* so prized by the Greek civic elite.[104]

Most of the statues set up to these athletic victors were in bronze and are long lost. We cannot know how they represented their subjects, though the marked taste for classicizing idealized statuary in the second century may suggest that some were modelled on images from the fifth and fourth centuries BC. Alternatively they may have shown their subjects not as idealized naked youths, but rather in the typical honorific dress of a tunic and himation. There must have been a wide range

[99] Wörrle, 'Neue Inschriftenfunde', 352, 4e and pl. 5.   [100] Ibid., 351, 2c; 360–1.

[101] See especially Pleket, 'Soziologie'; Robert, 'Discours d'ouverture'; O. van Nijf, 'Athletics, Festivals and Greek Identity in the Roman East', *PCPS* 45 (1999), 176–200; and id., 'Local Heroes'.

[102] On the impact of the idea of amateurism, see D. C. Young, *The Olympic Myth of Greek Amateur Athletics* (Chicago, 1984), and id., 'How the Amateurs Won the Olympics', in W. J. Raschke, ed., *The Archaeology of the Olympics: The Olympics and Other Festivals in Antiquity* (Madison, Wis., 1988), 55–75. It is especially clear in E. N. Gardiner, *Greek Athletic Sports and Festivals* (London, 1910), 17.

[103] See Pleket, 'Soziologie'; id., 'The Participants in the Ancient Olympic Games: Social Background and Mentality', in W. Coulson and H. Kyrieleis, eds., *Proceedings of an International Symposium on the Olympic Games, 5–9 September 1988* (Athens, 1992), 147–52; and van Nijf, 'Local Heroes', 320–7.

[104] On the importance of *paideia* as a badge of the elite see Schmitz, *Bildung und Macht*. He discusses public contests at 110–12 but deals primarily with literary *paideia* and does not discuss the role of athletics in elite self-representation. See also van Nijf, 'Local Heroes', 321, commenting on the same omission in Gleason, *Making Men*. More generally on *paideia* and education, see P. Brown, *Power and Persuasion in Late Antiquity: Towards a Christian Empire* (Madison, Wis., 1992); T. Barton, *Power and Knowledge: Astrology, Physiognomics and Medicine under the Roman Empire* (Ann Arbor, 1994); and R. A. Kaster, *Guardians of Language: The Grammarian and Society in Late Antiquity* (Berkeley, Los Angeles, and London, 1998).

of images used for these honorific statues, and the combination of visual details and the qualities celebrated in the inscriptions below would have worked together to give an individualized picture of the honorand.[105] While many of these images are now lost, there is one case where we can confidently reconstruct both appearance and setting.

PAST AND PRESENT IN APHRODISIAS AND SIDE

In the third century AD, the city of Aphrodisias decided to honour two victorious boxers by placing their statues at either end of the stage in the theatre. Their presence set up a number of resonances with the existing sculptural display. This appears to have been initially set up when the stage building was first constructed in the early empire, and was then gradually added to over the subsequent years.[106] This programme of imagery included a youthful figure representing the Demos of Aphrodisias and two tragic muses flanking a figure of Apollo, all deriving from the central part of the stage building. A number of figures of Nike probably served as acroteria.[107] An athletic statue also featured in this collection and may have decorated an upper niche of the *scenae frons* (Fig. 8.12).[108] It shows a figure standing with his weight on his right leg, the left arm by his side and the right bent at the elbow. He looks down towards his right side. It has been recognized as a variant of the Polycleitan 'Discophorus' type which has been interpreted either as an athlete holding the discus or as a figure of Hermes.[109] This particular statue wears a diadem around his head and does not sport the wings which identify other variants of the type as Hermes.[110] Instead, the athletic qualities of the statue are foremost here, manifested in his idealized body and modest downwards expression and the fillet

---

[105] For an account of how this worked in other honorific statues, see Smith, 'Honorific Portrait Statues', 63–70.

[106] Initial reports M. J. Mellink, *AJA* 72 (1968), 143; *AJA* 75 (1971), 177–8. For more detailed accounts of the development of the theatre and its sculptural display see J. M. Reynolds, 'Epigraphic Evidence for the Construction of the Theatre: 1st c. BC to mid 3rd c. AD', N. de Chaisemartin and D. Theodorescu, 'Recherches préliminaires sur la *frons scaenae* du théâtre', and K. T. Erim and R. R. R. Smith, 'Sculpture from the Theatre: A Preliminary Report', all in K. T. Erim and R. R. R. Smith, eds., *Aphrodisias Papers*, ii: *The Theatre, a Sculptor's Workshop, Philosophers and Coin-types*, JRA Supplement 2 (Ann Arbor, 1991), 15–28, 29–65, and 67–98.

[107] Erim and Smith, 'Sculpture', 67–79.   [108] Ibid., 72–4, no. 5.

[109] On the type see P. Zanker, *Klassizistische Statuen: Studien zur Veränderung des Kunstgeschmacks in der römischen Kaiserzeit* (Mainz, 1975), 4–7; P. C. Bol, 'Diskophoros', in H. Beck, P. C. Bol, and M. Bückling, eds., *Polyklet: der Bildhauer der griechischen Klassik* (Frankfurt, 1990), 111–17, cat. 19–30; and D. Kreikenbom, *Bildwerke nach Polyklet* (Berlin, 1990), 21–44. For a more sceptical view see M. Marvin, 'Roman Sculptural Reproductions of Polykleitos: The Sequel', in A. Hughes and E. Ranfft, eds., *Sculpture and its Reproductions* (London, 1997), 6–28.

[110] e.g. Kreikenbom, *Bildwerke*, cat. I 15, I 45.

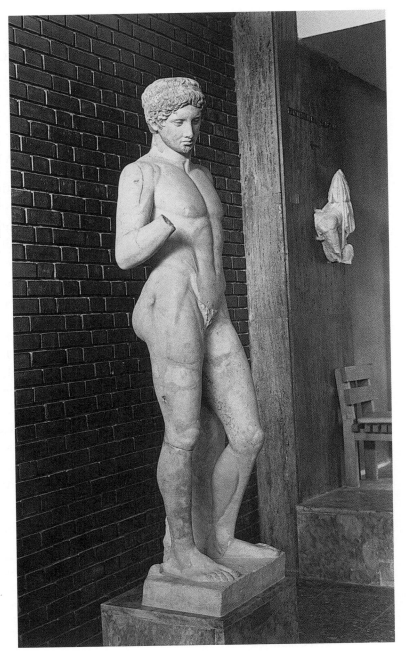

FIGURE 8.12 This classicizing statue is modelled on the Polycleitan Discophorus type. It formed part of the sculptural display of the theatre at Aphrodisias, providing a representation of athletic activity alongside images evoking intellectual or musical pursuits. H: 1.90m. Second century AD.

around his head. A number of portrait statues were also found in the excavations of the theatre.[111]

By the time that the two statues of local boxers were added, the sculptural display of the theatre combined images of the Demos of the city, tragic muses, Apollo,

[111] Erim and Smith, 'Sculpture', 82–6, nos. 16–20.

Victories, an athletic figure, and various portrait figures. The athlete fits into this programme as the representative of another important aspect of Greek culture to balance the depiction of figures associated with intellectual life. Crucial aspects of Hellenic identity, tragedy and athletics, were thus both represented. The use of a classicizing model for the statue also made the allusion to the classical past particularly apposite, by recalling the very physique of classical athletics.

At some point in the first half of the third century two portrait statues of victorious local boxers were set up at either end of the stage (Figs 8.13, 8.14).[112] Both are well-muscled figures. They wear the long gloves or 'caestus' worn by boxers and have portrait features. Both are bearded and have shaven heads, wearing the *cirrus in vertice* that appears on other depictions of athletes (a lock of hair high on the back of an otherwise shaven head). One of the statues (Piseas) is signed by the artist Polynices of Aphrodisias, while the other may have been produced by a different workshop.[113] They can be associated with two inscribed statue bases found at either end of the stage.[114] These bear the following inscriptions: 'The fatherland (honours) Candidianus, victor at Actia, circuit-victor (*periodonikēn*)' and 'The fatherland (honours) Piseas, son of Piseas, circuit-victor'. The description of both men as circuit-victors explains their entitlement to the honour of a public statue in the theatre. They had both won boxing victories in the four most prestigious international festivals, those at Olympia, Nemea, Isthmia, and Delphi.[115]

At the time these statues were set up the theatre had been adapted to hold gladiatorial games and wild beast hunts as well as musical contests.[116] Yet the popularity of these imported contests did not lessen the city's pride in its athletic heritage, and it is possible that the theatre was also used for athletic displays.[117] The respect with which Aphrodisias viewed her athletic victors is shown by the fact that the statues seem to have been carefully repaired and re-erected after damage at

---

[112] J. Inan and E. Alföldi-Rosenbaum, *Römische und frühbyzantinische Porträtplastik aus der Türkei: Neue Funde* (Mainz, 1979), 217–21, cats. 190–1; Erim and Smith, 'Sculpture', 84–6, nos. 19–20. The new reconstructions of the statues are published by J. A. Van Voorhis, 'Two Portrait Statues of Boxers and the Culture of Athletics at Aphrodisias in the Third Century CE', in C. Ratté and R. R. R. Smith, eds., *Aphrodisias Papers*, iv, JRA Supplement (Ann Arbor, forthcoming). She suggests that they were placed directly on the stage, in front of the end of the analemma wall.

[113] Inan and Alföldi-Rosenbaum, *Porträtplastik*, 219; Erim and Smith, 'Sculpture', 84, no. 19. Van Voorhis, 'Boxers', discusses the attribution of the statues.

[114] Rouché, *Performers and Partisans*, 207–8, nos. 74–5.

[115] See *Der Neue Pauly*, 'Periodos, periodonikēs', for bibliography.

[116] De Chaisemartin and Theodorescu, 'Recherches préliminaires', 38; C. Rouché, 'Inscriptions and the Later History of the Theatre', in Erim and Smith, *Aphrodisias Papers*, ii. 99–108, at 103.

[117] On gladiatorial games in the east the key account is still L. Robert, *Les gladiateurs dans l'Orient grec* (Paris, 1940; 2nd edn., Amsterdam, 1971). See also Rouché, *Performers and Partisans*, 60–80, and Woolf, 'Becoming Roman, Staying Greek'. For the honorific inscriptions set up to local and international athletic victors, see Rouché, *Performers and Partisans*, 198–221.

FIGURE 8.13 Contemporary athletic victors were also celebrated in the theatre, at least during the first half of the third century when two portraits of famous boxers were set up at either end of the stage. This statue is signed by Polynices of Aphrodisias and is linked with an inscription praising the boxer Piseas for victories in the four major panhellenic festivals. H: 1.77m. Second quarter of third century AD.

FIGURE 8.14. The second statue probably commemorates the boxer Candidianus, who is also praised for being a circuit-victor (*periodonikēs*). H: 1.50m. Mid-third century AD.

some point in their history.[118] Yet these modern-day athletic victors also set up a resonance with the idealized imagery of the stage building. They can be seen as the modern-day equivalents to the classical athlete represented there. They thus help to create a link between the present day of the early third century and the classical Greek past. The early third century was precisely the time when Philostratus was writing the *Gymnasticus*, a work which links the practices of his own time with the ancient past of athletics.[119] The contemporary-looking boxer statues interact with the Discophorus-type statue in a similar way. While that statue reminds us of athletics in the classical past, the honorific statues proclaim Aphrodisias' ability to continue to produce athletic victors in the contemporary world.

The prestige which could be gained through athletic victories in third-century Aphrodisias can also be seen in the fact that some victors chose to commemorate this aspect of their lives on their funerary monuments. This can be clearly seen on a sarcophagus from the city dated by Natalie de Chaisemartin to the second quarter of the third century (Fig. 8.15).[120] The front of the sarcophagus is dominated by the figure of a naked athlete who stands in the centre of the field. His head is turned to his right and he holds a crown in his left hand and another object, possibly a down-turned torch, in his right. On either side of the athlete the space is filled by wreaths of different types of foliage, similar to those which we find on victory monuments elsewhere. Numerous wreaths are shown to either side of the athlete, while more appear on each short side of the sarcophagus. Those on the sides and to the right of the athlete are placed above two crossed palms, a clear indication of past athletic victories. No inscriptions are currently visible inside the crowns, such as we see on another fragmentary sarcophagus from Aphrodisias, but it is quite possible that painted inscriptions were originally present.[121] The athletic nature of the deceased's victories is also made clear by the objects near his left foot. The large round object and two smaller cylindrical ones attended by a small child can be identified as a discus and jumping weights and may indicate that the athlete was a successful pentathlete.

The decoration of this sarcophagus is unlike that of most other Asia Minor sarcophagi and clearly seems to have been specially commissioned to record the athletic victories of a particular individual, presumably a citizen of Aphrodisias,

---

[118] Inan and Alföldi-Rosenbaum, *Porträtplastik*, 220–1. The inscribed bases seem later than the statues themselves. Van Voorhis, 'Boxers', suggests that this could be due either to the restoration of an older monument or to the reuse of these statues to commemorate the boxers Piseas and Candidianus.

[119] See A. Caretta, *Filostrato di Lemno: Il manuale dell'allenatore* (Novara, 1995), 15–16, on the date of the *Gymnasticus*, and discussion above, p. 75.

[120] N. de Chaisemartin, 'Appendix IV: Agonistic images on Aphrodisian sarcophagi', in Roueché, *Performers and Partisans*, 239–48 with pls. 22–4, at 239–45, no. 94.

[121] Roueché, *Performers and Partisans*, 200–2, no. 71; pl. 19. Other examples of inscribed wreaths can be seen on the Attic inscription now in the Metropolitan Museum in New York; Broneer, 'Isthmian Victory Crown', pl. 67, fig. 2.

FIGURE 8.15 The victories of another Aphrodisian athlete are commemorated on this unusual sarcophagus, which shows the athlete surrounded by victory crowns. L: 2.19m. First half of third century AD. Aphrodisias.

who would appear to have won 32 victories in athletic festivals.[122] While the crowns allude to the contemporary world of athletic competition, the athlete himself stands in a static pose, his head averted in a gesture of modesty which evokes classicizing athletic statuary. The sarcophagus presents the deceased as a successful athletic victor and worthy heir to the classical past.

We can see a similar interaction of classical and contemporary athletics in the city of Side in Pamphylia. During excavations here a room was found which shares a number of similarities with the so-called imperial rooms in Ephesus, discussed above. It lies on the central axis of a building known as Building M, a large court-yard surrounded by porticoes. It is flanked on either side by two smaller rooms. The importance of the room is indicated both by its lavish architectural decoration and by the fact that the columns immediately in front of the room are indented. Like the rooms in the Harbour Baths, Baths of Vedius and East Bath-Gymnasium at Ephesus, this room was originally decorated with a two-storeyed articulated

---

[122] For accounts of the sarcophagi produced in Asia Minor see H. Wiegartz, *Kleinasiatische Säulensarkophage: Untersuchungen zum Sarkophagtypus und zu den figürlichen Darstellungen*, IstanbulerForschungen 26 (Berlin, 1965); M. Waelkens, *Dokimeion: die Werkstatt der repräsentativen kleinasiatischen Sarkophage: Chronologie und Typologie ihrer Producktion*, Archäologische Forschungen 11 (Berlin, 1982), and, specifically on Aphrodisias, F. Isik, 'Die Sarkophage von Aphrodisias', in B. Andreae, ed., *Symposium über die antiken Sarkophage, Pisa 5.–12. September 1982*, Marburger Winckelmann-Programm (Marburg, 1984), 243–81.

FIGURE 8.16 A room in the complex known as Building M at Side had a lavishly decorated two-storey façade. This detail shows the remains of the architectural decoration. Building M, Side.

façade of projecting niches filled with statuary (Figs 8.16, 8.17). A large number of statues were found in the room, many of them fragmentary and showing fire damage.[123]

Both Mansel and Inan record the finds, which included seven statues on athletic subjects. Two statues of discus-throwers were found, one representing Myron's Discobolus (Fig. 8.18), the other an earlier type, known as the Ludovisi type after a hip-herm in the Museo Nazionale in Rome (Fig. 8.19).[124] Other athletic statues

[123] See A. M. Mansel, *Die Ruinen von Side* (Berlin, 1963), 109–21, for an account of the building and finds.

[124] J. Inan, *Roman Sculpture in Side* (Ankara, 1975), nos. 2, 1; Rausa, *Immagine*, 171, no. 1.1; 175, no. 4.9. See also J. Inan, 'Three Statues from Side', *Antike Kunst* 13 (1970), 17–33 with pls. 11–21, at 17–21, for the identification of the Ludovisi-type discobolus.

FIGURE 8.17 This reconstruction of the marble room in Building M suggests its original appearance, filled with statuary.

include a torso of the Polycleitan Diadoumenos (Fig. 8.20),[125] a torso of the Lysippan Apoxyomenus,[126] a torso of the sandalbinder type (Fig. 8.21) of Hermes or an athlete,[127] a torso of Hermes carrying a *kerykeion*,[128] and a number of fragments belonging to a naked male statue which had a support in the form of a herm.[129] Other fragments such as a hand holding a discus and a hand holding part of a fillet may also belong to some of these statues.[130] Another statue found in the room to the right of this one shows an oil-pouring youth and may also have been part of the display.[131]

Other statues found in the room depict the gods and include copies or variants of recognizable types: a head of Apollo, a torso of the Ares Borghese type, a draped

[125] Inan, *Sculpture in Side*, no. 7. [126] Ibid., no. 28; Rausa, *Immagine*, 208, no. 22.3.

[127] Inan, *Sculpture in Side*, no. 32. [128] Inan, 'Three Statues from Side', 21–6; *Sculpture in Side*, no. 3.

[129] Inan, *Sculpture in Side*, no. 245. [130] Ibid., nos. 270, 314.

[131] Similar to the Munich oil-pourer type, Inan, *Sculpture in Side*, no. 20; Rausa, *Immagine*, 213, no. 24.6. A. Linfert, *Von Polyklet zu Lysipp* (Giessen, 1966), 42–5, suggests that it may have shown an athlete cleaning himself with his strigil rather than pouring oil.

FIGURE 8.18 A number of athletic statues modelled on famous prototypes were found amid the remains from the marble room at Side. This torso comes from a copy of Myron's Discobolus, one of the most popular athletic statues in the second century AD. From Building M. H: 0.74m. Antonine.

female figure of the Hera Ephesia type, a torso of the Richelieu Hermes type, a statue of Hygeia, a torso of Nemesis, draped female figures of the Demeter type, a fragmentary statue of Asclepius, and a torso of Nike.[132] A torso of Marsyas was also found, and a number of fragments which suggest the presence of other figures such as Heracles, Apollo, and Hermes.[133] Some of the female draped statues may have

[132] Inan, *Sculpture in Side*, nos. 4, 10, 12, 22, 36, 37, 67, 69, 77, 94. Note, however, the review comments of A. Linfert, in *Bonner Jahrbucher* 179 (1979), 781–5, showing that some of these are variants rather than straight copies and disagreeing with some identifications.

[133] Inan, *Sculpture in Side*, nos. 55 (Marsyas), 421 (fragment of a club), 422 (fragment of a lyre), 384 (winged ankle). A child's leg (no. 381) may belong either to a portrait statue or to a figure of Eros.

FIGURE 8.19 The 'Ludovisi Discobolus' type shows another image of an athlete preparing to throw the discus and is also modelled on fifth-century BC forms. From Building M. H: 1.94m. Antonine.

served as portrait statues as probably did a torso of the small Herculaneum woman type,[134] and a cuirassed statue of an emperor occupied the central niche of the back wall.[135] Inan and Mansel date the statues to the Antonine period, although the head of the imperial statue was reworked at a later date.[136]

The room was thus decorated with a sculptural ensemble consisting of representations of the gods, particular individuals, the emperor, and idealized figures of classical athletes, with a high proportion of copies of classical Greek statues among

[134] Inan, *Sculpture in Side*, no. 54.   [135] Mansel, *Ruinen von Side*, 118.
[136] See J. Inan and E. Rosenbaum, *Roman and Early Byzantine Portrait Sculpture in Asia Minor* (London, 1966), 86–7, no. 63. Two other heads, possibly of Julio-Claudian figures, were also reworked (nos. 64–5).

FIGURE 8.20 This torso shows similarities with copies of Polycleitus' Diadoumenos and probably belonged to a statue of that type, evoking ideas of athletic victory. From Building M. H: 0.76m. Antonine.

them.[137] The function of the room is somewhat unclear since the purpose of the complex as a whole has not been determined. In its plan it resembles the gymnasia found in other cities in Asia Minor, particularly the palaestra of the Baths of Vedius in Ephesus, and the combination of statues also agrees with such rooms. Mansel thinks it likely that the complex in Side could have been part of a gymnasium since no other has as yet been found there, though no bathing suite has been found attached to the building, as is usual in Ephesus.[138] It has also been seen as a library.[139]

---

[137] For a proposed reconstruction of the display, see Linfert, Review of Inan, 783–4.

[138] Mansel, *Ruinen von Side*, 119. [139] Linfert, Review of Inan, 783.

FIGURE 8.21 The 'Sandalbinder', shown here, is another popular athletic type in second-century sculpture and helped to reinforce the classicizing, idealized mood of the sculptural display. From Building M. H: 0.76m. Antonine.

Whatever the function of the space, this room clearly served an important role as a showpiece of the city. The statuary display is notable for the high proportion of pieces which can be confidently identified as copies of classical Greek *opera nobilia*, most notably Myron's Discobolus and Polycleitus' Diadoumenus, whose fame in the second century is shown by their description in Lucian's *Lover of Lies*.[140] The athletic pieces, showing figures during and after athletic competition and the patron gods associated with the games, Hermes and Heracles, are set into a larger programme which stresses the importance of the Greek pantheon as well as the figure of the emperor himself. As we have seen elsewhere, here the Roman

[140] Lucian, *Lover of Lies* 18. See discussion above, p. 123.

FIGURE 8.22 A podium found at Side is decorated with agonistic images, including a scene of a symbolic prize crown inscribed ΙΕΡΑ ΠΥΘΙΑ (sacred Pythian games). It commemorates the establishment, under Gordian III, of a sacred international festival given isopythian status. W: 1.24m. Mid-third century AD.

emperor is inserted into the world of Greek culture, honoured as an equal of the Greek gods and as the patron of Greek learning and athletics. The choice of classicizing images also suggests an allusion to the cultural and artistic heritage of Greece which was so renowned during the Antonine period to which the decoration is dated.

Yet here, too, while the decoration alludes to the status of the classical past, when seen in its wider context the athletic images shown here may also have had contemporary resonances. So, like other cities of Asia Minor, Side seems to have had a flourishing agonistic life, recorded on both coins and inscriptions, though most of these date to the third century AD.[141] If some smaller contests also existed in the second century, as is likely, the classical athletic images displayed in this showpiece room would have helped to assert the place of these local contests within the wider history of Greek culture, reinforcing Side's claims to be seen as a truly Greek city. During the reign of Gordian III in the mid-third century AD Side seems to have

---

[141] See P. Weiss, 'Ein agonistisches Bema und die isopythischen Spiele von Side', *Chiron* 11 (1981), 315–46, at 335–9.

FIGURE 8.23 Two ceiling coffers from the nymphaeum outside the gates of Side also commemorate the Pythian festival. One shows a crown of flowers, inscribed ΙΕΡΟΣ ('sacred'). Mid-third century AD.

been awarded the honour of an international festival with isopythian status.[142] The impact of this festival, and the desire of the citizens of Side to advertise it and themselves, can be seen in the sculptural record of the city. The large prize crown awarded at the games is shown on a decorated platform dedicated by two citizens of Side (Fig. 8.22). It stands on a platform and is inscribed ΙΕΡΑ ΠΥΘΙΑ, 'sacred Pythian games'. More images of the crown decorated the ceiling coffers of the nymphaeum just outside the city gate.[143] In one it is shown decorated with flowers and inscribed ΙΕΡΟΣ, 'sacred' (written backwards, Fig. 8.23). In the other the crown is plain and has two palms and a pomegranate protruding from it.[144] Again it is inscribed, this time with the word ΟΙΚΟΥΜΕΝΙΚΟΣ, 'international' (Fig. 8.24).

[142] Weiss, 'Agonistisches Bema', 340–1.

[143] Mansel, *Ruinen von Side*, 53–64, had dated this to the Antonine period, but Weiss, 'Agonistisches Bema', 341–3, suggests a date in the third century, after the games instituted by Gordian, for at least part of the decoration.

[144] L. Robert, 'Inscriptions grecques de Sidè en Pamphylie', *Revue de Philologie* 32 (1958), 15–53, discusses these crowns at 20 n. 3.

FIGURE 8.24 A second coffer from the nymphaeum shows a plain crown with two palms and a pomegranate inside, inscribed ΟΙΚΟΥΜΕΝΙΚΟΣ (international). Like the other, it celebrates the high status of Side's festival. Mid-third century AD.

The sculptural decoration of the city of Side reveals an interest in both the classical tradition of athletics and the manifestation of this tradition in the city's festivals. It is only in the third century that Side seems to have displayed references to her new international festival on public architecture. Before then, however, victor statues of local athletes and inscriptions set up to honour elite benefactors would also have made the link between the classical past expressed in Building M and the embodiment of that past in the present. Yet a review of the monuments and images discussed in this chapter might suggest that there were also some changes in the representation of athletics in the course of the second and third centuries. Where athletic subjects appear in the sculptural displays of the second century, they are generally classicizing, idealized images, alluding to the priviliged position of athletics in the classical past. Yet from the end of the second century and especially in the third century coins and reliefs proudly announce the embodiment of this classical heritage in the festivals of the present, and especially the role which these could play in expressions of civic pride and loyalty to the imperial house.

CONCLUSIONS

This second part of the book has explored a number of the meanings that Greek athletics held for the inhabitants of the eastern Roman empire, both in the gymnasium and education, and in the world of athletic festivals. Some institutions such as the *ephēbeia* show a marked tendency towards archaism and helped to assert past victories or the traditional values of the cities in which they took place. The memory of the past is also enshrined in Pausanias' account of Olympia, whose dedications and victory monuments reassert her place as a Panhellenic meeting-point and the symbolic centre of Greece. Civic festivals too were a distinctive feature of Greek civic life, and a mark of belonging to the wider Greek world. Yet at the same time many festivals, celebrated either within the *ephēbeia* or by the city as a whole, were named after members of the imperial family, and accommodated the imperial power through vows, prayers, and statues. In all these areas, texts, images, and inscriptions both reflect and construct particular views of Greek athleticism, asserting its central place in the creation of good citizen soldiers, civic festivals, or the Hellenic lifestyle while also incorporating and celebrating the contemporary world.

NINE

Conclusions

The monuments, texts, and inscriptions discussed here all serve to prove the continuing vitality and relevance of Greek athletic culture within the world of the Roman empire. Yet this culture was also experienced and appropriated in differing ways across east and west, and over the course of time. Within the city of Rome and other western cities, Greek athletics found its place largely in the realms of leisure and entertainment, spectacles and bathing, whereas in the east it continued to play a more significant role in the creation and maintenance of civic and personal senses of identity. In this final chapter I will briefly expand on some of these issues, to consider how an examination of the uses of Greek athletics affects our wider picture of Roman attitudes to Greek culture, the Greeks' relationship with their own cultural past, and the negotiation between the two.

ROME: FANTASY AND CONTROL

The picture from Rome suggests that the imperial promotion of Greek athletic culture in Italy met an increasingly enthusiastic response. This was certainly a gradual process, begun in the reign of Augustus with the foundation of the *Sebasta* at Naples, which continued to receive imperial support under subsequent emperors. Naples' status as a Greek foundation made it an appropriate place for the institution of a Greek festival and the epigraphic evidence suggests that it came to gain a secure place on the agonistic circuit, attracting competitors from across the Mediterranean. Yet Naples' promotion of itself as living up to its Greek roots would also seem to tally with Roman desires, creating a safe space in which to indulge in one's fantasies of Greek life.[1]

By the reigns of Nero and Domitian, Greek athletic culture had spread from Campania to Rome, manifested in the establishment of Greek-style festivals by both emperors, but also in the increasingly Greek veneer given to exercise in the public baths. While literary evidence suggests that there was still some hostility to

[1] Cassius Dio 55.10.9; J. Kaimio, *The Romans and the Greek Language*, Commentationes Humanarum Litterarum 64 (Helsinki, 1979), 70–2.

the embrace of eastern customs in the late first and early second centuries AD, it simultaneously attests to the growing popularity of Greek body culture in the Roman baths. Mosaic evidence from the second and early third centuries from Rome and Ostia also suggests an increasing delight in the public spectacles of athletic competitions. The bathing public seems to have enjoyed the fantasy of seeing their own exercises as parallel to those of the athletic heroes of the current day, even if the competitors and victors in athletic festivals were still largely drawn from the eastern provinces.

The adoption of Greek-style festivals and physical training in Rome was a gradual process, gathering pace during the first and second centuries AD and reaching a peak in the Severan period. As with other Roman appropriations of elements of Greek culture, the functions and meanings of athleticism took on new forms to accommodate Roman needs. Greek athletics became part of the spectacle culture of ancient Rome, with successful athletes like M. Ulpius Domesticus or Aurelius Helix finding a fame amongst the populace of Rome and Ostia similar to that won by victorious charioteers or gladiators. While many of the athletic victors apparently came from the civic elites of the Greek east, their example rarely seems to have been followed by the equestrian and senatorial classes of Rome.[2] Instead the traditional Roman aversion to performance in public spectacles seems to have stopped all but a few from taking to the stadium themselves, and it is probably significant that the one example we do know of, Palfurius Sura, comes from the time of Nero when members of the elite were also encouraged to appear on stage.[3] The baths were a different matter, however. Here Romans of all classes could play out in their daily exercise regime a fantasy version of sporting success, free from the charge of public degradation.[4]

This dichotomy between spectatorship in public festivals and personal involvement in the baths suggests that while traditional hostility to the Greek gymnasium had certainly weakened by the third century AD, the ideological values with which athletic success and education were invested in Greek culture never took root in Rome. Cornelius Nepos' analysis of the Roman attitude to public competition and performance, made in the mid-first century BC, seems to have remained largely true throughout the Imperial period:

Almost everywhere in Greece, it was held to be a great honour to be proclaimed victor at Olympia . . . but among us all these things [acting and athletics] are regarded as disgraceful or lowly and quite removed from honourable behaviour. (pr. 5)

---

[2] On the status of Greek athletes see above, pp. 253–4.

[3] Scholiast to Juvenal, *Satire* 4.53; Tacitus, *Annals* 14.14–15; Suetonius, *Nero* 11.

[4] On the Roman attitude to public performance, see Edwards, *Politics*, 98–136, esp. 132 with further references.

Instead Greek athletics found its place in the sphere of leisure and private life, adding a welcome spice of exoticism to exercises in the baths and extending the range of public spectacles.[5]

An analysis of the idealizing athletic statues that decorated elite Roman villas also supports this picture of a growing interest in Greek athletic culture. Villas had traditionally provided a space for private indulgence in Greek culture, an area in which to exhibit the knowledge of Greek literature and thought which formed such a crucial part of elite Roman self-definition. The athletic statues which decorated bath and palaestra areas in elite villas built upon this philhellenism. Their evocation of fifth- and fourth-century BC forms conjured up the world of Classical Greece and the broader cultural associations of the Greek gymnasium. Yet the use of *athletic* statues to create this atmosphere also suggests the growing importance of athletic culture in the wider world. They show that athletics could now claim an equal role beside literature or philosophy as a crucial signifier of Greek culture. While Cicero's gymnasium appears to have been a thoroughly literary space, imperial villas reintegrate athletics into the Roman picture of Greek culture.

This sketch of Roman appropriations of Greek athletic culture shows both continuities and changes with the Republican period. The taboo against public performance and the preference for keeping expressions of philhellenism within the private sphere still seem to have been important. Yet this sphere grew to incorporate public festivals and bathing culture, allowing Romans to act out their fantasies of Greek life in the public baths at Rome as well as in their country villas or the Hellenized cities of Campania. I have suggested that the growing multiculturalism of Roman society, and the creation of a senatorial elite drawn from across the empire, could have helped to ease traditional worries about the preservation of Roman ancestral customs. As Rome solidified her control over the empire it was also inevitable that she should wish to share in all its benefits, including the vibrant festival culture sweeping throughout the Mediterranean. This was not a case of Greek culture taking over Rome, however, but of a careful adaptation of Greek customs and culture to service Roman needs and desires. Once copied and displayed in a Roman villa, the Greek victor statue that originally commemorated the achievement of a particular individual took on a more generic significance as a bearer of cultural or aesthetic values, designed to promote the self-image of the man whose villa it decorated. Physical exercise in the gymnasium lost its ideological associations with military training to become a leisure activity in the public baths. These adaptations share a number of parallels with other examples of the Roman use of Greek things, such as the use of Greek myths in domestic

---

[5] For a discussion of the concept of leisure in ancient Rome see J. Toner, *Leisure and Ancient Rome* (Cambridge, 1995), esp. 53–64 on the baths.

decoration or on sarcophagi to represent Roman values and give meaning to Roman lives.[6]

Athletics still seem to have been strongly signalled as 'Greek' in Rome, as we see from Pliny's comments about Romans exercising under a Greek trainer, or Juvenal's reference to Greek-style prizes of victory.[7] Indeed, the very 'foreignness' of athletics may have been what gave it exotic appeal. When we look at sensuous images of athletic boys, such as those at Domitian's villa, their status as Greek youths, reminiscent of the eastern slaves who attended Roman patrons, added an edge to their eroticism, making them simultaneously remote (figures from the classical past) and available (embodied in the slaves of the present). Indeed, we might see Roman attitudes to Greek culture as characterized by both yearning and control. The desire to immerse oneself in a Greek lifestyle can be seen in numerous anecdotes, such as the stories of elite Romans strolling around Greek gymnasia in Greek dress or Augustus' encouragement of the Romans on Capreae to dress up as Greeks, and the Greeks as Romans.[8] Yet at the same time this admiration for Greek culture was kept in check by the fact that it was now Rome who held political and military control.

Indeed, the institution of Greek-style festivals in Italy can be seen as emblematic of this double approach to Greek culture, admitting its pull over the Roman imagination, but also structuring and controlling that power by setting the games within Roman spectacle culture and under the authority of the Roman emperor. The institution of the *Sebasta* under Augustus also affected the balance of the Greek festival circuit. The traditional centre of this had always been Olympia, which continued to hold a pre-eminent place throughout the Roman period. Yet the institution of a new festival, created on the Olympic model and often featuring the emperors as agonothetes, also helped to shift the centre of Greek agonistic life to Italy and, eventually, to Rome. Domitian's Capitoline games can also be seen, in part, as a Roman version of the Olympic games, dedicated, like them, to Jupiter/Zeus.[9] As their appearance at the top of numerous victor lists shows, they came to hold a place at the very top of the festival hierarchy, challenging or equalling the status of the old *periodos* centres of Olympia, Delphi, Isthmia, and Nemea. The decision of the international athletic synod to set up their headquarters in Rome

[6] On floor mosaics see S. Muth, *Erleben von Raum—Leben im Raum: Zur Funktion mythologischer Mosaikbilder in der römisch-kaiserzeitlichen Wohnarchitektur* (Heidelberg, 1998). On sarcophagi see most recently P. Zanker and B. C. Ewald, *Mit Mythen leben: die Bilderwelt der römischen Sarkophage* (Munich, 2004).

[7] Pliny, *Panegyric* 13.5; Juvenal, *Satire* 3.68.

[8] Scipio: Livy 29.19.12, discussed by J.-L. Ferrary, *Philhellénisme et Impérialisme: Aspects idéologiques de la conquête romaine du monde Hellénistique* (Rome, 1988), 524–6; Tiberius: Suetonius, *Tiberius* 11; Augustus: Suetonius, *Augustus* 98.

[9] Tertullian, *De Spectaculis* 11.

under Hadrian and Antoninus Pius also proves how central a place Rome and the emperor had come to hold within Greek festival culture.

The imperial promotion of Greek athletic festivals in Italy can thus be seen in part as a form of control, firmly placing Rome and the emperor at the centre of a festival industry which became increasingly buoyant throughout the first three centuries AD. Visual, numismatic, and epigraphic evidence suggests that we can see a gradual increase in the foundation of new festivals over this period, moving from traditionally Greek areas which already possessed some festivals and now gained more, to their institution in areas with increasingly tenuous claims to Greek culture, such as Cilicia, Syria, and North Africa, to name only a few.[10] I have argued that festivals could play a central role within civic self-identities, allowing them to lay claim to a key signifier of Greek culture. Yet many of these festivals were acts of benefaction from the emperor, or bore imperial names, such as *Commodeia* or *Severeia*, and the monuments that commemorate civic festivals often also incorporate the imperial image. The emperor set himself, or was set, at the very heart of Greek festival culture.

Where we find athletics outside the Greek world, as in Gaul or North Africa, the decision to institute a Greek-style festival or exercise in the baths may have been influenced as much by the example of Rome and the emperors, as it was by the desire to lay claim to a Greek identity. In many cases we cannot single out one or another influence as being dominant. In Gaul, the influence of Rome, the Greek roots of some southern cities, and the activities of members of the elite elsewhere around the empire could all have exercised an influence. The imperial promotion or support of festivals around the empire also had the effect of shifting the balance, creating a worldwide festival culture in which areas outside the Greek east could also have a share.

THE GREEKS AND THEIR PAST: ATHLETICS IN THE SECOND SOPHISTIC

Some of the features that I have identified in the Roman attitude to Greek athletics could certainly have characterized athletic activity in the east of the empire too. Many of those who frequented bath-gymnasia in the cities of Greece or Asia Minor would have done so simply for exercise and relaxation, without pondering at length on how they were, in the process, acting out their cultural birthright. Fewer elite villas have been excavated in the eastern provinces than in the west, yet where they have been studied, like those of Herodes Atticus in Greece, there is little reason to suppose that their use and decoration differed greatly from those in Italy,

---

[10] Robert, 'Discours d'ouverture'.

and it has even been suggested that Herodes might have copied Hadrian in some aspects of the design of his villas.[11] The nature of one's audience may have played a crucial role here. While a figure like Herodes could use his education to assert his identity and status as a Greek, a teacher, and a sophist, he might also have used it on other occasions to build up connections with members of the elites from around the empire as a sign of a shared culture based on Greek *paideia*. The spectacular qualities of athletic festivals are also likely to have been valued just as much by eastern audiences as by those in the west. Mosaics celebrating the events of athletic and musical festivals are known from Greece as well as Italy, while a house in ancient Seleucia, near Antioch in Syria, featured a portrait of a famous athlete of the first century AD, Nicostratus of Aegeae, in the pavement of its portico.[12]

A number of parallels can thus be seen between the imagery associated with athletics in east and west, and in the ways that athletic activities were received and enjoyed. Yet the Greek engagement with athletic activity also goes far deeper than it does in the west. While we have seen that aspects of Greek athleticism could spread beyond the Greek east to Italy and elsewhere, their meanings to a Greek audience are integrally connected with issues of identity and the relationship that the Greeks of the Roman empire constructed with their classical past. This has become an area of particular interest in recent years. Studies of Greek rhetoric and literature in the Roman period show their overwhelming fascination with the ancient, and especially classical, past, whether this is expressed in romantic novels set entirely in a pre-Roman world or in the choice of themes from fifth and fourth-century BC Greek history as subjects for extempore public orations.[13] This has sometimes been seen as a form of nostalgia, a response to the realities of the Greek world's lack of political power by escape into memories of a happier past.[14] Others see it as a challenge, a sign of the imperial Greeks' self-confidence in their cultural claims and a means of gaining social and political power in the contemporary Roman world.[15] The way in which the elite used their knowledge of the past and command of the Attic dialect to define themselves as a group has also been noted.[16] More recent accounts, influenced by New Historicist approaches, stress instead

---

[11] Raeder, *Villa Hadriana*, 293. On the sculptural display of Herodes' villa in Arcadia, see G. Spyropoulos, *Drei Meisterwerke der Griechischen Plastik aus der Villa des Herodes Atticus zu Eva/Loukou* (Frankfurt am Main, 2001).

[12] Greece: S. E. Waywell, 'Roman Mosaics in Greece', *AJA* 83 (1979), 293–321 with pls. 45–52, at 316–17; Seleucia: D. Levi, *Antioch Mosaic Pavements* (Princeton, 1947), 115–16; J. Balty, 'La mosaïque antique au Proche-Orient I. Des origines à la Tétrarchie', *ANRW* II.12.2 (1981), 347–429, at 376, dating it to the Severan period.

[13] Among the many treatments, see Bowie, 'Greeks and their Past'; Swain, *Hellenism and Empire*, esp. 65–131. For an excellent discussion of the debate over the meanings of this archaism, see S. E. Alcock, *Archaeologies of the Greek Past: Landscapes, Monuments, and Memories* (Cambridge, 2002), 36–44.

[14] e.g. Bowie, 'Greeks and their Past'.   [15] e.g. Swain, *Hellenism and Empire*, 6–7.

[16] Schmitz, *Bildung und Macht*, 97–135. See also Gleason, *Making Men*, 21.

the variety of constructions of Greek culture and identity shown in the literature of the period.[17]

Analysis of the meanings and uses of Greek athletics makes an important contribution to this debate. The clear picture that emerges is of the continuing relevance and vitality of athletic activity in the Roman empire. This was a time when athletic festivals were thriving, successful athletes could gain worldwide renown, and athletes of the ancient past continued to receive cultic honours both in their home cities and at Olympia. That the claim to have produced an Olympic victor, either in the past or in the present day, could bring significant prestige to a city is clear from Pausanias' account of Greece and the victory inscriptions set up in cities around Greece and Asia Minor. The past is certainly of crucial importance here, but there is little sense of a retreat from the present into fond imaginings of the classical past. Some wistful or nostalgic tones can be detected, as in Dio's lament over the gymnasium-turned-cornfield in Euboea, or Pausanias' account of an abandoned sanctuary on Mount Lycaeus in Arcadia.[18] In general, however, monuments attesting to athletic victories of the past are used to prove a city's continuing claims to Greek culture and identity.

This link between past and present can be seen particularly clearly in the activities of the ephebes at Athens and Sparta and the ways that these asserted a sense of continuity with the Archaic or Classical past. 'Invented traditions', such as the whipping ritual at Sparta, served to draw attention to these cities in their Roman incarnations and suggested that their youths continued to embody the values and qualities strongly associated with past supremacy.[19] In particular, analysis of ephebic activities and the associations with which athletics is invested in the literary texts suggests that the long-standing connection between athletics and military training continued to pack an ideological punch in the Roman period. The scenes of *naumachiai* which appear on some Athenian ephebic reliefs show the continued importance to Athens of her naval heritage, and in particular her crucial defeat of the Persians at Salamis in 480 BC. The activities of the Athenian ephebes helped to suggest that the very qualities which made classical Athens great could still be seen in her imperial sons.

In a recent discussion of the Greeks' enduring interest in their role during the Persian Wars, Susan Alcock has suggested that these assertions of success against the barbarian foe had the potential to be seen as a form of resistance to Roman rule.[20] Plutarch certainly cautions against stirring up the masses by reminding

---

[17] T. Whitmarsh, *Greek Literature and the Roman Empire: The Politics of Imitation* (Oxford, 2001), esp. 30–2. See also König, *Athletics and Literature*.

[18] Dio Chrysostom, *Oration* 7.38–9; Pausanias 8.38.5.

[19] On this idea see E. Hobsbawm, 'Introduction: Inventing Tradition', in E. Hobsbawm and T. Ranger, eds., *The Invention of Tradition* (Cambridge, 1983), 1–14.

[20] Alcock, *Archaeologies*, 74–86, esp. 84–5.

them too much of past military successes.[21] Yet the Romans could also identify themselves with the Greeks in this narrative of the war against the barbarian, as we see with Lucius Verus and Caracalla's eastern campaigns.[22] Exaltation of the Greek past could be safely accommodated within Roman power and usually was, though in some few cases it may still have provided the means for subtle resistance.

Indeed, in some areas we can detect signs of a struggle between competing Greek and Roman constructions of Greece and Greek culture. Roman attitudes to Greek culture are often characterized by the simultaneous acknowledgement of the cultural superiority of classical Greece and the reminder that modern Greece has fallen from her erstwhile heights. This comes through very clearly in a letter by the younger Pliny to a colleague embarking on a term of office in Achaea, which contains the following advice: 'Remember what each city once was, without sneering because it has ceased to be so.'[23] Rome had a vested interest in preserving Achaea as a kind of museum culture, symbol of her classical past but largely lacking in contemporary relevance.[24] One result of this was a concentration on the cities of Sparta and Athens as centres of Hellenic culture. We see this in the institution by Hadrian of the Panhellenion at Athens. The rules and regulations of this body imply the superiority of mainland Greece, and particularly Athens, as the true centre of Greek culture.[25] The resistance of some Greeks to this imperial notion of Greece can be detected in the absence of the most prestigious cities of Asia Minor (Pergamum, Ephesus, and Smyrna) from the Panhellenion, and in the problems that its eponymous festival had in attracting competitors. As I suggest in my discussion of Pausanias, many Greeks seem to have preferred instead a vision of Greece which placed the Panhellenic sanctuary of Olympia and its athletic festival at her heart.

While one strategy to control the cultural power of Greece was to concentrate on the glories of her classical past, cities throughout the Greek world seem keen to use that past to assert their continued relevance in the world of the present. In addition to recognizing and celebrating the status of Olympia, cities set up new festivals, often modelled on those at Olympia and Delphi, to celebrate their civic gods and show their claims to Greek culture and identity. Processions could include statues of civic founders, asserting ancestral links with mainland Greece, while theatrical and athletic contests showed the performance of traditional elements of Greek

[21] Plutarch, *Precepts of Statecraft* 814a–c.

[22] A. J. S. Spawforth, 'Symbol of Unity? The Persian-Wars Tradition in the Roman Empire', in S. Hornblower, ed., *Greek Historiography* (Oxford, 1994), 233–47. See also above, p. 156, for Greek involvement in these campaigns.

[23] Pliny, *Letters* 8.24.5; discussed by Alcock, *Archaeologies*, 42–4.

[24] For discussions of Roman Greece, see especially S. E. Alcock, *Graecia Capta: The Landscapes of Roman Greece* (Cambridge, 1993), and ead., *Archaeologies*, esp. 36–98.

[25] See above, pp. 210–11, and particularly A. J. S. Spawforth, 'The Panhellenion Again', *Chiron* 29 (1999), 339–52.

culture.[26] Yet the emperors were also omnipresent, represented in the names of festivals, in the statues carried in procession, or in commemorative images. As I suggest above, the emperors placed themselves at the heart of festival culture, instituting or granting permission for the most prestigious crown games, appointing agonistic officials, and regulating the privileges granted to victorious performers and athletes. The symbolic importance of athletic and festival activity in constructions of Greek identity, and the ideological power which accrued to Panhellenic festival sites like Olympia, provided good reasons for the emperor to set himself at its heart, preventing the creation of a culture which bypassed Rome. Yet the Greeks themselves seem equally implicated in this process and were keen to boast of the favour shown by the possession of an imperial festival. In the dedications of buildings by elite euergetes, too, we often find the emperor's name included with that of the city and its patron deity, or his image inserted along with the donor's into idealizing displays. The elites of these cities were proud to show their loyalty to the imperial house, along with their respect for and knowledge of the different aspects of Greek culture. Indeed, the emperors themselves can be seen as the ultimate guardians of that culture by their acts of generosity to individual cities.[27]

The overall picture, then, seems to be one of assimilation and negotiation, rather than resistance or domination. Greek cities could use their claims to Greek culture as a way to claim prestige in the Roman world, while the emperors indicated their respect for that culture by their generosity in preserving it. Some tensions certainly existed. Not everyone bought into the imperial construction of Greece and imperial benefaction can be seen as a means of subtly controlling manifestations of civic pride which could otherwise lead to unrest. Yet in the majority of cases it probably suited all parties to sign up to an image of Greek cultural prestige preserved and enabled by Roman power. The role of the civic elites is a crucial one. Many of these also held posts within imperial administration and had ties of friendship with others from around the empire. They could use their education and adherence to Greek culture to show themselves as members of the elite, reap benefits for their communities, and simultaneously build links with others around the empire. Through their involvement in the *ephēbeia* elite youths also acted as the representatives of their cities, showing that these cities could still lay claim to the qualities of the past.

All this suggests that athletic culture, expressed through activities in the gymnasium and the contests of public festivals, continued to play a crucial role in the

---

[26] On statues, see the Salutaris inscription from Ephesus which records a procession that seems to have included the image of the city founder Androclus: G. M. Rogers, *The Sacred Identity of Ephesos: Foundation Myths of a Roman City* (London, 1991), 107–8.

[27] In accounts of imperial benefaction the historical importance of the recipient cities often seems to be an important factor, e.g. Tacitus, *Annals* 4.55–6.

formation of civic self-identities in the Roman period. As in the west, this use of athletics is characterized by appropriation and adaptation, involving the use of artefacts from the past (such as statues of Olympic victors) to give meaning to the present and the 'revival' or reinvention of practices to suit contemporary construc- tions of identity. The ways in which this was done also changed across space and time. While they did produce a few Olympic victors in the Imperial period, the cities of mainland Greece seem to have relied more heavily on past successes in their claims to contemporary prestige than the cities of Asia Minor did. These could boast a number of athletic victors, and also chose to celebrate and advertise their claims to Greek culture through the construction and decoration of new gym- nasium complexes and the foundation of new festivals. Some of these features can be found in Achaea too, but there is certainly a sense of a greater vitality in the wealthy cities of Asia Minor. Over time we can also see the appropriation of these signs of cultural identity spreading to areas with different claims to Greekness, such as Side in Pamphylia, or the Hellenized cities of Syria and Egypt, which I have not had space to examine here.[28] There are a number of other areas that would repay further study, such as the interplay and overlaps between Greek and Roman forms of spectacle in both Rome and the Greek east.[29] What I hope to have shown in this book, however, is that athletics was one of the central symbols of Greek culture in the Roman period and thus played a crucial role in constructions of Greek identity (on civic, regional, and individual levels) and in the Roman response to Hellenic culture. The examination of its meanings and appropriations helps to develop our growing picture of the ways that Greek culture was experienced across the Mediterranean world during the Roman empire.

---

[28] On gymnasium culture in Hellenistic and Roman Egypt, see B. Legras, *Néotês: Recherches sur les jeunes grecs dans l'Égypte Ptolémaïque et Romaine* (Paris, 1999).

[29] On gladiatorial games in the east, see L. Robert, *Les gladiateurs dans l'Orient grec* (Paris, 1940; 2nd edn., Amsterdam, 1971).

BIBLIOGRAPHY

ABBONANZA, L., 'Immagini della phantasia: Quadri di Filostrato maior tra pittura e scultura', *RömMitt* 108 (2001), 111–34.

ALCOCK, S. E., *Graecia Capta: The Landscapes of Roman Greece* (Cambridge, 1993).

—— 'Landscapes of Memory and the Authority of Pausanias', in *Pausanias Historien*, Entretiens sur l'Antiquité Classique 41 (Geneva, 1994), 241–67.

—— 'Nero at Play? The Emperor's Grecian Odyssey', in J. Elsner and J. Masters, eds., *Reflections of Nero: Culture, History and Representation* (London, 1994), 98–111.

—— 'The Peculiar Book Four and the Problem of the Messenian Past', in S. E. Alcock, J. F. Cherry, and J. Elsner, eds., *Pausanias: Travel and Memory in Roman Greece* (New York, 2001), 142–53.

—— *Archaeologies of the Greek Past: Landscape, Monuments, and Memories* (Cambridge, 2002).

ALCOCK, S. E., CHERRY, J. F., and ELSNER, J., eds., *Pausanias: Travel and Memory in Roman Greece* (New York, 2001).

ALFÖLDI-ROSENBAUM, E., 'A *Flamen Augustalis* on a Mosaic Pavement in the "Grandi Terme" of Aquileia', in J.-P. Darmon and A. Rebourg, eds., *La Mosaïque Gréco-Romaine*, iv (Paris, 1994), 101–5.

AMELING, W., *Herodes Atticus* (Hildesheim, 1983).

ANDERSON, G., *Lucian: Theme and Variation in the Second Sophistic* (Leiden, 1976).

—— *Philostratus: Biography and Belles Lettres in the Third Century AD* (London, 1986).

—— *The Second Sophistic: A Cultural Phenomenon in the Roman Empire* (London and New York, 1993).

ANDREAE, B., and CONTINELLO, B., *Die Skulpturen von Sperlonga*, Antike Plastik 14 (Berlin, 1974).

ARAFAT, K. W., 'Pausanias' Attitude to Antiquities', *ABSA* 87 (1992), 387–409.

—— 'Pausanias and the Temple of Hera', *ABSA* 90 (1995), 461–73.

—— *Pausanias' Greece: Ancient Artists and Roman Rulers* (Cambridge, 1996).

ARIETI, J. A., 'Nudity in Greek Athletics', *Classical World* 68 (1974–5), 431–6.

ARNOLD, D., *Die Polykletnachfolge* (Berlin, 1969).

ARNOLD, I. R., 'Agonistic Festivals in Italy and Sicily', *AJA* 64 (1960), 245–51.

ASHBY, T., 'The Villa d'Este at Tivoli', *Archaeologia* 61 (1908), 219–56.

AUGUET, R., *Cruauté et civilisation: Les jeux romaines* (Paris, 1970).

AURENHAMMER, M., *Skulpturen von Ephesos: Bildwerke aus Stein: Idealplastik I*, Forschungen in Ephesos 10/1 (Vienna, 1990).

AURIGEMMA, S., *Villa Adriana* (Rome, 1961).

BALDASSARRE, I., ed., *Pompei: Pitture e Mosaici*, viii (Rome, 1998).

BALTY, J., 'La mosaïque antique au Proche-Orient I. Des origines à la Tétrarchie', *ANRW* II.12.2 (1981), 347–429.

BANDY, S. J., ed., *Coroebus Triumphs: The Alliance of Sport and the Arts* (San Diego, 1988).

BARIGAZZI, A., ed., *Favorino di Arelate: Opere* (Florence, 1966).

BARNES, T. D., *Tertullian: A Historical and Literary Study* (Oxford, 1971).

BARTMAN, E., '*Décor et Duplicatio*: Pendants in Roman Sculptural Display', *AJA* 92 (1988), 211–25.

—— 'Sculptural Collecting and Display in the Private Realm', in E. K. Gazda, ed., *Roman Art in the Private Sphere* (Ann Arbor, 1991), 71–88.

—— *Ancient Sculptural Copies in Miniature* (Leiden, 1992).

—— 'Eros's Flame: Images of Sexy Boys in Roman Ideal Sculpture', in E. K. Gazda, ed., *The Ancient Art of Emulation: Studies in Artistic Originality and Tradition from the Present to Classical Antiquity* (Ann Arbor, 2002), 249–71.

BARTOLI, P. S., 'Memorie di varie escavazioni fatte in Roma e nei luoghi suburbani', in C. Fea, *Miscellanea filologica critica e antiquaria*, i (Rome, 1790), 222–73.

BARTON, C. A., *The Sorrows of the Ancient Romans: The Gladiator and the Monster* (Princeton, 1993).

BARTON, T., *Power and Knowledge: Astrology, Physiognomics and Medicine under the Roman Empire* (Ann Arbor, 1994).

BARTSCH, S., *Actors in the Audience: Theatricality and Doublespeak from Nero to Hadrian* (Cambridge, Mass., 1994).

BEARD, M., 'Le mythe (grec) à Rome: Hercule aux bains', in S. Georgoudi and J.-P. Vernant, eds., *Mythes grecs au figuré* (Paris, 1996), 81–104.

BEARD, M., NORTH, J., and PRICE, S., *Religions of Rome* (Cambridge, 1998).

BECATTI, G., *Mosaici e pavimenti marmorei*, Scavi di Ostia 4 (Rome, 1961).

BECK, H., and BOL, P. C., eds., *Polykletforschungen* (Berlin, 1993).

BENNDORF, O., 'Erzstatuen eines griechischen Athleten', *Forschungen in Ephesos*, i (Vienna, 1906), 181–204.

BERGMANN, B., and KONDOLEON, C., eds., *The Art of Ancient Spectacle* (New Haven and London, 1999).

BERTACCHI, L., *Basilica, Museo e Scavi—Aquileia* (Rome, 1994).

BETZ, A., 'Ephesia', *Klio* 52 (1970), 27–32.

BILINSKI, B., *L'agonistica sportiva nella grecia antica: aspetti sociali e ispirazioni letterarie* (Rome, 1959).

BILLAULT, A., ed., *Lucien de Samosata: Actes du colloque international de Lyon organisé au Centre d'Études Romaines et Gallo-Romaines les 30 septembre–1er octobre 1993* (Paris, 1994).

—— *L'Univers de Philostrate* (Brussels, 2000).

BLAGG, T., and MILLETT, M., eds., *The Early Roman Empire in the West* (Oxford, 1990).

BLAKE, M. E., 'Roman Mosaics of the Second Century in Italy', *Memoirs of the American Academy in Rome* 13 (1936), 69–214.

BLOCH, H., *I bolli laterizi e la storia edilizia* (Rome, 1938).

BOATWRIGHT, M. T., *Hadrian and the City of Rome* (Princeton, 1987).

—— 'The City Gate of Plancia Magna in Perge', in E. D'Ambra, ed., *Roman Art in Context: An Anthology* (Englewood Cliffs, NJ, 1993), 189–207.

—— *Hadrian and the Cities of the Roman Empire* (Princeton, 2000).

BOEGEHOLD, A. L., 'Group and Single Competitions at the Panathenaia', in J. Neils, ed., *Worshipping Athena: Panathenaia and Parthenon* (Madison, Wis., 1996), 95–105.

BOHRINGER, F., 'Cultes d'athlètes en Grèce classique: propos politiques, discours mythiques', *REA* 81 (1979), 5–18.

BOL, P. C., 'Diskophoros', in H. Beck, P. C. Bol, and M. Bückling, eds., *Polyklet: der Bildhauer der griechischen Klassik* (Frankfurt, 1990), 111–17.

BOL, R., *Das Statuenprogramm des Herodes-Atticus-Nymphäums*, Olympischen Forschungen 15 (Berlin, 1984).

BOMGARDNER, D. L., *The Story of the Roman Amphitheatre* (London, 2000).

BOMPAIRE, J., *Lucien Écrivain: Imitation et création* (Paris, 1958).

BONANNO ARAVANTINOU, M., 'Un frammento di sarcofago romano con fanciulli atleti nei Musei Capitolini: Contributo allo studio dei sarcofagi con scene di palestra', *Bollettino d'Arte* 15 (1982), 67–84.

BONFANTE, L., 'Nudity as a Costume in Classical Art', *AJA* 93 (1989), 543–70.

BOWERSOCK, G. W., *Greek Sophists in the Roman Empire* (Oxford, 1969).

—— ed., *Approaches to the Second Sophistic* (University Park, Pa., 1974).

—— 'Philosophy in the Second Sophistic', in G. Clark and T. Rajak, eds., *Philosophy and Power in the Graeco-Roman World: Essays in Honour of Miriam Griffin* (Oxford, 2002), 157–70.

BOWIE, E. L., 'The Greeks and their Past in the Second Sophistic', *Past and Present* 46 (1970), 3–41; reprinted in M. I. Finley, ed., *Studies in Ancient Society* (London, 1974), 166–209.

—— 'The Vedii Antonini and the Temple of Hadrian', *Proceedings of the Tenth International Congress of Classical Archaeology* (Ankara, 1973), 866–74.

—— 'Apollonios of Tyana: Tradition and Reality', *ANRW* II.16.2 (Berlin and New York, 1978), 1652–99.

—— 'The Importance of the Sophists', *YCS* 27 (1982), 29–60.

—— 'Past and Present in Pausanias', in *Pausanias Historien*, Entretiens sur l'Antiquité Classique 41 (Geneva, 1994), 207–30.

—— 'Inspiration and Aspiration: Date, Genre, and Readership', in S. E. Alcock, J. F. Cherry, and J. Elsner, eds., *Pausanias: Travel and Memory in Roman Greece* (New York, 2001), 21–32.

BRADLEY, K. R., 'The Chronology of Nero's Visit to Greece AD 66/67', *Latomus* 37 (1978), 61–72.

BRANHAM, R. B., *Unruly Eloquence: Lucian and the Comedy of Traditions* (Cambridge, Mass., and London, 1989).

BRENOT, A., *Recherches sur l'éphébie attique et en particulier sur la date de l'institution* (Paris, 1920).

BRONEER, O., 'The Isthmian Victory Crown', *AJA* 66 (1962), 259–63.

BROWN, P., *Power and Persuasion in Late Antiquity: Towards a Christian Empire* (Madison, Wis., 1992).

BRUNT, P., 'The Bubble of the Second Sophistic', *BICS* 39 (1994), 25–52.

BRUSIN, G., 'Aquileia—Scavi in un grande edificio pubblico', *NSc* (1923), 224–31.

BRUUN, C., and GALLINA ZEVI, A., eds., *Ostia e Portus nelle loro relazioni con Roma*, Acta Instituti Romani Finlandiae 27 (Rome, 2002).

BULGARINI, F., *Notizie storiche, antiquarie, statistiche ed agronomiche intorno all' antichissima città di Tivoli e suo territorio* (Rome, 1848).

CALDELLI, M. L., 'Curia athletarum, iera xystike synodos e organizzazione delle terme a Roma', *ZPE* 93 (1992), 75–87.

—— *L'Agon Capitolinus* (Rome, 1993).

—— *Gli agoni alla greca nelle regioni occidentali dell'impero: La Gallia Narbonensis* (Rome, 1997).

—— 'Varia agonistica ostiensia', in G. Paci, ed., *Epigrafia Romana in area Adriatica: Actes de la IXe. rencontre franco-italienne sur l'épigraphie du monde romain* (Macerata, 1998), 205–47.

CALZA, G., and BECATTI, G., *Ostia*, 9th edn., rev. M. Floriani Squarciapino (Rome, 1974).

CALZA, R., *I ritratti*, Scavi di Ostia 5 (Rome, 1964).

CAMERON, A., *Bread and Circuses: The Roman Emperor and his People* (Oxford, 1974).

—— *Circus Factions* (Oxford, 1976).

CANTARELLA, E., *Bisexuality in the Ancient World*, trans. C. Ó Cuilleanáin (New Haven and London, 1992).

CARANDINI, A., RICCI, A., and DE VOS, M., *Filosofiana: The Villa of Piazza Armerina* (Palermo, 1982).

CARETTA, A., *Filostrato di Lemno: Il manuale dell'allenatore* (Novara, 1995).

CAREY, S., 'A Tradition of Adventures in the Imperial Grotto', *Greece and Rome* 49 (2002), 44–61.

CARTLEDGE, P., and SPAWFORTH, A., *Hellenistic and Roman Sparta: A Tale of Two Cities* (London, 1989).

CASTAGNOLI, F., 'Il capitello della Pigna Vaticana', *BullCom* 71 (1943–5), 1–30.

CASTELLI, L., 'Trovamenti di antichità classica nella Villa Pontificia di Castelgandolfo', *Illustrazione Vaticana* 4 (1933), 578–80.

CASTRIOTA, D., *Myth, Ethos and Actuality: Official Art in Fifth-Century BC Athens* (Madison, Wis., 1992).

CASTRIOTES, P., *Glypta tou Ethnikou Mouseiou* (Athens, 1908).

CHAISEMARTIN, N. DE, 'Appendix IV: Agonistic Images on Aphrodisian Sarcophagi', in C. Roueché, *Performers and Partisans at Aphrodisias in the Roman and Late Roman periods*, JRS Monograph 6 (London, 1993), 239–48 with pls. 22–4.

—— and THEODORESCU, D., 'Recherches préliminaires surs la *frons scaenae* du théâtre', in K. T. Erim and R. R. R. Smith, eds., *Aphrodisias Papers*, ii: *The Theatre, a Sculptor's Workshop, Philosophers and Coin-types*, JRA Supplement 2 (Ann Arbor, 1991), 29–65.

CHANDLER, R., *Marmora Oxoniensia* (Oxford, 1763).

CHARBONNEAUX, J., 'Quatre marbres antiques du Musée du Louvre', *Monuments Piots* 45 (1951), 33–51.

—— *La sculpture grecque et romaine au Musée du Louvre* (Paris, 1963).

CHASTAGNOL, A., *Le sénat romain à l'époque impériale: Recherches sur la composition de l'Assemblée et le statut de ses membres* (Paris, 1992).

CIMA, M., and LA ROCCA, E., eds., *Le tranquille dimore degli dei. Le residenza imperiale degli horti Lamiani* (Venice, 1986).

CLARIDGE, A., *Rome: An Oxford Archaeological Guide* (Oxford, 1998).

CLARKE, J. R., *Roman Black-and-White Figural Mosaics* (New York, 1979).

—— 'Mosaic workshops at Pompeii and Ostia Antica', in P. Johnson, R. Ling, and D. J. Smith, eds., *Fifth International Colloquium on Ancient Mosaics, held at Bath, England, on September 5–12, 1987*, JRA Supplement 9 (Ann Arbor, 1994), 89–102.

COHEN, D., 'Law, Society and Homosexuality in Classical Athens', *Past and Present* 117 (1987), 3–21.

—— *Law, Sexuality and Society: The Enforcement of Morals in Ancient Athens* (Cambridge, 1991).

COHOON, J. W., ed., *Dio Chrysostom*, ii, Loeb Classical Library (Cambridge, Mass., 1939).

COLEMAN, K., 'Fatal Charades: Roman Executions Staged as Mythological Enactments', *JRS* 80 (1990), 44–73.

—— 'Launching into History: Aquatic Displays in the Early Empire', *JRS* 83 (1993), 48–74.

COULSON, W., and KYRIELEIS, H., eds., *Proceedings of an International Symposium on the Olympic Games, 5–9 September 1988* (Athens, 1992).

CRESCENZI, L., 'La Villa di Domiziano a Castel Gandolfo', *Archeologia Laziale* 2 (1979), 99–106.

CROWTHER, N. B., 'Athletic Dress and Nudity in Greek Athletics', *Eranos* 80 (1982), 163–8.

—— 'Greek Games in Republican Rome', *AC* 52 (1983), 268–73.

—— 'Studies in Greek Athletics', *Classical World* 78 (1984–5), 497–558.

—— 'Male "Beauty" Contests in Greece', *AC* 54 (1985), 285–91.

—— 'Studies in Greek Athletics', *Classical World* 79 (1985–6), 73–135.

—— 'Recent Trends in the Study of Greek Athletics', *AC* 59 (1990), 246–55.

—— 'Euexia, Eutaxia, Philoponia: Three Contests of the Greek Gymnasium', *ZPE* 85 (1991), 301–4.

CSAPO, E., and SLATER, W. J., *The Context of Ancient Drama* (Ann Arbor, 1995).

CUMONT, F., *Recherches sur le symbolisme funéraire des Romains* (Paris, 1942).

D'AMBRA, E., ed., *Roman Art in Context: An Anthology* (Englewood Cliffs, NJ, 1993).

D'ANDRIA, F., and RITTI, T., *Hierapolis Scavi e Ricerche*, ii: *Le Sculture del Teatro*, Archeologica 55 (Rome, 1985).

D'ARMS, J., *Romans on the Bay of Naples* (Cambridge, Mass., 1970).

DAMSKY, B. L., 'The Stadium Aureus of Septimius Severus', *American Journal of Numismatics* 2 (1990), 77–105.

DARMON, J.-P., and REBOURG, A., eds., *La Mosaïque Gréco-Romaine IV* (Paris, 1994).

DAVIDSON, J., *Courtesans and Fishcakes: The Consuming Passions of Classical Athens* (London, 1997).

—— 'Dover, Foucault and Greek Homosexuality: Penetration and the Truth of Sex', *Past and Present* 170 (2001), 3–51.

DAWKINS, R. M., 'The Sanctuary', in id., ed., *The Sanctuary of Artemis Orthia at Sparta* (London, 1929), 1–51.

—— ed., *The Sanctuary of Artemis Orthia at Sparta* (London, 1929).

DE FRANCESCHINI, M., *Villa Adriana: Mosaici, Pavimenti, Edifici* (Rome, 1991).

DE GRUMMOND, N. T., and RIDGWAY, B. S., eds., *From Pergamon to Sperlonga: Sculpture and Context* (Berkeley, Los Angeles, and London, 2000).

DE MARCELLUS, H. V., 'The Origins and Nature of the Attic Ephebeia to 200 BC', D.Phil thesis (Oxford, 1994).

DELAINE, J., *The Baths of Caracalla: A Study in the Design, Construction and Economics of Large-Scale Building Projects in Imperial Rome*, JRA Supplement 25 (Portsmouth, RI, 1997).

—— 'Benefactions and Urban Renewal: Bath Buildings in Roman Italy', in J. DeLaine and D. E. Johnston, eds., *Roman Baths and Bathing*, i, JRA Supplement 37 (Portsmouth, RI, 1999), 67–74.

—— 'Introduction: Bathing and Society', in J. DeLaine and D. E. Johnston, eds., *Roman Baths and Bathing*, i, JRA Supplement 37 (Portsmouth, RI, 1999), 7–16.

—— and JOHNSTON, D. E. eds., *Roman Baths and Bathing*, i, JRA Supplement 37 (Portsmouth, RI, 1999).

DELLA CORTE, M., 'La "Villa rustica N. Popidi Flori" esplorata dalla signora Giovanna Zurlo-Pulzella, nel fondo di sua proprietà in contrada Pisanella, comune di Boscoreale, l'anno 1906', *NSc* (1921), 442–60.

—— *Iuventus: un nuovo aspetto della vita pubblica di Pompei finora inesplorato* (Arpino, 1924).

DELORME, J. *Gymnasion: Étude sur les monuments consacrés à l'éducation en Grèce* (Paris, 1960).

DESSAU, H., 'Due iscrizioni ostiensi', *Bullettino dell'Istituto di corrispondenza archeologica* (1881), 131–41.

DEUBNER, L., *Attische Feste* (Berlin, 1932).

DILLON, S., 'The Portraits of a Civic Benefactor in 2nd-c. Ephesos', *JRA* 9 (1996), 261–74.

—— 'Subject Selection and Viewer Reception of Greek Portraits from Herculaneum and Tivoli', *JRA* 13 (2000), 21–40.

DOMERGUE, C., LANDES, C., and PAILLER, J.-M., eds., *Spectacula*, i: *Gladiateurs et amphithéatre: Actes du colloque tenu à Toulouse et à Lattes les 26, 27, 28 et 29 mai 1987* (Lattes, 1990).

DOVER, K., *Greek Homosexuality* (London, 1978).

DREES, L., *Olympia, Gods, Artists and Athletes* (London, 1967).

DUMONT, A., *L'Essai sur l'éphébie attique* (Paris, 1876).

DUNBABIN, K. M. D., *The Mosaics of Roman North Africa* (Oxford, 1978).

—— *The Mosaics of the Greek and Roman World* (Cambridge, 1999).

EBERT, J., *Griechische Epigramme auf Sieger an gymnischen und hippischen Agonen* (Berlin, 1972).

EDMONDSON, J. C., 'The Cultural Politics of Public Spectacle in Rome and the Greek East, 167–166 BCE', in B. Bergmann and C. Kondoleon, eds., *The Art of Ancient Spectacle* (New Haven and London, 1999), 77–95.

EDWARDS, C., *The Politics of Immorality* (Cambridge, 1993).

EICHLER, F., 'Die Bronzestatue aus Ephesos in verbesserte Wiederherstellung', *Jahrbuch der Kunsthistorischen Sammlung in Wien* 50 (1953), 15–22.

ELLIS, H., *The Townley Gallery* (London, 1846).

ELSNER, J., *Art and the Roman Viewer* (Cambridge, 1995).

—— 'Image and Ritual: Reflections on the Religious Appreciation of Classical Art', *CQ* 46 (1996), 515–31.

—— 'Hagiographic Geography: Travel and Allegory in the *Life of Apollonius of Tyana*', *JHS* 117 (1997), 22–37.

—— 'Structuring "Greece": Pausanias' *Periegesis* as a Literary Construct', in S. E. Alcock, J. F. Cherry, and J. Elsner, eds., *Pausanias: Travel and Memory in Roman Greece* (New York, 2001), 3–20.

ENNAÏFER, M., *Le cité d'Althiburos et l'édifice des Asclepieia* (Tunis, 1976).

ENSOLI, S., 'Iside a Tivoli', in *Iside: Il mito, il mistero, la magia* (Milan, 1997), 418–20.

—— 'Prêtres d'Isis en marbre rouge antique: Antinoüs dans la "Palestra" de la Villa Adriana', in J. Ch.-Gaffiot and H. Lavagne, eds., *Hadrien: Trésors d'une villa impériale* (Paris, 1999), 79–83.

ERIM, K. T. and SMITH, R. R. R., 'Sculpture from the Theatre: A Preliminary Report', in K. T. Erim and R. R. R. Smith, eds., *Aphrodisias Papers*, ii: *The Theatre, a Sculptor's Workshop, Philosophers and Coin-types*, JRA Supplement 2 (Ann Arbor, 1991), 67–98.

—— —— eds., *Aphrodisias Papers*, ii: *The Theatre, a Sculptor's Workshop, Philosophers and Coin-types*, JRA Supplement 2 (Ann Arbor, 1991).

ERRINGTON, R. M., 'Aspects of Roman Acculturation in the East under the Republic', in *Alte Geschichte und Wissenschaftsgeschichte: Festschrift für Karl Christ* (Darmstadt, 1988), 140–57.

EWALD, B. C., 'Death and Myth: New Books on Roman Sarcophagi', *AJA* 103 (1999), 344–8.

FAGAN, G. G., *Bathing in Public in the Roman World* (Ann Arbor, 1999).

FARRINGTON, A., 'Imperial Bath Buildings in South-West Asia Minor', in S. Macready and F. H. Thompson, eds., *Roman Architecture in the Greek World*, Society of Antiquaries Occasional Papers 10 (London, 1987), 50–9.

—— 'Olympic Victors and the Popularity of the Olympic Games in the Imperial Period', *Tyche* 12 (1997), 15–46.

—— 'The Introduction and Spread of Roman Bathing in Greece', in J. DeLaine and D. E. Johnston, eds., *Roman Baths and Bathing*, i JRA Supplement 37 (Portsmouth, RI, 1999), 57–65.

FERRARY, J.-L., *Philhellénisme et Impérialisme: Aspects idéologiques de la conquête romaine du monde Hellénistique* (Rome, 1988).

FINLEY, M. I., and PLEKET, H. W., *The Olympic Games: The First Thousand Years* (London, 1976).

FISHER, N., 'Gymnasia and the Democratic Values of Leisure', in P. Cartledge, P. Millett, and S. von Reden, eds., *Kosmos: Essays in Order, Conflict, and Community in Classical Athens* (Cambridge, 1998), 84–104.

FLACELIÈRE, M. R., 'Hadrien et Delphes', *CRAI* (1971), 175–85.

FLINTERMANN, J. J., *Power, Paideia and Pythagoreanism* (Amsterdam, 1995).

FLORIANI SQUARCIAPINO, M., 'Nuovi Mosaici Ostiensi', *AttiPontAccRomRend* 58 (1985–6), 87–144.

—— 'Un Altro Mosaico Ostiense con Atleti', *AttiPontAccRomRend* 59 (1986–7), 161–79.

FOLLET, S., *Athènes au IIe et au IIIe siècle: Études chronologiques et prosopographiques* (Paris, 1976).

—— 'Lucien et l'Athènes des Antonins', in A. Billault, ed., *Lucien de Samosata: Actes du colloque international de Lyon organisé au Centre d'Études Romaines et Gallo-Romaines les 30 septembre–1er octobre 1993* (Paris, 1994), 131–9.

FONTENROSE, J., 'The Hero as Athlete', *California Studies in Classical Antiquity* 1 (1968), 73–104.

FORBES, C. A., *Neoi: A Contribution to the Study of Greek Associations* (Middletown, Conn., 1913).

—— "ΟΙ ΑΦ᾽ ΗΡΑΚΛΕΟΥΣ in Epictetus and Lucian', *American Journal of Philology* 60 (1939), 473–4.

—— 'Ancient Athletic Guilds', *Classical Philology* 50 (1955), 238–52.

FORNARI, F., 'Roma: Scoperte di antichità nel suburbio', *NSc* (1916), 311–20.

FOSS, C., 'Appendix: Inscriptions Related to the Complex', in F. K. Yegül, *The Bath-Gymnasium Complex at Sardis* (Cambridge, Mass., 1986), 167–72.

FOUCAULT, M., *The History of Sexuality*, ii: *The Use of Pleasure*, trans. R. Hurley (New York, 1985).

—— *The History of Sexuality*, iii: *The Care of the Self*, trans. R. Hurley (London, 1986).

FOWDEN, G., 'City and Mountain in Late Roman Attica', *JHS* 108 (1988), 48–59.

FRAZER, J. G., *Pausanias's Description of Greece* (London, 1898).

FRIESEN, S. J., *Twice Neokoros: Ephesus, Asia and the Cult of the Flavian Imperial Family* (Leiden, 1993).

GALLI, G., 'Relazioni', *AttiPontAccRomRend* 10 (1934), 68–89.

GARDINER, E. N., *Greek Athletic Sports and Festivals* (London, 1910).

—— *Athletics of the Ancient World* (London, 1930).

GASPARRI, C., 'Lo Stadio Panatenaico', *Annuario della Scuola Archeologica di Atene* 52–3 (1974–5), 313–93.

—— 'Sculture provenienti dalle Terme di Caracalla e di Diocleziano', *Rivista dell' Istituto Nazionale di Archeologia e Storia dell' Arte* III.6–7 (1983–4), 133–50.

GASSOWSKA, B., 'Cirrus in vertice', in *Mélanges offerts à Kazimierz Michalowski* (Warsaw, 1966), 421–7.

GATTI, G., 'Scoperte di antichità in Roma e nel suburbio', *NSc* (1888), 434–59.

—— 'Scoperte recentissime', *BullCom* (1888), 327–34.

GAZDA, E. K., ed., *The Ancient Art of Emulation: Studies in Artistic Originality and Tradition from the Present to Classical Antiquity* (Ann Arbor, 2002).

GERKAN, A. VON, and KRISCHEN, F., eds., *Milet i:9: Thermen und Palaestren* (Berlin, 1928).

GLEASON, M., *Making Men: Sophists and Self-presentation in Ancient Rome* (Princeton, 1995).

GOLDEN, M., *Sport and Society in Ancient Greece* (Cambridge, 1998).

—— *Sport in the Ancient world from A to Z* (London and New York, 2004).

GOLDHILL, S., *Foucault's Virginity: Ancient Erotic Fiction and the History of Sexuality* (Cambridge, 1995).

—— 'Introduction: Setting an Agenda: "Everything is Greece to the wise"', in id., ed., *Being Greek under Rome: Cultural Identity, the Second Sophistic and the Development of Empire* (Cambridge, 2001), 1–25.

—— 'The Erotic Eye: Visual Stimulation and Cultural Conflict', in id., ed., *Being Greek under Rome: Cultural Identity, the Second Sophistic and the Development of Empire* (Cambridge, 2001), 154–94.

—— ed., *Being Greek under Rome: Cultural Identity, the Second Sophistic and the Development of Empire* (Cambridge, 2001).

GRAINDOR, P., 'Les cosmètes du Musée d'Athènes', *BCH* 39 (1915), 241–401.

—— 'Études sur l'éphébie attique sous l'Empire', *Musée Belge* 26 (1922), 165–228.

—— *Album d'inscriptions attiques d'époque impériale* (Gand, 1924).

—— *Un milliardaire antique: Hérode Atticus et sa famille* (Cairo, 1930).

GRAINDOR, P., *Athènes de Tibère à Trajan* (Cairo, 1931).

GRIFFIN, M. T., *Nero: The End of a Dynasty* (London, 1984).

GRIMAL, P., *Les jardins romains*, 3rd edn. (Paris, 1984).

GROS, P., 'Rome ou Marseilles? Le problème de l'hellénisation de la Gaule transalpine aux deux derniers siècles de la République', in M. Bats, ed., *Marseilles grecque et la Gaule* (Aix, 1992), 369–79.

GRUEN, E. S., *Culture and National Identity in Republican Rome* (Ithaca, 1993).

GSELL, S., *Musée de Tébessa* (Paris, 1902).

GUARDUCCI, M., 'Una nuova officina di lucernette romane: gli *Aeoli*', *RömMitt* 89 (1982), 103–31.

—— 'Nuove osservazioni sulle lucernette degli Aeoli', *RömMitt* 93 (1986), 301–3.

GUSMAN, P., *La Villa Imperiale de Tibur* (Paris, 1904).

HABICHT, C., *Pausanias' Guide to Ancient Greece*, 2nd edn. (Berkeley, Los Angeles, and London, 1988).

HALFMANN, H., *Die Senatorien aus dem östlichen Teil des Imperium Romanum bis zum Ende des 2. Jahrhunderts n. Chr* (Göttingen, 1979).

HALL, A. S., and MILNER, N. P., 'Education and Athletics: Documents Illustrating the Festivals of Oenoanda', in D. French, ed., *Studies in the History and Topography of Lycia and Pisidia: In Memoriam A. S. Hall*, British Institute of Archaeology at Ankara Monograph 19 (London, 1994), 7–47.

—— —— and COULTON, J. J., 'The Mausoleum of Licinnia Flavilla and Flavianus Diogenes of Oinoanda: Epigraphy and Architecture', *Anatolian Studies* 46 (1996), 111–44.

HALLETT, C. H., 'Kopienkritik and the Works of Polykleitos', in W. Moon, ed., *Polykleitos, the Doryphoros and Tradition* (Madison, Wis., 1995), 121–60.

HANNESTAD, N., Review of P. Zanker, *Klassizistische Statuen: Studien zur Veränderung des Kunstgeschmacks in der römischen Kaiserzeit* (Rhien, 1974), in *JRS* 67 (1977), 121–2.

HARDIE, P., *Virgil* (Oxford, 1998).

HARL, K., *Civic Coins and Civic Politics in the Roman East AD 180–275* (Berkeley, Los Angeles, and London, 1987).

HARRIS, H. A., *Greek Athletes and Athletics* (London, 1964).

—— *Sport in Greece and Rome* (London, 1972).

HARRISON, S., *Apuleius: A Latin Sophist* (Oxford, 2000).

HAÜBER, C., 'I vecchi ritrovamenti (prima del 1870)', in M. Cima and E. La Rocca, eds., *Le tranquille dimore degli dei: La residenza imperiale degli horti Lamiani* (Venice, 1986), 167–72.

HEINZE, R., 'Anacharsis', *Philologus* 50 (1891), 458–68.

HERRMANN, H.-V., 'Die Siegerstatuen von Olympia', *Nikephoros* 1 (1988), 119–83.

HINE, D., *Puerilities: Erotic Epigrams of the Greek Anthology* (Princeton and Oxford, 2001).

HIRZEL, H., 'Musaico tuscolano', *Annali dell'Istituto di corrispondenza archeologica* (1863), 397–412.

HOBSBAWM, E., 'Introduction: Inventing Tradition', in E. Hobsbawm and T. Ranger, eds., *The Invention of Tradition* (Cambridge, 1983), 1–14.

HOFF, M. C., and ROTROFF, S. I., eds., *The Romanization of Athens: Proceedings of a Conference held at Lincoln, Nebraska*, Oxbow Monograph 94 (Oxford, 1997).

HÖLSCHER, T., *Römische Bildsprache als semantisches System* (Heidelberg, 1987).

HOPKINS, K., *Death and Renewal* (Cambridge, 1983).

HOWARD, S., *The Lansdowne Herakles*, 2nd edn. (Malibu, Calif., 1978).

HUMPHREY, J. H., *Roman Circuses: Arenas for Chariot Racing* (London, 1986).

HUSKINSON, J., *Roman Children's Sarcophagi: Their Decoration and its Social Significance* (Oxford, 1996).

HYDE, W. W., *Olympic Victor Monuments and Greek Athletic Art* (Washington, 1921).

INAN, J., 'Three Statues from Side', *Antike Kunst* 13 (1970), 17–33 with pls. 11–21.

—— *Roman Sculpture in Side* (Ankara, 1975).

—— 'Der sandalenbindende Hermes', *Antike Plastik* 22 (1993), 105–16.

—— and ALFÖLDI-ROSENBAUM, E., *Römische und frühbyzantinische Porträtplastik aus der Türkei: Neue Funde* (Mainz, 1979).

—— and ROSENBAUM, E., *Roman and Early Byzantine Portrait Sculpture in Asia Minor* (London, 1966).

INSALACO, A., 'I mosaici degli atleti dalle terme di Caracalla', *Archeologia Classica* 41 (1989), 293–327.

ISIK, F., 'Die Sarkophage von Aphrodisias', in B. Andreae, ed., *Symposium über die antiken Sarkophage, Pisa 5.–12. September 1982*, Marburger Winckelmann-Programm (Marburg, 1984), 243–81.

JACOB, C., 'The Greek Traveler's Areas of Knowledge: Myth and Other Discourses in Pausanias' Description of Greece', *Yale French Studies* 59 (1980), 65–85.

JACQUEMIN, A., 'Pausanias, le sanctuaire d'Olympie et les archéologues', in D. Knoepfler and M. Piérart, eds., *Éditer, traduire, commenter: Pausanias en l'an 2000* (Geneva, 2001), 283–300.

JOHNSTON, A., 'Hierapolis Revisited', *Numismatic Chronicle* 144 (1984), 52–80.

JONES, B. W., *Domitian and the Senatorial Order: A Prosopographical Study of Domitian's Relationship with the Senate, AD 81–96* (Philadelphia, 1979).

JONES, C. P., 'The Levy at Thespiae under Marcus Aurelius', *Greek, Roman and Byzantine Studies* 12 (1971), 45–8.

—— 'A Syrian in Lyon', *AJP* 99 (1978), 336–52.

—— *The Roman World of Dio Chrysostom* (Cambridge, Mass., 1978).

—— 'Two Inscriptions from Aphrodisias', *Harvard Studies in Classical Philology* 85 (1981), 107–29.

—— *Culture and Society in Lucian* (Cambridge, Mass., 1986).

—— 'The Panhellenion', *Chiron* 26 (1996), 29–56.

—— 'The Pancratiasts Helix and Alexander on an Ostian Mosaic', *JRA* 11 (1998), 293–8.

—— 'A Decree of Thyatira in Lydia', *Chiron* 29 (1999), 1–21.

—— 'Pausanias and his Guides', in S. E. Alcock, J. F. Cherry, and J. Elsner, eds., *Pausanias: Travel and Memory in Roman Greece* (New York, 2001), 33–9.

JÜTHNER, J., *Die athletischen Leibesübungen der Griechen*, ed. F. Brein (Vienna, 1965, 1968).

—— ed., *Philostratos über Gymnastik* (Leipzig, 1909).

KAIMIO, J., *The Romans and the Greek Language*, Commentationes Humanarum Litterarum 64 (Helsinki, 1979).

KASTER, R. A., *Guardians of Language: The Grammarian and Society in Late Antiquity* (Berkeley, Los Angeles, and London, 1998).

KEAY, S., and TERRENATO, N., eds., *Italy and the West: Comparative issues in Romanization* (Oxford, 2001).

KEIL, J., 'Inschriften', *Forschungen von Ephesos* 3 (Vienna, 1923), 91–168.

—— 'Skulpturengruppen in Ephesos', *JÖAI* 39 (1952), 42–6.

KENNELL, N. M., *The Gymnasium of Virtue: Education and Culture in Ancient Sparta* (Chapel Hill, 1995).

KHANOUSSI, M., 'Spectaculum pugilum et gymnasium. Compte rendu d'un spectacle de jeux athlétiques et de pugilat, figuré sur une mosaïque de la région de Gafsa (Tunisie)', *CRAI* (1988), 543–61.

—— 'Ein römisches Mosaik aus Tunisien mit ein Darstellung eines agonistischen Wettkampfes', *Antiken Welt* 22.3 (1991), 146–53.

—— 'Les spectacles de jeux athlétiques et de pugilat dans l'Afrique romaine', *RömMitt* 98 (1991), 315–22.

KINDSTRAND, J. F., *Anacharsis: The Legend and the Apophthegmata* (Uppsala, 1981).

KLEINER, G., *Die Ruinen von Milet* (Berlin, 1968).

KOCH, G., and SICHTERMANN, H., *Römische Sarkophage: Handbuch der Archäologie* (Munich, 1982).

KOCH, H., *Studien zum Theseustempel in Athen* (Berlin, 1955).

KOESTER, H., ed., *Ephesos: Metropolis of Asia* (Valley Forge, Pa., 1995).

KÖNIG, J., 'Athletic Training and Athletic Festivals in the Greek Literature of the Roman Empire', D.Phil. thesis (Cambridge, 2000).

—— 'Favorinus' *Corinthian Oration* in its Corinthian context', *PCPS* 47 (2001), 141–68.

—— *Athletics and Literature in the Roman Empire* (Cambridge, forthcoming).

KOORTBOJIAN, M., 'Forms of Attention: Four Notes on Replication and Variation', in E. K. Gazda, ed., *The Ancient Art of Emulation: Studies in Artistic Originality and Tradition from the Present to Classical Antiquity* (Ann Arbor, 2002), 173–204.

KOTULA, T., 'Utraque lingua eruditi: Une page relative à l'histoire de l'éducation dans l'Afrique romaine', in J. Bibauw, ed., *Hommage à Marcel Renard*, ii (Brussels, 1968), 386–92.

KRAMÉROWSKIS, V., and LANDES, C., eds., *Spectacula*, ii: *le théâtre antique et ses spectacles: Actes du colloque tenu au Musée archéologique Henri Prades de Lattes les 27, 28, 29 et 30 avril 1989* (Lattes, 1992).

KREIKENBOM, D., *Bildwerke nach Polyklet* (Berlin, 1990).

KURKE, L., 'The Economy of Kudos', in C. Dougherty and L. Kurke, eds., *Cultural Poetics in Archaic Greece: Cult, Performance, Politics* (Cambridge, 1993), 131–63.

KYLE, D., 'Directions in Ancient Sport History', *Journal of Sport History* 10 (1983), 7–34.

—— *Athletics in Ancient Athens* (Leiden, 1987).

LANCHA, J., *Recueil général des mosaïques de la Gaule*, iii: *Province de Narbonnaise*, ii: *Vienne* (Paris, 1981).

—— *Les mosaïques de Vienne* (Lyons, 1990).

—— *Mosaïque de culture dans l'occident Romain (Ie–IVe s.)* (Rome, 1997).

LANCIANI, R., *New Tales of Old Rome* (Boston, 1901).

—— *La Villa Adriana, guida e descrizione* (Rome, 1906).

—— 'Le antichità del territorio Laurentino nella reale tenuta di Castelporziano', *Monumenti Antichi* 16 (1906), 242–74 with pls. 1–3.

LANDES, C., ed., *Le stade romain et ses spectacles* (Lattes, 1994).

LANDWEHR, C., *Die antiken Gipsabgüsse aus Baiae: griechische Bronzestatuen in Abgüssen römischer Zeit* (Berlin, 1985).

LATTANZI, E., *I ritratti dei cosmeti nel museo nazionale di Atene* (Rome, 1968).

LATTIMORE, S., 'The Bronze Apoxyomenos from Ephesos', *AJA* 76 (1972), 13–16.

—— 'Two Statues of Herakles', *J. Paul Getty Museum Journal* 2 (1975), 17–26.

—— 'The Nature of Early Greek Victor Statues', in S. J. Bandy, ed., *Coroebus Triumphs: The Alliance of Sport and the Arts* (San Diego, 1988), 245–56.

LAUTER, H., *Zur Chronologie römischer Kopien nach Originalen des V. Jahrh* (Bonn, 1966).

LAVAGNE, H., 'Rome et les associations dionysiaques en Gaule (Vienne et Nîmes)', in *L'association dionysiaque dans les sociétés anciennes* (Rome, 1986), 129–48.

LAZZARINI, M. L., 'I Greci di Ostia', *Scienze dell'Antichità: Storia, Archeologia, Antropologia* 6–7 (1992–3), 137–41.

LE GLAY, M., 'Vienne Antique', in H. Stern and M. Le Glay, eds., *La Mosaïque Gréco-Romaine II* (Paris, 1975), 125–34.

—— 'Hercule et la *Iuuentus* Viennoise: A propos de la mosaïque des athlètes vainqueurs', in *Mosaïque: Recueil d'hommages à Henri Stern* (Paris, 1983), 265–71.

LEADER-NEWBY, R., and NEWBY, Z., eds., *Art and Inscriptions in the Ancient World* (forthcoming).

LEBLANC, O., 'Le décor des latrines des "Thermes des Lutteurs" à Saint-Romain-en-Gal (Rhône)', in *Actes des séminaires de l'association française de peintures murales antiques 1990–1991–1993 (Aix-en-Provence, Narbonne et Chartres)*, special edition, *Revue Archéologique de Picardie* 10 (1995), 239–63.

LEE, H. M., 'Athletics and the Bikini Girls from Piazza Armerina', *Stadion* 10 (1984), 45–76.

—— 'The Later Greek Boxing Glove and the "Roman" Caestus: A Centennial Reevaluation of Jüthner's "Über Antike Turngeräthe" ', *Nikephoros* 10 (1997), 161–78 with pls. 2–7.

LEGRAS, B., *Néotés: Recherches sur les jeunes grecs dans l'Égypte Ptolémaïque et Romaine* (Paris, 1999).

LEIWO, M., *Neapolitana: A Study of Population and Language in Graeco-Roman Naples*, Commentationes Humanarum Litterarum 102 (Helsinki, 1994).

LEVI, D., *Antioch Mosaic Pavements* (Princeton, 1947).

LIGORIO, P., *Descrittione della superba e magnificentissima Villa Hadriana*, reproduced in J. G. Graevius, ed., *Thesaurus Antiquitatum et Historiarum Italiae* VIII/4 (Leiden, 1723).

[LIGORIO, P.], 'Trattato delle Antichità di Tivoli et della Villa Hadriana', preserved in manuscripts Vatican, Vat Lat 5295; Barb Lat 4849, and British Library, Add MS 22001.

LINFERT, A., *Von Polyklet zu Lysipp* (Giessen, 1966).

—— Review of J. Inan, *Roman Sculpture in Side* (Ankara, 1975), in *Bonner Jahrbucher* 179 (1979), 781–5.

—— 'Aus Anlaß neuer Repliken des Westmacottschen Epheben und des Dresdner Knaben', in H. Beck and P. C. Bol, eds., *Polykletforschungen* (Berlin, 1993), 141–92.

LING, R., *The Insula of the Menander at Pompeii*, i (Oxford, 1997).

LIVERANI, P., 'L'*Antiquarium* di Villa Barberini a Castel Gandolfo', *AttiPontAccRomRend* 61 (1988–9), 103–30.

—— *L'Antiquarium di Villa Barberini a Castel Gandolfo* (Vatican City, 1989).

—— 'Il Doriforo del Braccio Nuovo e l'Efebo tipo Westmacott di Castel Gandolfo: Nota sul restauro e sul contesto', in H. Beck and P. C. Bol, eds., *Polykletforschungen* (Berlin, 1993), 117–40.

LOPREATO, P., 'L'edificio romana della "Braida Murada": Nuove scoperte', *Aquileia Chiama* 29 (1992), 2–4.

—— 'Le grandi terme di Aquileia: I mosaici del frigidarium', in J.-P. Darmon and A. Rebourg, eds., *La Mosaïque Gréco-Romaine IV* (Paris, 1994), 87–99.

LORAUX, N., *L'invention d'Athènes: Histoire de l'oration funèbre dans la 'cité classique'* (Paris and New York, 1981).

LUGLI, G., 'La villa di Domiziano sui Colli Albani', *BullCom* 45 (1917), 29–78.

—— 'La villa di Domiziano sui Colli Albani', *BullCom* 46 (1918), 3–68.

—— 'La villa di Domiziano sui Colli Albani', *BullCom* 47 (1919), 153–205.

—— 'La villa di Domiziano sui Colli Albani', *BullCom* 48 (1920), 3–72.

MACDONALD, W., and PINTO, J. A., *Hadrian's Villa and its Legacy* (New Haven and London, 1995).

MACDONNELL, M., 'The Introduction of Athletic Nudity: Thucydides, Plato and the Vases', *JHS* III (1991), 182–93.

MAFFEI, S., *Luciano di Samosata: Descrizioni di opere d'arte* (Turin, 1994).

MÄHL, E., *Gymnastik und Athletik im Denken der Römer* (Amsterdam, 1974).

MANCIOLI, D., *Giochi e spettacoli* (Rome, 1987).

MANDERSCHEID, H., *Die Skulpturenausstattung der kaiserzeitlichen Thermenanlagen* (Berlin, 1981).

—— *Bibliographie zum römischen Badewesen unter besonderer Berücksichtigung der öffentlichen Thermen* (Munich, 1988).

MANN, C., *Athlet und Polis im archaischen und frühklassischen Griechenland* (Göttingen, 2001).

MANSEL, A. M., *Die Ruinen von Side* (Berlin, 1963).

MARROU, H. I., *ΜΟΥΣΙΚΟΣ ΑΝΗΡ: Étude sur les scènes de la vie intellectuelle figurant sur les monuments funéraires des Romains* (Grenoble, 1938).

—— *A History of Education in Antiquity*, trans. G. Lamb, 2nd edn. (London, 1977).

MARVIN, M., 'Freestanding Sculpture from the Baths of Caracalla', *AJA* 87 (1983), 347–83.

—— 'Copying in Roman Sculpture: The Replica Series', in E. D'Ambra, ed., *Roman Art in Context: An Anthology* (Englewood Cliffs, NJ, 1993), 161–88.

—— 'Roman Sculptural Reproductions of Polykleitos: The Sequel', in A. Hughes and E. Ranfft, eds., *Sculpture and its Reproductions* (London, 1997), 7–28.

MATTHEWS, V. J., 'Sulla and the Games of the 175th Olympiad (80 BC)', *Stadion* 5 (1979), 239–43.

MEIGGS, R., *Roman Ostia*, 2nd edn. (Oxford, 1973).

MICHAELIS, A., *Ancient Marbles in Great Britain*, trans. C. A. M. Fennell (Cambridge, 1882).

—— *A Catalogue of the Ancient Marbles at Lansdowne House*, ed. A. H. Smith (London, 1899).

MIHAILOV, G., *Inscriptiones Graecae in Bulgaria repertae*, i² (Sofia, 1970).

MILLAR, F., 'P. Herennius Dexippus: The Greek World and the Third-Century Invasions', *JRS* 59 (1969), 12–29.

—— *The Emperor in the Roman World*, 2nd edn. (London, 1992).

—— *The Roman Near East* (Cambridge, Mass., and London, 1993).

MILLAR, S. G., 'Excavations at the Panhellenic Site of Nemea: Cults, Politics and Games', in W. J. Raschke, ed., *The Archaeology of the Olympics: The Olympics and Other Festivals in Antiquity* (Madison, Wis., 1988), 141–51.

MILLER, S. G., *Arete: Greek Sports from Ancient Sources*, 2nd edn. (Berkeley and Los Angeles, 1991).

—— *Ancient Greek Athletics* (New Haven and London, 2004).

MIRANDA, E., 'Tito a Napoli: una dedica onoraria', *Epigraphica* 50 (1988), 222–6.

MITCHELL, S., 'Iconium and Ninica: Two Double Communities in Roman Asia Minor', *Historia* 28 (1979), 409–38.

—— 'Festivals, Games and Civic Life in Roman Asia Minor', *JRS* 80 (1990), 183–93.

MOMMSEN, A., *Feste der Stadt Athen in Altertum* (Leipzig, 1898).

MOON, W., ed., *Polykleitos, the Doryphoros and Tradition* (Madison, Wis., 1995).

MORENO, P., *Scultura ellenistica* (Rome, 1994).

MORETTI, L., *Iscrizioni agonistiche greche* (Rome, 1953).

—— *Olympionikai: i vincitori negli antichi agoni olimpici*, Atti della Accademia Nazionale dei Lincei 8 (Rome, 1957).

—— *Inscriptiones Graecae Urbis Romae*, i (Rome, 1968).

—— 'Supplemento al catalogo degli Olympionikai', *Klio* 52 (1970), 295–303.

—— 'Nuovo Supplemento al catalogo degli Olympionikai', *Miscellanea Greca e Romana* 12 (1987), 67–91.

—— 'I Greci a Roma', *Opuscula Instituti Romani Finlandiae* 4 (1989), 6–16.

—— 'Nuovo Supplemento al catalogo degli Olympionikai', in W. Coulson and H. Kyrieleis, eds., *Proceedings of an International Symposium on the Olympic Games, 5–9 September 1988* (Athens, 1992), 119–28.

MÜLLER, S., *Das Volk der Athleten: Untersuchungen zur Ideologie und Kritik des Sports in der griechisch-römischen Antike* (Trier, 1995).

MULVEY, L., 'Visual Pleasure and Narrative Cinema', in ead., *Visual and Other Pleasures* (Basingstoke, 1989), 14–26; first published in *Screen* (1975).

MUTH, S., *Erleben von Raum—Leben im Raum: zur Funktion mythologischer Mosaikbilder in der römisch-kaiserzeitlichen Wohnarchitektur* (Heidelberg, 1998).

NEILS, J., 'The Panathenaia and Kleisthenic Ideology', in W. D. E. Coulson, O. Palagia, T. L. Shear Jr., H. A. Shapiro, and F. J. Frost, eds., *The Archaeology of Athens and Attica under the Democracy*, Oxbow Monograph 37 (Oxford, 1994), 151–60.

NEUDECKER, R., Review of H. Manderscheid, *Die Skulpturenausstattung der kaiserzeitlichen Thermenanlagen* (Berlin, 1981), in *Gnomon* 57 (1985), 171–8.

—— *Die skulpturen-Ausstattung römischer Villen in Italien* (Mainz, 1988).

NEWBOLD, R. F., 'Cassius Dio and the Games', *AC* 44 (1975), 589–604.

NEWBY, Z., 'Greek Athletics as Roman Spectacle: The Mosaics from Ostia and Rome', *PBSR* 70 (2002), 177–203.

—— 'Sculptural Display in the so-called Palaestra of Hadrian's Villa at Tivoli', *RömMitt* 109 (2002), 59–82.

—— 'Art and Identity in Asia Minor', in S. Scott and J. Webster, eds., *Roman Imperialism and Provincial Art* (Cambridge, 2003), 192–213.

NIELSEN, I., *Thermae et Balnea: The Architecture and Cultural History of Roman Public Baths* (Aarhus, 1990).

NISBET, G., *Greek Epigram in the Roman Empire: Martial's Forgotten Rivals* (Oxford, 2003).

NOACK, F., and LEHMANN-HARTLEBEN, K., *Baugeschichtliche Untersuchungen am Stadtrand von Pompeji* (Berlin and Leipzig, 1936).

NOCK, A. D., 'Sarcophagi and Symbolism', *AJA* 50 (1946), 140–70; reprinted in id., *Essays on Religion and the Ancient World*, ed. Z. Stewart (Oxford, 1972), ii. 606–41.

NOGARA, B., *I mosaici antichi conservati nei palazzi pontifici del Vaticano e del Laterano* (Milan, 1910).

—— 'Recente scoperte di statuaria classica nel villa papale di Castel Gandolfo già Barberini', in C. Galassi Paluzzi, ed., *Atti del III Congresso Nazionale di Studi Romani*, i (1935), 31–88.

NORTH, J. A., 'These He Cannot Take', *JRS* 73 (1983), 169–74.

OGILVIE, R. M., *The Library of Lactantius* (Oxford, 1978).

OLIN, M., 'Gaze', in R. S. Nelson and R. Shiff, eds., *Critical Terms for Art History* (Chicago and London, 1996), 208–19.

OLIVER, J. H., *Marcus Aurelius: Aspects of Civic and Cultural Policy in the East*, Hesperia Supplement 13 (Princeton, 1970).

—— 'Athenian Lists of Ephebic Teams', *Archaiologike Ephemeris* (1971), 66–74.

—— 'The Empress Plotina and the Sacred Thymelic Synod', *Historia* 24 (1975), 125–8.

—— *Greek Constitutions of Early Roman Emperors from Inscriptions and Papyri*, Memoirs of the American Philosophical Society 178 (Philadelphia, 1989).

OUDOT-LUTZ, E., 'La représentation des Athéniens dans l'oeuvre de Lucien', in A. Billault, ed., *Lucien de Samosata: Actes du colloque international de Lyon organisé au Centre d'Études Romaines et Gallo-Romaines les 30 septembre–1er octobre 1993* (Paris, 1994), 141–8.

PALAGIA, O., 'Seven Pilasters of Heracles from Sparta', in S. Walker and A. Cameron, eds., *The Greek Renaissance in the Roman Empire*, BICS Supplement 55 (London, 1989), 122–9.

PALM, J., *Rom, Römertum und Imperium in der griechischen Literatur der Kaiserzeit* (Lund, 1959).

PANDERMALIS, D., 'Zur Programm des Statuenausstattung in der Villa dei Papyri' *AthMitt* 86 (1971), 173–209.

PAPEN, F. G. VON, 'Die Spiele von Hierapolis', *Zeitschrift für Numismatik* 26 (1908), 161–82.

PARIBENI, R., 'Boscoreale: Villa rustica rinvenuta nella contrada Centopiedi, al Tirone', *NSc* (1903), 64–7.

—— 'Tivoli: Rinvenimenti di sculture a Villa Adriana', *NSc* (1932), 120–5.

PARKE, H. W., *Festivals of the Athenians* (London, 1977).

PARKER, R., *Athenian Religion: A History* (Oxford, 1996).

PASCHETTO, L., *Ostia Colonia Romana: Storia e Monumenti* (Rome, 1912).

PAUSZ, R.-D., and REITINGER, W., 'Das Mosaik der gymnischen Agone von Batten Zammour, Tunisien', *Nikephoros* 5 (1992), 119–23.

PAVESE, C. O., 'L'atleta di Ephesos', in H. Friesinger and F. Krinzinger, eds., *100 Jahre Österreichische Forschungen in Ephesos: Akten des Symposions Wien 1995*, Archäologisches Forschungen 1 (Vienna, 1999), 579–84.

PAVOLINI, C., *La vita quotidiana a Ostia* (Bari, 1986).

PEEK, W., 'Zu einem Epheben-Epigramm aus Athen', *Athens Annals of Archaeology* 6 (1973), 125–7.

PELEKIDES, C., *Histoire de l'éphébie attique des origines à 31 avant Jésus-Christ* (Paris, 1962).

PELLETIER, A., *Vienne antique de la conquête romaine aux invasions alamanniques (IIe siècle avant–IIIe siècle après J.-C.)* (Roanne, 1982).

PICOZZI, M. G., 'Una replica della testa dell' "Atleta Amelung" da Castel Gandolfo: Problemi ed Ipotesi', *AttiPontAccRomRend* 48 (1975–6), 95–125.

PINDER, E., 'Musaico tuscolano', *Bullettino dell'Istituto di correspondenza archeologica comunale di Roma* (1862), 179–82.

PLATT, V., ' "Honour Takes Wing": Deceptive Inscriptions in Imperial Greece', in R. Leader-Newby and Z. Newby, eds., *Art and Inscriptions in the Ancient World* (forthcoming).

PLEKET, H. W., 'Some Aspects of the History of the Athletic Guilds', *ZPE* 10 (1973), 197–227.

—— 'Zur Soziologie des antiken Sports', *Mededelingen van het Nederlands Instituut te Rome* 36 (1974), 57–87.

—— 'Games, Prizes, Athletes and Ideology: Some Aspects of the History of Sport in the Greco-Roman World', *Stadion* (=*Arena*) 1 (1975), 49–89.

—— 'The Participants in the Ancient Olympic Games: Social Background and Mentality', in W. Coulson and H. Kyrieleis, eds., *Proceedings of an International Symposium on the Olympic Games, 5–9 September 1988* (Athens, 1992), 147–52.

POLIAKOFF, M. B., *Combat Sports in the Ancient World: Competition, Violence and Culture* (New Haven and London, 1987).

POLLITT, J. J., 'The Impact of Greek Art on Rome', *Proceedings of the American Philological Association* 108 (1978), 155–74.

—— *Art in the Hellenistic Age* (Cambridge, 1986).

PORTER, J. I., 'Ideals and Ruins: Pausanias, Longinus and the Second Sophistic', in S. E. Alcock, J. F. Cherry, and J. Elsner, eds., *Pausanias: Travel and Memory in Roman Greece* (New York, 2001), 63–92.

POTTER, D. S., 'Entertainers in the Roman Empire', in D. S. Potter and D. J. Mattingly, eds., *Life, Death and Entertainment in the Roman Empire* (Ann Arbor, 1999), 256–325.

PRETZLER, M., 'Myth and History at Tegea: Local Tradition and Community Identity', in T. H. Nielsen and J. Roy, eds., *Defining Ancient Arcadia* (Copenhagen, 1999), 89–129.

PRICE, S. R. F., *Rituals and Power: The Roman Imperial Cult in Asia Minor* (Cambridge, 1984).

PRITCHETT, W. K., *Pausanias Periegetes*, ii (Amsterdam, 1999).

PUTORTÌ, N., 'Reggio di Calabria: Nuove scoperte in città', *NSc* (1924), 89–103.

RAEDER, J., *Die statuarische Ausstattung der Villa Hadriana bei Tivoli* (Frankfurt am Main, 1983).

RASCHKE, W. J., 'Images of Victory: Some New Considerations of Athletic Monuments', in ead., ed., *Archaeology of the Olympics: The Olympics and Other Festivals in Antiquity* (Madison, Wis., 1988), 38–54.

—— ed., *The Archaeology of the Olympics: The Olympics and Other Festivals in Antiquity* (Madison, Wis., 1988).

RAUSA, F., *L'immagine del vincitore: L'atleta nella statuaria greca dell'età arcaica all'ellenismo* (Rome, 1994).

RAWSON, E., *Intellectual Life in the Late Roman Republic* (London, 1985).

REED, N. B., 'The *Euandria* Competition Reconsidered', *Ancient World* 15 (1987), 59–64.

REYNOLDS, J. M., 'Epigraphic Evidence for the Construction of the Theatre: 1st c. BC to mid 3rd c. AD', in K. T. Erim and R. R. R. Smith, eds., *Aphrodisias Papers*, ii: *The Theatre, a Sculptor's Workshop, Philosophers and Coin-types*, JRA Supplement 2 (Ann Arbor, 1991), 15–28.

RHOMIOPOULOU, K., *Hellenoromaika glypta tou ethnikou archaiologikou mouseiou* (Athens, 1997).

RICCI, A., *La villa dei Quintilii* (Rome, 1998).

RIDGWAY, B. S., *Roman Copies of Greek Sculpture: The Problem of the Originals* (Ann Arbor, 1984).

—— 'Paene ad exemplum: Polykleitos' Other Works', in W. Moon, ed., *Polykleitos, the Doryphoros and Tradition* (Madison, Wis., 1995), 177–99.

—— 'The Sperlonga Sculptures: The Current State of Research', in N. T. de Grummond and B. S. Ridgway, eds., *From Pergamon to Sperlonga: Sculpture and Context* (Berkeley, Los Angeles, and London, 2000), 78–91.

RITTI, T., *Hierapolis Scavi e Ricerche*, i: *Fonti Letterarie ed Epigrafiche*, Archeologica 53 (Rome, 1985).

ROBERT, L., 'Catalogue Agonistique des Romaia de Xanthos', in id., *Opera Minora Selecta*, vii. 681–94.

—— 'Recherches Épigraphiques. 1. Aristos Hellēnōn', *REA* 31 (1929), 13–20; reprinted in id., *Opera Minora Selecta*, ii. 758–67.

—— 'Inscriptions grecques d'Asie Mineure', in W. M. Calder and J. Keil, eds., *Anatolian Studies presented to W. H. Buckler* (Manchester, 1939), 227–48; reprinted in id., *Opera Minora Selecta*, i. 611–32.

—— *Les gladiateurs dans l'Orient grec* (Paris, 1940; 2nd edn. Amsterdam, 1971).

—— 'Les boules dans les types monétaires agonistiques', *Hellenica* 7 (1949), 93–104.

—— 'Inscriptions grecques de Sidè en Pamphylie', *Revue de Philologie* 32 (1958) 15–53; reprinted in id., *Opera Minora Selecta*, v. 758–67.

—— 'Un relief inscrit au musée de Stamboul', in id., *Hellenica* 11–12 (Paris, 1960), 369–80.

—— 'Les épigrammes satiriques de Lucilius sur les athlètes: Parodie et réalités', in *L'épigramme grecque*, Entretiens sur l'Antiquité Classique 14 (Geneva, 1968), 181–295; reprinted in id., *Opera Minora Selecta*, vi. 317–431.

—— 'Deux concours grecs à Rome', *CRAI* (1970), 6–27; reprinted in id., *Opera Minora Selecta*, v. 647–68.

—— 'Deux inscriptions de Tarse et d'Argos', *BCH* 101 (1977), 80–132.

—— 'La titulature de Nicée et de Nicomédie: la gloire et la haine', *Harvard Studies in Classical Philology* 81 (1977) 1–39; reprinted in id., *Opera Minora Selecta*, vii. 211–49.

—— 'Une vision de Perpétue martyre à Carthage en 203', *CRAI* (1982), 228–76; reprinted in id., *Opera Minora Selecta*, v. 791–839.

—— 'Discours d'ouverture', in *Praktika of the Eighth International Congress of Greek and Latin Epigraphy* (Athens, 1984), i. 35–45.; reprinted in id., *Opera Minora Selecta*, vi. 709–19.

ROBERTSON, N., 'A Point of Precedence at Plataia: The Dispute between Athens and Sparta over Leading the Procession', *Hesperia* 55 (1986), 88–102.

ROBINSON, R. S., *Sources for the History of Greek Athletics in English Translation* (Cincinnati, 1955).

ROGERS, G. M., *The Sacred Identity of Ephesos: Foundation Myths of a Roman City* (London, 1991).

ROMANO, D. G., 'The Panathenaic Stadium and Theatre of Lykourgos: An Examination of the Facilities on the Pnyx Hill', *AJA* 89 (1985), 441–54.

ROMANO, M., 'L'epigrafe ateniese a Phayllos (IG, I³, 2, 823)', *ZPE* 123 (1998), 105–16.

ROMEO, I., 'The Panhellenion and Ethnic Identity in Hadrianic Greece', *Classical Philology* 97 (2002), 21–40.

ROSSI, V., ed., *Filostrato, 'Eroico'* (Venice, 1997).

ROUECHÉ, C., 'Inscriptions and the Later History of the Theatre', in K. T. Erim and R. R. R. Smith, eds., *Aphrodisias Papers*, ii: *The Theatre, a Sculptor's Workshop, Philosophers and Coin-types*, JRA Supplement 2 (Ann Arbor, 1991), 99–108.

—— *Performers and Partisans at Aphrodisias in the Roman and Late Roman Periods*, JRS Monograph 6 (London, 1993).

ROUSSEL, P., 'Les chlamydes noires des éphèbes Athéniens', *REA* 43 (1941), 163–5.

RUMSCHEID, J., *Kranz und Krone: Zu Insignien, Siegespreisen und Ehrenzeichen der römischen Kaiserzeit* (Tübingen, 2000).

RUSSELL, D. A., *Greek Declamation* (Cambridge, 1983).

—— and WILSON, N. G., eds., *Menander Rhetor* (Oxford, 1981).

SALOMIES, O., 'People in Ostia: Some Onomastic Observations and Comparisons with Rome', in C. Bruun and A. Gallina Zevi, eds., *Ostia e Portus nelle loro relazioni con Roma*, Acta Instituti Romani Finlandiae 27 (Rome, 2002), 135–59.

SALZA PRINA RICOTTI, E., 'Villa Adriana in Pirro Ligorio e Francesco Contini', *Atti della Accademia Nazionale dei Lincei: Memorie* 8.17 (1973), 3–47.

—— 'Villa Adriana nei suoi limiti e nella sua funzionalità', *AttiPontAccRomMem* 14 (1982), 25–55.

—— *Villa Adriana: Il sogno di un imperatore* (Rome, 2001).

SANSONE, D., *Greek Athletics and the Genesis of Sport* (Berkeley, Los Angeles, and London, 1988).

SAURON, G., 'Templa Serena. A propos de la Villa des Papyri d'Herculaneum: les Champes-Elysées épicuriens', *MEFRA* 92 (1980), 277–301.

SCANLON, T. F., *Greek and Roman Athletics: A Bibliography* (Chicago, 1984).

—— 'Combat and Contest: Athletic Metaphors for Warfare in Greek Literature', in S. J. Bandy, ed., *Coroebus Triumphs: The Alliance of Sport and the Arts* (San Diego, 1988), 230–44.

—— *Eros and Greek Athletics* (Oxford, 2002).

SCHERRER, P., 'The City of Ephesos from the Roman Period to Late Antiquity', in H. Koester, ed., *Ephesos: Metropolis of Asia* (Valley Forge, Pa., 1995), 1–25.

—— 'The Historical Topography of Ephesos', in D. Parrish, ed., *Urbanism in Western Asia Minor: New Studies on Aphrodisias, Ephesos, Hierapolis, Pergamon, Perge and Xanthos*, JRA Supplement 45 (Portsmouth, RI, 2001), 57–87.

SCHMITZ, T., *Bildung und Macht: zur sozialen und politischen Funktion der zweiten Sophistik in der griechischen Welt der Kaiserzeit*, Zetemata 97 (Munich, 1997).

SCHNEIDER, R. M., 'Orientalische Tischdiener als römische Tischfusse', *AA* (1992), 295–305.

SCHRÖDER, B., *Der Sport in Altertum* (Berlin, 1927).

SCHWARTZ, J., *Biographie de Lucien de Samosata* (Brussels, 1965).

SERWINT, N. J., 'Greek Athletic Sculpture from the Fifth and Fourth Centuries BC: An Iconographic Study', Ph.D. thesis (Princeton, 1987).

SHEAR, J. L., 'Polis and Panathenaia: The History and Development of Athena's Festival', Ph.D. thesis (Pennsylvania, 2001).

—— 'Reusing Statues, Rewriting Inscriptions, and Bestowing Honours in Roman Athens', in R. Leader-Newby and Z. Newby, eds., *Art and Inscriptions in the Ancient World* (forthcoming).

SHERK, R. K., *Roman Documents from the Greek East: Senatus Consulta and Epistulae to the Age of Augustus* (Baltimore, 1969).

SHIPLEY, G., *The Greek World after Alexander 323–30 BC* (London and New York, 2000).

SIDEBOTTOM, H., 'Pausanias: Past, Present, and Closure', *CQ* 52.2 (2002), 494–9.

SIMON, E., *Festivals of Attica: An Archaeological Commentary* (Madison, Wis., 1983).

SINN, U., *Olympia: Cult, Sport, and Ancient Festival*, trans. T. Thornton (Princeton, 2000).

—— LADSTÄTTER, G., MARTIN, A., and VÖLLIG, T., 'Bericht über das Forschungsprojekt "Olympia während der römischen Kaiserzeit und in der Spätantike" III. Die Arbeiten im Jahr 1994', *Nikephoros* 7 (1994), 229–50.

SLAVAZZI, F., 'I programmi decorativi della villa: Temi, colori, riflessi', in *Adriano: Architettura e Progetto* (Milan, 1999), 63–7.

SMALLWOOD, E. M., *Documents Illustrating the Principates of Gaius, Claudius and Nero* (Cambridge, 1967).

SMITH, A. H., 'Gavin Hamilton's Letters to Charles Townley', *JHS* 21 (1901), 306–21.

SMITH, R. R. R., 'Typology and Diversity in the Portraits of Augustus', *JRA* 9 (1996), 31–47.

—— 'Cultural Choice and Political Identity in Honorific Portrait Statues in the Greek East in the Second Century AD', *JRS* 88 (1998), 56–93.

SNODGRASS, A. N., 'Pausanias and the Chest of Kypselos', in S. E. Alcock, J. F. Cherry, and J. Elsner, eds., *Pausanias: Travel and Memory in Roman Greece* (New York, 2001), 127–41.

SOGLIANO, A., 'Pompei: Degli edifizi recentemente scoperti e degli oggetti raccolti negli scavi dal settembre 1888 al marzo 1889', *NSc* (1889), 114–36, at 114–22.

SOLIN, H., *Beiträge zur Kenntnis der griechischen Personennamen in Rom*, Commentationes Humanarum Litterarum 48 (Helsinki, 1971).

SPAWFORTH, A. J. S., 'Sparta and the Family of Herodes Atticus: A Reconsideration of the Evidence', *ABSA* 75 (1980), 203–20.

—— 'Notes on the Third Century AD in Spartan Epigraphy', *ABSA* 79 (1984), 263–88.

—— 'Agonistic Festivals in Roman Greece', in S. Walker and A. Cameron, eds., *The Greek Renaissance in the Roman Empire*, BICS Supplement 55 (London, 1989), 193–7.

—— 'Symbol of Unity? The Persian-Wars Tradition in the Roman Empire', in S. Hornblower, ed., *Greek Historiography* (Oxford, 1994), 233–47.

—— 'The Panhellenion Again', *Chiron* 29 (1999), 339–52.

—— and WALKER, S., 'The World of the Panhellenion I: Athens and Eleusis', *JRS* 75 (1985), 78–104.

—— —— 'The World of the Panhellenion II: Three Dorian Cities', *JRS* 76 (1986), 88–105.

SPECHT, E., 'Kranz, Krone oder Korb für den Sieger', in *Altmodische Archäologie: Festschrift für Friedrich Brein (Forum Archaeologiae: Zeitschrift für klassische Archäologie* (14 March 2000), available via http://farch.net).

SPIVEY, N., *The Ancient Olympics* (Oxford, 2004).

SPYROPOULOS, G., *Drei Meisterwerke der Griechischen Plastik aus der Villa des Herodes Atticus zu Eva/Loukou* (Frankfurt am Main, 2001).

STEINER, D., 'Moving Images: Fifth-Century Victory Monuments and the Athlete's Allure', *Classical Antiquity* 17 (1998), 123–49.

—— *Images in Mind: Statues in Archaic and Classical Greek Literature and Thought* (Princeton and Oxford, 2001).

STERN, H., *Recueil général des mosaïques de la Gaule*, ii: *Province de Lyonnaise*, i: *Lyon* (Paris, 1967).

STESKAL, M., and LA TORRE, M., 'Das Vediusgymnasium in Ephesos', *JÖAI* 70 (2001), 221–44.

STEVENSON, J., ed., *A New Eusebius: Documents Illustrating the History of the Church*, ed. W. H. C. Frend (London, 1987).

STEWART, A., 'The Canon of Polykleitos: A Question of Evidence', *JHS* 98 (1978), 122–31.

—— 'Lysippan Studies 3. Not by Daedalos?', *AJA* 82 (1978), 473–82.

—— *Greek Sculpture: An Exploration* (New Haven and London, 1990).

—— *Art, Desire and the Body in Ancient Greece* (Cambridge, 1997).

SVORONOS, J. N., *Das Athener National Museum*, German trans. (Athens, 1937).

SWADDLING, J., *The Ancient Olympic Games* (London, 1980; 2nd edn. 1999).

SWAIN, S., *Hellenism and Empire: Language, Classicism, and Power in the Greek World AD 50–250* (Oxford, 1996).

—— 'Defending Hellenism: Philostratus, *In Honour of Apollonius*', in M. Edwards, M. Goodman, and S. Price, eds., *Apologetics in the Roman Empire* (Oxford, 1999), 157–96.

—— 'Bilingualism in Cicero? The Evidence of Code-Switching', in J. N. Adams, M. Janse, and S. Swain, eds., *Bilingualism in Ancient Society: Language Contact and the Written Text* (Oxford, 2002), 128–67.

SWEET, W. E., *Sport and Recreation in Ancient Greece* (Oxford and New York, 1987).

TAMM, B., *Neros Gymnasium in Rom* (Stockholm, 1970).

THUILLIER, J.-P., 'Le programme "Atlétique" des *Ludi Circenses* dans la Rome Républicaine', *Revue des Études Latines* 60 (1982), 105–22.

—— *Les Jeux athlétiques dans la civilisation étrusque* (Rome, 1985).

—— 'La nudité athlétique (Grèce, Etrurie, Rome)', *Nikephoros* 1 (1988), 29–48.

—— *Le Sport dans la Rome Antique* (Paris, 1996).

—— 'Le *cirrus* et la barbe: Questions d'iconographie athlétique romaine', *MEFRA* 110 (1998), 351–80.

THÜR, H., 'The Processional Way in Ephesos as a Place of Cult and Burial', in H. Koester, ed., *Ephesos: Metropolis of Asia* (Valley Forge, Pa., 1995), 157–99.

TOBIN, J., 'Some New Thoughts on Herodes Atticus's Tomb, his Stadium of 143/4, and Philostratus *VS* 2.550', *AJA* 97 (1993), 81–9.

—— *Herodes Attikos and the City of Athens: Patronage and Conflict under the Antonines* (Amsterdam, 1997).

TONER, J., *Leisure and Ancient Rome* (Cambridge, 1995).

TORELLI, M., 'Da Sparta a Villa Adriana: le terme d'Arapissa, il ginnasio del Platanistas e il Teatro Marittimo', in M. Gnade, ed., *Stips Votiva: Papers presented to C. M. Stibbe* (Amsterdam, 1991), 225–32.

TOUCHETTE, L., 'The Mechanics of Roman Copy Production?', in G. R. Tsetskhladze, A. J. N. W. Prag, and A. M. Snodgrass, eds., *Periplous: Papers on Classical Art and Archaeology Presented to Sir John Boardman* (London, 2000), 344–52.

TOURRENC, S., 'La mosaïque des "athlètes vainqueurs" ', in H. Stern and M. Le Glay, eds., *La Mosaïque Gréco-Romaine II* (Paris, 1975), 135–53.

TRAVERSARI, G., *Gli Spettacoli in Acqua nel Teatro Tardo-Antico* (Rome, 1960).

—— *Il Museo Archeologico di Venezia: I ritratti* (Rome, 1968).

TRAVLOS, J., *A Pictorial Dictionary of Ancient Athens* (London, 1971).

TRENDELENBURG, A., *Pausanias in Olympia* (Berlin, 1914).

TURCAN, R., 'Les sarcophages romains et le problème du symbolisme funéraire', *ANRW* 16.2 (1978), 1700–35.

VALERI, C., 'Brevi note sulle Terme di Porta Marina a Ostia', *Archeologica Classica* 52 (2001), 307–22.

—— 'Arredi scultorei dagli edifice termali di Ostia', in C. Bruun and A. Gallina Zevi, eds., *Ostia e Portus nelle loro relazioni con Roma*, Acta Instituti Romani Finlandiae 27 (Rome, 2002), 213–28.

VAN NIJF, O., 'Athletics, Festivals and Greek Identity in the Roman East', *PCPS* 45 (1999), 176–200.

—— 'Inscriptions and Civic Memory in the Roman East', in A. E. Cooley, ed., *The Afterlife of Inscriptions* (London, 2000), 21–36.

—— 'Local Heroes: Athletics, Festivals and Elite Self-Fashioning in the Roman East', in S. Goldhill, ed., *Being Greek under Rome: Cultural Identity, the Second Sophistic and the Development of Empire* (Cambridge, 2001), 306–34.

VAN VOORHIS, J. A., 'Two Portrait Statues of Boxers and the Culture of Athletics at Aphrodisias in the Third Century CE', in C. Ratte and R. R. R. Smith, eds., *Aphrodisias Papers*, iv JRA Supplement (Ann Arbor, forthcoming).

VERMEULE, C. C., *Greek Sculpture and Roman Taste* (Ann Arbor, 1977).

VEYNE, P., 'La famille et l'amour sous le haut-empire Romain', *Annales: Économies, Sociétés, Civilisations* 33 (1978), 35–63.

—— 'Homosexuality in Ancient Rome', in P. Ariès and A. Béjin, eds., *Western Sexuality: Practice and Precept in Past and Present Times*, trans. A. Forster (Oxford, 1985), 26–35.

—— *Did the Greeks Believe in their Myths? An Essay on the Constitutive Imagination*, trans. P. Wissing (Chicago, 1988).

—— *Bread and Circuses: Historical Sociology and Political Pluralism*, trans. B. Pearce (London, 1990).

VIDAL-NAQUET, P., 'The Black Hunter and the Origin of the Athenian Ephebia', in id., *The Black Hunter: Forms of Thought and Forms of Society in the Greek World*, trans. A. Szegedy-Maszak (Baltimore and London, 1986), 106–28.

VILLE, G., *La Gladiature en Occident des Origines à la Mort de Domitien* (Rome, 1981).

VIRGILI, P., 'Le stade de Domitien', in C. Landes, ed., *Le stade romain et ses spectacles* (Lattes, 1994), 107–19.

VISCONTI, C. L., 'Escavazioni di Ostia dall'anno 1855 al 1858', *Annali dell'Istituto di corrispondenza archeologica* 29 (1857), 281–340.

—— 'Trovamenti di oggetti d'arte e di antichità figurata', *BullCom* (1886), 49–53.

WACE, A. J. B., 'Excavations at Sparta: The Roman Baths (Arapissa)', *ABSA* 12 (1905–6), 407–14.

WAELKENS, M., *Dokimeion: die Werkstatt der repräsentativen kleinasiatischen Sarkophage, Chronologie und Typologie ihrer Produktion*, Archäologische Forschungen 11 (Berlin, 1982).

WALKER, S., and CAMERON, A., eds., *The Greek Renaissance in the Roman Empire*, BICS Supplement 55 (London, 1989).

WALLACE-HADRILL, A., *Suetonius: The Scholar and his Caesars* (London, 1983).

—— 'Greek Knowledge, Roman Power', *Classical Philology* 83 (1988), 224–33.

—— 'Rome's Cultural Revolution', *JRS* 79 (1989), 157–64.

—— 'Roman Arches and Greek Honours: The Language of Power at Rome', *PCPS* 36 (1990), 143–81.

—— 'Mutatio morum: The Idea of a Cultural Revolution', in T. Habinek and A. Schiesaro, eds., *The Roman Cultural Revolution* (Cambridge, 1997), 3–22.

—— 'To be Roman, go Greek: Thoughts on Hellenization at Rome', in M. Austin, J. Harries, and C. Smith, eds., *Modus Operandi: Essays in Honour of Geoffrey Rickman*, BICS Supplement 71 (London, 1998), 79–91.

—— 'The Villa as Cultural Symbol', in A. Frazer, ed., *The Roman Villa: Villa Urbana* (Philadelphia, Pa., 1998), 43–53.

—— 'Vivere alla greca per essere Romani', in S. Settis, ed., *I Greci*, ii. iii (Torino, 1998), 938–63.

WARDEN, P. G., 'The Sculptural Program of the Villa of the Papyri', *JRA* 4 (1991), 257–61.

—— and ROMANO, D. G., 'The Course of Glory: Greek Art in a Roman Context at the Villa of the Papyri at Herculaneum', *Art History* 17 (1994), 228–54.

WARD-PERKINS, J. B., *Roman Architecture* (New York, 1977).

WAYWELL, S. E., 'Roman Mosaics in Greece', *AJA* 83 (1979), 293–321 with pls. 45–52.

WEBER, M., *Antike Badekultur* (Munich, 1996).

WEEBER, K.-W., *Panem et Circenses: Massenunterhaltung als Politik im antiken Rom*, 2nd edn. (Mainz, 1994).

WEIS, H. A., 'Odysseus at Sperlonga: Hellenistic Hero or Roman Heroic Foil?', in N. T. de Grummond and B. S. Ridgway, eds., *From Pergamon to Sperlonga: Sculpture and Context* (Berkeley, Los Angeles, and London, 2000), 111–65.

WEISMANN, W., *Kirche und Schauspiele: die Schauspiele im Urteil der lateinischen Kirchenväter unter besonderer Berücksichtigung von Augustin* (Würzburg, 1972).

WEISS, P., 'Ein agonistisches Bema und die isopythischen Spiele von Side', *Chiron* 11 (1981), 315–46.

WELCH, K., 'Greek Stadia and Roman Spectacles: Asia, Athens and the Tomb of Herodes Atticus', *JRA* 11 (1998), 117–45.

WELCKER, F. G., *Alte Denkmäler*, i (Göttingen, 1849).

WERNER, H., *Die Sammlung antiker Mosaiker in den Vatikanischen Museen* (Vatican City, 1998).

WESSNER, P., ed., *Scholia in Iuvenalem Vetustiora* (Lipsiae, 1931).

WHITE, L. M., 'Urban Development and Social Change in Imperial Ephesos', in H. Koester, ed., *Ephesos: Metropolis of Asia* (Valley Forge, Pa., 1995), 27–79.

WHITMARSH, T., ' "Greece Is the World": Exile and Identity in the Second Sophistic', in S. Goldhill, ed., *Being Greek under Rome: Cultural Identity, the Second Sophistic and the Development of Empire* (Cambridge, 2001), 269–305.

—— *Greek Literature and the Roman Empire: The Politics of Imitation* (Oxford, 2001).

WHITTAKER, H., 'Pausanias and His Use of Inscriptions', *Symbolae Osloenses* 66 (1991), 171–86.

WIEDEMANN, T., *Emperors and Gladiators* (London and New York, 1992).

WIEGARTZ, H., *Kleinasiatische Säulensarkophage: Untersuchungen zum Sarkophagtypus und zu den figürlichen Darstellungen*, Istanbuler Forschungen 26 (Berlin, 1965).

WILLERS, D., *Hadrians panhellenisches Programm: archäologische Beiträge zur Neugestaltung Athens durch Hadrian* (Basel, 1990).

WILLIAMS, C. A., *Roman Homosexuality: Ideologies of Masculinity in Classical Antiquity* (Oxford, 1999).

WILLIAMS, G., *Tradition and Originality in Roman Poetry* (Oxford, 1968).

WILSON, PAUL, 'A Corpus of Ephebic Inscriptions from Roman Athens 31 BC–267 AD', Ph.D. thesis (Monash, 1992).

WILSON, PETER, *The Athenian Institution of the Khoregia: The Chorus, the City and the Stage* (Cambridge, 2000).

WINNEFELD, H., *Die Villa des Hadrian bei Tivoli* (Berlin, 1895).

WOJCIK, M. R., *La Villa dei Papyri ad Ercolano* (Rome, 1986).

WOLTERS, P., 'Ein Denkmal der Partherkriege', *AthMitt* 28 (1903), 291–300.

WOODWARD, A. M., 'Excavations at Sparta. III. The Inscriptions', *ABSA* 26 (1923–5), 159–239.

—— 'Inscriptions', in R. M. Dawkins, ed., *The Sanctuary of Artemis Orthia at Sparta* (London, 1929), 285–377.

WOOLF, G., 'Becoming Roman, Staying Greek: Culture, Identity and the Civilising Process in the Roman East', *PCPS* 40 (1994), 116–43.

—— *Becoming Roman: The Origins of Provincial Civilization in Gaul* (Cambridge, 1998).

—— 'The Roman Cultural Revolution in Gaul', in S. Keay and N. Terrenato, eds., *Italy and the West: Comparative issues in Romanization* (Oxford, 2001), 173–86.

WÖRRLE, M., *Stadt und Fest in kaiserzeitliche Kleinasien* (Munich, 1988).

—— 'Neue Inschriftenfunde aus Aizanoi I', *Chiron* 22 (1992), 337–76.

YEGÜL, F. K., 'A Study in Architectural Iconography: Kaisersaal and the Imperial Cult', *Art Bulletin* 64 (1982), 7–31.

—— *The Bath-Gymnasium Complex at Sardis* (Cambridge, Mass., 1986).

—— *Baths and Bathing in Classical Antiquity* (Cambridge, Mass., 1992).

YOUNG, D. C., *The Olympic Myth of Greek Amateur Athletics* (Chicago, 1984).

—— 'How the Amateurs Won the Olympics', in W. J. Raschke, ed., *The Archaeology of the Olympics: The Olympics and Other Festivals in Antiquity* (Madison, Wis., 1988), 55–75.

ZANKER, P., *Klassizistische Statuen: Studien zur Veränderung des Kunstgeschmacks in der römischen Kaiserzeit* (Mainz, 1974).

—— 'Zur Funktion und Bedeutung griechischer Skulptur in der Römerzeit', in H. Flashar, ed., *Le Classicisme à Rome aux Iers siècles avant et après J.-C.*, Entretiens sur l'Antiquité Classique 25 (Geneva, 1979), 283–314.

—— *The Power of Images in the Age of Augustus*, trans. A. Shapiro (Ann Arbor, 1988).

—— *The Mask of Socrates: The Image of the Intellectual in Antiquity*, trans. A. Shapiro (Berkeley, Los Angeles, and Oxford, 1995).

—— and EWALD, B. C., *Mit Mythen leben: die Bilderwelt der römischen Sarkophage* (Munich, 2004).

ZEVI, F., and GRANELLI, A., 'Le Terme di Nettuno: Stratigrafia e fase edilizie pre-adrianee', *Mededelingen van het Nederlands Instituut te Rome* 58 (1999), 80–2.

ZIEGLER, R., *Städtisches Prestige und kaiserliche Politik: Studien zum Festwesen in Ostkilikien im 2. und 3. Jahrhundert n. Chr.* (Düsseldorf, 1985).

INDEX

Entries in bold type refer to illustrations. Roman names are listed according to *nomen* or *cognomen*

Achaea 224, 279, 281
Acriae 220
Actia festival at Nicopolis 27, 31
acting 30, 43, 55
Aemilius Paullus, L. 26
Aezanoi 253–4
Africa, *see* North Africa
agōgē, *see* Sparta
Agon Capitolinus, *see* Capitoline Games at Rome
Agon Herculeus 37, 74–5
Agon Minervae 37
Agon Solis 37
agōnes, *see* festivals
Agricola 77
Agrippa, *see* Rome, Baths of Agrippa
Aianteia festival at Salamis 180, 229; *see also* Salamis
Alcandridas, P. Aelius of Sparta 221–2
Alexander Severus 37, 63, 67, 69, 74–5
Alexander the Great 37, 124
Alexandria 229
Althiburus 85
amateurism 10, 254
Amelung athlete statue type 100 n. 54, 113, **114**
Anacharsis 146; *see also* Lucian, *Anacharsis*
Androclus 244, 280 n. 26
Anicius Gallus, L. 26
Antinous 55, 178
Antoninus Pius 35, 36, 50, 137, 240, 244 n. 58
Aphrodisias 12, 252, 255–61
Aphrodite of Cnidus, *see* Praxiteles
Apollonius of Tyana 157, 166
Apuleius 5, 86
Aquileia 62–3, 64–7, **65, 66**
archaism 156, 157–8, **160**, 178, 200, 277
Argos 212, 217, 218, 221
aristos Hellēnōn 170, 221, 228
Aristotle 38, 56, 95, 125
Arrachion of Phigalia 153, 218
Arrichion, *see* Arrachion

Artemis Orthia 151, 152, 204; *see also* Sparta, Sanctuary of Artemis Orthia
Artists of Dionysus, *see* guild of actors
Asclepieia festival at Carthage 85
Asclepius 55, 70, 92, 217, 243, 264
Asia Minor 11, 13, 229–70, 281
Astylus of Croton 219–20, 223 n. 79, 226–7
Athenaea festival at Athens 178
Athens 11–12, 84, 122, 210–11, 214, 244
    Diogenium gymnasium 169
    Lyceum gymnasium 145, 146, 169
    Panathenaic stadium 195, 200, 244
    ephēbeia 168–201
    ephebic reliefs 171–92, **172, 173, 175, 176, 181, 184, 190**
    see also Pausanias on Athens
athletes
    and their cities 223–8, 253
    fame of 58–9, 62, 273; *see also* cultic honours to athletes
    female 59
    Roman 26 n. 31, 30–1, 42–3, 54
    and statues 76, 126–8, 148, 223–8, 253; *see also* victory statues
    status of 9–10, 253–4
athletic victors
    crowning of 41, 49, 56, 105, 250–1
    rewards for 36, 226–7; *see also* guild of athletes; prizes
athletics
    ideals associated with 95, 127, 128, 137, 252–3
    as spectacle 26, 59, 143, 273, 277
    and warfare 40, 43–4, 76, 148–50, 151, 155–6, 169–70, 188–92, 200–1, 215, 223, 227–8, 278
Attalids 34
atticism 9, 84, 277
Augustus 4, 23, 27, 28, 31, 32, 34, 204, 235, 238
Aurelian 37, 63
Aurelius Achilles 252–3

Aurelius Alcamenes 178, 198
Aurelius Alexander 58
Aurelius Helix 58, 75, 226, 273

ball games 46, 151, 154, 163
bathing culture 45–6, 274
baths
    in Greek east 157, 164–6, 230–1; *see also*
        Ephesus; Miletus
    in Italy 27–30, 33, 41, 42, 45; *see also* Ostia;
        Rome
    sculptural display of 70, 71, 89, 92, 231–2;
        see also gymnasium, sculptural display of;
        mosaics
beauty 126–8, 148
benefaction, *see* euergetism
bilingualism 5, 86–7, 235
Boscoreale, villa of N. Popidius Florus 47
boxing 30, 40, 41, 93, 148, 154, 208, 257
    in Italy 25, 26 n. 27
    in North Africa 85
boxing gloves 50, 54, 257
Britain 140

Caligula, *see* Gaius
Callimachus (sculptor) 93
Campania 46–8; *see also* Naples; Pompeii
Candidianus of Aphrodisias 257, **259**
Capitoline Games at Rome 16, 24, 27, 31, 32,
    35, 36, 37, 40, 42, 43, 53 n. 38, 58, 61, 78,
    84, 137
Capsa, *see* Gafsa
Caracalla 70, 74, 75, 156, 200, 238, 249; *see also*
    Rome, Baths of Caracalla
Carthage 85
Caryatids 122
Castel Gandolfo
    Domitian's Villa 96–106, 130–4
    Ninfeo Bergantino 105, 132–4
Cato the Elder 3
Celsus Polemaeanus, Ti. Julius 139, 237
Centopiedi 48
Chaeron of Pellene 149–50
chariot races 16, 21, 39, 42, 59, 273
Chionis of Sparta 219–20, 221, 222
Christians 24, 39, 83
Cicero 5, 33, 38, 39, 40, 90–1, 124, 136
circuit-victor, see *periodonikēs*
circus 53; *see also* chariot races
cirrus 50, 54, 63, 65, 81, 257

civic identity, *see* identity, Greek civic
civic rivalries 247–8, 204
Claudius 31, 34, 48, 78
Cleombrotus of Sybaris 223 n. 79
coinage 37, **37**, 247–8, **248**, 268, 270
Commodus 178 n. 23
Commodeia festival at Caesarea in
        Mauretania 85
Contini, Francesco 108
copies, *see* sculpture, Greek, Roman copies of
Corinth 83–4, 212, 244
Coroebus of Elis 223
cosmētēs 171–7, 190
Costoboci 227–8
Creugas 154, 217, 218
Critius (sculptor) 123, 214
crowns 32, 57–8, 66, 68, 85, 248, 260–1, 269,
    269, **270**; *see also* prizes
cultic honours to athletes 152, 216, 219, 223–6
Cylon of Athens 214
Cynisca of Sparta 218
Cyniscus of Mantinea 104

Damianus, *see* Flavius Damianus
Damoxenus 154, 218
deaths 153, 154
Deinosthenes of Sparta 220
Delphi 210, 211–13, 224, 244, 247
Demeter 204
d'Este, Ippolito 111
diet 24
Dio Chrysostom 126–8, 144
Dionysius of Halicarnassus 25
Discobolus, *see* discus-thrower; Ludovisi
        Discobolus; Myron Discobolus statue
discus-thrower statue 111–13, 255, 262, **264–5**;
        see also Ludovisi Discobolus; Myron
        Discobolus statue
Domesticus, Marcus Ulpius 35, 61, 273
Domitian 23, 24, 31, 32–3, 37, 96, 132–4, 139;
        see also Castel Gandolfo, Domitian's villa
Dresden youth statue type 99, **101–2**, 104,
        105, 120, 130

Earinus 134
education 3, 42, 147–50, see also *ephēbeia*
Egypt 11, 229
Elagabalus 36, 63, 67, 74
Elataea 227–8
Eleusis 179, 190 n. 74, 194, 195, 211

Eleutheria festival at Plataea 170, 191
elite self-representation 86–7, 277; *see also* Greek elite; identity
Emesa 5, 74
endurance 148, 151–4, 199
Ennius 40
ephēbeia 149–50, 155, 156 n. 48; *see also* Athens, *ephēbeia*; Sparta, *agōgē*
Ephesus 11, 12, 211, 230–46, 253
    Baths of Vedius 123, 231, 235–40, **236**, 243–4, 245, 266
    East Baths-Gymnasium 231, 235–8, **237**, 240–3, 245
    Harbour Baths 231–5, **234**, 244, 245
Ephesus apoxyomenus statue type **98**, 99, 104, 105, 232, **233**
Epicharinus 214–15
epigrams 73–4, *see also* Lucillius
Epitaphia festival at Athens 179, 188, 189, 191
erotics, *see* homoeroticism
Etruscan games 25
euandria 148
Euarestes, Julius Lucius Pilius 252
euergetism 8, 9, 13, 78, 84, 86, 193–5, 200, 235, 240–1, 244–5, 246, 251–2
    by emperor 45, 59, 251, 280
euexia 148
Euphranor, statue of Paris 132
Euripides 8
Eurycles, M. Ulpius Appuleius 253
Euryleonis of Sparta 218
Eusebeia Games at Puteoli 36
eutaxia 148
Eutyches, P. Pompeius 60

fantasy 31–2, 55, 56, 272, 274
Farnese Bull 70, 72
Farnese Heracles 71–4, **73**, 184
Faustina 243, 246
Favorinus 83–4
Fede, Count 113
festival culture 84, 86, 275–6
festivals
    in eastern provinces 246–52, 268–70, 271
    ephebic involvement in at Athens 171, 174–9
    imperial involvement in 13–14, 34, 48, 177–8, 247, 251, 275–6, 280
    introduction to Rome and Italy 24–34, 36–7, 137, 272–3
    introduction to western provinces 36, 76–87
freedom 147, 149, 150, 151, 170
Flavianus Flavillianus, L. Septimius 253
Flavius Damianus 240, 243
Fronto, P. Sthenius 252, 253

Gafsa, athletic mosaic 84–7
Gaius (Caligula) 22, 23
Gaius Caesar 28, 76–7
Galba 22
Galen 24, 38, 75
Ganymede 132–4
Gaul 76–84, 140
    Greek culture in 83–4, 140
    hellenization of 77–8, 82–4
    population of 83
    romanization of 77–8, 84
gladiatorial contests 21, 59, 257, 273
Glaucus 208
Gordian III 37, 63, 268
Granianus, Aelian 217, 228
Greek elite
    involvement in athletics 44, 253–4
    self-promotion 186–7, 253–4
    see also euergetism; identity, Greek elite
Greek Renaissance 7–11; *see also* Second Sophistic
guild
    of actors 34, 76, 78 n. 136, 251
    of athletes 31 n. 52, 34–6, 76, 82, 137
gymnasium 229–30
    evoked in Roman baths 28, 53–4, 55, 56
    evoked in Roman villas 90–1, 95, 105–6, 121, 125, 136, 138, 274; *see also* Castel Gandolfo, Domitian's Villa; Tivoli, Hadrian's Villa
    link with philosophy 53–4, 55, 90–1
    sculptural display of 231–2, 235, 243, 245–6, 265–7; *see also* Ephesus; Side

Hadrian 12, 35, 36, 50, 96, 121, 195, 210–11, 212, 228, 279; *see also* Tivoli, Hadrian's Villa
Haloia festival at Athens 178
Hamilton, Gavin 55, 116, 119
Helix, *see* Aurelius Helix
hellenism, *see* philhellenism
Hellenistic art 93
Hellenistic kings 26, 34, 89, 91

hellenization 2; *see also* Gaul, hellenization of
 of Rome 3–7, 33, 44
 as badge of elite 84, 140
Heracles
 at Athens 178, 184–5, 197–9
 at Sparta 155, 163–6
 images of 70, 71, 79–80, 82, 90, 128, 264;
  see also Farnese Heracles
 as patron of athletes 35, 74, 75, 76, 107, 119,
  224, 235, 267
Heraia festival at Argos 36
Herculaneum, Villa of the Papyri 91
Herennius Dexippus 179, 186
Herennius Dexippus, P. 186, 200–1
Hermes 70, 107, 119, 235, 264, 267; *see also*
 Sandalbinder statue type
Hermolycus 214–15, 221
herms 53, 80, 90, 91
Herodes Atticus 9, 119 n. 9, 139, 163, 191,
 193–200, 244–5, 276–7
Herodotus 156, 214, 221
heroes as athletes 119, 225–6; *see also* cultic
 honours to athletes
Hesiod 147
Hierapolis 12, 14, 248–51
hippodrome garden 99, 105
Hipposthenes of Sparta 218–19, 221
Homer 8, 147
homoeroticism
 as association of athletics 30, 40, 64, 129,
  144
 in gymnasium 126, 128
 as response to statues 125, 134, 275
 in Roman art 129
 in Roman culture 132–4, 130
Horace 4, 28, 88
Hygeia 55, 70, 243, 264

identity 3, 11
 Greek 1–2, 8–11, 83–4, 144, 145, 228, 271,
  277–8, 280–1
 Greek civic 9–10, 31, 162–3, 191–2, 200–1,
  202, 204, 212 n. 31, 220–1, 222–8, 247,
  269–70, 279, 281
 Greek elite 9, 10, 252, 280; *see also* elite self-
  representation; Greek elite
 Roman 44, 84, 143, 274
 Roman elite 3, 5, 40, 90, 140
immortality 41–2; *see also* athletes, fame of;
 cultic honours to athletes

Imperial Cult 32, 36, 66, 238–9, 240, 247–8,
 271
imperial family, dedications and honours to
 85, 177–8, 194–5, 234, 235, 238–9, 246,
 249, 251, 267–8, 271, 280
imperial rooms, *see* marble rooms
Isis 111
Isthmia 211–12, 224, 244

Jenkins, Thomas 116
Jews 2
Julia Domna 5, 74, 75, 238, 249
Julius Caesar 23, 25 n. 20, 40
Junius Mauricus 40
Jupiter 24, 25, 32
Juvenal 4, 22, 41, 46, 139

Kaisersaal, *see* marble rooms

Ladas 217–18, 221
lamps **29**
Lansdowne Heracles 116, **118**, 119
Lepcis Magna 74
library 266
Ligorio, Pirro 107–8, 109, 111
literature, Greek imperial 1, 8; *see also* Lucian;
 Pausanias; Philostratus
Livy 25
Lucan 40
Lucian 83 n. 154
 Anacharsis 144–52, 154, 169–70
 Lover of Lies 123, 267
 On Salaried Posts on Great Houses 41, 139
 Ps-Lucian, *Amores* 128–9
Lucillius 29
Lucius Verus 156, 194–5
ludi 25, 27, 49 n. 21
Ludovisi Discobolus statue type 262, **265**
luxury 40, 64, 92, 140, 156
Lycurgus 151, 155, 163, 169, 192
Lyons 82
Lysippus 72, 93, 116 n. 97; *see also* Farnese
 Heracles; Sandalbinder statue type
 Apoxyomenus statue 28, 89
 Heracles statuette 124

Macedonia 156
Magerius 86
Mandrogenes of Magnesia 154
Marathon 188–9, 194

marble rooms 235–9, 245, 261–3
marble style 237
Marcus Aurelius 105, 194–5, 243, 246
Marefoschi, Cardinal 113, 116
Marius 38, 39
Mark Antony 27, 34
Marseilles 77–8, 143
Martial 46, 78, 124
Massilia, *see* Marseilles
Megara 215–16
Melancomas 127
Messene 222–3
Methydrium 220
Miletus 243, 246
military training 28, 40, 41; see also *ephēbeia*;
    athletics and warfare
Milo of Croton 109
Mithridates 26
Mnesibulus of Elataea 227–8
Morus 60 n. 66, 63
mosaics 46–70, 79–82, 85–6, 86–7, 137
    named athletes on 58–62, 63–4, 67, 277
    portraits of athletics on 62–8, 277
Mummius 209, 212
Munichia 180, 182, 185, 188, 229
Muses 87, 243, 246, 252, 255
musical contests 16, 29, 32, 82, 252
Myron 93; *see also* Amelung athlete statue
    type
    Discobolus statue 56, 70, 74, 80, 92,
      113–16, **115**, 121, 122–5, 244, 246, 262, **264**
    statue of Chionis of Sparta 219
    statue of Ladas 218, 221

nakedness of athletes 25, 40, 43, 216
Naples 27, 31, 46, 48, 77, 78, 143, 272
naval contests 178, 179–92
Nemausus, *see* Nîmes
Nemea 211–12, 224
Neptune 50, 64
Nero 23, 24, 28–31, 48; *see also* Neronian
    Games at Rome; Rome, Baths of Nero
Neronian Games at Rome 28–31, 40, 43, 54
Nesiotes 123, 214 n. 38
nicknames of athletes 63
Nicopolis 27
Nicostratus of Aegeae 62 n. 74, 277
Nîmes 28, 76–7
Nobilior, M. Fulvius 25
North Africa 5, 24, 84–7, 140

nostalgia 126, 156, 213, 277, 278
nudity, *see* nakedness of athletes

Odessus, *see* Varna
Oebotas of Dyme 219, 223–4, 225, 226–7
Oenoanda 246 n. 67, 247 n. 68, 252, 253
Olympeia festival at Aquileia 66
Olympia 121, 203, 205–10, 213, 220–2, 224,
    244, 247
Olympic Games 24, 26, 30, 33, 202, 209–10,
    221
oratory 178, 189, 196, 198; *see also* sophists
Orsippus of Megara 215–16, 219, 221, 223
Ostia
    bath complexes 6, 45
    Baths of Buticosis 51
    Baths of Neptune 49, 50–1, **51**, 52, 54
    Baths of Porta Marina 49, 51–6, **53**, 123
    Baths of the Seven Sages 51 n. 32
    Baths of the Trinacria 49
    Forum Baths 49–50
    Terme Marittime 49, 56–8, **57**
    Via Severiana Baths 62, 63–4, **64**
    Inn of Alexander Helix 58–9, **59**, 69
    population of 62, 48
    spectacle culture of 48–9
otium 6, 90
Ovid 28

paideia 5, 86–7, 140, 174, 254, 277
Palfurius Sura 30–1, 43, 273
Panathenaea festival at Athens 146, 148 n. 17,
    179, 180, 182, 185, 191
pancration 41, 148, 153, 155, 170, 196, 198
Panhellenion 192 n. 82, 210–11, 212
panhellenism 76, 150, 170, 192, 203, 209, 213,
    279
Parapotamii 220–1
Parthians 156
past, relationship with 74, 76, 152, 156–7, 162,
    187–92, 200–1, 203, 208, 213, 217, 222,
    227, 246, 260, 270, 277–81
Pausanias 202–3
    on Athens 211, 214–15
    on Delphi 211, 212
    on Olympia 203, 205–10, 211, 213
    on Olympic victors 149–50, 153, 214–15
    on panhellenism 170–1, 203–4, 212
    on Sparta 152, 154–5, 163, 218–20, 222
Pellene 149

Peloponnesian War 204
pentathlon 56, 85, 95, 112, 125, 260
Pergamum 211, 238
Perge 243
peri alkēs festival at Athens 178, 185, 195–9
periodos 36, 146, 211
periodonikēs 60, 154 n. 40, 228, 257
Perseus of Macedon 26
Persian wars 12, 170, 156, 188–9, 191, 192, 202, 203, 209, 213, 214–15, 223, 278–9
Petronius 124
Phaylus of Croton 212–13, 215
Pheidias 93
philhellenism 3, 31–2, 96, 136, 274
Philostratus 75
    Gymnasticus 24, 75–6, 152–3, 153–4, 155, 156–7, 170, 260
    Heroicus 226
    Imagines 153
    Life of Apollonius of Tyana 12, 75, 152, 157, 209, 228
physical training
    at Rome 40–1, 42–4, 46, 137, 273
    in Greece 147–9, 229; see also *ephēbeia*; gymnasium
Piazza Armerina 51, 59
Piranesi 108
Piseas of Aphrodisias 257, **258**
Plancia Magna 243
Plataea 170, 191, 209, 221, 223, 228
Plato 8, 38, 90, 125, 189
Pliny the Younger 23, 39, 40–1, 46, 78, 105, 231, 279
Plotina 76
Plutarch 43, 194, 212
Polybius 26
Polycleitus 93
    Diadoumenus statue 123, 263, **266**
    Discophorus statue 255–6
    Doryphorus statue 70, 74, 92, 93, 121 n. 110
    Heracles statue 71, **72**
    statue of Cyniscus 99–100; see also Westmacott athlete statue type
Polydamas of Scotoussa 75, 149, 170, 225
Polynices of Aphrodisias 257
Pompeii 46
    House of Menander (I.x.4) 48
    Palaestra (VIII.ii.23) 47, **47**
    Stabian Baths 27–8, 46

Pompey the Great 25, 38
Praxiteles 93
    Aphrodite of Cnidus 92, 122
    statue of satyr 130–2, **131**
prizes 52–3, 58, 80, 82, 85, 146–7, 157, 174, 247
Promachus of Pellene 75, 149–50, 153, 170, 215
Protesilaos 226
Puteoli 36
Pythagoras of Rhegium 113
Pythian Games, *see* Delphi
Pythian Games at Carthage 85
Pythian Games at Hierapolis, *see* Hierapolis
Pythian Games at Side **268**, 269, **270**

Quintilii brothers 139

Rabirius 97 n. 45
race in armour 170, 178, 219, 221, 228
Reggio di Calabria 61 n. 73
Regilla 244
resistance to Rome 10, 211, 228, 277, 278–9; see also Roman Empire, Greek response to
Rhodes 227
Roman Empire 7, 33, 140, 274
    Greek response to 10, 14, 277, 280; see also resistance to Rome
Roman Republic 6, 25, 27, 33, 88–91, 136, 274
romanization 87, 231, 276; see also Gaul, romanization of
Rome, *see also* hellenization of Rome; philhellenism
    Baths of Agrippa 28, 29, 33, 41, 46, 89
    Baths of Caracalla 46, 62–3, 67–76, **68**, **69**, 123
    Baths of Nero 29–30, 33, 37, 41, 46, 63, 74
    Baths of Titus 46
    Baths of Trajan 35, 46
    Caelian Hill Bath complex 60
    Campus Martius 23, 27, 28, 41
    Horti Lamiani 123
    odeum of Domitian 32
    palace of Domitian 105
    stadium of Domitian 32, 37, 63, 105
    Via Nomentana Bath complex 60
    Via Portuense bath complex 60–1, **61**
    attitudes to athletics in 33, 37, 38–41, 43–4, 137–9, 149, 273; see also Tacitus, Pliny the Younger

population of 4–5, 33, 62, 139–40
spectacle culture of 21–4, 33

Salamis 180, 182, 188–9, 213
Sandalbinder statue type 263, **267**, 116, **117**
Santa Severa 61 n. 73
sarcophagi 41–2, **42**, 139, 189 n. 70, 260–1,
    275
Sardis 238, **239**
sculpture, *see also* victory statues
    display of 89, 91–3; *see also* baths, sculptural
        display of; villas, sculptural display of;
        gymnasium, sculptural display of
    Greek in Rome 89, 90
    Greek, Roman copies of 56, 89, 90, 92–3,
        122–5, 265, 267; *see also* Myron,
        Discobolus statue
    idealized 88–9, 246, 270
Sebasta Festival at Naples 27, 31, 33, 36, 46,
    48
Second Sophistic 8, 144, 199; *see also*
    archaism; Greek Renaissance; past,
    relationship with
Seleucia 62 n. 74, 277
senators 4–5, 78–9, 84, 139–40
Seneca 38, 39, 46
Septimius Severus 5, 37, 74, 243, 249, 251
Severan dynasty 5, 63, 74, 137, 273; *see also*
    names of individual emperors
Severeia festival at Caesarea in Mauretania 85
Shelburne, Lord 56, 116
Sicyon 216–17
Side 11, 123, 261–70
Smirat 86
Smyrna 211
Solon, *see* Lucian, *Anacharsis*
sophists 8, 9, 12; *see also* Favorinus; Flavius
    Damianus; Herodes Atticus
Sostratus of Pellene 224
Sparta 11–12, 83, 157, 218–19, 221–2; *see also*
    Pausanias on Sparta
    agōgē 150–63, 169, 171, 192
    Arapissa baths complex 163–6
    gymnasium of Eurycles 164
    Platanistas grove and contest 154–5, 163,
        165, 199
    sanctuary of Artemis Orthia 157–60, **158**,
        162; *see also* Artemis Orthia
    sickle dedications 157–9, **159**, **160**
    whipping contest 151–3, 158

spectatorship 42, 39; *see also* athletics as
    spectacle
Sperlonga 132
St Colombe 82
St-Romaine-en-Gal 79, 82
stadium 105; *see also* hippodrome garden;
    Rome, Domitian's stadium
Statius 132–4
statues of athletes, *see* victor statues
stoic attitudes to athletics 39
Suetonius 23–4
Sulla 26
Sulpicius Maximus, Q. 138
Sybaris 223 n. 79
Syracuse 226
Syria 11

Tacitus 30–1, 40, 43, 54
Tarquinius Priscus 25
Tegea 204
Termessus 229
Tertullian 24, 39, 86
Theagenes of Thasos 219, 224–5, 226
theatre 43, 82, 109, 121, 130, 147
    decoration of 249–51, 255–60
Theocritus 4
Theseus 75, 234, **235**
    at Athens 178, 188, 194, 195, 198–9
Tiberius 22, 23, 89
Titus 31, 48
Tivoli, Hadrian's villa 106–22, 165
Tor Paterno 122
torch race 59, 178, 179, 180, 184, 188
Townley, Charles 55, 116
trainers of athletes 76, 153–4
Trajan 23, 76, 231, 234
Trimalchio 124
Tusculum, Lancelloti Mosaic 52 n. 36

Valerius Asiaticus 78–9
Varna 191, 229
Vedia Phaedrina 240
Vedius Antoninus, P. 240, **241–2**, 243
Venus (Aphrodite) 92, 243
Vespasian 23, 34
victory statues 9, 93, 121, 125, 126, 152, 159–62,
    205–9, 213, 214–15, 216–18, 219, 223–7,
    252, 254–5, 257–60, **258–9**
victory dedications 157–62, 180–1, 192–3,
    214–27

Vienna (Gaul), *see* Vienne
Vienne 40, 78–82, **80**, **82**
villas
   naming of areas 90, 107
   sculptural display of 6, 89–92, 95–6, 122–5,
      274, 276–7
   see also Castel Gandolfo, Domitian's Villa;
      Tivoli, Hadrian's Villa
Vindex 124
violence 153–5

Virgil 4
virtue, *see* athletics, ideals associated with
Vitruvius 38, 39

warfare, *see* athletics and warfare
Westmacott Athlete statue type 99, **100**, 104,
      120, 130
wrestling 41, 170, 196, 198

Zanes 205–6